THIRD EDITION

THEORETICAL FOUNDATIONS OF
HEALTH EDUCATION
and HEALTH PROMOTION

Manoj Sharma, MBBS, MCHES, PhD, FAAHB

Professor, Public Health

Jackson State University

JONES & BARTLETT
LEARNING

World Headquarters
Jones & Bartlett Learning
5 Wall Street
Burlington, MA 01803
978-443-5000
info@jblearning.com
www.jblearning.com

Jones & Bartlett Learning books and products are available through most bookstores and online booksellers. To contact Jones & Bartlett Learning directly, call 800-832-0034, fax 978-443-8000, or visit our website, www.jblearning.com.

10505-6

Production Credits

VP, Executive Publisher: David D. Cella
Publisher: Cathy L. Esperti
Editorial Assistant: Taylor Ferracane
Associate Director of Production: Julie C. Bolduc
Production Manager: Tina Chen
Associate Production Editor: Kristen Rogers
Director of Marketing: Andrea DeFronzo
VP, Manufacturing and Inventory Control: Therese Connell
Composition: Cenveo® Publisher Services

Project Management: Cenveo® Publisher Services
Cover Design: Kristin E. Parker
Associate Director of Rights & Media: Joanna Lundeen
Rights & Media Specialist: Jamey O'Quinn
Media Development Editor: Shannon Sheehan
Cover Image: © shotty/Shutterstock
Printing and Binding: Edwards Brothers Malloy
Cover Printing: Edwards Brothers Malloy

Library of Congress Cataloging-in-Publication Data
Library of Congress Cataloging-in-Publication Data unavailable at time of printing.

6048

Printed in the United States of America
20 19 18   10 9 8 7 6 5 4

© shotty/Shutterstock

CONTENTS

FROM THE AUTHOR

I have great pleasure in presenting this third edition of *Theoretical Foundations of Health Education and Health Promotion* to my readers. I have been really pleased with its success over the years. In 2015, Amazon ranked it #14 in sales in health books under education and teaching. The reviews mentioned on Amazon's website, and those that I have received from students nationally, from colleagues all over the world, from international collaborators, and from reviewers of this book, have all been largely positive and constructive. Based on this feedback I have made several changes to this *Third Edition*. I hope my readers, who include undergraduate students, graduate students, practitioners, and researchers, will continue to give this edition the same love, admiration, and support as previous editions of this book. This book should be a required reading by all students, practitioners, and researchers in the disciplines of public health and education as it presents all of the relevant health education and health promotion theories in a simple, practical, easy-to-apply format.

PREFACE

Theoretical Foundations of Health Education and Health Promotion, Third Edition provides an accessible, uniform approach to understanding the theories commonly used in health education and health promotion. Each theory is described in a consistent and uniform manner and discussed in simple language with an emphasis on practical applications. The book is designed for use in a quarter- or semester-long course. The information presented here is in consonance with the core competencies for health education specialists described by the National Commission for Health Education Credentialing (NCHEC) and provides a useful review for those preparing to take the certification examination both at the CHES and MCHES levels. The book is also useful for those preparing for the Certified in Public Health (CPH) exam administered by the National Board of Public Health Examiners (NBPHE).

NEW TO THIS EDITION:

I would first like to mention that my coauthor from previous editions, Dr. John Romas, has retired, and I am the sole author of this book. In this revision, on the suggestion of the students and reviewers, I have added:

- **NEW!** Chapter 11 is a new chapter that addresses some of the newer theories in health education and health promotion. These include:
  - The integrative model of behavioral prediction (IM)
  - Emotional intelligence theory
  - The information-motivation-behavioral skills (IMB) model
  - Self-determination theory (SDT)
  - The construct of self-esteem
  - The community coalition action theory (CCAT), and
  - The theory of gender and power
- **NEW!** The multi-theory model (MTM) for health behavior change is a new model that I hope readers will find useful and stimulating enough to test in their research or practice.
- Diverse examples and activities have been added to each theory to make this edition more attractive not only to health education specialists but also to public health professionals,

nursing educators, dietitians, nutrition educators, health coaches, lay health volunteers, and all health care professionals involved with health education and health promotion.

- **NEW UPDATES** include:
  - Addition of the 2015 Health Education Specialist Practice Analysis (HESPA) study in Chapter 1
  - Inclusion of SHAPE America in Chapter 1
  - Inclusion of Delta Omega in Chapter 1
  - Addition of the social ecological model in Chapter 2
  - Expansion of CDCynergy in Chapter 2
  - Expansion of intervention mapping in Chapter 2
  - Addition of a diagram on the transtheoretical model in Chapter 4
  - Elaboration of social network and social support theory in Chapter 6
  - Simplification of Chapter 7
  - Addition of current information on social marketing in Chapter 8, and
  - Addition of diagrams and tables in Chapter 9
  - Also added are newer interventions, newer references, and updated websites in all chapters.

FEATURES AND BENEFITS:

Each chapter offers several learning tools to aid readers in understanding and learning to apply theory-based behavior change interventions:

- **Key concepts and chapter objectives** begin each chapter and help readers focus their attention and retain important information.
- **Chapter summaries** conclude each chapter and provide an opportunity for readers to prepare for exams and master key concepts effectively by reinforcing important topics and important terms. Important terms and their definitions are also provided in the glossary at the end of the book.
- **Boxed quotations** highlight the theorists or important aspects of the theory and provide a direct flavor of the actual theory.
- Each chapter begins with a discussion of the **historical genesis and constitutive constructs of the theory**. This foundation is followed by a clear delineation of the constructs of the theory, which helps readers understand the process by which the theory is reified and used in health education and health promotion. This process of simplification of constructs helps the health education and health promotion student to apply these constructs in designing programs.
- **Application Exercises** in each chapter present a case study that urges readers to apply concepts discussed in the chapter and to retrieve additional applications from the literature.
- Each discussion of theory is accompanied by a **practical Skill-Building Activity** in the context of planning and evaluation along with a set of application questions. This activity will assist readers in mastering the application of the theory to community, school, worksite, or patient care settings.
- **Up-to-date examples of applications** from current literature are included throughout the text and serve as ideas for designing interventions and resources for initiating a literature review.

- Each chapter includes a **Websites to Explore** section that encourages readers to participate in specific interactive activities to enhance their learning on the topic.

INSTRUCTOR RESOURCES:

- A set of updated PowerPoint slides for each chapter that instructors can use for classroom lectures.
- Instructors also have access to updated TestBank questions for each chapter.

© shotty/Shutterstock

ACKNOWLEDGMENTS

We want to thank all of the reviewers who read through this text and provided invaluable advice:

Elizabeth Ash, MA, Morehead State University;

David Brown, EdD, MA, MCHES, Jackson State University;

Kirk Dearden, DrPH, MPH, Boston University School of Public Health;

Carl Fertman, PhD, CHES, University of Pittsburgh;

Deborah A. Fortune, PhD, CHES, North Central Carolina University;

Pamela Y. Frasier, MSPH, PhD, Radford University;

Jewel Goodman Shepherd, PhD, MPA, CHES, Old Dominion University;

Wendelyn Inman, PhD, Tennessee State University;

Jerome Kotecki, PhD, Ball State University;

Janet Ludwig, PhD, Hawthorn University;

Karen Lyke, MS, CCN, DSc, DANLA, Hawthorn University, Maryland University of Integrative Health;

Brandi S. Niemeier, PhD, University of Wisconsin-Whitewater;

Elizabeth Reifsnider, PhD, RN, WHNP-BC, PHCNS-BC, FAAN, College of Nursing and Health Innovation, Arizona State University;

Dr. Jacqueline E. Sharpe, Old Dominion University;

Brad Welch, MEd, CHES, University of New Orleans;

Joshua H. West, PhD, MPH, Brigham Young University;

Julie Zaruba Fountaine, MS, College of St. Scholastica.

SPECIAL APPRECIATION

A special appreciation is extended to graduate students at the Jackson State University, University of Cincinnati, and Walden University who have used this book and provided excellent suggestions.

Finally, I am thankful to Dr. Paul Branscum of the University of Oklahoma and Dr. Adam Knowlden of the University of Alabama for reviewing Chapter 11 of this book and providing valuable feedback.

INTRODUCTION TO HEALTH EDUCATION, HEALTH PROMOTION, AND THEORY

KEY CONCEPTS

- behavior
- certified health education specialist (CHES)
- certified in public health (CPH)
- code of ethics
- community-related concepts
- concepts related to antecedents of behavior
- dietitian
- health
- health behavior

- health coach
- health education
- health literacy
- health promotion
- master certified health education specialist (MCHES)
- nursing educator
- theory

AFTER READING THIS CHAPTER YOU SHOULD BE ABLE TO

- Define health, health behavior, health education, and health promotion
- Identify the limitations of the traditional definition of health
- Differentiate between health education and health promotion
- Define concepts related to antecedents of behavior
- Delineate community-related concepts
- List the responsibilities of certified health education specialists
- Explain the role of theory in health education and health promotion
- Name different types of theories and provide examples
- Identify 10 national health education organizations

HEALTH, BEHAVIOR, AND HEALTH BEHAVIOR

Health is an age-old concept. In Old English the idea appeared as *haelen* ("to heal"), and in Middle English as *helthe*, meaning to be sound in body, mind, and spirit. The classic Greek definition of medicine was to "prolong life and prevent disease," or in other words to keep people healthy (Cook, 2004). Similarly, medicine in ancient India was called Ayurveda, or the science of life or health. By the 17th century, most medical textbooks commonly used the word *restoration*. By the end of the 19th century, the word *health* was considered colloquial and was replaced with the word *hygiene*, which was considered more scientific (Cook, 2004).

After the Second World War, the word *health* resurfaced with the formation of the World Health Organization (WHO), a global entity. Around the same time, the Hygienic Laboratory in the United States was renamed the National Institutes of Health. In 1948, WHO defined health in its constitution as "a state of complete physical, mental, and social well-being and not merely the absence of disease or infirmity" (WHO, 1974, p. 29). This definition of health has received a lot of criticism over the years for a number of reasons.

First, the use of the word *state* is misleading. Health is dynamic and changes from time to time. For example, a person may be healthy in the morning and then develop a headache in the afternoon and thus not be in the "state" of health. Second, the dimensions mentioned in the definition are inadequate to capture the variations in health. One such dimension is the spiritual dimension (Perrin & McDermott, 1997). Bensley (1991) has identified six perspectives related to the spiritual dimension of health: (1) sense of fulfillment, (2) values and beliefs of community and self, (3) wholeness in life, (4) well-being, (5) God or a controlling power, and (6) human–spiritual interaction. None of these concepts are included in WHO's definition. Another dimension that is not mentioned is the political dimension. Do the rich get sick more often, or do the poor? Who controls greater resources to health? Do the rich or the poor have a greater burden of mortality? All these and many other questions pertaining to the politics of health must be explicitly mentioned in the definition for it to be meaningfully complete.

> **Health is a state of complete physical, mental, and social well-being and not merely the absence of disease or infirmity.**
>
> —World Health Organization (1974, p. 29)

Third, the word *well-being* is very subjective. A definition must be more objective, and subjectivity should be minimized. Fourth, the way in which health is defined makes it very difficult to measure. McDowell and Newell (1987) pointed out that "just as language molds the way we think[,] our health measurements influence (and are influenced by) the way we define and think about health" (p. 14); in other words, health and measurement are inextricably linked. Fifth, WHO's definition of health presents an idealistic or utopian view. It would be impossible to find anyone who embodies all the attributes presented in the definition. Thus the definition of health lacks practical applications.

Sixth, in the WHO definition health is presented as an end product, whereas most people perceive health as a means of achieving something that they value more highly. For example, people want to be healthy so that they can raise their families. Finally, the WHO definition of health is written from an individualistic perspective in which health is defined for one person. It lacks a community orientation, which is much needed for something as complex as health. These limitations of the WHO definition are summarized in **Table 1-1**.

The original WHO definition has been modified in subsequent discussions at the world level. In November 1986, the first International Conference on Health Promotion was held in Ottawa,

Table 1-1	Limitations of the World Health Organization's Definition of Health
Health is dynamic, not a state.	
The dimensions are inadequate.	
The definition is subjective.	
Measurement is difficult.	
The definition is idealistic rather than realistic.	
Health is not an end but a means.	
The definition lacks a community orientation.	

Canada (WHO, 1986). At that conference the Ottawa Charter for Health Promotion was drafted. In the charter, health was defined more broadly:

> [H]ealth has been considered less as an abstract state and more as a means to an end which can be expressed in functional terms as a resource which permits people to lead an individually, socially, and economically productive life. Health is a resource for everyday life, not the object of living. It is a positive concept emphasizing social and personal resources as well as physical capabilities (WHO, 1986, p. 1).

A more contemporary definition describes health as "a means to achieve desirable goals in life while maintaining a multidimensional (physical, mental, social, political, economic, and spiritual) equilibrium that is operationalized for individuals, as well as for communities." This definition is more inclusive.

Another important basic concept is **behavior**. *Merriam-Webster's Dictionary* defines behavior as "anything that an organism does involving action and response to stimulation." The key word is "action." A behavior is any overt action, conscious or unconscious, with a measurable frequency, intensity, and duration. "Frequency" refers to how many times the behavior occurs in a given time period. For example, we may classify someone as being active who participates in some sort of physical activity 5 days a week. "Intensity" refers to how intensely or how hard the behavior is performed. For example, we may say that a behavior is mildly intense, moderately intense, or vigorous depending on the effect it has on the heart rate or the number of calories burned. "Duration" refers to the amount of time spent on each session. For example, physical activity may last for 20 minutes on any given day.

Any behavior is influenced by factors at five levels. The first level pertains to individual factors. For example, a person's attitude helps determine his or her behavior. A person who is partaking in physical activity may believe that physical activity is refreshing. The second level pertains to interpersonal factors. For example, the person may be exercising because his or her spouse requested it. The third level pertains to institutional or organizational factors. For example, there may be a policy at the workplace that requires every person to work out for an hour, and that may be the reason the person is performing the physical activity. The fourth level pertains to community factors. For example, if the only available parking is 10 minutes away from where the person lives or works, this may be the main reason the person is physically active. The final level in determining behavior is the role of public policy factors. For example, laws and policies requiring the use of seat belts while driving may make a person perform that particular behavior.

A behavior is any overt action, conscious or unconscious, with a measurable frequency, intensity, and duration.

Now let us focus our attention on defining **health behavior**. The World Health Organization (1998, p. 8) defines health behavior as "any activity undertaken by an individual regardless of actual or perceived health status, for the purpose of promoting, protecting or maintaining health, whether or not such behavior is objectively effective toward that end." David Gochman (1982, p. 167; 1997, p. 3) defines health behavior as "those personal attributes such as beliefs, expectations, motives, values, perceptions, and other cognitive elements; personality characteristics, including affective and emotional states and traits; and behavioral patterns, actions, and habits that relate to health maintenance, to health restoration, and to health improvement." Three key foci of health behavior are clear in these definitions: maintenance of health, restoration of health, and improvement of health.

These foci correspond to the three levels of prevention: namely, primary prevention, secondary prevention, and tertiary prevention (Modeste & Tamayose, 2004; Pickett & Hanlon, 1998). **Primary prevention** refers to preventive actions taken prior to the onset of a disease or injury with the intention of removing the possibility of its ever occurring. **Secondary prevention** refers to actions that block the progression of an injury or disease at its incipient stage. **Tertiary prevention** refers to actions taken after the onset of disease or injury with the intention of assisting the individual with the disease or disability. The actions for primary, secondary, and tertiary level care are taken at individual, interpersonal, organizational, community, and public policy levels. Hence health behavior can be defined as all actions with a potentially measurable frequency, intensity, and duration performed at the individual, interpersonal, organizational, community, or public policy level for primary, secondary, or tertiary prevention.

Some health behaviors have positive attributes, such as promoting physical activity or eating five or more servings of fruits and vegetables. Other health behaviors focus on extinguishing negative attributes, such as smoking or binge drinking. These behaviors can be categorized as risk behaviors and protective behaviors. The World Health Organization (1998, p. 18) defines risk behaviors as "specific forms of behavior which are proven to be associated with increased susceptibility to a specific disease or ill-health." For example, indiscriminate sexual behavior is a risk behavior for sexually transmitted diseases, including HIV/AIDS. Protective behaviors aim to protect a person from developing ill health or a specific disease. For example, a person may be immunized against tetanus and thus prevent the disease. Green and Kreuter (2005) divided protective behaviors into two categories: health-directed and health-related behaviors. Health-directed behaviors are actions a person consciously pursues for health improvement or health protection, such as seeking an immunization, getting a physical examination, eating a low-fat food, or using a condom. Health-related behaviors are actions performed for reasons other than health but that have health effects. An example is an individual who is trying to lose weight in order to improve his or her appearance.

HEALTH EDUCATION AND HEALTH PROMOTION

Health education professionals facilitate modification of health behaviors. **Health education** has been defined in several ways. Downie, Fyfe, and Tannahill (1990) defined it as "[c]ommunication activity aimed at enhancing positive health and preventing or diminishing ill-health in individuals and groups through influencing the beliefs, attitudes and behavior of those with power and of the community at large" (p. 28). The 2000 Joint Committee on Health Education and Promotion Terminology (Gold & Miner, 2002, p. 3) defined health education as "any combination of planned learning experiences based on sound theories that provide individuals, groups, and communities the opportunity to acquire information and the skills needed to make quality health decisions." The World Health Organization (1998, p. 4) defined health education as "compris[ing] consciously constructed opportunities for learning involving some form of communication designed to improve health literacy, including improving knowledge, and developing life skills which are conducive to individual and community health." Green and Kreuter (2005, p. G-4) defined health education as "any planned combination of learning experiences designed to predispose, enable, and reinforce voluntary behavior conducive to health in individuals, groups or communities."

From these definitions some things are clear. First, health education is a systematic, planned application, which qualifies it as a science. Second, the delivery of health education involves a set of techniques rather than just one, such as preparing health education informational brochures, pamphlets, and videos; delivering lectures; facilitating role plays or simulations; analyzing case studies; participating and reflecting in group discussions; reading; and interacting in computer-assisted training. In the past, health education encompassed a wider range of functions, including community mobilization, networking, and advocacy, which are now embodied in the term **health promotion**. Third, the primary purpose of health education is to influence antecedents of behavior so that healthy behaviors develop in a voluntary fashion (without any coercion). The common antecedents of behavior are awareness, information, knowledge, skills, beliefs, attitudes, and values. Finally, health education is performed at several levels. It can be done one-on-one, such as in a counseling session; it can be done with a group of people, such as through a group discussion; it can be done at an organizational level, such as through an employee wellness fair; or it can be done at the community level, such as through a multiple-channel, multiple-approach campaign.

Healthy People 2020 **reflects assessments of major risks to health and wellness, changing public health priorities, and emerging issues related to our nation's health preparedness and prevention.**

—U.S. Department of Health and Human Services (2009)

Since the publication of *Healthy People: The Surgeon General's Report on Health Promotion and Disease Prevention* (U.S. Department of Health and Human Services [USDHHS], 1979), the term *health promotion* has gained popularity and continues to gain strength. This term has been used in the *Objectives for the Nation* (USDHHS, 1980), *Healthy People 2000* (USDHHS, 1990), *Healthy People 2010* (USDHHS, 2000), and *Healthy People 2020* (USDHHS, 2009) reports. **Table 1–2** summarizes the 38 focus areas in *Healthy People 2020*, which underscore the importance of health promotion.

Green and Kreuter (2005, p. G-4) defined health promotion as "any planned combination of educational, political, regulatory and organizational supports for actions and conditions of living conducive to the health of individuals, groups or communities." The 2000 Joint Committee on Health Education and Promotion Terminology (Gold & Miner, 2002, p. 4) defined health promotion as "any planned combination of educational, political, environmental, regulatory, or organizational mechanisms that support actions and conditions of living conducive to the health of individuals, groups, and communities." The *Ottawa Charter for Health Promotion* (WHO, 1986, p. 1) defined health promotion as "the process of enabling people to increase control over, and to improve, their health." The Ottawa Charter identified five key action strategies for health promotion:

- Build healthy public policy.
- Create physical and social environments supportive of individual change.
- Strengthen community action.

Table 1-2 Focus Areas in *Healthy People 2020*	
Access to health services	HIV
Adolescent health	Immunization and infectious diseases
Arthritis, osteoporosis, and chronic back conditions	Injury and violence prevention
Blood disorders and blood safety	Maternal, infant, and child health
Cancer	Medical product safety
Chronic kidney diseases	Mental health and mental disorders
Diabetes	Nutrition and weight status
Disability and secondary conditions	Occupational safety and health
Early and middle childhood	Older adults
Educational and community-based programs	Oral health
Environmental health	Physical activity and fitness
Family planning	Public health infrastructure
Food safety	Quality of life and well-being
Genomics	Respiratory diseases
Global health	Sexually transmitted diseases
Health care–associated infections	Substance abuse
Health communication and health information technology	Social determinants of health
Hearing and other sensory or communication disorders	Tobacco use
Heart disease and stroke	Vision

- Develop personal skills such as increased self-efficacy and feelings of empowerment.
- Reorient health services to the population and partnership with patients.

These action areas were confirmed in the *Jakarta Declaration on Leading Health Promotion into the 21st Century* in 1997 (WHO, 1997). In addition, the Jakarta Declaration identified five priorities for health promotion:

- Promote social responsibility for health.
- Increase investments for health development.
- Expand partnerships for health promotion.
- Increase community capacity and empower the individual.
- Secure an infrastructure for health promotion.

Once again, all these depictions of health promotion have some things in common. First, just like health education, health promotion is a systematic, planned application that qualifies as a science. Second, it entails methods beyond mere education such as community mobilization, community organization, community participation, community development, community empowerment, networking, coalition building, advocacy, lobbying, policy development, formulating legislation, and developing social norms. Third, unlike health education, health promotion does not endorse voluntary change in behavior but utilizes measures that compel an individual's behavior change. These measures are uniform and mandatory. Often the behavior change in health promotion comes from measures that an individual may not like, for example, an increase in insurance premium for a smoker. Finally, health promotion is done at the group or community level.

> **Health for all: The attainment by all people of the world of a level of health that will permit them to lead a socially and economically productive life.**
>
> —World Health Organization (1986, p. 4)

RESPONSIBILITIES AND COMPETENCIES FOR HEALTH EDUCATORS

The history of health education dates to the late 19th century, when the first academic programs emerged for training school health educators (Allegrante et al., 2004). The 2003 "Directory of Institutions Offering Undergraduate and Graduate Degree Programs in Health Education" listed 258 institutions offering baccalaureate, master's, and doctoral degrees in health education (American Association for Health Education, 2003).

As the profession of health education has grown, greater interest has arisen in establishing standards and holding professionals accountable to those standards. In February 1978, a conference for health educators was convened in Bethesda, Maryland, to analyze the similarities and differences in preparing health educators from different practice settings and to discuss the possibility of developing uniform guidelines (National Commission for Health Education Credentialing [NCHEC], Society for Public Health Education [SOPHE], & American Association for Health Education [AAHE], 2006; U.S. Department of Health, Education and Welfare, 1978). Soon after, the Role Delineation Project was implemented, which looked at the role of the entry-level health education specialist and identified the desirable responsibilities, functions, skills, and knowledge for that level. These were verified by a survey of practicing health educators. The process led to the publication of *A Framework for the Development of Competency-Based Curricula for Entry-Level Health Educators* (NCHEC, 1985).

In 1986, the second Bethesda Conference provided consensus for the certification process, and in 1988, the National Commission for Health Education Credentialing was established. In 1989, a charter certification phase was introduced, during which time health educators could become certified by submitting letters of support and academic records. From 1990 to the present, the NCHEC has conducted competency-based national certification examinations. An individual who meets the required health education training qualifications, successfully passes the certification exam, and meets continuing education requirements is known as a **certified health education specialist (CHES)**. In 2015, there were approximately 12,000 CHES and 1,000 **master certified health education specialists (MCHES)** (J. Wessner, personal communication, June 19, 2015). **Table 1-3** summarizes the responsibilities for health education specialists (NCHEC, 2015b).

In 1992, the AAHE and SOPHE began to determine graduate-level competencies, and a Joint Committee for the Development of Graduate-Level Preparation Standards was formed. *A Competency-Based Framework for Graduate Level Health Educators* was published in 1999 (AAHE, NCHEC, & SOPHE, 1999; Rehrig, 2010).

Table 1-3	Seven Areas of Responsibilities for Health Education Specialists
I. Assess needs, assets, and capacity for health education/promotion.	
II. Plan health education/promotion.	
III. Implement health education/promotion.	
IV. Conduct evaluation and research related to health education/promotion.	
V. Administer and manage health education/promotion.	
VI. Serve as a health education/promotion resource person.	
VII. Communicate, promote, and advocate for health, health education/promotion, and the profession.	

In 1998 the profession launched the National Health Educator Competencies Update Project (CUP), a 6-year project to reverify the entry-level health education responsibilities, competencies, and subcompetencies and to verify the advanced-level competencies and subcompetencies (Airhihenbuwa et al., 2005; Gilmore, Olsen, Taub, & Connell, 2005). The CUP model identified three levels of practice: (1) entry (competencies and subcompetencies performed by health educators with a baccalaureate or master's degree and less than 5 years of experience), (2) advanced 1 (competencies and subcompetencies performed by health educators with a baccalaureate or master's degree and more than 5 years of experience), and (3) advanced 2 (competencies and subcompetencies performed by health educators with a doctoral degree and 5 years or more of experience). The CUP model contains seven areas of responsibility, 35 competencies, and 163 subcompetencies, many of which are similar to previous models. The CUP model also identified six settings for health education (**Table 1-4**).

In 2010, the AAHE, NCHEC, and SOPHE undertook the Health Educator Job Analysis (HEJA) project, which was a multiphased national study (NCHEC, 2010). The HEJA project verified the three levels of practice identified in the CUP model, namely entry, advanced 1, and advanced 2, and reaffirmed the seven major areas of responsibilities.

In 2015, the Health Education Specialist Practice Analysis (HESPA) study was completed (NCHEC, 2015a). The purpose of this study was to validate the practice of entry-level and advanced-level health education specialists to determine whether there were any changes in health education practice since HEJA 2010 so that the certification process, professional preparation, and continuing education of health education specialists could be improved. The study identified 36 competencies and 258 subcompetencies, of which 141 subcompetencies were for entry, 76 for advanced 1, and 41 for advanced 2 levels.

Table 1-4	Settings for Health Education Identified in the CUP Model
Community	
School (K–12)	
Health care	
Business/industry	
College/university	
University health services	

Health education is an important and integral function of public health. The Institute of Medicine (1988) defined three core functions of public health in its *Future of Public Health* report:

1. *Assessment*. Every public health agency should regularly and systematically collect, assemble, analyze, and make available information on the health of the community.
2. *Policy development*. Every public health agency should assist in the development of comprehensive public health policies.
3. *Assurance*. Every public health agency should ensure that services necessary to achieve agreed-upon goals in communities are provided either directly or by regulations or by other agencies.

Building on these identified functions, the Public Health Functions Steering Committee (1994) identified six public health goals and 10 essential public health services. The six goals are to (1) prevent epidemics and the spread of disease, (2) protect against environmental hazards, (3) prevent injuries, (4) promote and encourage healthy behaviors, (5) respond to disasters and assist communities in recovery, and (6) assure the quality and accessibility of health services. The 10 essential public health services are to (1) monitor health status to identify community health problems; (2) diagnose and investigate health problems and health hazards in the community; (3) inform, educate, and empower people about health issues; (4) mobilize community partnerships to identify and solve health problems; (5) develop policies and plans that support individual and community health efforts; (6) enforce laws and regulations that protect health and ensure safety; (7) link people to needed personal health services and ensure the provision of health care when it is otherwise unavailable; (8) ensure the availability of a competent public health and personal health care workforce; (9) evaluate the effectiveness, accessibility, and quality of personal and population-based health services; and (10) research new insights and innovative solutions to health problems. It can be seen from both these lists that health education is a core and integral function of public health and that health educators are key public health functionaries.

The Institute of Medicine published *The Future of the Public's Health in the 21st Century* in 2002, which echoed the vision articulated in *Healthy People 2010* (USDHHS, 2000): healthy people in healthy communities. It emphasized the following key areas of action:

- Adopt a focus on population health that includes multiple determinants of health.
- Strengthen the public health infrastructure.
- Build partnerships.
- Develop systems of accountability.
- Emphasize evidence.
- Improve communication.

Once again, all of these functions underscore the inextricable linkage between public health and health education. Health education is an important subset of public health. Just as there is an NCHEC, since 2005 the National Board of Public Health Examiners (NBPHE, 2015) has ensured that graduates from schools and programs of public health accredited by the Council on Education for Public Health (CEPH) have gained the required knowledge and skills related to public health. NBPHE is responsible for developing, preparing, administering, and evaluating a voluntary certification exam. People who pass this exam earn the credential **certified in public health (CPH)**. The first exam was conducted in 2008 and certified about 500 individuals. The exam consists of questions from five core areas (biostatistics, epidemiology, environmental health sciences, health policy and management, and social and behavioral sciences) along with seven cross-cutting areas (communication and informatics, diversity and culture, leadership, public health biology, professionalism, programs planning, and systems thinking).

Other professionals besides health education specialists and public health professionals also practice health education. Among these are **nursing educators**, who provide patient education and sometimes community health education, and **dietitians** (registered dietitians, nutrition educators), who provide nutrition education in both patient care and community settings. A new field that is emerging utilizes **health coaches**, who work one-on-one with individuals to help them achieve their health goals through lifestyle and behavior adjustments. All five of these professionals—namely, health education specialists, public health professionals, nursing educators, dietitians, and health coaches—will find this book extremely helpful in practicing evidence-based behavior change approaches in their respective fields.

CODE OF ETHICS FOR THE HEALTH EDUCATION PROFESSION

Ethics is a major area of philosophy that deals with the study of morality, and in recent years, interest in ethics has increased in all walks of life. Practicing ethical behavior provides a standard for performance in any profession. In the profession of health education, the earliest effort to develop a code of ethics was the 1976 code of ethics developed by the Society for Public Health Education (Taub, Kreuter, Parcel, & Vitello, 1987). A coalition of national health education organizations, composed of the American Academy of Health Behavior (AAHB), the American Association for Health Education (AAHE), the American College Health Association (ACHA), the American Public Health Association's (APHA) Public Health Education and Health Promotion (PHEHP) section, APHA's School Health Education and Services (SHES) section, the American School Health Association (ASHA), the Directors of Health Promotion and Education (DHPE), Eta Sigma Gamma, the Society for Public Health Education (SOPHE), and the Society of State Directors of Health, Physical Education and Recreation (SSDHPER; now known as the Society of State Leaders of Health and Physical Education) has developed a unified **code of ethics for health educators** (Coalition of National Health Education Organizations, 2004). The code of ethics has six areas, which are summarized in **Table 1-5**.

HEALTH EDUCATION ORGANIZATIONS

Eleven health education organizations exist at the national level. The following subsections provide a brief description of each of these organizations.

AMERICAN ACADEMY OF HEALTH BEHAVIOR (AAHB)

The American Academy of Health Behavior was established in 1998. The mission of this organization is to advance the practice of health education and health promotion through health behavior research. Its specific objectives are to:

Table 1-5	Articles in the Code of Ethics for the Health Education Profession

Responsibility to the public: Supports principles of self-determination and freedom of choice for the individual

Responsibility to the profession: Exhibits professional behavior

Responsibility to employers: Accountable for professional activities and actions

Responsibility in the delivery of health education: Respects the rights, dignity, confidentiality, and worth of people

Responsibility in research and evaluation: Conducts oneself in accordance with federal and state laws, organizational and institutional policies, and professional standards

Responsibility in professional preparation: provides quality education that benefits the profession and the public

- Foster and disseminate findings of health behavior, health education, and health promotion research through sponsorship of scientific meetings, symposia, and publications
- Recognize outstanding achievements in the areas of health behavior, health education, and health promotion research
- Facilitate collaborative research efforts by bringing its members in contact with each other through a membership directory, professional meetings, professional publications, and electronic media
- Advance health education and health promotion by influencing health policy and allocation of resources (government agencies, private foundations, universities, etc.) and by developing and disseminating a cohesive body of knowledge in the area of health behavior research

Its website is www.aahb.org.

AMERICAN COLLEGE HEALTH ASSOCIATION (ACHA)

The American College Health Association was established in 1920. The mission of the organization is to be the principal advocate and leadership organization for college and university health. The association provides advocacy, education, communications, products, and services, as well as promoting research and culturally competent practices to enhance its members' ability to advance the health of all students and the campus community. Its main objectives are to:

- Support and promote systems and programs that produce optimum health outcomes for college students and campus communities
- Be the primary source of information, education, and consultation on health and health promotion issues affecting college and university students within the campus community
- Be the leading source of evidence-based knowledge about the field of college health
- Be the principal advocate for national public policy affecting the health of all college students and campus communities
- Develop and maximize the use of human, financial, and technological resources to ensure and sustain growth

Its website is www.acha.org.

AMERICAN PUBLIC HEALTH ASSOCIATION'S (APHA) PUBLIC HEALTH EDUCATION AND HEALTH PROMOTION (PHEHP) SECTION

The Public Health Education and Health Promotion section was established in 1920. The parent organization, the American Public Health Association, was formed in 1872. The section has more than 3,000 members. Its specific objectives are to:

- Be a strong advocate for health education, disease prevention, and health promotion directed to individuals, groups, and communities in all activities of the association
- Encourage the inclusion of health education, disease prevention, and health promotion activities in all of the nation's health programs
- Stimulate thought, discussion, research, and programmatic applications aimed at improving the public's health
- Improve the quality of research and practice in all public health programs of health education, disease prevention, and health promotion
- Provide networking opportunities for persons whose professional interests and training include, but are not limited to, the disciplines of health education, health communication, health promotion, social marketing, behavioral and social sciences, and public relations
- Provide section members with opportunities to become informed and engaged in all of the activities and matters of concern to the association
- Facilitate collaboration with all of the association's boards, committees, special primary interest groups, caucuses, sections, and affiliates
- Provide section members with such benefits as the annual meeting program, continuing education opportunities, newsletters, and a structure for exercising association leadership
- Identify and recognize individuals who make outstanding and substantial contributions to health education, disease prevention, and health promotion

Its website is www.apha.org/apha-communities/member-sections/public-health-education-and-health-promotion.

AMERICAN PUBLIC HEALTH ASSOCIATION'S SCHOOL HEALTH EDUCATION AND SERVICES (SHES) SECTION

The School Health Education and Services section was established in 1942 and has more than 300 members. Its specific objectives are to:

- Provide a section within the association that works independently, with other association substructures, and with external organizations toward the improvement of early childhood, school, and college health programs
- Interpret the functions and responsibilities of health agencies to day care, preschool, school, and college personnel
- Interpret early childhood, school, and college health education and service objectives to other public health personnel and assist them in integrating the objectives in their community
- Provide a forum for discussion of practices and research in early childhood, school, and college health

- Encourage the provision of health promotion programs within the school and college settings that address the needs of children and school personnel
- Encourage among interested association members the study and discussion of procedures and problems in early childhood, school, and college health services, health education, and environmental health programs

Its website is www.apha.org/apha-communities/member-sections/school-health-education -and-services.

AMERICAN SCHOOL HEALTH ASSOCIATION (ASHA)

The American School Health Association was established in 1927 and has a membership of more than 3,000. The mission of ASHA is to protect and promote the health of children and youth by supporting coordinated school health programs as a foundation for school success. Its specific objectives are to:

- Promote interdisciplinary collaboration among all who work to protect and improve the health, safety, well-being, and school success of children, youth, families, and communities
- Provide professional development opportunities for all those associated with school health programs
- Provide advocacy for building and strengthening effective school health programs
- Advance a research agenda that promotes quality school health programs
- Fulfill these initiatives by acquiring human, fiscal, and material resources

Its website is www.ashaweb.org.

DELTA OMEGA HONORARY SOCIETY IN PUBLIC HEALTH

This is the honorary society of public health. It was established in 1924 at Johns Hopkins University within the School of Hygiene and Public Health (now known as the Bloomberg School of Public Health). Delta Omega has about 17,000 members. Its mission is to promote excellence in practice, research, education, and academic achievement in the field of public health.

Its website is www.deltaomega.org.

DIRECTORS OF HEALTH PROMOTION AND EDUCATION (DHPE)

The Directors of Health Promotion and Education was established in 1946 and has more than 200 members. Its specific objectives are to:

- Serve as a channel through which directors of public health education programs of states and territories of the United States may exchange and share methods, techniques, and information for the enrichment and improvement of public health education programs
- Establish position statements and make recommendations on legislation and public policy related to and having implications for public health education
- Participate with the Association of State and Territorial Health Officials (ASTHO) in promoting health and preventing disease

- Identify methods of improving the quality and practice of education, public health education, and health promotion
- Elicit cooperation and coordination with national, public, private, and voluntary agencies related to public health programs
- Provide a forum for continuing education opportunities in public health education and health promotion

Its website is www.dhpe.org.

ETA SIGMA GAMMA (ESG)

Eta Sigma Gamma was established in 1967. It is the national professional health education honorary society. The specific objectives of this organization are to:

- Support the planning, implementation, and evaluation of health education programs and resources
- Stimulate and disseminate scientific research
- Motivate and provide health education services
- Recognize academic achievement
- Support health education advocacy initiatives
- Promote professional standards and ethics
- Promote networking activities among health educators and related professionals

Its website is www.etasigmagamma.org.

SHAPE AMERICA (SOCIETY OF HEALTH AND PHYSICAL EDUCATORS)

This is the new name (since 2014) of the organization that was previously known as American Alliance for Health, Physical Education, Recreation and Dance (AAHPERD). The organization was formed in 1885 and has undergone seven name changes. SHAPE America is the country's largest organization of physical educators. Its vision is "Healthy People—Physically Educated and Physically Active!" The mission of SHAPE America is to enhance professional practice and augment research related to health and physical education, physical activity, dance, and sport.

Its website is www.shapeamerica.org.

SOCIETY FOR PUBLIC HEALTH EDUCATION (SOPHE)

The Society for Public Health Education was established in 1950 and has more than 4,000 members. The primary mission of SOPHE is to provide leadership to the profession of health education and to contribute to the health of all people through advances in health education theory and research and excellence in health education practice, and to promote public policies conducive to health. The specific objectives of this organization are to:

- Expand the reach and effectiveness of advocacy efforts beyond SOPHE membership
- Promote the use of health education to eliminate health disparities

- Review, expand, and promote a dynamic research agenda for health education and behavioral sciences
- Support and enhance the professional preparation and training of health educators and public health professionals
- Proactively market health education
- Continually elevate SOPHE's performance in operations, governance, and resource development to achieve the strategic plan

Its website is www.sophe.org.

SOCIETY OF STATE LEADERS OF HEALTH AND PHYSICAL EDUCATION (SSLHP)

This is the new name of the organization formerly known as the Society of State Directors of Health, Physical Education and Recreation (SSDHPER). The Society was established in 1926. Its mission is to provide leadership in facilitating and promoting initiatives to achieve national health and education goals and objectives. Members of SSLHP supervise and coordinate programs in health, physical education, and related fields within state departments of education. Associate membership is available to individuals interested in the goals and programs of the society, but who do not work within a state education agency. Its specific objectives are to:

- Help shape national and state policy defining and supporting comprehensive school health and physical education programs
- Link state health, physical education, and recreation leaders with their counterparts in other states
- Forge school–family–community linkages in support of school health, physical education, and recreation programs
- Foster professional growth and the development of leadership and advocacy skills
- Help resolve complex issues in education and health reform
- Provide leadership in the effort to link postsecondary institutions to school districts for improvement in curriculum, instruction, and assessment
- Provide a supportive network of professional and social relationships among members
- Provide training and workshops for members to help them increase capacity to improve comprehensive school health education and programs within their states

Its website is www.thesociety.org.

BASIC VOCABULARY IN HEALTH EDUCATION AND HEALTH PROMOTION

Health education and health promotion have their roots in several disciplines: biological science, behavioral science, economics, political science, and other social sciences. As in any other field, certain terms and jargon are common to health promotion and health education professionals. Some of these terms are presented in this section. These terms are used when we talk of the antecedents of health behavior change.

AWARENESS

A concept commonly used by health educators is developing awareness of health topics. To undergo any behavior change, the person first needs to become aware of what he or she is going to change. The *American Heritage Dictionary* defines being aware as "being mindful or heedful." The word *aware* implies knowledge gained through one's own perceptions or other means of information. **Awareness** refers to becoming conscious about an action, idea, object, person, or situation. An example of building awareness is a health educator screening a film about avian flu (bird flu) in a community in which there have been no cases of avian flu and no one knows about this disease. When people are already aware of an issue—for example, that smoking is harmful to health—there is no need to build awareness regarding that issue.

INFORMATION

After becoming aware of the need to make a behavior change, the person starts to gather facts about the change. The collection of facts related to an action, idea, object, person, or situation is called **information**. Health educators provide information on various health topics through pamphlets, brochures, flyers, compact discs, videos, and so forth.

KNOWLEDGE

After gathering information for making a behavior change, the person needs to learn facts and gain insights related to the action, idea, object, person, or situation. These facts and insights are called **knowledge**. Knowledge is part of the cognitive domain, and Bloom (1956) identified six categories of cognitive learning. The first level is knowledge, which entails recalling data or information—for example, reciting the symptoms of a disease or knowing safety procedures. The second level is comprehension, or understanding the meaning, translation, interpolation, and interpretation of instructions and problems. An example is the ability to state a problem in one's own words. The third level is application, which entails using a concept in a new situation. It also means applying what was learned in the classroom setting to novel situations in the workplace. The fourth level is analysis, in which the person is able to separate concepts into component parts so that their organizational structure may be understood. For example, a health educator collects information about a community and then prioritizes the needs to decide what program to offer in the community. The fifth level is synthesis, in which the parts are put together to form a whole, with emphasis on creating a new meaning or structure. The sixth and final level is evaluation, where one makes judgments about the value of ideas or materials. Knowledge can be tested using true/false or multiple-choice questions.

> **Science is organized knowledge.**
>
> —Herbert Spencer

SKILLS

Performing any action requires a set of psychomotor **skills**. Performance entails physical movement, coordination, and use of the motor skill. Development of these skills requires practice and is measured in terms of speed, precision, distance, procedures, or techniques in execution (Simpson, 1972). Seven categories, ranging from the simplest to the most complex skill, have been identified:

1. *Perception.* The ability to use sensory cues to guide motor activity.
2. *Set.* The readiness to act. It includes mind-set, which predetermines a person's response to different situations.
3. *Guided response.* Early stages in learning a complex skill, which include imitation and trial and error.
4. *Mechanism.* Learned responses have become habitual, and the movements can be performed with some confidence and proficiency.
5. *Complex overt response.* Performance without hesitation; automatic performance.
6. *Adaptation.* Skills are well developed, and the individual can modify movement patterns to fit special requirements.
7. *Origination.* The person creates new movement patterns to fit a particular situation or specific problem.

Psychomotor skills are required in almost all health education programs. These are tested by demonstration and re-demonstration. For example, in a cardiopulmonary resuscitation program, the instructor first shows the correct technique and then checks to see whether the participants have learned the technique correctly.

HEALTH LITERACY

The 2000 Joint Committee on Health Education and Promotion Terminology (Gold & Miner, 2002, p. 5) defined **health literacy** as "the capacity of an individual to obtain, interpret, and understand basic health information and services and the competence to use such information and services in ways that are health enhancing." Zarcadoolas, Pleasant, and Greer (2003) have suggested a four-part model to understand health literacy:

1. *Fundamental literacy/numeracy.* Competence in understanding and using printed language, spoken language, numerals, and basic mathematical symbols or terms. This domain is involved in a wide range of cognitive, behavioral, and social skills and abilities.
2. *Literacy pertaining to science and technology.* Understanding the basic scientific and technological concepts, technical complexity, the phenomenon of scientific uncertainty, and the phenomenon of rapid change.
3. *Community/civic literacy.* Understanding about sources of information, agendas, and methods of interpreting those agendas. It enables people to engage in dialogue and decision making. It includes media interpretation skills and understanding civic and legislative functions.
4. *Cultural literacy.* Understanding collective beliefs, customs, worldviews, and social identity relationships to interpret and produce health information.

The Patient Protection and Affordable Care Act of 2010, Title V, defines health literacy as the degree to which an individual has the capacity to obtain, communicate, process, and understand basic health information and services to make appropriate health decisions (Centers for Disease Control & Prevention, 2015).

BELIEFS

Beliefs are convictions that a phenomenon is true or real (Rokeach, 1970). In other words, beliefs are statements of perceived fact or impressions about the world. These are neither correct nor incorrect. For example, a student may enter a classroom and say that the classroom is big. She may be used to smaller classrooms, and thus from her perspective the current classroom seems big. Another student may enter the same classroom and say that it is small. He may be used to bigger classrooms and, thus, from his perspective the classroom is small.

ATTITUDES

Attitudes are relatively constant feelings, predispositions, or sets of beliefs directed toward an idea, object, person, or situation (Mucchielli, 1970). Put another way, attitudes are beliefs with an evaluative component. Attitudes have an affective component and demonstrate what one likes and what one does not like. For example, the student who found the room too small might qualify that belief by saying that it is "an ugly, small room." Since an evaluation has been made that the student dislikes the room, it becomes an attitude. Likewise, another student might find the same room to be a cozy, small room and thus demonstrate an attitude of liking the room.

Attitudes are usually measured by self-reporting scales, such as Likert scales. Likert scales list several sentences about an object and then ask respondents whether they strongly agree, agree, disagree, or strongly disagree with each statement. The scores are then summed to measure the respondent's attitude toward that object.

VALUES

A collection of beliefs and attitudes makes up a value system. **Values** are enduring beliefs or systems of beliefs regarding whether a specific mode of conduct or end state of behavior is personally or socially preferable (Rokeach, 1970). Let us take the example of the student who likes cozy, small classrooms. He also likes the students and the instructor in the classroom and likes the textbook that has been assigned by his instructor. He likes to read and to complete his assignments on time. Such a student can be said to have a value system that values education.

COMMUNITY MOBILIZATION

A **community** is a collection of people identified by a set of shared values. Working with communities is fundamental to the practice of health education. The first step in working with a community is **community mobilization**, which involves persuading community members to attend or participate in any activity planned by the health educator. The purpose of community mobilization is to enhance awareness on a given issue at the community level. Activities such as organizing a talk in the community, arranging a health fair, and bringing together key leaders of the community for a panel discussion are all methods used in community mobilization.

COMMUNITY ORGANIZATION

The second step for action at a community level is **community organization**. The term *community organization* was coined by American social workers in the late 1800s to describe their efforts with immigrants and indigent people (Minkler & Wallerstein, 1997). In community organization, community members identify needs, set objectives, prioritize issues, develop plans, and implement projects for community improvement in health and related matters. Green and Kreuter (2005, p. G-2) define community organization as "the set of procedures and processes by which a population and its institutions mobilize and coordinate resources to solve a mutual problem or to pursue mutual goals." Activities such as group discussions and committee meetings are common at this stage.

COMMUNITY PARTICIPATION

When community members actively participate in planning or implementing projects, it is called **community participation**. Community participation can take place regarding health-related matters or other civic matters. Community members must be in leadership roles for true community participation. Arnstein (1971) has identified seven different types of participation in a ladder of participation. At the bottom of the ladder there is no participation—only manipulation. Token participation entails the levels of information, consultation, and placation. Development of partnerships, delegation of power, and citizen control are levels of participation that are desirable.

COMMUNITY DEVELOPMENT

At the stage of **community development**, local initiative and leadership in a community have been organized and stimulated so that changes in health or other matters are occurring. The key word in the concept of community development is *change* at the community level. Change can be measured by assessing changes in services or the provision of new services or by replacing existing policies or by incorporating new policies.

COMMUNITY EMPOWERMENT

The concept of **community empowerment** is closely related to the Ottawa Charter definition of community action for health. The World Health Organization (1998, p. 6) defines it as "a process through which people gain greater control over decisions and actions affecting their health." In essence, empowerment is a process whereby individuals gain mastery over their lives in the context of changing their social and political environments. Empowerment can be a social, cultural, psychological, or political process. Individual empowerment is different from community empowerment. Individual empowerment is mainly about an individual gaining control over his or her personal life. Community empowerment entails individuals collectively gaining greater influence and control over the determinants of health and the quality of life in their community.

NETWORKING

An important function of health promotion is to establish a network. Creating interdependent relationships with individuals, groups, and organizations to accomplish mutually set objectives in health or other matters is called **networking**.

COALITION BUILDING

No single organization can effectively achieve changes in the health status of a community; collaboration between agencies, groups, and organizations is needed. A grouping of separate organizations in a community united to pursue a common goal related to health or other matters affecting a large number of people is called a **coalition**. It takes time and concerted effort to develop such coalitions; this art is called *coalition building*, and it is a vital function for achieving health promotion goals.

ADVOCACY

Advocacy is active support of an idea or cause that entails especially the act of pleading or arguing for something. Green and Kreuter (2005, p. G-1) define advocacy as "working for political, regulatory, or organizational change on behalf of a particular interest group or population." Advocacy in health involves creating a shift in public opinion and mobilizing the essential resources to support any issue or policy that affects the health of a community or a constituency. It is a vital function for achieving health promotion goals.

LOBBYING

Lobbying is working with and influencing policy makers to develop an issue or a policy affecting the health of a community. It is an important activity in health promotion. Oftentimes health lobbyists have to compete with more powerful and resource-rich lobbyists from business or industry.

POLICY DEVELOPMENT

Policies are made by institutions or governments (local, state, or federal). Health promotion professionals work with institutional heads or other lawmakers to develop health policies. The process of developing a policy with ramifications for the health of communities is called **policy development**.

LEGISLATION

Legislation refers to the laws passed by elected officials at the local, state, or federal level. Legislation has ramifications for the health of a large number of people. Health promotion professionals work at every step of the way to influence laws that foster healthy behaviors and help in extinguishing negative and unhealthy behaviors.

DEVELOPMENT OF SOCIAL NORMS

Creating social acceptance for a practice, behavior, condition, policy, law, or environment that may affect the health in a community is called **development of social norms**. Health promotion professionals develop social norms so that healthy behaviors become acceptable and normative.

ROLE OF THEORY IN HEALTH EDUCATION AND HEALTH PROMOTION

Several disciplines influence health education and health promotion in many ways. But health education is influenced primarily by the behavioral sciences, and health promotion is deeply embedded in the social sciences. It is from these behavioral and social sciences that the practice of health education and health promotion borrows the strategic planning of its methods.

The core concepts in behavioral and social sciences are organized in the form of theories. Theories are developed as a result of research. Kerlinger and Lee (2000, p. 8) have defined theory as "a set of interrelated concepts, definitions, and predispositions that present a systematic view of events or situations by specifying relations among variables in order to explain and predict the events or situations." In health education and health promotion, we are primarily interested in predicting or explaining changes in behaviors or environments. A theoretical foundation is becoming almost mandatory for practitioners of health education and health promotion. These days, even for entry-level health educators, competency in developing a logical scope and sequence plan for health education is a requirement (NCHEC, SOPHE, & AAHE, 2006). Graduate-level health educators must base their practice on accepted theory. Theories help us articulate assumptions and hypotheses about the strategies and targets of interventions (National Cancer Institute, 2005).

Polit and Hungler (1999) have classified theories into three types. Macro theories, or grand theories, purport to explain and describe large segments of the environment or human experience. Talcott Parsons's (1951) theory on social functioning is an example of a macro theory. Middle-range theories describe or explain phenomena such as specific behaviors. Albert Bandura's (1986, 2004) social cognitive theory is an example of a midrange theory. Finally, descriptive theories describe or explain a single discrete phenomenon, such as Hans Selye's (1974) explanation of general adaptation syndrome.

Glanz, Rimer, and Viswanath (2008) have classified theories as explanatory theories, or theories of the problem, and change theories, or theories of action. Explanatory theories help describe and identify why a problem exists and search for modifiable constructs. Change theories guide the development of interventions and form the basis of evaluation.

Theories start from discussions of concepts or ideas that are abstract entities. These are not measurable or observable. The concepts are adopted into theories and become known as constructs. For example, in social cognitive theory (Bandura, 1986, 2004), "self-efficacy" is a construct. When specific properties are assigned to the construct, it becomes an indicator. For example, a questionnaire examining self-efficacy may contain 10 items, which constitute what the construct means. A variable or quantitative score can be derived from each indicator, and this will vary from one individual to other. For example, in the 10-item questionnaire each item may be ranked from 1 to 5, and the summation may yield a score between 10 and 50. The constructs of a theory are constantly refined by empirical testing. A theory must be able to demonstrate predictive power. Behavioral theories must be able to make significant changes on affect (feelings or conation), thought (cognition), and action (volition). Ideally a theory provides practical guidance on what, why, and how. An ideal theory must be testable and must be generalizable. The constructs of the theory must be able to explain phenomena, which for health education and health promotion are behaviors or environmental conditions. **Figure 1-1** shows a generic depiction of a behavioral theory.

There is nothing so practical as a good theory.

—Kurt Lewin

Theories derived from behavioral or social science help the practice of health education and health promotion in several ways. First, the use of a theory helps in developing program objectives that are measurable. For example, if the health education program uses social cognitive theory (Bandura, 1986, 2004) to change physical activity behavior in elementary school students, then the objectives can be based on the following three constructs derived from the theory: (1) At the end of the program 80% of the participants are able to demonstrate positive change in their physical activity expectations score from before to after the intervention, (2) at the end of the program 80% of the participants are able to demonstrate positive change in their physical activity self-efficacy score from before to after the intervention, and (3) at

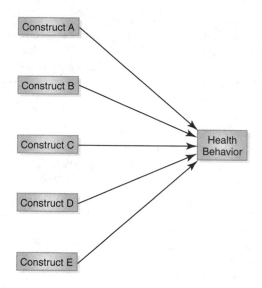

FIGURE 1-1 Generic depiction of a behavioral theory.

the end of the program 80% of the participants are able to demonstrate positive change in their physical activity self-control score from before to after the intervention.

Second, a theory helps in identifying the method to use in health education or health promotion. For example, to change self-efficacy, the behavior must be taught in small steps, so demonstration could be used as a method. Third, a theory helps in deciding the timing of the intervention. For example, interventions that prevent use of tobacco should be implemented at the middle school level because that is when the behavior is beginning. Fourth, a theory helps in choosing the right mix of strategies and methods. In the earlier example, we were able to choose three constructs of the social cognitive theory because the theory suggests that those three constructs are important for early-stage adolescents.

Fifth, a theory aids communication between professionals. The constructs of each theory remain the same in different applications, so readers can understand what was done across the studies. Sixth, the use of a theory helps in replication of the program because the same constructs can be used from one intervention to the other. Finally, behavioral and social science theories help educators to design programs that are more effective (have greater impact) and more efficient (take less time). These benefits are summarized in **Table 1-6**.

Table 1-6	Benefits of Theory in Health Education and Health Promotion
Helps in discerning measurable program outcomes	
Specifies methods for behavior change	
Identifies the timing for interventions	
Helps in choosing the right mix of strategies	
Enhances communication between professionals	
Improves replication	
Improves program efficiency and effectiveness	

Table 1-7	The SMART Way to Write Objectives
S = Specific (what exactly is being changed and in whom)	
M = Measurable (percentage of participants who will change)	
A = Action verb (list, describe, identify, explain)	
R = Realistic (must be achievable)	
T = Time frame (end of the session, end of one year)	

APPLICATION EXERCISE

Go to your library webpage and see if you have access to MEDLINE, CINAHL, and ERIC databases. If you have access, then conduct this exercise using those three databases. If not, go to the following website which has public domain MEDLINE (PubMed): www.ncbi.nlm.nih.gov/pubmed.

Choose a health behavior that interests you, such as a physical activity behavior or a behavior of eating fruits and vegetables. Then choose a target population such as schoolchildren or worksite. Add the key words "theory" and "intervention" to your key words for a "behavior" and a "target population," and conduct a search for a theory-based health education or health promotion intervention. Choose one article from your library or Internet search, and summarize it in 500 words.

SKILL-BUILDING ACTIVITY

Think of either a positive behavior or a negative behavior amenable to modification by health education. Choose a target population for whom this behavior would be most relevant. Now, using the SMART way of writing objectives shown in **Table 1-7**, write at least three program objectives that would help bring about positive change in this behavior in your target population.

SUMMARY

Health is a means to achieve desirable goals in life while maintaining a multidimensional (physical, mental, social, political, economic, and spiritual) equilibrium that is operationalized for individuals as well as for communities. Health behaviors are actions with potentially measurable frequency, intensity, and duration performed at the individual, interpersonal, organizational, community, or public policy level for primary, secondary, or tertiary prevention. Health education is the systematic application of a set of techniques to voluntarily and positively influence health through changing the antecedents of behavior (awareness, information, knowledge, skills, beliefs, attitudes, and values) in individuals, groups, or communities. Health promotion is the process of empowering people to improve their health by providing educational, political, legislative, organizational, social, and community supports.

Health education and health promotion professionals assess individual and community needs; plan health education strategies, interventions, and programs; implement health education strategies, interventions, and programs; conduct evaluation and research related to health education; administer health education strategies, interventions, and programs; serve as health education resources; and communicate and advocate for health and health education. All these functions can be aided by the use of theories from the behavioral and social sciences. Theories help to discern measurable program outcomes, specify methods for behavior change, identify the timing for interventions, choose the right mix of strategies, enhance communication between professionals, improve replication, and improve program efficiency and effectiveness.

IMPORTANT TERMS

advocacy
attitudes
awareness
behavior
beliefs
certified health education specialist (CHES)
certified in public health (CPH)
coalition
code of ethics for health educators
community
community development
community empowerment
community mobilization
community organization
community participation
development of social norms
dietitian
health
health behavior

health coach
health education
health literacy
health promotion
information
knowledge
legislation
lobbying
master certified health education specialist (MCHES)
networking
nursing educator
policy development
primary prevention
secondary prevention
skills
tertiary prevention
values

REVIEW QUESTIONS

1. How has the World Health Organization defined health? Discuss the limitations of this definition of health.
2. Differentiate between health education and health promotion.
3. Differentiate among primary, secondary, and tertiary prevention.
4. What are the areas of responsibilities for entry-level health educators?
5. What are the differences in responsibilities for entry-level health educators and graduate-level health educators?
6. Identify at least five settings for health education.
7. Discuss at least five areas in the code of ethics for the health education profession.
8. Discuss the objectives of any one national-level health education organization.
9. Differentiate between attitudes and beliefs.

10. Differentiate between community mobilization and community empowerment.

11. Define theory. What are the benefits of using a theory in health education and health promotion?

WEBSITES TO EXPLORE

American Public Health Association (APHA)

www.apha.org/

The American Public Health Association (APHA) is the oldest and largest organization of public health professionals in the world, representing more than 50,000 members from more than 50 public health occupations including health education. APHA is an association of individuals and organizations that works to improve the public's health and to achieve equity in health status for all. APHA promotes the scientific and professional foundation of public health practice and policy, advocates for the conditions of a healthy global society, emphasizes prevention, and enhances the ability of members to promote and protect environmental and community health. *Visit this website and read about the latest public health news.*

Eta Sigma Gamma (ESG)

www.etasigmagamma.org/

Eta Sigma Gamma was founded on the campus of Ball State University in Muncie, Indiana, on August 14, 1967. It is the national health education honorary society. The principal purpose of Eta Sigma Gamma is to elevate the standards, ideals, competence, and ethics of professionally trained men and women in and for the health science discipline. *Visit this website and find out more about the national officers of this organization. Does your university have a chapter? Find information on starting a chapter at your college or explore the criteria for joining an existing chapter.*

National Board of Public Health Examiners (NBPHE)

www.nbphe.org/

The mission of NBPHE is to test the knowledge and skills of students and graduates from schools and programs of public health accredited by the Council on Education for Public Health (CEPH). *Explore this website and find the date of the next exam. Evaluate what you need to do to become eligible for this exam.*

National Commission for Health Education Credentialing (NCHEC)

www.nchec.org/

The mission of NCHEC is to improve the practice of health education and to serve the public and profession of health education by certifying health education specialists, promoting professional development, and strengthening professional preparation and practice. This organization credentials health educators in the United States. Requirements for the Certified Health Education Specialist (CHES) examination, dates for examinations, requirements for continuing education, and a forum for job seekers and employers are presented on the website. *Explore this website and find the date of the next exam. Evaluate what you need to do to become eligible for this exam.*

Society of Health and Physical Educators (SHAPE America)

www.shapeamerica.org/

SHAPE America was founded in 1855 and has undergone seven name changes since; its present name dates from 2014. SHAPE America is one of the largest organizations of physical educators. Its mission is to advance professional practice and promote research related to health and physical education, physical activity, dance, and sport. *Visit this website and find out the different types of membership. Locate your district and find out some of the activities that are occurring there.*

Society for Public Health Education (SOPHE)

www.sophe.org/

SOPHE was founded in 1950 and is an independent, international professional association made up of a diverse membership of health education professionals and students. Its mission is to provide leadership to the profession of health education and health promotion and to contribute to the health of all people through advances in health education theory and research, excellence in health education practice, and the promotion of public policies conducive to health. The website presents news and announcements, benefits of joining, opportunities for continuing education, and advocacy. *Explore this website and find the date of the next SOPHE midyear or annual meeting. Visit the resources and links and learn about other health education organizations.*

World Health Organization (WHO)

www.who.int/en/

The website has information about the formation and organization of WHO, health information about all countries, alphabetical information about common health topics, a list of WHO publications, and a database of all WHO publications and WHO sites. *Read the constitution of the World Health Organization. Reflect on the successes and failures of this organization since its inception in 1948.*

REFERENCES

Airhihenbuwa, C. O., Cottrell, R. R., Adeyanju, M., Auld, M. E., Lysoby, L., & Smith, B. J. (2005). The National Health Educator Competencies Update Project: Celebrating a milestone and recommending next steps to the profession. *American Journal of Health Education, 36*, 361–370.

Allegrante, J. P., Airhihenbuwa, C. O., Auld, M. E., Birch, D. A., Roe, K. M., & Smith, B. J. (2004). Toward a unified system of accreditation for professional preparation in health education: Final report of the National Task Force on Accreditation in Health Education. *Health Education and Behavior, 31*, 668–683.

American Association for Health Education. (2003). Directory of institutions offering undergraduate and graduate degree programs in health education. 2003 edition. *American Journal of Health Education, 34*(4), 219–235.

American Association for Health Education, National Commission for Health Education Credentialing, & Society for Public Health Education. (1999). *A competency-based framework for graduate-level health educators.* Allentown, PA: National Commission for Health Education Credentialing.

Arnstein, S. R. (1971). Eight rungs on the ladder of citizen participation. In E. S. Cahn & B. A. Passett (Eds.), *Citizen participation: Effecting community change* (p. 70). New York: Praeger.

Bandura, A. (1986). *Social foundations of thought and action.* Englewood Cliffs, NJ: Prentice-Hall.

Bandura, A. (2004). Health promotion by social cognitive means. *Health Education and Behavior, 31*, 143–164.

Bensley, R. J. (1991). Defining spiritual health: A review of the literature. *Journal of Health Education, 22*(5), 287–290.

Bloom, B. S. (1956). *Taxonomy of educational objectives. Handbook I: The cognitive domain.* New York: David McKay.

Centers for Disease Control and Prevention, (2015). Learn about health literacy. Retrieved from http://www.cdc .gov/healthliteracy/learn/

Coalition of National Health Education Organizations. (2004). Code of ethics. Retrieved from http://www.hsc.usf .edu/CFH/cnheo/ethics.htm

Cook, H. (2004). Historical keywords. Health. *Lancet, 364*, 1481.

Downie, R., Fyfe, C., & Tannahill, A. (1990). *Health promotion: Models and values.* Oxford, UK: Oxford University Press.

Gilmore, G. D., Olsen, L. K., Taub, A., & Connell, D. (2005). Overview of the National Health Educator Competencies Update Project, 1998–2004. *Health Education and Behavior, 32*, 725–737.

Glanz, K., Rimer, B. K., & Viswanath, K, (2008). *Health behavior and health education. Theory, research, and practice* (4th ed.). San Francisco: Jossey-Bass.

Gochman, D. S. (1982). Labels, systems, and motives: Some perspectives on future research. *Health Education Quarterly, 9*, 167–174.

Gochman, D. S. (1997). Health behavior research: Definitions and diversity. In D. S. Gochman (Ed.), *Handbook of health behavior research: Vol. 1. Personal and social determinants.* New York: Plenum Press.

Gold, R. S., & Miner, K. R., for the 2000 Joint Committee on Health Education and Promotion Terminology. (2002). Report of the 2000 Joint Committee on Health Education and Promotion Terminology. *Journal of School Health, 72*, 3–7.

Green, L. W., & Kreuter, M. W. (2005). *Health program planning: An educational and ecological approach* (4th ed.). Boston: McGraw-Hill.

Institute of Medicine. (1988). *Future of public health.* Washington, DC: National Academy Press.

Institute of Medicine. (2002). *The future of the public's health in the 21st century.* Washington, DC: National Academy Press.

Kerlinger, F. N., & Lee, H. B. (2000). *Foundations of behavioral research* (4th ed.). Fort Worth, TX: Harcourt College.

McDowell, I., & Newell, C. (1987). The theoretical and technical foundations of health measurement. In I. McDowell & C. Newell (Eds.), *Measuring health: A guide to rating scales and questionnaires* (pp. 10–42). New York: Oxford University Press.

Minkler, M., & Wallerstein, N. (1997). Improving health through community organization and community building. A health education perspective. In M. Minkler (Ed.), *Community organizing and community building for health.* New Brunswick, NJ: Rutgers University Press.

Modeste, N. M., & Tamayose, T. (Eds.). (2004). *Dictionary of public health promotion and education. Terms and concepts* (2nd ed.). San Francisco: Jossey-Bass.

Mucchielli, R. (1970). *Introduction to structural psychology.* New York: Funk and Wagnalls.

National Board of Public Health Examiners. (2015). National Board of Public Health Examiners. Retrieved from http://www.nbphe.org

National Cancer Institute. (2005). *Theory at a glance: A guide for health promotion practice* (2nd ed.). Washington, DC: U.S. Department of Health and Human Services.

National Commission for Health Education Credentialing. (1985). *A framework for the development of competency based curricula for entry-level health educators.* New York: Author.

National Commission for Health Education Credentialing. (2010). Health educator job analysis 2010. Executive summary and recommendations. Retrieved from http://nchec.sitewrench.com/assets/2251/health_educator_job _analysis_ex_summary-final-2-19-10.pdf

National Commission for Health Education Credentialing. (2015a). Health education specialist practice analysis (HESPA) study: Executive summary. Retrieved from http://nchec.sitewrench.com/assets/2251/executive _summary.pdf

National Commission for Health Education Credentialing. (2015b). Responsibilities and competencies for health education specialists. Retrieved from http://nchec.sitewrench.com/responsibilities-and-competencies

National Commission for Health Education Credentialing, Society for Public Health Education, & American Association for Health Education. (2006). *Competency-based framework for health educators—2006*. Whitehall, PA: Author.

Parsons, T. (1951). *The social system*. New York: Free Press.

Perrin, K. M., & McDermott, R. J. (1997). The spiritual dimension of health: A review. *American Journal of Health Studies, 13*(2), 90–99.

Pickett, G., & Hanlon, J. J. (1998). *Public health: Administration and practice* (10th ed.). St. Louis, MO: Mosby.

Polit, D. F., & Hungler, B. P. (1999). *Nursing research: Principles and methods* (6th ed.). Philadelphia: Lippincott.

Public Health Functions Steering Committee. (1994). Public health in America. Retrieved from http://www.health.gov/phfunctions/public.htm

Rehrig, M. (2010, Winter). The long awaited advanced credential, MCHES, Don't miss out. *The CHES Bulletin, 21*(1), 1.

Rokeach, M. (1970). *Beliefs, attitudes and values*. San Francisco: Jossey-Bass.

Selye, H. (1974). *The stress of life*. New York: McGraw-Hill.

Simpson, E. J. (1972). *The classification of educational objectives in the psychomotor domain*. Washington, DC: Gryphon House.

Taub, A., Kreuter, M., Parcel, G., & Vitello, E. (1987). Report from the AAHE/SOPHE Joint Committee on Ethics. *Health Education Quarterly, 14*(1), 79–90.

U.S. Department of Health, Education and Welfare. (1978). *Preparation and practice of community, patient, and school health educators: Proceedings of the workshop on commonalities and differences*. Washington, DC: Division of Allied Health Professions.

U.S. Department of Health and Human Services. (1979). *Healthy People: The surgeon general's report on health promotion and disease prevention*. Washington, DC: Author.

U.S. Department of Health and Human Services. (1980). *Promoting health—preventing disease. Objectives for the nation*. Washington, DC: Author.

U.S. Department of Health and Human Services. (1990). *Healthy People 2000. National health promotion and disease prevention objectives*. Washington, DC: Author.

U.S. Department of Health and Human Services. (2000). *Healthy People 2010* (Vols. *1–2*). Washington, DC: Author.

U.S. Department of Health and Human Services. (2009). *Healthy People 2020: The road ahead*. Retrieved from http://www.healthypeople.gov/HP2020/default.asp

World Health Organization. (1974). Constitution of the World Health Organization. *Chronicle of the World Health Organization, 1*, 29–43.

World Health Organization. (1986). *Ottawa charter for health promotion, 1986*. Geneva, Switzerland: Author.

World Health Organization. (1997). *The Jakarta Declaration on leading health promotion into the 21st century*. Geneva, Switzerland: Author.

World Health Organization. (1998). Health promotion glossary. Retrieved from http://www.who.int/hpr/NPH/docs/hp_glossary_en.pdf

Zarcadoolas, C., Pleasant A., & Greer, D. S. (2003). Elaborating a definition of health literacy: A commentary. *Journal of Health Communication, 8*, 119–120.

Chapter 2

PLANNING MODELS IN HEALTH EDUCATION AND HEALTH PROMOTION

KEY CONCEPTS

- assessment protocol for excellence in public health (APEXPH)
- CDCynergy
- comprehensive health education model (CHEM)
- intervention mapping model
- model
- model for health education planning (MHEP)
- model for health education planning and resource development (MHEPRD)
- multilevel approach to community health (MATCH)
- PEN-3 model
- planned approach to community health (PATCH)
- PRECEDE-PROCEED model
- social-ecological models

AFTER READING THIS CHAPTER YOU SHOULD BE ABLE TO

- Differentiate between a theory and a model
- Apply the PRECEDE-PROCEED model of planning in health education and health promotion
- Identify the main components of the planned approach to community health (PATCH) model
- Describe the multilevel approach to community health (MATCH) model
- Narrate the steps and processes in the intervention mapping model
- Explain the assessment protocol for excellence in public health (APEXPH) model
- Explicate the comprehensive health education model (CHEM)
- Describe the model for health education planning (MHEP)
- Elaborate on the model for health education planning and resource development (MHEPRD)

- Explain the PEN-3 model
- Summarize the CDCynergy model
- Explain the social-ecological model

DIFFERENCES BETWEEN A MODEL AND A THEORY

A theory helps health education and health promotion programs identify program objectives, specify methods for facilitating behavior change, provide guidance about the timing of the methods, and select the methods of intervention. These are all very specific functions in the broad area of planning. Planning skills are one of the seven essential responsibilities of health educators. In addition to setting objectives and selecting methods, planning functions may include assessing needs, prioritizing needs, allocating resources, matching human resources to tasks, and so on. To achieve these goals, health promotion and health education planning relies on various models.

A **model** can be characterized as a theory in its early stages. Models are eclectic, creative, simplified, miniaturized applications of concepts for addressing problems. Model makers present their ideas but may not yet have the empirical evidence through testing and experimentation that are required of a theory. Sometimes a model is thoroughly tested, yet the word "model" sticks as part of its name. Unlike theories, models do not provide guidance for micro-level management. An example of a model is the PRECEDE-PROCEED model (Green & Kreuter, 2005), which is used in planning health promotion and health education programs. This model provides guidance for planning at the macro level: what behaviors to target, what resources to tap, how to mobilize the community, and so on. A theory such as social cognitive theory provides guidance at the micro level; it tells which attitudes to change for making the behavior change, what activities to do with the target audience, what educational methods to employ, and so forth. **Table 2-1** summarizes the differences between a model and a theory.

> **Planning is bringing the future into the present so that you can do something about it now.**
>
> —Alan Lakein

The essential competencies identified by the Health Education Specialist Practice Analysis (HESPA) (National Commission for Health Education Credentialing, 2015) for health education

Table 2-1	Comparison Between a Model and a Theory
Theory	**Model**
Explains or predicts phenomena	Simplified, miniaturized application of concepts for addressing problems
Micro-level guidance	Macro-level guidance
Empirically tested	Not enough empirical evidence
Based in previous literature	Creative
Usually parsimonious	Usually tries to cover a lot
Does not contain any model	May embody one or more theories
Example: Social cognitive theory	Example: PRECEDE-PROCEED model

Table 2-2	Competencies Identified by the Health Education Specialist Practice Analysis (HESPA) (National Commission For Health Education Credentialing, 2015) for Health Education Specialists Who Are Planning Health Education and Promotion
2.1	Involve priority populations, partners, and other stakeholders in the planning process.
2.2	Develop goals and objectives.
2.3	Select or design strategies and interventions.
2.4	Develop a plan for delivery of health education/promotion.
2.5	Assess factors that influence implementation of health education and promotion.

specialists who are planning health education and promotion are summarized in **Table 2-2**. To fulfill these competencies at the macro level, planning models are needed; to accomplish these functions at the micro level, theories are needed.

This chapter focuses on models that are used in planning health promotion and health education programs at the macro level. Later chapters emphasize micro-level planning using behavioral and social science theories. We begin with an overview of the various planning models and the process of planning. The models discussed in this chapter are the PRECEDE-PROCEED model (Green & Kreuter, 2005); planned approach to community health (PATCH) model (U.S. Department of Health and Human Services [USDHHS], 2005); multilevel approach to community health (MATCH) model (Simons-Morton, Greene, & Gottlieb, 1995); intervention mapping model (Bartholomew, Parcel, Kok, & Gottlieb, 2006); assessment protocol for excellence in public health (APEXPH) model (National Association of County and City Health Officials, 1991); comprehensive health education model (CHEM) (Sullivan, 1973); model for health education planning (MHEP) (Ross & Mico, 1980); model for health education planning and resource development (MHEPRD) (Bates & Winder, 1984); PEN-3 model (Airhihenbuwa, 1993); and the CDCynergy model (Centers for Disease Control and Prevention [CDC], 2004). Linnan and colleagues (2005) surveyed instructors at 253 accredited graduate and undergraduate health education programs to gather information about planning and the professional preparation of health educators. Among survey respondents, 88% used the PRECEDE-PROCEED model in their teaching, and 62% used the planned approach to community health (PATCH) model. The following discussion presents the models in the order of their popularity as identified by these survey respondents.

PRECEDE-PROCEED MODEL

One of the most popular models in health education is the **PRECEDE-PROCEED model**; approximately 1,000 applications of this model had been published in the health field as of the early 2000s (Green & Kreuter, 2005). The acronym PRECEDE stands for predisposing, reinforcing, and enabling constructs in educational/environmental diagnosis and evaluation. The acronym PROCEED stands for policy, regulatory, and organizational constructs in educational and environmental development.

The model originated in the 1970s from applications in hypertension trials (Green, Levine, & Deeds, 1975; Green, Levine, Wolle, & Deeds, 1979), cost-benefit evaluations of health education programs (Green, 1974), family planning studies (Green, 1970), and immunization campaigns (Rosenstock, Derryberry, & Carriger, 1959). The model was initially called PRECEDE (predisposing, reinforcing, and enabling constructs in educational diagnosis and evaluation) and remained popular under that name throughout the 1980s (Green, Kreuter, Deeds, & Partridge, 1980). In the 1980s the movement for health promotion grew very strong; in response, the model evolved, and a number of health promotion functions were added. As a result, it came to be known as PRECEDE-PROCEED. In the 1990s the role of socioenvironmental approaches was strengthened even further, and the model emphasized the ecological approach. The latest edition of this model was published in 2005 (Green & Kreuter, 2005). For a detailed discussion of this model, see *Health Program Planning: An Educational and Ecological Approach* (Green & Kreuter, 2005). **Figure 2-1** depicts the model.

The eight phases of the PRECEDE-PROCEED model provide guidance in planning any health program. The first phase is *social assessment*. An assessment of community perceptions provides a starting point for identifying quality of life concerns, and methods such as asset mapping, social reconnaissance, nominal group process, the Delphi method, focus groups, central location intercept interviews, and surveys may be employed. Asset mapping is an assessment of the strengths, capacities, and skills of individuals and the existing resources in a community. In social reconnaissance, a point of entry into the community is chosen and local players are identified; this is followed by preparation of research and briefing materials and identification of leaders and representatives. This is followed in turn by field interviews and then analysis, reporting, and follow-up. In the

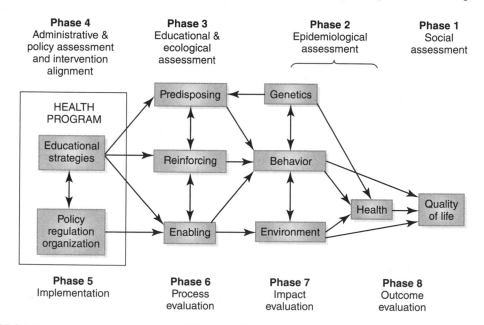

FIGURE 2-1 Generic representation of the PRECEDE-PROCEED model for health, program planning, and evaluation that shows the main lines of causation from program inputs and determinants of health to outcomes by the direction of the arrows.

nominal group process, community participants are recruited and are asked to reflect on a single question. The responses are collected and then ranked in importance by the participants to establish a priority list. In the Delphi method, a panel of experts is recruited and sent a questionnaire. Subsequent mailings of the questionnaire aim at deriving consensus, and the choices are narrowed at each iteration. Focus group discussions are small group discussions on a given topic moderated by a facilitator. Central location intercept interviews are conducted at shopping malls, churches, and other places where target population members can be found. These interviews typically include structured, close-ended questions. Surveys also consist of asking questions of the target population and can be done by mail, e-mail, online, or other means.

The second phase is *epidemiological assessment*, and it includes identifying the specific health problems that are contributing to or interacting with the quality of life concerns identified in the social assessment. This phase also identifies the causative factors in the three categories of genetics, behavior, and environment. Epidemiology assessment consists of two parts—descriptive and analytical—and attempts to gather information on both these aspects. In **descriptive epidemiology**, facts regarding the time, place, and population attributes of the health problem are collected through mortality (death), morbidity (illness), and disability rates. **Analytical epidemiology** examines the determinants of health. In this model analytical work translates into identifying behaviors and environments. Behaviors are of three types: proximal, or direct, actions affecting health; actions influencing the health of others; and distal actions affecting the organizational or policy environment. To diagnose behaviors that need to be targeted, the behavioral factors are rated in terms of importance and changeability. Behavioral objectives are developed for those behaviors that are judged to be more changeable and more important. To diagnose environments, environmental factors are rated in terms of importance and changeability. Environmental objectives also are determined by focusing on the more changeable and more important ones listed.

The third phase is *educational and ecological assessment*. In this phase, factors are classified into the hallmark categories of this model as predisposing, enabling, or reinforcing factors. **Predisposing factors** are antecedents to behavioral change that provide motivation for the behavior (for example, knowledge, beliefs, attitudes, values, perceptions). **Enabling factors** are antecedents to behavioral or environmental change that allow a motivation or environmental policy to be realized (for example, availability of resources, accessibility, laws, legislations, skills). **Reinforcing factors** follow a behavior and provide continuing reward for sustaining the behavior (for example, family, peers, teachers, employers, health providers, community leaders, or decision makers). In this phase the factors are identified and sorted, priorities are determined, and once again priorities within categories are identified using the criteria of changeability and importance.

The fourth phase is *administrative and policy assessment and intervention alignment*. In this phase the program components are aligned with priorities, resources needed to run the program are identified, barriers that may influence the program are addressed, and policies needed to run the program are developed. In aligning priority determinants with program components, ecological levels are first matched with program components, followed by mapping specific interventions, and finally pooling previous interventions to patch any gaps. This phase assesses aspects such as time, personnel, and budget.

The fifth phase is *implementation*. In this phase several factors may hinder or augment the impact of the program. These factors pertain to the program (such as resources and goals), the implementing organization (such as employee attributes, organizational goals, and organizational climate), the political milieu, and the environment (such as timing and other organizations).

The sixth phase is *process evaluation*. In this phase, the first evaluation is whether the intervention has been implemented in the manner in which it was planned. For example, if 10 activities were planned, have all of them been implemented, and to what extent have they been implemented? Second, the reception of the program at the site where it has been implemented is evaluated. Third, the attitudes of the recipients of the program are considered. How satisfied have they been with the program? What did they like and what did they dislike about the program? Fourth, the response of the person implementing the program is determined. What difficulties did he or she face while implementing the program? What things were easy to do? Finally, the competencies of the personnel involved are assessed. For example, if health education work was done, was it done by a certified health education specialist or someone else?

The seventh phase is *impact evaluation*. Impact evaluation assesses the immediate effect of the program on its target behaviors or environments and their predisposing, enabling, and reinforcing antecedents. For example, a program designed to combat obesity in a community would measure physical activity and consumption of fruits and vegetables.

The final phase is *outcome evaluation*. In this phase, changes in health status (such as mortality, morbidity, and disability indicators) and quality of life concerns (such as perceived quality of life and unemployment) are measured.

The PRECEDE-PROCEED model has been used in a variety of applications in health promotion and health education programming, including coalition building (Fisher et al., 1996), enhancing community participation (Lengerich et al., 2007; Watson, Horowitz, Garcia, & Canto, 2001), combatting domestic violence (Ekhtiari, Shojaeizadeh, Foroushani, Ghofranipour, & Ahmadis, 2014), planning multiple-channel interventions (Hall & Best, 1997), developing health instruments (Chang, Brown, Nitzke, & Baumann, 2004), conducting needs assessments (Brouse, Basch, Wolf, & Shmukler, 2004; Hu, Wallace, Jones, & Liu, 2009; Li, Cao, Lin, Li, Wang, & He, 2009), implementing health risk appraisals at worksites (Bailey, Rukholm, Vanderlee, & Hyland, 1994), planning disease prevention programs at worksites (Wilkens, 2003), planning employee assistance programs at worksites (Dille, 1999), planning health programs in school settings (MacDonald & Green, 2001), weight management programs (Cole & Horacek, 2009, 2010), training health care staff (Larson, Cohn, Meyer, & Boden-Albala, 2009; Macrina, Macrina, Horvath, Gallaspy, & Fine, 1996), improving self-care (Chiang, Huang, Yeh, & Lu, 2004), implementing patient education on anticoagulant therapy (Shaha et al., 2015), and ensuring compliance behaviors (Kang, Han, Kim, & Kim, 2006). **Table 2–3** summarizes these applications.

The developers of this model, Larry Green and Marshall Kreuter, teamed up with Robert Gold to develop a computerized software program designed to help health educators in academia who teach community health courses and assist practitioners in the field to plan and implement community health programs. The software is called EMPOWER (enabling methods of planning and organizing within everyone's reach) (Gold, Green, & Kreuter, 1998). The program provides a specific example in the area of breast cancer prevention and control and walks the user through the various steps of the PRECEDE-PROCEED model.

The PRECEDE-PROCEED model is by far the most popular and most researched model in the field of health promotion and health education. It has been in existence for four decades, and professional health

> The hallmarks of the PRECEDE-PROCEED model are: (1) flexibility and scalability, (2) evidence-based process and evaluability, (3) its commitment to the principle of participation, and (4) its provision of a process for appropriate adaptation of evidence-based "best practices."
>
> —Green and Kreuter (2005, p. 18)

Table 2-3	Applications of the PRECEDE-PROCEED Model
Coalition building	
Enhancing community participation	
Combatting domestic violence	
Planning multiple-channel interventions	
Developing health instruments	
Conducting needs assessments	
Implementing health risk appraisals at worksites	
Planning disease prevention programs at worksites	
Planning employee assistance programs (EAPs) at worksites	
Planning health programs in school settings	
Weight management programs	
Training health care staff	
Improving self-care	
Implementing patient education on anticoagulant therapy	
Ensuring compliance behaviors	

educators are familiar with this model. It is very comprehensive and covers all areas of planning. The initiation of the model utilizes community inputs and participation, which is a big plus. The phased evaluation is also a strong feature of the model.

However, the model does have a few limitations. First, it is too comprehensive to be fully implemented in many situations. Health promotion and education funding may be allocated for work in a specific area, with no provision for social assessment or epidemiological assessment. In such cases, the model is implemented in a piecemeal fashion. Second, health promotion and education programs are often implemented on a limited basis. These programs may not account for changes in health outcomes, making evaluation impossible. Third, the model is a mixture of several theories, and it is not possible to discern which component of the model is working and to what extent. Finally, comparative studies with other models have not been done. Therefore, the relative utility of this model cannot be ascertained.

PLANNED APPROACH TO COMMUNITY HEALTH MODEL

The **planned approach to community health (PATCH) model** was developed in the mid-1980s by the Centers for Disease Control and Prevention in partnership with state and local health departments and several community groups (USDHHS, 2005). It is an effective community health planning model that is used by many states and communities and several countries. PATCH aims at increasing the capacity of communities to plan, implement, and evaluate community-based health promotion programs. Thus, capacity building is a very important part of the model. The PATCH model builds on the PRECEDE model (Kreuter, 1992), but is more user friendly and does not

PATCH was built on the same philosophy as the World Health Organization's Health for All and the Ottawa Charter for Health Promotion, which specifies that health promotion is the process of enabling people to increase control over their health and to improve their health.

—U.S. Department of Health
and Human Services
(2005, p. I-H-I)

use academic terminology. A key strategy of the PATCH model is that it builds linkages within the community and between the community and the state health department, universities, and other regional and national organizations.

After its initial development in 1984–1985, a pilot program using the PATCH model was tested in six states by the CDC. Based on the feedback received, it was revised and then delivered in 11 additional states. In 1988, evaluation studies were performed by the University of North Carolina, the Research Triangle Institute, and the PATCH National Working Group, and in all three studies the PATCH model was found to be effective. Since 1991, the CDC has not directly delivered the PATCH program in communities; instead, the CDC provides training and consultation to state health departments. Currently, most state health departments have a state coordinator and staff trained in the PATCH model. **Table 2-4** summarizes the five key elements of the PATCH model.

Active participation of community members is vital in the PATCH model. People participate in analyzing community data, setting priorities, planning intervention activities, and making decisions on the health priorities of their communities. Using qualitative and quantitative data to identify a community's health status and needs is also important in the PATCH model. Community members are engaged in analyzing the factors that contribute to a health problem, in linking with *Healthy People 2020* objectives (U.S. Department of Health and Human Services, 2009), and in designing health promotion interventions. Examples of these interventions are educational programs, mass media campaigns, and policy advocacy. These interventions are conducted in various settings, such as schools, health care facilities, community sites, and workplaces. Community members then conduct timely evaluations. Finally, the community becomes empowered and can replicate the process for more than one health condition.

The PATCH model has five distinct phases for planning a health program. The first phase is *mobilizing the community*. In this phase the target community is defined, participants are actively recruited from the community, partnerships are formed, and a demographic profile of the community is completed. Efforts are made to ensure that the participants who have been recruited are representative of the demographic profile of the community. In this phase a steering committee is also formed and community leaders are involved.

The second phase is *collecting and organizing data*. In this phase, community members obtain data on mortality, morbidity, community opinion, and behaviors. The quantitative data is collected from sources such as vital statistics and surveys, and the qualitative data is collected from community leaders and others. The data are analyzed and shared with the community.

Table 2-4	Key Elements of the PATCH Model
Community members participate in the process.	
Data guides the development of programs.	
Participants develop a comprehensive health promotion strategy.	
Evaluation emphasizes feedback and program improvement.	
Community capacity for health promotion is increased.	

The third phase is *choosing health priorities*. In this phase the community group analyzes the social, economic, political, and environmental factors that affect the behaviors that are detrimental for health. As a result of this analysis, they identify priorities and develop objectives.

The fourth phase is *developing a comprehensive intervention plan*. In this phase the community group identifies resources, assesses existing programs, reviews existing policies, and appraises conditions. Then the group develops intervention objectives and an intervention plan. The intervention plan includes details of strategies, a time line, and an activity plan for things such as recruiting volunteers, publicizing activities, evaluating activities, and informing the community about results.

The fifth phase is *evaluation*. The purpose is to monitor and assess progress achieved during the phases of PATCH and to evaluate interventions. The unique feature here is that the community determines the end points of evaluation, and feedback is provided to the community.

Goodman, Steckler, Hoover, and Schwartz (1993) studied PATCH projects to see how communities traversed the various stages of PATCH. They found the approach to be effective, but recommended the following changes to enhance the effectiveness of the PATCH model:

1. Conduct a community capacity assessment prior to initiating a community needs assessment.
2. Do not rely solely on behavioral risk factor surveys.
3. Analyze needs assessment data quickly, and share the assessment with the community as soon as possible.
4. Allow for flexibility and modifications by the community when determining the priority of health objectives.
5. Provide technical assistance throughout the project, not just in the beginning.
6. Fund at least one full-time local coordinator, and encourage extensive capacity building.
7. Emphasize multiple interventions around one chronic condition at a time.
8. Emphasize program institutionalization.

Suen, Christenson, Cooper, and Taylor (1995) studied the performance of 2,888 local health departments regarding core public health functions. They categorized the core functions of local health departments as follows: (1) health-related data collection, surveillance, and outcomes monitoring; (2) protection of environment, housing, food, and water; (3) investigation and control of diseases and injuries; (4) public information and education; (5) accountability and quality assurance; (6) laboratory services; (7) training and education; and (8) leadership, policy development, and administration. They found that the performance index was greater for all eight functions in those local health departments using health planning models such as the PATCH model. PATCH is indeed a very user-friendly model at the local health department level. For more specific details of this model, see the *Planned Approach to Community Health: Guide for the Local Coordinator* (USDHHS, 2005). The PATCH model has not been reported in the literature in recent years, and it is losing its popularity.

MULTILEVEL APPROACH TO COMMUNITY HEALTH MODEL

In the late 1980s, Simons-Morton, Greene, and Gottlieb (1995) introduced the **multilevel approach to community health (MATCH) model**. It is a very practical, yet comprehensive, model. It places the health educator at the center of planning and can be implemented without an

Table 2-5	Phases of the MATCH Model
Phase 1. Goals selection	
Phase 2. Intervention planning	
Phase 3. Program development	
Phase 4. Implementation preparations	
Phase 5. Evaluation	

extensive local needs assessment. Few reports on the use of this model are available other than those by the authors. **Table 2-5** summarizes the five phases in the MATCH model.

The first phase is *goals selection*, and it includes four steps: (1) selecting health status goals by looking at prevalence, perceived and actual importance, changeability, and availability of programmatic resources; (2) selecting the target population by looking at health problem prevalence, accessibility, and programmatic interests; (3) identifying health behavior goals by looking at prevalence, association, and changeability; and (4) identifying environmental goals by looking at access to services, availability of programs and resources, enabling policies, practices, regulations, and barriers.

The second phase is *intervention planning*, which includes the following four steps: (1) identifying the targets of intervention at the community level, (2) selecting intervention objectives, (3) identifying mediators of the intervention objectives (such as knowledge, skills, attitudes, and practices), and (4) selecting intervention approaches by applying theories.

The third phase is *program development*, and it also includes four steps: (1) creating program units or components that include paying attention to the target population, intervention targets, intervention objectives, structural units, and channels; (2) selecting or developing curricula and creating intervention guides that include learning objectives, content, teaching/learning methods, and materials; (3) developing session plans in which educational objectives are delineated with teaching/learning activities, materials, and specific instructions; and (4) creating or acquiring instructional materials in which existing materials are reviewed and selected and new materials developed after pilot testing.

The fourth phase is *implementation preparation* and comprises two steps. The first step includes facilitating, adopting, implementing, and maintaining a health behavior by developing a specific proposal; developing the need, readiness, and environmental supports for change; providing evidence of the efficacy of the intervention; identifying change agents and opinion leaders; and establishing constructive working relationships with decision makers. The second step in this phase concerns selecting and training implementers.

> Whereas PRECEDE-PROCEED emphasizes formal needs assessment, MATCH as formulated by Simons-Morton and associates (1995) is a framework that gives more attention to implementation.
>
> —Simons-Morton, Greene, and Gottlieb (1995, p. 132)

The fifth and final phase is *evaluation*. There are three levels of evaluation: (1) process evaluation, which assesses recruitment, session, and program implementation, quality of learning activities, and immediate outcomes; (2) impact evaluation, which examines antecedents of behaviors and environments, changes in behaviors and environments, and any side effects of the program; and (3) outcome evaluation, which assesses health outcomes, cost effectiveness, and policy recommendations. For more details on this model, see *Introduction to Health Education and Health Promotion* (Simons-Morton, Greene, & Gottlieb, 1995). In recent years the MATCH model has not been reported in the literature and is losing its popularity.

INTERVENTION MAPPING

In the 1990s, Bartholomew and colleagues proposed a model for health education and health promotion planning called **intervention mapping** (Bartholomew Eldridge et al., 2015). This socioecological approach looks at individual behaviors in an environmental context. Intervention mapping has been used for several types of programs in health promotion and education. Some examples of such programs are breast and cervical cancer screening (Fernandez, Gonzales, Tortolero-Luna, Partida, & Bartholomew, 2005), diabetes self-management education (Song, Choi, Kim, Seo, & Lee, 2015), diet and physical activity promotion (Brug, Oenema, & Ferreira, 2005; van Stralen, de Vries, Mudde, Bolman, & Lechner, 2009), fruit and vegetable promotion (Perez-Rodrigo et al., 2005), HIV and sexually transmitted disease (STD) prevention (Mkumbo et al., 2009; Tortolero et al., 2005), school-based physical activity injury prevention (Collard, Chinapaw, van Mechelen, & Verhagen, 2009), supporting healthy lifestyles for leg ulcer patients (Heinen, Bartholomew, Wensing, Kerkhof, & Achterberg, 2006), sexual and reproductive health (Aaro et al., 2006), socioeconomic health inequities (Abbema, Van Assema, Kok, De Leeuw, & De Vries, 2004), promoting exercise therapy for urinary incontinence patients (Alewijnse, Mesters, Metsemakers, & van den Borne, 2002), rehabilitation of cancer patients (McEwen et al., 2015), violence prevention (Murray, Kelder, Parcel, Frankowski, & Orpinas, 1999), and weight gain prevention (Kremers et al., 2005; Verweij, Proper, Weel, Hulshof, & van Mechelen, 2009). These applications are summarized in **Table 2-6**.

Intervention mapping is a six-step process:

> **In Intervention Mapping we argued for a social ecological approach in which health is viewed as a function of individuals and of the environments in which individuals live, including family, social networks, organizations, communities, and societies.**
>
> —Batholomew, Parcel, Kok, and Gottlieb (2006, p. 9)

1. *Performing needs assessment or problem analysis.* An assessment is made of health, quality of life, behavior, and environment, along with an assessment of community capacity. In this step, program outcomes are established, and a participatory planning group is formed that includes the planners, implementers, and participants.
2. *Creating matrices of change objectives based on the determinants of behavioral and environmental conditions.* In this step, performance and change objectives are established and rated in terms of changeability and importance. An example of a behavioral change objective for a nutrition education program might read, "At the end of the program, 90% of the children will quit drinking sweetened beverages."
3. *Selecting theory-based intervention methods and practical strategies.* In this step, the program is reviewed with interested participants, theoretical methods are identified, program methods are chosen, and design strategies that match change objectives are chosen. This step includes five sub-steps. In the first sub-step the planning group generates ideas. In the second sub-step the theoretical methods are identified for the change objectives. In the third and fourth sub-steps practical methods are chosen. In the final step each change objective is matched with a theoretical method and a practical method.
4. *Translating methods and strategies into an organized program.* In this step, consultation with program participants and implementers is done; program scope, sequence, theme, and materials are listed; protocols are designed; and program materials are prepared and pretested with the target audience.

Table 2-6	Applications of Intervention Mapping
Breast and cervical cancer screening	
Diabetes self-management education	
Diet and physical activity promotion	
Fruit and vegetable promotion	
HIV and STD prevention	
School-based physical activity injury prevention	
Supporting healthy lifestyles in leg ulcer patients	
Sexual and reproductive health	
Socioeconomic health inequities	
Promoting exercise therapy for urinary incontinence patients	
Rehabilitation of cancer patients	
Violence prevention	
Weight gain prevention	

5. *Planning for the adoption, implementation, and sustainability of the program.* In this step adopters and users are identified; adoption, implementation, and sustainability performance objectives are decided; and interventions are designed to affect program use.
6. *Generating an evaluation plan.* In this step the program is described, along with program outcomes, effect questions, and process questions. Then indicators and measures are developed, and evaluation designs are specified.

For complete details on this model, see *Planning Health Promotion Programs: An Intervention Mapping Approach* (Bartholomew Eldridge et al., 2015).

ASSESSMENT PROTOCOL FOR EXCELLENCE IN PUBLIC HEALTH MODEL

The **assessment protocol for excellence in public health (APEXPH) model** was developed by the National Association of County and City Health Officials (NACCHO) with funding from the CDC in the late 1980s (NACCHO, 1991). The users for this planning model are intended to be local health departments. The model helps in building organizational capacity and establishes a leadership role for local health departments. The unique features of this model are as follows:

- It is a form of self–assessment tool.
- It leads to development of a practical plan of action.
- It focuses on the local health department's capacity and the community's actual and perceived needs.
- It helps the local health department to build its relationships with other local government agencies and community, state, and federal agencies.

- It provides a protocol through which a health department can assess health needs, set priorities, develop policy, and assure that health needs are met.
- It fits local situations and resources.

APEXPH is a three-part process. The first part is an *organizational capacity assessment*. In this part an internal review of the local health department is done to determine the administrative capacity of the department, and a plan of action is created. The second part is the *community process*, in which key members of the community are involved to assess the health of the community. In this part a community advisory committee is established to identify and prioritize key health problems. Then health data are collected and analyzed, followed by setting goals and objectives and identifying local resources. The third part is *completing the cycle*. The organizational action plan and community health plan are monitored and evaluated, and the three core functions of assessment, policy development, and assurance are institutionalized. Some applications of this model have been reported on in Kentucky (Kalos, Kent, & Gates, 2005), Illinois (Turnock, Handler, Hall, Lenihan, & Vaughn, 1995), and Michigan (Vaughn, Richards, Christenson, Taylor, & Eyster, 1994). Additionally, an application of the APEXPH model has been reported in the post-war frozen conflict situation in Nagorno-Karabakh, an ethnically Armenian territory locked within post-Soviet Azerbaijan (Thompson, Dorian, & Harutyunyan, 2010).

> **APEXPH is a voluntary process for organizational and community self-assessment, planned improvements, and continuing evaluation and reassessment.**
>
> —National Association of County and City Health Officials (1991)

COMPREHENSIVE HEALTH EDUCATION MODEL

One of the earliest planning models is the **comprehensive health education model (CHEM)**, developed in the early 1970s by Sullivan (1973). The chief advantage of this model lies in its simplicity. This model is no longer in use and is included in this discussion mainly for historical reasons. The model comprises six steps:

1. *Involving people*. The target population and the personnel required to carry out the program are identified, and a working relationship between the two is established.
2. *Setting goals*. Programmatic goals and objectives are established that mirror health education practices and resources in the target population.
3. *Defining problems*. The planners determine the gaps between what is and what ought to be and prioritize problems.
4. *Designing plans*. The most appropriate approach is identified, program objectives are set, a time line is defined, activities and resources are selected, and a pretest is conducted.
5. *Conducting activities*. The program is implemented.
6. *Evaluating results*. The evaluation results are used for continuing or changing the program.

As the planners move through each of these steps, they must consider the interaction of the health problem with the chosen behaviors, reflect on the available best practices, contemplate the limitations of health education, and identify resources needed to conduct the program. In recent years the CHEM has not been reported in the literature, and it is mentioned here mainly for historical reasons.

MODEL FOR HEALTH EDUCATION PLANNING

Another early model in health education planning, developed in the 1960s, is the **model for health education planning (MHEP)** (Ross & Mico, 1980). This model also is not used much in current practice. There are six phases in the model, each of which has three dimensions: the content dimension (subject matter), the method dimension (steps and techniques), and the process dimension (interactions):

1. *Program initiation.* Planners develop an understanding of the target population's problem, develop a relationship with the population, and create awareness of the problem.
2. *Needs assessment.* Planners identify past assessment efforts, collect new data, analyze data, and describe the problem.
3. *Goal setting.* Goals are based on the problems identified in the needs assessment. Goals must be appropriate and realistic. In addition, input from those who will be affected is gathered, and strategies are developed for implementing the identified goals.
4. *Planning/programming.* Planners translate the strategies into a rational implementation plan or program, design systems and tools for managing the activities, and arrange for commitments among all the involved parties.
5. *Implementation.* The activities are initiated, training and technical assistance is provided, problem solving is carried out, and reporting is done.
6. *Evaluation.* Evaluation measures are clarified, data are collected and analyzed, and refinements to the program and process are made.

One application of this model has been for continuing education of occupational health nurses (Moore & Short, 1994). Other than that it has not been applied much in recent years.

MODEL FOR HEALTH EDUCATION PLANNING AND RESOURCE DEVELOPMENT (MHEPRD)

The **model for health education planning and resource development (MHEPRD)** was proposed by Bates and Winder (1984) in the early 1980s, but it is not among the more popular models and is little used in health education practice today. The hallmarks of this model are that it considers planning a cyclical process, it separates processes from the end products, and it considers evaluation not as a separate step but as an integrated element throughout the model. There are five phases in the model:

1. *Health education plans.* An end result of the needs assessment (which in this model is called a policy analysis process) and an ongoing evaluation process.
2. *Demonstration programs.* Developed through a development process and an ongoing evaluation process.
3. *Operational programs.* The validation process determines which programs should be continued and thus made operational and which ones must be dropped. The ongoing evaluation process continues in this phase. This phase also entails development of an implementation plan.

4. *Research programs.* Implementation of those programs that are based on sound research continues in the implementation process.

5. *Information and statistics.* The data generated once again go through the policy analysis process in phase 1 and guide further planning.

In recent years the MHEPRD has not been reported in the literature, and it is mentioned here mainly for historical reasons.

PEN-3 MODEL

The **PEN-3 model** was developed as a child survival program for African countries (Airhihenbuwa, 1993, 1995). Later its use was extended to several other applications with minority populations, such as breast and cervical cancer screening in Latina women (Erwin, Johnson, Feliciano-Libid, Zamora, & Jandorf, 2005; Erwin et al., 2007), breast self-examination among Iranian women (Naghibi, Shojaizadeh, Montazeri, & Yazdani Cherati, 2015), cervical cancer screening in African American women (Williams, Moneyham, Kempf, Chamot, & Scarinci, 2015), cancer screening in African American men (Abernethy et al., 2005), breast cancer education for African American women (Kline, 2007), breast cancer screening promotion in native Hawaiian women (Ka'opua, 2008), dietary behaviors in African Americans (James, 2004; Kannan, Sparks, Webster, Krishnakumar, & Lumeng, 2010), health factors in Latino immigrants (Garces, Scarinci, & Harrison, 2006), and smoking practices in African Americans (Beech & Scarinci, 2003). **Table 2-7** summarizes these applications.

The model consists of three dimensions, each of which contains the acronym PEN. The model is depicted in **Figure 2-2**. The three dimensions are interrelated and interdependent. The first dimension, cultural identity, has the following PEN:

P *Person.* Health education should be committed to improving the health of every person.

E *Extended family.* Health education should be directed toward not just the immediate family but also the extended family or kin group of the person.

Table 2-7   Applications of the Pen-3 Model
Breast and cervical cancer screening in Latina women
Breast self-examination among Iranian women
Cervical cancer screening in African American women
Cancer screening in African American men
Breast cancer education for African American women
Breast cancer screening promotion in native Hawaiian women
Child survival in African countries
Dietary behavior in African Americans
Health factors in Latino immigrants
Smoking practices in African Americans

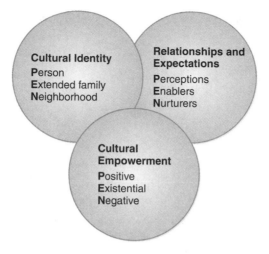

FIGURE 2-2 The PEN-3 model.

N *Neighborhood*. Health education should be directed toward improving health in neighborhoods and communities. Involvement of community leaders is vital for culturally appropriate health programming.

The second dimension of the PEN-3 model used to be called educational diagnosis of health behavior, but its new name is "relationships and expectations" (Webster & Airhihenbuwa, 2005). This dimension evolved from the health belief model (Hochbaum, 1958), the theory of reasoned action (Fishbein & Ajzen, 1975), and the PRECEDE-PROCEED model (Green & Kreuter, 2005). In this dimension the PEN acronym is as follows:

P *Perceptions*. These pertain to knowledge, beliefs, attitudes, and values that may facilitate or hinder motivation for changing a given behavior. Here the health programs must start with the perceived perceptions of the person rather than the real needs identified by the planners for the latter to be meaningful and acceptable.

E *Enablers*. These are societal or systemic forces that may augment the health behavior or hinder it by creating barriers. These include available resources, accessibility, referrals, and types of service.

N *Nurturers*. These are reinforcing factors that an individual may receive from significant others. These significant others could be members of the extended family, peers, employers, health personnel, religious leaders, or government officials.

The third dimension of the PEN-3 model used to be called the cultural appropriateness of health beliefs, but is now called "cultural empowerment" (Webster & Airhihenbuwa, 2005). Thus, this model is particularly useful for work with minority populations and yields a culturally appropriate program. The PEN acronym in this dimension is as follows:

P *Positive*. These are the positive perceptions, enablers, and nurturers that help the person, family, or community to engage in positive health practices. These positive health practices lead to empowerment at the individual level, family level, and community level.

E *Existential*. These consist of practices that are neither good nor bad and thus do not need to be changed.

N *Negative*. These are the negative perceptions, enablers, and nurturers that help the person, family, or community to engage in negative practices that impair health.

In planning, this model goes through several phases. The first phase is health education, in which the planners must decide whether the health education effort is directed toward individuals, extended families, or communities. In the second phase, the planners collect data by surveys or interviews and identify the beliefs and practices related to perceptions, enablers, and nurturers. The third phase entails classifying these beliefs into three categories: positive, existential, or negative. In the final phase, the planners classify beliefs into those that are rooted in cultural patterns and those that are newly formed and select culturally appropriate health education strategies.

CDCYNERGY

CDCynergy, created in the 1990s by the Centers for Disease Control and Prevention, is a multimedia CD-ROM used for planning, managing, and evaluating public health communication programs (CDC, 2004). It originated as a planning model for communication programs but has now been expanded and tailored for a variety of public health planning applications. Systematic training for its usage and application is conducted by the Society for Public Health Education (SOPHE). The training curriculum includes a template for creating a health communication plan, examples of real-world public health interventions, a glossary of health communication terminology, and resources useful for developing and evaluating health intervention and communication plans (SOPHE, 2002).

The CDCynergy process is a six-phase process:

1. *Problem definition and description*. The problem is defined, and resources are considered.
2. *Problem analysis*. Goals are set.
3. *Communication program planning*. The primary and secondary target audiences are chosen, and communication objectives are set.
4. *Program and evaluation development*.
5. *Program implementation and management*.
6. *Feedback*. Feedback is given and used to refine the program.

More recently a lighter version of CDCynergy for social marketing applications, called CDCynergy Lite, has also been made available. The tool takes the practitioner step by step through the process, giving instructions on "What It Is" and "How It Is Done," with tools and templates for each step. The first step in CDCynergy Lite is *problem description*. In this step, the user writes a problem statement, lists and maps the causes of the health problem, identifies potential audiences, and conducts a SWOT (strengths, weaknesses, opportunities, and threats) analysis that assesses the factors in the broader situation that could have an impact on the implementation of the program or its ultimate success. The second step is *market research* (also called *consumer or audience research*), which is designed to enhance the understanding of the target audience's characteristics, attitudes, beliefs, values, behaviors, determinants, benefits, and barriers to behavior change in order to create a strategy for social marketing programs. This entails defining the research questions, developing a market research plan, conducting and analyzing market research, and summarizing the research results.

The third step in CDCynergy Lite is developing a *market strategy*, which is a plan of action for the entire social marketing program. It entails selecting the primary and secondary target audience segments, defining current and desired behaviors for each audience segment, prioritizing audience/behavior pairs, and describing the benefits the program will offer. The fourth step is *interventions*, which are methods used to promote behavior change (e.g., developing a website to promote physical activity in youth). This entails selecting members and assigning roles for the planning team; writing specific, measurable objectives for each intervention activity; and writing a program plan, including time line and budget, for each intervention.

The fifth step in CDCynergy Lite is *evaluation*. It entails identifying the program elements to monitor, selecting key evaluation questions, determining data collection methods, developing a data analysis plan, and developing a time line and budget. The final step is *implementation*. It entails preparing for launch, producing the program materials, hiring and training the staff, and launching the program.

SOCIAL-ECOLOGICAL MODELS

These models owe their origin to the work of Urie Bronfenbrenner (1974, 1994), a developmental psychologist. He asserted that in order to understand human development the entire ecological system must be considered. He discussed five subsystems that compose layers of the ecological system. The first is the *microsystem,* which consists of the immediate environment, such as family, school, peer group, and worksite. The second layer, called the *mesosystem,* comprises the linkages and processes between two or more settings, such as the relationship between home and school, school and workplace, and so on. The third layer is the *exosystem,* which consists of the linkages and processes with two or more settings, one of which does not contain the person but has indirect influences on him or her. For example, in the case of a child, the relationship between home and father's workplace would be the exosystem. The fourth layer, called the *macrosystem,* includes the culture comprising customs, lifestyles, belief systems, and so on. The final layer is the *chronosystem,* which includes changes over time in the environment. Examples would include changes over the life course in family structure, socioeconomic status, place of residence, employment, and so forth.

The concept of ecological approach has been applied in health promotion program planning, where it has been acknowledged that multiple factors influence health behavior and these factors interact among themselves; as a result behavior-specific, multilevel interventions must be planned (Golden, McLeroy, Green, Earp, & Lieberman, 2015; Sallis, Owen, & Fisher, 2008). A generic **social-ecological model** can be conceptualized as consisting of six levels of interventions. The first level for such interventions is the *intrapersonal level*, where individual-level factors are targeted. The second level for such interventions is the *interpersonal level*, where the interactions between individuals are targeted. The third level for such interventions is the *social level*, where social factors are targeted. The fourth level is the *cultural level*, where cultural factors are targeted. The fifth level is the *organizational level*, where organizational factors are targeted. The final level is the *policy/environmental level*, where policy level and environmental change factors are targeted. This model is depicted in **Figure 2-3**.

Some examples of applications of social-ecological models in health promotion include the Stand Up Australia program, an intervention designed to reduce workplace sitting (Neuhaus et al.,

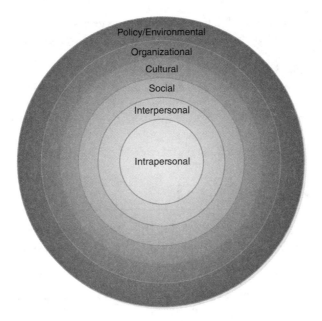

FIGURE 2-3 Social-ecological model for planning multilevel health behavior interventions.

2014); Colorado LEAP Study, an intervention study designed to prevent early childhood obesity (Bellows et al., 2013); and Healthy Living Cambridge Kids (HLCK), a multicomponent intervention targeting community, school, family, and individuals to promote healthy weight and fitness (Chomitz et al., 2010).

OTHER MODELS

Some less commonly used models in health promotion and education are the effectiveness-based model from social work (Kettner, Moroney, & Martin, 1999), the evidence-based/risk factor analysis model (Dever, 1997), the social marketing assessment and response tool (SMART) (Neiger, Thackeray, Barnes, & McKenzie, 2003), and total quality improvement (TQI) (Batten, 1992). These models are rarely used in health promotion and health education.

APPLICATION EXERCISE

To learn more about applications, find a full-text article of one of the models and analyze how the steps of the model were used in that application. For example, Mkumbo and colleagues (2009) used intervention mapping to develop and implement a school-based sexuality and HIV/AIDS education program in Tanzania. The first step of this model entails performing a needs assessment, which they conducted in a participatory manner, involving the researchers, the curriculum developers, the teachers, and the students. The second step entails creating matrices of change objectives based on the determinants of behavioral and environmental conditions. The third and fourth steps entail choosing theory-based methods and developing a program. The authors developed a program comprising five lessons, organized around 23 sessions, with the aim of delaying the onset of sexual intercourse and increasing correct and consistent condom use among young people. The fifth step is planning for the adoption, implementation, and sustainability of the program; and the sixth step is evaluation. The last two steps in this application are unclear. This is an application of a Western model in a sub-Saharan African country.

Read this article and prepare a critique of 250 words.

SKILL-BUILDING ACTIVITY

Let us take the most popular model for planning health education and health promotion programs, the PRECEDE-PROCEED model, and apply it to a practical situation. Let us assume we are interested in developing a physical activity promotion program for African American women in a midwestern city. **Figure 2-4** depicts each phase of the model and how it can be applied.

In the first phase, you could choose a focus group discussion with the target audience for social assessment. The focus group discussion would identify the target audience's quality of life concerns, common leisure time physical activities, and program expectations. In the first part of the second phase, epidemiological assessment, you could collect local data from the county health department, statewide health data, and national health data about overweight and obesity and a sedentary lifestyle, and compile mortality and morbidity (incidence and prevalence) statistics of diseases associated with a sedentary lifestyle. In the second part of the second phase, only a behavioral factor of moderate-intensity leisure time physical activity can be chosen from the genetic, behavioral, and environmental factors.

In the third phase, educational and ecological assessment, you can select predisposing factors of knowledge about benefits of physical activity, attitudes of self-efficacy, and decisional balance based on the stages of change model (Prochaska & DiClemente, 1983). Physically active peers can be used as reinforcing factors. In the enabling factors category, the program can build skills for aerobics and make a free class available.

In the fourth phase of administrative and policy assessment, permission and use of facilities at a local health center can be obtained, participants can be recruited at the health center, and policy changes would be planned. In the fifth phase, program implementation, one health educator could conduct eight weekly educational sessions with 30 participants at a total cost of $5,000.

In the sixth phase, process evaluation, you could use tally sheets to gauge the degree of implementation and perform a satisfaction survey of participants. In the seventh phase, impact evaluation, you could compare participants' knowledge and attitude scores before and after the intervention, test their skills after the intervention, and assess the acceptance and credibility of peers after the intervention. Since the program is modest and short in duration, the eighth phase of outcome evaluation cannot be done.

Using this approach, plan to work on a health issue of your choice with a target population of your choice. You can apply the PRECEDE-PROCEED model or use another model to plan your program. **Table 2-8** provides a set of questions to assist you in choosing activities that correspond to different phases of the PRECEDE-PROCEED model.

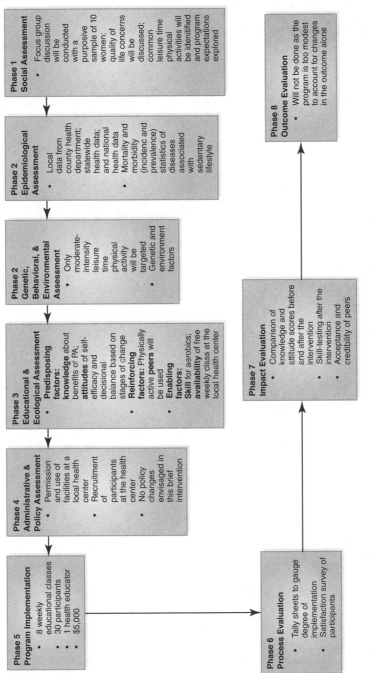

FIGURE 2-4 Application of the PRECEDE-PROCEED model for changing moderate-intensity leisure time physical activity in a small group of African American women in a midwestern city through a brief first-time educational intervention.

Table 2-8	Choosing Activities for Health Education Program Planning Using the PRECEDE-PROCEED Model

1. What will be the best activity to facilitate social assessment?
   - Asset mapping
   - Social reconnaissance
   - Focus group discussion
   - Delphi method
   - Nominal group process
   - Central location intercept interviews
   - Surveys
   - Public service data
   - Other

2. What data will be needed to conduct epidemiological assessment?
   - Mortality data
   - Morbidity data
   - Disability data
   - Behavioral data
   - Environmental data
   - Genetic data
   - Other

3. What factors should be considered in educational and ecological assessment?
   - Predisposing
     - Knowledge
     - Beliefs
     - Attitudes
     - Values
     - Others
   - Reinforcing
     - Peers
     - Parents
     - Decision makers
     - Employers
     - Others
   - Enabling
     - Availability
     - Accessibility
     - Legislation
     - Skills
     - Others

4. What should be considered in administrative and policy assessment?
   - Alignment with priorities
   - Assessment of resources
   - Identification of barriers
   - Assessment of policies
   - Other

Table 2-8	Choosing Activities for Health Education Program Planning Using the PRECEDE-PROCEED Model (*continued*)

5. What should be considered in implementation?
   - Time
   - Personnel
   - Budget
   - Other

6. What should be considered in process evaluation?
   - Degree of fidelity
   - Reception at the site
   - Recipient response
   - Implementer's response
   - Competencies of personnel

7. What should be considered in impact evaluation?
   - Predisposing antecedents
   - Reinforcing antecedents
   - Enabling antecedents
   - Behaviors
   - Environments

8. What should be considered in outcome evaluation?
   - Health status
   - Quality of life

SUMMARY

Planning is an essential responsibility for health educators. Theories from behavioral and social sciences help in micro-level planning (setting objectives and identifying methods), but the macro-level, or overall, planning is done by models. Models are miniaturized and simplified applications of concepts for addressing problems and usually contain inputs from several theories. This chapter discussed several planning models: the PRECEDE-PROCEED model, the planned approach to community health (PATCH) model, the multilevel approach to community health (MATCH) model, the intervention mapping model, the assessment protocol for excellence in public health (APEXPH) model, the comprehensive health education model (CHEM), the model for health education planning (MHEP), the model for health education planning and resource development (MHEPRD), the PEN-3 model, CDCynergy, and social-ecological models.

The most popular model is the PRECEDE-PROCEED model, which has been applied in a variety of settings for coalition building, enhancing community participation, planning multiple-channel interventions, developing health instruments, conducting needs assessments, implementing health risk appraisals at worksites, planning disease prevention programs at worksites, planning employee assistance programs at worksites, planning health programs in school settings, training health care staff, and improving self-care and compliance behaviors.

PATCH is a community health planning model that works equally well at state and local levels and builds capacity. MATCH is a model that emphasizes implementation and is feasible in situations where an extensive needs assessment cannot be done. Intervention mapping builds on a socio-ecological approach that looks at individual behaviors in an environmental context. APEXPH is a useful model at the local level. CHEM, MHEP, and MHEPRD are not commonly used and have been discussed mainly from a historical perspective. The PEN-3 model is culturally sensitive and helps in culturally appropriate planning. CDCynergy is a health communication model that has been tailored to a variety of other applications. Social-ecological models consider the person in an ecological environment and design interventions at multiple levels.

IMPORTANT TERMS

analytical epidemiology

assessment protocol for excellence in public health (APEXPH) model

CDCynergy

comprehensive health education model (CHEM)

descriptive epidemiology

enabling factors

intervention mapping

model

model for health education planning (MHEP)

model for health education planning and resource development (MHEPRD)

multilevel approach to community health (MATCH) model

PEN-3 model

planned approach to community health (PATCH) model

PRECEDE-PROCEED model

predisposing factors

reinforcing factors

social-ecological models

REVIEW QUESTIONS

1. Differentiate between a model and a theory.
2. Define the PRECEDE-PROCEED model. How would you design a program to prevent smoking in adolescents using the PRECEDE-PROCEED model?
3. What are the competencies for health educators who are planning health education strategies, interventions, and programs?
4. Describe the essential features of the PATCH model.
5. Discuss the five phases of the MATCH model.
6. Identify the six steps of intervention mapping.
7. What does the acronym APEXPH mean? Briefly discuss this model.
8. Differentiate between the comprehensive health education model and the model for health education planning.
9. Describe the PEN-3 model.
10. Summarize the main features of CDCynergy.
11. Define the social-ecological model. Develop a social-ecological model for promoting physical activity in college students.

WEBSITES TO EXPLORE

Centers for Disease Control and Prevention (CDC)

www.cdc.gov/

The Centers for Disease Control and Prevention (CDC), founded in 1946, is one of the major components of the U.S. Department of Health and Human Services. We have seen in this chapter that the CDC helped in formation of the PATCH model and provided funding for the APEXPH model. This website contains reliable health-related information on almost all important public health topics. *Explore this website to see the numerous activities of the CDC. Type in the word* PATCH *in its search engine to find historic information about the PATCH model.*

Intervention Mapping

www.interventionmapping.com/

Intervention mapping is a protocol for developing effective behavior change interventions. *Explore this website. Locate the tab with publications on intervention mapping. Review a few abstracts describing applications of intervention mapping. If you are interested in this approach, you can become a member of the Intervention Mapping mailing list on this website.*

National Association of County and City Health Officials (NACCHO)

www.naccho.org/

NACCHO is the national organization representing local public health agencies. The assessment protocol for excellence in public health (APEXPH) model was developed by NACCHO. The website provides news and information about events pertaining to local health departments, programs and activities, publications and tools, public health advocacy, a press room, and membership. *In the publications and tools section, locate the information on how to order the APEXPH workbook.*

PRECEDE-PROCEED Model

www.lgreen.net/precede.htm

The PRECEDE-PROCEED model has evolved since the 1970s, using inputs from several professionals around the country. This website includes a brief history of the genesis and evolution of the model. *Explore this website to find out about the new features in the current edition of the book that describes this model.*

Social-Ecological Model: Violence Prevention

www.cdc.gov/violenceprevention/overview/social-ecologicalmodel.html

This a real-world social-ecological model developed by the Centers for Disease Control and Prevention (CDC) for violence prevention. It uses a four-level social-ecological model (individual, relationship, community, societal) to understand violence and the effect of potential prevention strategies. *Review this website and develop a social-ecological model for another health behavior.*

REFERENCES

Aaro, L. E., Flisher, A. J., Kaaya, S., Onya, H., Fuglesang, M., Klepp, K. I., et al. (2006). Promoting sexual and reproductive health in early adolescence in South Africa and Tanzania: Development of a theory- and evidence-based intervention programme. *Scandinavian Journal of Public Health, 34*(2), 150–158.

Abbema, E. A., Van Assema, P., Kok, G. J., De Leeuw, E., & De Vries, N. K. (2004). Effect evaluation of a comprehensive community intervention aimed at reducing socioeconomic health inequalities in The Netherlands. *Health Promotion International, 19*(2), 141–156.

Abernethy, A. D., Magat, M. M., Houston, T. R., Arnold, H. L., Jr., Bjorck, J. P., & Gorsuch, R. L. (2005). Recruiting African American men for cancer screening studies: Applying a culturally based model. *Health Education and Behavior, 32*(4), 441–451.

Airhihenbuwa, C. O. (1993). Health promotion for child survival in Africa: Implications for cultural appropriateness. *Hygie, 12*(3), 10–15.

Airhihenbuwa, C. O. (1995). *Health and culture: Beyond the Western paradigm.* Thousand Oaks, CA: Sage Publications.

Alewijnse, D., Mesters, I. E., Metsemakers, J. F., & van den Borne, B. H. (2002). Program development for promoting adherence during and after exercise therapy for urinary incontinence. *Patient Education and Counseling, 48*(2), 147–160.

Bailey, P. H., Rukholm, E. E., Vanderlee, R., & Hyland, J. (1994). A heart health survey at the worksite: The first step to effective programming. *AAOHN Journal, 42,* 9–14.

Bartholomew Eldridge, L. K., Markham C. M., Ruiter, R. A. C., Fernandez, A. C., Kok, G., & Parcel, G. S. (2006). *Planning health promotion programs: An intervention mapping approach* (4th ed.). San Francisco: Jossey-Bass.

Bates, I. J., & Winder, A. E. (1984). *Introduction to health education.* Mountain View, CA: Mayfield.

Batten, J. D. (1992). *Building a total quality culture.* Menlo Park, CA: Crisp.

Beech, B. M., & Scarinci, I. C. (2003). Smoking attitudes and practices among low-income African-Americans: Qualitative assessment of contributing factors. *American Journal of Health Promotion, 17*(4), 240–248.

Bellows, L. L., Johnson, S. L., Davies, P. L., Anderson, J., Gavin, W. J., & Boles, R. E. (2013). The Colorado LEAP study: Rationale and design of a study to assess the short term longitudinal effectiveness of a preschool nutrition and physical activity program. *BMC Public Health, 13,* 1146.

Bronfenbrenner, U. (1974). Developmental research, public policy, and the ecology of childhood. *Child Development, 45*(1), 1–5.

Bronfenbrenner, U. (1994). Ecological models of human development. In *International encyclopedia of education* (2nd ed., Vol. *3*). Oxford: Elsevier.

Brouse, C. H., Basch, C. E., Wolf, R. L., & Shmukler, C. (2004). Barriers to colorectal cancer screening: An educational diagnosis. *Journal of Cancer Education, 19*(3), 170–173.

Brug, J., Oenema, A., & Ferreira, I. (2005). Theory, evidence and intervention mapping to improve behavior nutrition and physical activity interventions. *International Journal of Behavioral and Nutrition and Physical Activity, 2*(1), 2.

Centers for Disease Control and Prevention. (2004). CDCynergy overview. Retrieved May 31, 2006, from http://www.cdc.gov/communication/cdcynergy.htm

Chang, M. W., Brown, R. L., Nitzke, S., & Baumann, L. C. (2004). Development of an instrument to assess predisposing, enabling, and reinforcing constructs associated with fat intake behaviors of low-income mothers. *Journal of Nutrition, Education and Behavior, 36,* 27–34.

Chiang, L. C., Huang, J. L., Yeh, K. W., & Lu, C. M. (2004). Effects of a self-management asthma educational program in Taiwan based on PRECEDE PROCEED model for parents with asthmatic children. *Journal of Asthma, 41*(2), 205–215.

Chomitz, V. R., McGowan, R. J., Wendel, J. M., Williams, S. A., Cabral, H. J,, King, S. E., et al. (2010). Healthy Living Cambridge Kids: A community-based participatory effort to promote healthy weight and fitness. *Obesity, 18*(Suppl. 1), S45–S53.

Cole, R. E., & Horacek, T. (2009). Applying precede-proceed to develop an intuitive eating nondieting approach to weight management pilot program. *Journal of Nutrition Education & Behavior, 41*(2), 120–126.

Cole, R. E., & Horacek, T. (2010). Effectiveness of the "My Body Knows When" intuitive-eating pilot program. *American Journal of Health Behavior, 34*(3), 286–297.

Collard, D. C., Chinapaw, M. J., van Mechelen, W., & Verhagen, E. A. (2009). Design of the iPlay study: Systematic development of a physical activity injury prevention programme for primary school children. *Sports Medicine, 39*(11), 889–901.

Dever, G. E. (1997). *Improving outcomes in public health practice: Strategy and methods.* Gaithersburg, MD: Aspen.

Dille, J. H. (1999). Worksite influenza immunization. Successful program. *AAOHN Journal, 47*(7), 292–300.

Ekhtiari, Y. S., Shojaeizadeh, D., Foroushani, A. R., Ghofranipour, F., & Ahmadis, B. (2014). Effect of an intervention on attitudes towards domestic violence among Iranian girls. *Journal of Pakistan Medical Association, 64*(9), 987–992.

Erwin, D. O., Johnson, V. A., Feliciano-Libid, L., Zamora, D., & Jandorf, L. (2005). Incorporating cultural constructs and demographic diversity in the research and development of a Latina breast and cervical cancer education program. *Journal of Cancer Education, 20*(1), 39–44.

Erwin, D. O., Johnson, V. A., Trevino, M., Duke, K., Feliciano, L., & Jandorf, L. (2007). A comparison of African American and Latina social networks as indicators for culturally tailoring a breast and cervical cancer education intervention. *Cancer, 109*(2 Suppl.), 368–377.

Fernandez, M. E., Gonzales, A., Tortolero-Luna, G., Partida, S., & Bartholomew, L. K. (2005). Using intervention mapping to develop a breast and cervical cancer screening program for Hispanic farmworkers: Cultivando La Salud. *Health Promotion Practice, 6*(4), 394–404.

Fishbein, M., & Ajzen, I. (1975). *Belief, attitude, intention, and behavior: An introduction to theory and research.* Reading, MA: Addison Wesley.

Fisher, E. B., Jr., Strunk, R. C., Sussman, L. K., Arfken, C., Sykes, R. K., Munro, J. M., et al. (1996). Acceptability and feasibility of a community approach to asthma management: The Neighborhood Asthma Coalition (NAC). *Journal of Asthma, 33*(6), 367–383.

Garces, I. C., Scarinci, I. C., & Harrison, L. (2006). An examination of sociocultural factors associated with health and health care seeking among Latina immigrants. *Journal of Immigrant and Minority Health, 8*(4), 377–385.

Gold, R. S., Green, L. W., & Kreuter, M. W. (1998). *EMPOWER: Enabling methods of planning and organizing within everyone's reach.* Sudbury, MA: Jones and Bartlett.

Golden, S. D., McLeroy, K. R., Green, L. W., Earp, J. A., & Lieberman, L. D. (2015). Upending the social ecological model to guide health promotion efforts toward policy and environmental change. *Health Education & Behavior, 42*(1 Suppl.), 8S–14S.

Goodman, R. M., Steckler, A., Hoover, S., & Schwartz, R. (1993). A critique of contemporary community health promotion approaches: Based on a qualitative review of six programs in Maine. *American Journal of Health Promotion, 7*(3), 208–220.

Green, L. W. (1970). Identifying and overcoming barriers to the diffusion of knowledge about family planning. *Advances in Fertility Control, 5*, 21–29.

Green, L. W. (1974). Toward cost-benefit evaluations of health education: Some concepts, methods and examples. *Health Education Monographs, 2*(Suppl. 1), 34–64.

Green, L. W., & Kreuter, M. W. (2005). *Health program planning: An educational and ecological approach* (4th ed.). Boston: McGraw-Hill.

Green, L. W., Kreuter, M. W., Deeds, S. G., & Partridge, K. B. (1980). *Health education planning: A diagnostic approach.* Palo Alto, CA: Mayfield.

Green, L. W., Levine, D. M., & Deeds, S. G. (1975). Clinical trials of health education for hypertensive outpatients: Design and baseline data. *Preventive Medicine, 4*, 417–425.

Green, L. W., Levine, D. M., Wolle, J., & Deeds, S. G. (1979). Development of randomized patient education experiments with urban poor hypertensives. *Patient Counseling and Health Education, 1*, 106–111.

Hall, N., & Best, J. A. (1997). Health promotion practice and public health: Challenge for the 1990s. Heart Health Think Tank Group. *Canadian Journal of Public Health*, *88*, 409–415.

Heinen, M. M., Bartholomew, L. K., Wensing, M., Kerkhof, P., & Achterberg, T. (2006). Supporting adherence and healthy lifestyles in leg ulcer patients: Systematic development of the Lively Legs program for dermatology outpatient clinics. *Patient Education and Counseling*, *61*(2), 279–291.

Hochbaum, G. M. (1958). *Public participation in medical screening programs: A sociopsychological study* (PHS Publication No. 572). Washington, DC: U.S. Government Printing Office.

Hu, J., Wallace, D. C., Jones, E., & Liu, H. (2009). Cardiometabolic health of Chinese older adults with diabetes living in Beijing, China. *Public Health Nursing*, *26*(6), 500–511.

James, D. C. (2004). Factors influencing food choices, dietary intake, and nutrition-related attitudes among African Americans: Application of a culturally sensitive model. *Ethnicity and Health*, *9*(4), 349–367.

Kalos, A., Kent, L., & Gates, D. (2005). Integrating MAPP, APEXPH, PACE-EH, and other planning initiatives in Northern Kentucky. *Journal of Public Health Management and Practice*, *11*(5), 401–406.

Kang, J. H., Han, H. R., Kim, K. B., & Kim, M. T. (2006). Barriers to care and control of high blood pressure in Korean-American elderly. *Ethnicity and Disease*, *16*(1), 145–151.

Kannan, S., Sparks, A. V., Webster, J. D., Krishnakumar, A., & Lumeng, J. (2010). Healthy eating and Harambee: Curriculum development for a culturally-centered bio-medically oriented nutrition education program to reach African American women of childbearing age. *Maternal and Child Health Journal*, *14*(4), 535–547.

Ka'opua, L. S. (2008). Developing a culturally responsive breast cancer screening promotion with Native Hawaiian women in churches. *Health & Social Work*, *33*(3), 169–177.

Kettner, P., Moroney, R., & Martin, L. (1999). *Designing and managing programs: An effectiveness based approach* (2nd ed.). Thousand Oaks, CA: Sage.

Kline, K. N. (2007). Cultural sensitivity and health promotion: Assessing breast cancer education pamphlets designed for African American women. *Health Communication*, *21*(1), 85–96.

Kremers, S. P., Visscher, T. L., Brug, J., Chinapaw M. J., Schouten, E. G., Schuit, A. J., et al. (2005). Netherlands research programme weight gain prevention (NHF-NRG): Rationale, objectives and strategies. *European Journal of Clinical Nutrition*, *59*(4), 498–507.

Kreuter, M. W. (1992). PATCH: Its origin, basic concepts, and links to contemporary public health policy. *Journal of Health Education*, *23*(3), 135–139.

Larson, E. L., Cohn, E. G., Meyer, D. D., & Boden-Albala, B. (2009). Consent administrator training to reduce disparities in research participation. *Journal of Nursing Scholarship*, *41*(1), 95–103.

Lengerich, E. J., Kluhsman, B. C., Bencivenga, M., Allen, R., Miele, M. B., & Farace, E. (2007). Development of community plans to enhance survivorship from colorectal cancer: Community-based participatory research in rural communities. *Journal of Cancer Survivorship*, *1*(3), 205–211.

Li, Y., Cao, J., Lin, H., Li, D., Wang, Y., & He, J. (2009). Community health needs assessment with precede-proceed model: A mixed methods study. *BMC Health Services Research*, *9*, 181.

Linnan, L. A., Sterba, K. R., Lee, A. M., Bontempi, J. B., Yang, J., & Crump, C. (2005). Planning and the professional preparation of health educators: Implications for teaching, research, and practice. *Health Promotion Practice*, *6*, 308–319.

MacDonald, M. A., & Green, L. W. (2001). Reconciling concept and context: The dilemma of implementation in school-based health promotion. *Health Education and Behavior*, *28*(6), 749–768.

Macrina, D., Macrina, N., Horvath, C., Gallaspy, J., & Fine, P. R. (1996). An educational intervention to increase use of the Glasgow Coma Scale by emergency department personnel. *International Journal of Trauma Nursing*, *2*(1), 7–12.

McEwen, S. E., Davis, A. M., Jones, J. M., Martino, R., Poon, I., Rodriguez, A. M., et al. (2015). Development and preliminary evaluation of a rehabilitation consult for survivors of head and neck cancer: An intervention mapping protocol. *Implementation Science*, *10*(1), 6.

Mkumbo, K., Schaalma, H., Kaaya, S., Leerlooijer, J., Mbwambo, J., & Kilonzo G. (2009). The application of intervention mapping in developing and implementing school-based sexuality and HIV/AIDS education in a developing country context: The case of Tanzania. *Scandinavian Journal of Public Health*, *37*(Suppl. 2), 28–36.

Moore, P. V., & Short, J. (1994). Planning a continuing education program: The model for health education planning. *AAOHN Journal, 42*(9), 430–434.

Murray, N. G., Kelder, S. H., Parcel, G. S., Frankowski, R., & Orpinas, P. (1999). Padres Trabajando por la Paz: A randomized trial of a parent education intervention to prevent violence among middle school children. *Health Education Research, 14*(3), 421–426.

Naghibi, S. A., Shojaizadeh, D., Montazeri, A., & Yazdani Cherati, J. (2015). Sociocultural factors associated with breast self-examination among Iranian women. *Acta Medica Iranica, 53*(1), 62–68.

National Association of County and City Health Officials. (1991). *Assessment Protocol for Excellence in Public Health (APEXPH) workbook.* Washington, DC: Author.

National Commission for Health Education Credentialing. (2015). Areas of responsibilities, competencies, and sub-competencies for health education specialists—2015. Retrieved September 28, 2015, from http://nchec .sitewrench.com/assets/2251/hespa_competencies_and_sub-competencies.pdf

Neiger, B. L., Thackeray, R., Barnes, M. D., & McKenzie J. F. (2003). Positioning social marketing as a planning process for health education. *American Journal of Health Studies, 18*(2/3), 75–81.

Neuhaus, M., Healy, G. N., Fjeldsoe, B. S., Lawler, S., Owen, N., Dunstan, D. W., et al. (2014). Iterative development of Stand Up Australia: A multi-component intervention to reduce workplace sitting. *International Journal of Behavioral and Nutritional Physical Activity, 11*, 21.

Perez-Rodrigo, C., Wind, M., Hildonen, C., Bjelland, M., Aranceta, J., Klepp, K. I., et al. (2005). The pro children intervention: Applying the intervention mapping protocol to develop a school based fruit and vegetable promotion programme. *Annals of Nutrition and Metabolism, 49*(4), 267–277.

Prochaska, J. O., & DiClemente, C. C. (1983). Stages and processes of self change of smoking: Toward an integrative model of change. *Journal of Consulting and Clinical Psychology, 51*, 390–395.

Rosenstock, I. M., Derryberry, M., & Carriger, B. (1959). Why people fail to seek poliomyelitis vaccination. *Public Health Reports, 74*, 98–103.

Ross, H., & Mico, P. (1980). *Theory and practice in health education.* Palo Alto, CA: Mayfield.

Sallis, J. F., Owen, N., & Fisher, E. B. (2008). Ecological models of health behavior. In K. Glanz, B. K. Rimer, & K. Viswanath (Eds.), *Health behavior and health education. Theory, research, and practice* (4th ed., pp. 465–486). San Francisco: Jossey-Bass.

Shaha, M., Wüthrich, E., Stauffer, Y., Herczeg, F., Fattinger, K., Hirter, K., et al. (2015). Implementing evidence-based patient and family education on oral anticoagulation therapy: A community-based participatory project. *Journal of Clinical Nursing, 24*(11-12), 1534–1545.

Simons-Morton, B. G., Greene, W. H., & Gottlieb, N. H. (1995). *Introduction to health education and health promotion* (2nd ed.). Prospect Heights, IL: Waveland.

Society for Public Health Education. (2002). CDCynergy training. Retrieved May 30, 2006, from http://www .sophe.org/public/cdcynergy/cdc_description.html

Song, M., Choi, S., Kim, S. A., Seo, K., & Lee, S. J. (2015). Intervention mapping protocol for developing a theory-based diabetes self-management education program. *Research & Theory for Nursing Practice, 29*(2), 94–112.

Suen, J., Christenson, G. M., Cooper, A., & Taylor, M. (1995). Analysis of the current status of public health practice in local health departments. *American Journal of Preventive Medicine, 11*(Suppl. 6), 51–54.

Sullivan, D. (1973). Model for comprehensive, systematic program development in health education. *Health Education Report, 1*(1), 4–5.

Thompson, M. E., Dorian, A. H., & Harutyunyan, T. L. (2010). Identifying priority healthcare trainings in frozen conflict situations: The case of Nagorno Karabagh. *Conflict & Health, 4*(1), 21.

Tortolero, S. R., Markham, C. M., Parcel, G. S., Peters, R. J., Jr., Escobar-Chaves, S. L., Basen-Engquist, K., et al. (2005). Using intervention mapping to adapt an effective HIV, sexually transmitted disease, and pregnancy prevention program for high-risk minority youth. *Health Promotion Practice, 6*(3), 286–298.

Turnock, B. J., Handler, A., Hall, W., Lenihan, D. P., & Vaughn, E. (1995). Capacity-building influences on Illinois local health departments. *Journal of Public Health Management and Practice, 1*(3), 50–58.

U.S. Department of Health and Human Services. (2005). *Planned Approach to Community Health: Guide for the local coordinator.* Atlanta, GA: U.S. Department of Health and Human Services, Centers for Disease Control and Prevention, National Center for Chronic Disease Prevention and Health Promotion. Retrieved May 23, 2006, from http://www.cdc.gov/nccdphp/publications/ PATCH/index.htm

U.S. Department of Health and Human Services. (2009). *Healthy People 2020: The road ahead.* Retrieved from http://www.healthypeople.gov/HP2020/default.asp

van Stralen, M. M., de Vries, H., Mudde, A. N., Bolman, C., & Lechner, L. (2009). The working mechanisms of an environmentally tailored physical activity intervention for older adults: A randomized controlled trial. *International Journal of Behavioral Nutrition and Physical Activity, 6,* 83.

Vaughn, E. H., Richards, T. B., Christenson, G. M., Taylor, M. S., & Eyster, J. (1994). An information manager for the Assessment Protocol for Excellence in Public Health. *Public Health Nursing, 11*(6), 399–405.

Verweij, L. M., Proper, K. I., Weel, A. N., Hulshof, C. T., & van Mechelen, W. (2009). Design of the Balance Systematic development, evaluation and implementation of an occupational health guideline aimed at the prevention of weight gain among employees. *BMC Public Health, 9,* 461.

Watson, M. R., Horowitz, A. M., Garcia, I., & Canto, M. T. (2001). A community participatory oral health promotion program in an inner-city Latino community. *Journal of Public Health Dentistry, 61,* 34–41.

Webster, J. D., & Airhihenbuwa, C. O. (2005). PEN-3 model: A cultural framework for organizing CBPR principles and practice. Paper presented at 133rd Annual Meeting of American Public Health Association. Abstract retrieved from http://apha.confex.com/apha/133am/techprogram/paper_107991.htm

Wilkens, P. M. (2003). Preventing work-related musculoskeletal disorders in VDT users: A comprehensive health promotion program. *Work, 20*(3), 171–178.

Williams, M., Moneyham, L., Kempf, M. C., Chamot, E., & Scarinci, I. (2015). Structural and sociocultural factors associated with cervical cancer screening among HIV-infected African American women in Alabama. *AIDS Patient Care and STDS, 29*(1), 13–19.

THE HEALTH BELIEF MODEL

KEY CONCEPTS

- cues to action
- health belief model (HBM)
- illness behaviors
- perceived barriers
- perceived benefits
- perceived severity

- perceived susceptibility
- perceived threat
- preventive or health behaviors
- self-efficacy
- sick role behaviors
- value expectancy theories

AFTER READING THIS CHAPTER YOU SHOULD BE ABLE TO

- Describe the historical genesis of the health belief model (HBM)
- List six constructs of the HBM
- Summarize the applications of the HBM in health education and health promotion
- Identify educational methods and match these to modify each construct from the HBM
- Apply the HBM in changing a health behavior of your choice

The **health belief model (HBM)** is one of the first theories developed exclusively for health-related behaviors. Although labeled a "model," the HBM meets all the criteria for a theory. The HBM originated in the 1950s and has been thoroughly tested in a variety of situations since that time. Today it is one of the most popular models as it provides specific guidance at the micro level for planning the "how to" part of interventions. Based on experimentation over the years, the HBM has expanded and borrowed from other theories to strengthen its predictive and explanatory potential. See Chapter 2 for a discussion of the differences between a model and a theory.

This chapter begins with a description of the historical aspects of the genesis of the HBM. Next we describe the various constructs that make up the model. Then we discuss the applications of the HBM in behavioral research, primary prevention, and secondary prevention. Finally, the limitations of the model are discussed, and a skill-building application using the HBM is presented.

HISTORICAL PERSPECTIVE

The HBM originated from the work of a group of social psychologists in the U.S. Public Health Service in the 1950s: Godfrey Hochbaum, Stephen Kegels, and Irwin Rosenstock (Rosenstock, 1974a). These social psychologists were confronted with the problem that very few people were participating in preventive and disease detection programs. The Public Health Service sent out chest x-ray units to neighborhoods to conduct free screening for tuberculosis, yet few people took advantage of the service. To explain this phenomenon and to help recruit more participation from people, the group looked at the existing theories and then developed the HBM.

Development of the HBM was influenced by the theory of Kurt Lewin and his colleagues (Lewin, 1935; Lewin, Dembo, Festinger, & Sears, 1944) that behavior depends on two variables: (1) the value placed by an individual on an outcome (value) and (2) the individual's estimate of the likelihood that a given action will result in that outcome (expectancy). It is a goal-setting theory based on level of aspiration, in which the individual sets the target of future performance based on past performance (Maiman & Becker, 1974). Such theories are called **value expectancy theories**, and the HBM falls into this category. Maiman and Becker (1974) noted that the HBM was conceptually similar to five other theories of decision making prominent in the 1950s: Atkinson's (1957) risk-taking model, Edwards's (1954) subjective expected utility model, Feather's (1959) decision making under uncertainty model, Rotter's (1954) reinforcement model, and Tolman's (1955) performance behavior theory.

Atkinson's (1957) risk-taking model described behavior as a multiplicative relationship among expectancy, incentive, and motive. Expectancy is the person's anticipation of outcomes from an action, which can be positive or negative. Incentives are rewards that will accrue when the person performs the behavior. Motives are characteristics that encourage the person to pursue positive incentives and avoid negative incentives. Edwards's (1954) subjective expected utility model purports that action is based on the subjective value (or utility) of attaining the goal and the subjective probability (or likelihood) of attaining that goal.

Feather's (1959) decision making under uncertainty model utilizes three constructs: (1) attainment attractiveness, which is the individual's preference to pursue a goal; (2) success probability, which is the likelihood that a given goal is attainable; and (3) choice potential, which is the behavior to be done. Rotter's (1954) reinforcement model purports that behavior is based on the expectancy that a certain action will lead to a certain outcome and on reinforcement from previous learning.

Finally, Tolman's (1955) theory describes six variables (three positive and three negative) that influence the performance of any behavior: (1) need-push for food, (2) positive valence of expected food, (3) expectation of food, (4) need-push against work, (5) negative valence of expected work, and (6) expectation of work.

Maiman and Becker (1974) noted that these models all predict behavior based on two variables: the value the individual placed on a particular goal (attractiveness of the goal) and the individual's estimate regarding the likelihood of attaining that goal (subjective probability). Thus all these theories are value expectancy theories.

> **The Health Belief Model relates psychological theories of decision making (which attempt to explain action in a choice situation) to an individual's decision about alternative health behaviors.**
>
> —Maiman and Becker (1974, p. 9)

Kasl and Cobb (1966) classified three kinds of behaviors regarding health. The first are **preventive (or health) behaviors**, which consist of actions taken for the purpose of preventing disease or detecting disease in an asymptomatic phase by a person who believes him- or herself to be healthy. Initially, the HBM was developed mainly to address these preventive behaviors (Rosenstock, 1974b). The second group are **illness behaviors**, which consist of actions taken by a person who feels sick and indulges in the behavior for the purpose of defining the state of his or her health and for discovering suitable remedies. The third group are **sick role behaviors**, which consist of actions taken by people who are sick for the purpose of getting well. The HBM also has been applied to illness behaviors (Kirscht, 1974), sick role behaviors (Becker, 1974), and behaviors related to chronic illness (Kasl, 1974).

In the 1970s a review measured the various dimensions of the HBM on standardized scales (Maiman, Becker, Kirscht, Haefner, & Drachman, 1977), and in the 1980s the model was strengthened further, mostly by the work of Marshall Becker and colleagues (Janz & Becker, 1984). In the late 1980s the model was expanded to include self-efficacy (Rosenstock, Strecher, & Becker, 1988). Since then the model has been applied to a variety of health behaviors.

CONSTRUCTS OF THE HEALTH BELIEF MODEL

Theories from behavioral and social sciences have what are known as "constructs," and these building blocks can be distinctly identified. The constructs of HBM are depicted in **Figure 3-1**. The HBM has six constructs, the first of which is **perceived susceptibility**. This refers to the subjective belief that a person has with regard to acquiring a disease or reaching a harmful state as a result of indulging in a particular behavior. Individuals vary considerably with regard to their perception of susceptibility to any given illness or harmful condition. On one extreme are individuals who completely deny any possibility of their acquiring the disease. In the middle are people who may admit to the possibility of acquiring the disease, but believe it is not likely to happen to them. At the other extreme are people who are so fearful of acquiring the disease that they believe they will in all probability acquire it. The more susceptible a person feels, the greater the likelihood of his or her taking preventive measures.

Perceived susceptibility has a strong cognitive component and is partly dependent on knowledge (Rosenstock, 1974a). According to the HBM, health educators need to build perceived susceptibility by elaborating on the possibility of negative consequences and personalizing those risks for their participants. For example, in a smoking prevention program, health educators might

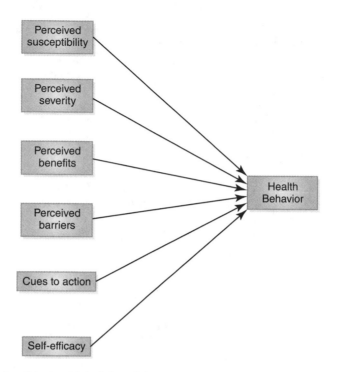

FIGURE 3-1 Constructs of the health belief model.

mention that smoking causes lung cancer and, based on the relative risk calculated from epidemiological studies, mention that this risk is 22 times higher for a smoker than for a nonsmoker. A word of caution needs to be kept in mind: in building perceived susceptibility, one should not create unrealistic or exaggerated fears about the condition.

The second construct of the HBM is **perceived severity**, which refers to a person's subjective belief in the extent of harm that can result from the disease or harmful state as a result of a particular behavior. This perception also varies from person to person. One person might perceive the disease from a purely medical perspective and thus be concerned with signs, symptoms, any limitations arising out of the condition, the temporary or permanent nature of the condition, its potential for causing death, and so on; whereas another individual might look at the disease from a broader perspective, such as the adverse effects it might have on his or her family, job, and relationships.

Perceived severity also has a strong cognitive component, which is dependent on knowledge (Rosenstock, 1974a). According to the HBM, health educators need to build perceived severity by describing the serious negative consequences and personalizing them for participants. For example, in a nutrition education class, health educators might mention that consuming large amounts of saturated fats may lead to development of heart disease and share a story about a member of the community who suffered a heart attack. In addition to describing the clinical consequences, the effects on family, job, and relationships would also be shared. The constructs of perceived severity and perceived susceptibility are often grouped together and called **perceived threat**.

The third construct of the HBM is **perceived benefits**, which refers to belief in the advantages of the methods suggested for reducing the risk or seriousness of the disease or harmful state resulting from a particular behavior. The relative effectiveness of known available alternatives plays a role in shaping actions. An alternative is likely to be seen as beneficial if it reduces the perceived susceptibility or perceived severity of the disease (Rosenstock, 1974a). In facilitating the construct of perceived benefits, health educators need to specify the exact action to be taken and specify the advantages or benefits that would result from that course of action. For example, health educators teaching about breast self-examination would describe the exact technique and the benefits, such as the ability to detect cancer or other diseases early, feeling good about oneself, feeling in control of one's health, and feeling more responsible toward oneself and one's family.

The fourth construct, which goes hand-in-hand with the construct of perceived benefits, is **perceived barriers**. Perceived barriers refer to beliefs concerning the actual and imagined costs of following the new behavior. An individual may believe that a new action is effective in reducing perceived susceptibility or perceived severity of the disease but may consider the action to be expensive, inconvenient, unpleasant, painful, or upsetting (Rosenstock, 1974a). Health educators need to reduce such barriers so the person will take the recommended actions. They may do so by giving reassurance, correcting misperceptions, and providing incentives. For example, in a smoking cessation class, health educators might continually reassure participants that they can overcome the habit of smoking, correct the misperception that tobacco addiction is impossible to break by giving examples of persons who have broken the habit, and provide monetary incentives for participants to continue in the smoking cessation class.

The fifth construct in the HBM is **cues to action**, which are the precipitating forces that make a person feel the need to take action. Such cues may be internal (e.g., perception of a bodily state) or external (e.g., interpersonal interactions, media communication, or receiving a postcard from the doctor for a follow-up examination) (Rosenstock, 1974a). If the perceived susceptibility or perceived severity is low, then a very intense stimulus is needed as a cue to action. When the perceived susceptibility or perceived severity is high, then even a slight stimulus is adequate.

The final construct, **self-efficacy**, was added to the model in the 1980s (Rosenstock et al., 1988). Self-efficacy is the confidence that a person has in his or her ability to pursue a behavior. It is behavior specific and is in the present. It is not about the past or future. We will learn more about this construct in Chapter 7 in the discussion of social cognitive theory, from which it was borrowed.

Four strategies can be used to build self-efficacy:

1. *Breaking down the complex behavior into practical and doable small steps.* For example, instead of telling women to perform breast self-examination, the women could be taught the entire procedure in small steps.
2. *Using a demonstration from a credible role model.* For example, in facilitating an educational program about quitting alcohol, a popular movie star (with whom the participants identify) who has successfully gone through the rehabilitation process could share his or her story to help enhance the self-efficacy of the participants.

The Health Belief Model (HBM) hypothesizes that health-related action depends upon the simultaneous occurrences of three classes of factors:

1. The existence of sufficient motivation (or health concern) to make health issues salient or relevant.
2. The belief that one is susceptible (vulnerable) to a serious health problem or to the sequelae of that illness or condition. This is often termed perceived threat.
3. The belief that following a particular health recommendation would be beneficial in reducing the perceived threat, and at a subjectivity-acceptable cost.

—Rosenstock, Strecher, and Becker (1988, p. 177)

3. *Using persuasion and reassurance*. If a person has failed in the past to make a behavior change, those failures can be attributed to external reasons. For example, in a smoking cessation program, a health educator could ask participants to identify their past failures with smoking cessation and then mention that they could have failed because of bad timing, having too many tasks at hand at that time, the season in which they were attempting the change, and so on.

4. *Reducing stress*. Any behavior change is associated with some amount of stress, which hinders the change process. When this stress is negative, or distress, it hinders the learning process. Reducing distress is an effective means of building self-efficacy. For example, if participants find breast self-examination to be stressful, they can be encouraged to relax by taking a shower or listening to music or practicing progressive muscle relaxation before performing the behavior.

Table 3-1 summarizes the key constructs of the health belief model.

Table 3-1	Key Constructs of the Health Belief Model	
Construct	**Definition**	**How to Modify?**
Perceived susceptibility	Subjective belief that a person may acquire a disease or enter a harmful state as a result of a particular behavior	• Mention negative consequences (e.g., smoking causes lung cancer) • Personalize the risks for participants (e.g., the chances of developing lung cancer if you are a smoker are 22 times more than a nonsmoker, based on a relative risk computed by epidemiological studies)
Perceived severity	Belief in the extent of harm that can result from the acquired disease or harmful state as a result of a particular behavior	• Mention serious negative consequences (e.g., eating saturated fats causes heart disease) • Personalize the seriousness for the education participants (e.g., share a story about a person who died from a heart attack in the community)
Perceived benefits	Belief in the advantages of the methods suggested for reducing the risk or seriousness of the disease or harmful state resulting from a particular behavior	• Specify the exact action (e.g., the individual will carry out breast self-examination in every quadrant every month after taking a shower) • Specify the positive benefits that will accrue from the behavior (e.g., doing breast self-examination monthly will allow you to detect cancer or other diseases early, to feel good about yourself, to feel in control of your health, and to feel more responsible toward yourself and your family)
Perceived barriers	Belief concerning actual and imagined costs of performing the suggested behavior	• Reassure the education recipients that the behavior has minimal cost (e.g., for breast self-examination, state that it would only mean spending another 15 minutes while taking a shower)

Table 3-1	Key Constructs of the Health Belief Model (*continued*)	
Construct	**Definition**	**How to Modify?**
		• Correct any misperceptions that education participants may have (e.g., a person may think a gall bladder ultrasound is an invasive procedure; correcting that misperception may increase the likelihood of the person getting that test) • Provide incentives for indulging in the behavior (e.g., free cholesterol testing may be offered to increase the chances that more people will get tested)
Cues to action	Precipitating force that makes a person feel the need to take action	• Implement a reminder system to encourage the behavior (e.g., post a note or call the person on the phone)
Self-efficacy	Confidence in one's ability to acquire the new behavior	• Practice in small steps (e.g., breaking down complex behavior of self-examination into doable small steps) • Have a role model demonstrate the behavior (e.g., show a video of a well-known movie star with whom the target audience can identify performing the same behavior) • Use persuasion and reinforcement (e.g., tell participants that they have what it takes to perform the behavior, and attribute failures to external forces) • Reduce stress associated with implementing a new behavior (e.g., have participants take a relaxing shower before doing a breast self-examination)

APPLICATIONS OF THE HEALTH BELIEF MODEL

It is not possible to summarize all the applications of the HBM since the 1950s because so many practitioners and researchers have used it. However, the applications can be divided into three general categories:

1. Behavioral research model building and instrument development
2. Primary prevention through health education regarding prevention of diseases or for specific protection against diseases, such as immunization
3. Screening for diseases, compliance with treatment, and other secondary prevention tasks

> The Health Belief Model was originally formulated to explain (preventive) health behavior.
>
> —Rosenstock (1974b, p. 27)

Examples of behavioral research in which the HBM was used include developing an AIDS health belief scale (Zagumny & Brady, 1998), identifying factors associated with infant mortality (Eshleman, Poole, & Davidhizar, 2005), refining an instrument for breast cancer screening

(Champion, 1993; Medina-Shepherd & Kleier, 2010), involvement of dental practitioners in the prevention of eating disorders (DiGioacchino, Keenan, & Sargent, 2000), modeling for physical activity behavior (Juniper, Oman, Hamm, & Kerby, 2004; Rahmati-Najarkolaei, Tavafian, Gholami Fesharaki, & Jafari, 2015), modeling childhood obesity prevention behaviors (Vaitinadin, Rosen, Ying, Wilson, & Sharma, 2015), predictive modeling to prevent severe acute respiratory syndrome (SARS) (Wong & Tang, 2005), predictors of health behaviors in college students (Von Ah, Ebert, Ngamvitroj, Park, & Kang, 2004), modeling of sexual behavior (Lin, Simoni, & Zemon, 2005), modeling of smoking in college students (Kofahi & Haddad, 2005), sociopsychological modeling for diabetes (Gillibrand & Stevenson, 2006), and using a sodium adherence dietary scale (Welch, Bennett, Delp, & Agarwal, 2006). **Table 3-2** summarizes these applications.

The HBM has been used for primary prevention for promoting bicycle helmet use (Lajunen & Rasanen, 2004), promoting condom use in female sex workers (Buckingham, Moraros, Bird, Meister, & Webb, 2005), decreasing tanning bed use (Greene & Brinn, 2003), promoting healthy dietary behavior (Chew, Palmer, & Kim, 1998), genetic testing (Raz, Atar, Rodnay, Shoham-Vardi, & Carmi, 2003), health coaching (George & Tanner, 2014), promoting hepatitis B vaccination (Bigham et al., 2006), promoting influenza vaccination (Lau, Yang, Tsui, & Kim, 2006), promoting measles immunization (Pielak & Hilton, 2003), osteoporosis prevention (Khani Jeihooni, Hidarnia, Kaveh, & Hajizadeh, 2015; Nieto-Vázquez, Tejeda, Colin, & Matos, 2009), pesticide safety (Martinez, Gratton, Coggin, Rene, & Waller, 2004), prevention of periodontal disease (Ndiokwelu, 2004), solar disinfection of drinking water (Rainey & Harding, 2005), and tuberculosis prevention (Rodriguez-Reimann, Nicassio, Reimann, Gallegos, & Olmedo, 2004). **Table 3-3** summarizes these applications.

Some examples in which the HBM has been used for secondary prevention are for adherence to malaria chemoprophylaxis (Farquharson, Noble, Barker, & Behrens, 2004), anxiety reduction in nulliparous pregnant women (Shahnazi, Sabooteh, Sharifirad, Mirkarimi, & Hassanzadeh, 2015), breast self-examination and mammography (Dundar et al., 2006; Tavafian, Hasani, Aghamolaei, Zare, & Gregory, 2009; Torbaghan, Farmanfarma, Moghaddam, & Zarei, 2014), cervical cancer

Table 3-2	Applications of the Health Belief Model in Behavioral Research
AIDS health belief scale	
Factors associated with infant mortality	
Instrument for breast cancer screening	
Involvement of dental practitioners in the prevention of eating disorders	
Modeling for physical activity behavior	
Modeling childhood obesity prevention behaviors	
Predictive modeling to prevent severe acute respiratory syndrome (SARS)	
Predictors of health behaviors in college students	
Modeling of sexual behavior	
Modeling of Smoking in college students	
Sociopsychological modeling for diabetes	
Sodium adherence dietary scale	

Table 3-3	Applications of the Health Belief Model in Primary Prevention
Bicycle helmet use	
Condom use in female sex workers	
Decreasing tanning bed use	
Dietary behavior	
Genetic testing	
Health coaching	
Hepatitis B vaccination	
Influenza vaccination	
Measles immunization	
Osteoporosis prevention	
Pesticide safety	
Prevention of periodontal disease	
Solar disinfection of drinking water	
Tuberculosis prevention	

screening (Ben-Natan & Adir, 2009; Park, Chang, & Chung, 2005), cognitive status examination for Alzheimer's disease (Werner, 2003), colorectal cancer screening (Almadi et al., 2015; Austin et al., 2009; Greenwald, 2006; Omran & Ismail, 2010; Sohler, Jerant, & Franks, 2015), compliance with anticoagulant warfarin therapy (Orensky & Holdford, 2005), compliance with antiviral therapy in hepatitis B patients (Wai et al., 2005), HIV testing (de Paoli, Manongi, & Klepp, 2004), medication compliance in schizophrenia (Seo & Min, 2005), medication adherence in AIDS (Cox, 2009), medication adherence in hypertension (Yue, Li, Weilin, & Bin, 2015), medication use in osteoporosis (Unson, Fortinsky, Prestwood, & Reisine, 2005), patient acceptance of continuous positive airway pressure (CPAP) therapy in sleep apnea (Tyrrell, Poulet, Pe Pin, & Veale, 2006), prostate cancer screening (Doukas, Localio, & Li, 2004), recurrent injury prevention in trauma patients (Van Horn, 2005), screening for bone loss in epileptic patients (Elliott & Jacobson, 2006), and tuberculosis screening (Poss, 1999). **Table 3-4** summarizes these applications.

Table 3-4	Applications of the Health Belief Model in Secondary Prevention
Adherence to malaria chemoprophylaxis	
Anxiety reduction in nulliparous pregnant women	
Breast self-examination and mammography	
Cervical cancer screening	
Cognitive status examination for Alzheimer's disease	
Colorectal cancer screening	
Compliance with anticoagulant warfarin therapy	

(continues)

Table 3-4	Applications of the Health Belief Model in Secondary Prevention (*continued*)
Compliance with antiviral therapy in hepatitis B patients	
HIV testing	
Medication compliance in schizophrenia	
Medication adherence in AIDS	
Medication adherence in hypertension	
Medication use in osteoporosis	
Patient acceptance of continuous positive airway pressure (CPAP) therapy in sleep apnea	
Prostate cancer screening	
Recurrent injury prevention in trauma patients	
Screening for bone loss in epileptic patients	
Tuberculosis screening	

LIMITATIONS OF THE HEALTH BELIEF MODEL

The HBM is particularly useful for planning programs for disease avoidance and injury avoidance, but it does not lend itself very well to promotion of behaviors, particularly long-term behavior change. Harrison, Mullen, and Green (1992) conducted a meta-analysis of the relationships among four HBM dimensions (perceived susceptibility, perceived severity, perceived benefits, and perceived costs) and health behaviors in 16 studies. They computed mean effect sizes for all studies and found weak effect sizes and lack of homogeneity in a majority of the studies. They concluded that the model lacked consistent predictive power mainly because it focuses on a limited number of factors. Cultural factors, socioeconomic status, and previous experiences also shape health behaviors, and those factors are not accounted for in the model. A study by Mullen, Hersey, and Iverson (1987) found less predictive power for the HBM when compared with the theory of reasoned action, the theory of planned behavior, and the PRECEDE-PROCEED model. This conclusion once again underscores the need for the HBM to expand its predictors. To some extent, that has been done by adding the construct of self-efficacy.

Another problem with the HBM (which is also true for other models) is that different questions are used in different studies to determine the same beliefs, thereby making it difficult to compare studies. Janz, Champion, and Strecher (2002) noted that the constructs of the HBM do not all carry equal value. For example, perceived barriers are the single most important predictors of behaviors in the HBM. Often it is not possible to easily influence the barriers, and thus the model will not work.

Ogden (2003) noted that the HBM is a pragmatic model but has criticized its conceptual basis. First, she noted that some studies of the HBM have found no role of perceived susceptibility, indicating that its constructs are not specific and cannot be tested. Second, she described two types of truth in the philosophy of science: synthetic truth, which can be known through exploration and testing; and analytic truth, which is known by definition. She contended that the HBM focuses on analytic truth; thus its conclusions are not supported by observation. Finally, she noted that completing questions about an individual's cognition in the operationalization of the HBM may change that person's thinking rather than tap into how the individual was originally thinking. In a rejoinder to Ogden's article, Ajzen and Fishbein (2004) refuted all these assertions.

APPLICATION EXERCISE

Applications of the HBM in behavioral research, primary prevention, and secondary prevention have been cited throughout the chapter. Choose one study in an area that interests you and obtain the full-text article to see how this model has been applied.

One example is the development of an instrument for breast cancer screening behaviors by Champion (1993). She delimited her instrument development parameters to the constructs of the HBM; namely, perceived susceptibility, perceived severity, perceived benefits, perceived barriers, cues to action, and self-efficacy. She developed items for each construct and used a Likert scale. She established construct validity of the scale through a panel of national experts and performed a factor analysis. Cronbach's alpha reliability coefficients for various construct scales ranged from .80 to .93. Test-retest correlations ranged from .45 to .70.

Locate the full-text article for this study and prepare a 250-word critique. In your critique reflect on the validity and reliability of the scale. Is the scale face valid? Is the scale content valid? Is the scale construct valid? Has concurrent validity been tested? Is the scale internally consistent? Are test-retest reliability coefficients adequate? How can this scale be improved further? If you had to develop a scale using the HBM, what steps would you undertake?

SKILL-BUILDING ACTIVITY

Let us see how we can apply the HBM to the issue of safer sex practices among college students. **Figure 3-2** depicts each of the constructs from the HBM and links these with the educational processes and behavior objectives in this example.

The health education intervention would start with modifying the construct of perceived susceptibility, which can be done by showing a video about college students suffering from HIV/AIDS and sexually transmitted diseases (STDs). The video must show people who are similar to the target audience in their characteristics. The construct of perceived severity can be built by making a presentation using statistics and a case study that underscores the serious negative consequences. These consequences can be medical as well as involving school, work, family, and relationships. To influence perceived benefits, make sure students have all the information they need to take the action: for example, where to get condoms, how to choose them, how to store them, when to use them, how to put them on, how to remove them, and how to dispose of them. To modify perceived barriers, have the students brainstorm all real and imagined barriers. Then discuss in a large group how each of these barriers can be overcome to abstain from sex, use condoms, or use alternatives to sex. In addition, as an incentive, the students could be provided with a small supply of free condoms. To influence cues to action, visual reminders would be used. Youth would be provided with key chains with the messages so that they could remember to perform the chosen healthy behaviors. To build self-efficacy, a video with a credible role model could be shown that depicts the behaviors in small

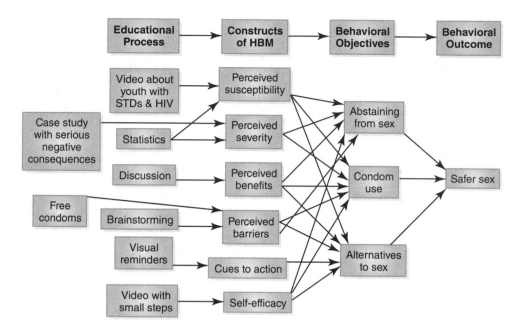

FIGURE 3-2 How the health belief model can be used to modify sexual behavior in youth to promote safer sex.

steps; reinforces the messages about abstinence, condom use, and alternatives to sex; and provides practical advice to reduce stress and anxiety in times of making love.

Using this approach, apply the HBM to a health behavior issue for a target group of your choice. **Table 3–5** provides a set of questions to assist you in choosing an appropriate educational method that corresponds to different constructs of the HBM.

TABLE 3-5	Choosing the Educational Methods for Health Education Program Planning Using the Health Belief Model

1. What is the best educational method to facilitate perceived susceptibility?
   - Lecture underscoring negative consequences
   - Presenting statistics
   - Case study with negative consequences
   - Video film highlighting negative consequences
   - Other

2. What is the best educational method to facilitate perceived severity?
   - Lecture
   - Presenting statistics
   - Case study
   - Video film
   - Other

TABLE 3-5	Choosing the Educational Methods for Health Education Program Planning Using the Health Belief Model (*continued*)

3. What is the best educational method to facilitate perceived benefits?
   - Lecture
   - Small group discussion
   - Large group discussion
   - Other

4. What is the best educational method to facilitate perceived barriers?
   - Brainstorming
   - Small group discussion
   - Large group discussion
   - Incentives
   - Other

5. What is the best educational method to facilitate cues to action?
   - Visual reminders
   - Phone call
   - Personal reminder
   - Other

6. What is the best educational method to facilitate self-efficacy?
   - Demonstration
   - Role play
   - Video with a credible role model
   - Stress reduction techniques
     - Progressive muscle relaxation
     - Visual imagery
     - Autogenic training
     - Yoga
     - Other
   - Other

SUMMARY

The health belief model is the first theory that was developed exclusively for health-related behaviors. It had its start in an exploration of the reasons people were not accessing free screening for tuberculosis. The HBM predicts behavior based on the constructs of perceived susceptibility, perceived severity, perceived benefits, perceived costs, cues to action, and self-efficacy. Perceived susceptibility refers to the subjective belief a person has regarding the likelihood of acquiring a disease or harmful state as a result of indulging in a particular behavior. Perceived severity refers to the subjective belief in the extent of harm that can result from the acquired disease or harmful state as a result of a particular behavior. Perceived susceptibility and perceived severity are together called perceived threat. Perceived benefits are beliefs in the advantages of the methods suggested for reducing the risk or seriousness of the disease or harmful state resulting from a particular behavior. Perceived barriers are beliefs concerning the actual and imagined costs of following the new behavior. Cues to action are the precipitating forces that make a person feel the need to take action. Self-efficacy is the confidence that a person has in his or her ability to pursue a behavior. The HBM has been widely used in behavioral research, primary prevention, and secondary prevention.

IMPORTANT TERMS

cues to action
health belief model (HBM)
illness behaviors
perceived barriers
perceived benefits
perceived severity

perceived susceptibility
perceived threat
preventive (or health) behaviors
self-efficacy
sick role behaviors
value expectancy theories

REVIEW QUESTIONS

1. Discuss the historical genesis of the health belief model.
2. Describe the constructs of the health belief model.
3. Define self-efficacy. How is self-efficacy built?
4. Differentiate between perceived severity and perceived susceptibility.
5. How can the construct of perceived barriers be modified?
6. Discuss the limitations of the health belief model.

WEBSITES TO EXPLORE

Health Belief Model

http://std.about.com/od/education/a/healthbelief.htm

This website describes the HBM and gives examples of applications of its constructs. *Review this website and develop a program that applies HBM to promote condom use.*

Meta-Analysis of the HBM

http://her.oxfordjournals.org/cgi/content/abstract/7/1/107

This website presents an abstract of a study that included a meta-analysis of the relationships between four HBM constructs (perceived susceptibility, perceived severity, perceived benefits, and perceived barriers) and health behavior involving 16 studies. *Locate the full-text article from your library and read it. Comment on the usefulness of the HBM based on this article.*

Reflections on the Health Belief Model

www.ncbi.nlm.nih.gov/pubmed/6392204

This website presents an abstract of an article by Janz and Becker (1984) that reflects on the HBM. *Locate the full-text of the article from your library. Identify the advantages and disadvantages of the HBM based on reading this article. The article was published in 1984; do you think it is still relevant today?*

University of Twente: Health Belief Model

www.cw.utwente.nl/

www.utwente.nl/cw/theorieenoverzicht/Theory%20Clusters/Health%20Communication/Health_Belief_Model/

Visit this website of the University of Twente in the Netherlands (the first URL listed). Translate the page into English if needed. At the upper right on the page is the website's search engine. In the search box type the words *Health Belief Model*, and it will take you to a page that describes the model. (You can also go directly go to the page by using the second URL.) It discusses the application of HBM to sexuality education. *Review the application and comment on its strengths and weaknesses.*

REFERENCES

Ajzen, I., & Fishbein, M. (2004). Questions raised by a reasoned action approach: Comment on Ogden (2003). *Health Psychology, 23*, 431–434.

Almadi, M. A., Mosli, M. H., Bohlega, M. S., Al Essa, M. A., AlDohan, M. S., Alabdallatif, T. A., et al. (2015). Effect of public knowledge, attitudes, and behavior on willingness to undergo colorectal cancer screening using the health belief model. *Saudi Journal of Gastroenterology, 21*(2), 71–77.

Atkinson, J. W. (1957). Motivational determinants of risk taking behavior. *Psychological Review, 64*, 359–372.

Austin, K. L., Power, E., Solarin, I., Atkin, W. S., Wardle, J., & Robb, K. A. (2009). Perceived barriers to flexible sigmoidoscopy screening for colorectal cancer among UK ethnic minority groups: A qualitative study. *Journal of Medical Screening, 16*(4), 174–179.

Becker, M. H. (1974). The health belief model and sick role behavior. In M. H. Becker (Ed.), *The health belief model and personal health behavior* (pp. 82–92). Thorofare, NJ: Charles B. Slack.

Ben-Natan, M., & Adir, O. (2009). Screening for cervical cancer among Israeli lesbian women. *International Nursing Review, 56*(4), 433–441.

Bigham, M., Remple, V. P., Pielak, K., McIntyre, C., White, R., & Wu, W. (2006). Uptake and behavioural and attitudinal determinants of immunization in an expanded routine infant hepatitis B vaccination program in British Columbia. *Canadian Journal of Public Health, 97*(2), 90–95.

Buckingham, R. W., Moraros, J., Bird, Y., Meister, E., & Webb, N. C. (2005). Factors associated with condom use among brothel-based female sex workers in Thailand. *AIDS Care, 17*(5), 640–647.

Champion, V. L. (1993). Instrument refinement for breast cancer screening behaviors. *Nursing Research, 42*, 139–143.

Chew, F., Palmer, S., & Kim, S. (1998). Testing the influence of the health belief model and a television program on nutrition behavior. *Health Communication, 10*(3), 227–245.

Cox, L. E. (2009). Predictors of medication adherence in an AIDS clinical trial: Patient and clinician perceptions. *Health and Social Work, 34*(4), 257–264.

de Paoli, M. M., Manongi, R., & Klepp, K. I. (2004). Factors influencing acceptability of voluntary counselling and HIV-testing among pregnant women in northern Tanzania. *AIDS Care, 16*(4), 411–425.

DiGioacchino, R. F., Keenan, M. F., & Sargent, R. (2000). Assessment of dental practitioners in the secondary and tertiary prevention of eating disorders. *Eating Behaviors, 1*(1), 79–91.

Doukas, D. J., Localio, A. R., & Li, Y. (2004). Attitudes and beliefs concerning prostate cancer genetic screening. *Clinical Genetics, 66*(5), 445–451.

Dundar, P. E, Ozmen, D., Ozturk, B., Haspolat, G., Akyildiz, F., Coban, S., et al. (2006). The knowledge and attitudes of breast self-examination and mammography in a group of women in a rural area in western Turkey. *BMC Cancer, 6*, 43.

Edwards, W. (1954). The theory of decision making. *Psychological Bulletin, 51*, 380–417.

Elliott, J. O., & Jacobson, M. P. (2006). Bone loss in epilepsy: Barriers to prevention, diagnosis, and treatment. *Epilepsy and Behavior, 8*(1), 169–175.

Eshleman, M. J., Poole, V., & Davidhizar, R. (2005). An investigation of factors associated with infant mortality in two midwest counties. *Journal of Practical Nursing, 55*(3), 5–10.

Farquharson, L., Noble, L. M., Barker, C., & Behrens, R. H. (2004). Health beliefs and communication in the travel clinic consultation as predictors of adherence to malaria chemoprophylaxis. *British Journal of Health Psychology, 9*(Pt. 2), 201–217.

Feather, N. T. (1959). Subjective probability and decision under uncertainty. *Psychological Review, 66*, 150–164.

George, M., & Tanner, J. F. (2014). Promotion to change lifestyle: Securing participation and success. *Health Marketing Quarterly, 31*(4), 293–311.

Gillibrand, R., & Stevenson, J. (2006). The extended health belief model applied to the experience of diabetes in young people. *British Journal of Health Psychology, 11*, 155–169.

Greene, K., & Brinn, L. S. (2003). Messages influencing college women's tanning bed use: Statistical versus narrative evidence format and a self-assessment to increase perceived susceptibility. *Journal of Health Communication, 8*(5), 443–461.

Greenwald, B. (2006). Promoting community awareness of the need for colorectal cancer screening: A pilot study. *Cancer Nursing, 29*(2), 134–141.

Harrison, J. A., Mullen, P. D., & Green, L. W. (1992). A meta-analysis of studies of the health belief model with adults. *Health Education Research, 7*(1), 107–116.

Janz, N. K., & Becker, M. H. (1984). The health belief model: A decade later. *Health Education Quarterly, 11*, 1–47.

Janz, N. K., Champion, V. L., & Strecher, V. J. (2002). The health belief model. In K. Glanz, B. K. Rimer, & F. M. Lewis (Eds.), *Health behavior and health education: Theory, research, and practice* (3rd ed., pp. 45–66). San Francisco: Jossey-Bass.

Juniper, K. C., Oman, R. F., Hamm, R. M., & Kerby, D. S. (2004). The relationships among constructs in the health belief model and the transtheoretical model among African-American college women for physical activity. *American Journal of Health Promotion, 18*(5), 354–357.

Kasl, S. V. (1974). The health belief model and behavior related to chronic illness. In M. H. Becker (Ed.), *The health belief model and personal health behavior* (pp. 106–127). Thorofare, NJ: Charles B. Slack.

Kasl, S. V., & Cobb, S. (1966). Health behavior, illness behavior, and sick role behavior. I. Health and illness behavior. *Archives of Environmental Health, 12*(2), 246–266.

Khani Jeihooni, A., Hidarnia, A., Kaveh, M. H., & Hajizadeh, E. (2015). The effect of a prevention program based on health belief model on osteoporosis. *Journal of Research in Health Sciences, 15*(1), 47–53.

Kirscht, J. P. (1974). The health belief model and illness behavior. In M. H. Becker (Ed.), *The health belief model and personal health behavior* (pp. 60–81). Thorofare, NJ: Charles B. Slack.

Kofahi, M. M., & Haddad, L. G. (2005). Perceptions of lung cancer and smoking among college students in Jordan. *Journal of Transcultural Nursing, 16*(3), 245–254.

Lajunen, T., & Rasanen, M. (2004). Can social psychological models be used to promote bicycle helmet use among teenagers? A comparison of the health belief model, theory of planned behavior and the locus of control. *Journal of Safety Research, 35*(1), 115–123.

Lau, J. T., Yang, X., Tsui, H. Y., & Kim, J. H. (2006). Prevalence of influenza vaccination and associated factors among community-dwelling Hong Kong residents of age 65 or above. *Vaccine, 24*(26), 5526–5534.

Lewin, K. (1935). *A dynamic theory of personality: Selected papers.* New York: McGraw-Hill.

Lewin, K., Dembo, T., Festinger, L., & Sears, P. S. (1944). Level of aspiration. In J. M. Hunt (Ed.), *Personality and the behavior disorders: A handbook based on experimental and clinical research* (pp. 333–378). New York: The Ronald Press.

Lin, P., Simoni, J. M., & Zemon, V. (2005). The health belief model, sexual behaviors, and HIV risk among Taiwanese immigrants. *AIDS Education & Prevention, 17*(5), 469–483.

Maiman, L. A., & Becker, M. H. (1974). The health belief model: Origins and correlates in psychological theory. In M. H. Becker (Ed.), *The health belief model and personal health behavior* (pp. 9–26). Thorofare, NJ: Charles B. Slack.

Maiman, L. A., Becker, M. H., Kirscht, J. P., Haefner, D. P., & Drachman, R. H. (1977). Scales for measuring health belief model dimensions: A test of predictive value, internal consistency, and relationships among beliefs. *Health Education Monographs, 5*, 215–230.

Martinez, R., Gratton, T. B., Coggin, C., Rene, A., & Waller, W. (2004). A study of pesticide safety and health perceptions among pesticide applicators in Tarrant County, Texas. *Journal of Environmental Health, 66*(6), 34–37, 43.

Medina-Shepherd, R., & Kleier, J. A. (2010). Spanish translation and adaptation of Victoria Champion's Health Belief Model Scales for breast cancer screening-mammography. *Cancer Nursing, 33*(2), 93–101.

Mullen, P. D., Hersey, J. C., & Iverson, D. C. (1987). Health behavior models compared. *Social Science and Medicine, 24*, 973–981.

Ndiokwelu, E. (2004). Applicability of Rosenstock-Hochbaum health behaviour model to prevention of periodontal disease in Enugu students. *Odontostomatologie Tropicale, 27*(106), 4–8.

Nieto-Vázquez, M., Tejeda, M. J., Colin, J., & Matos, A. (2009). Results of an osteoporosis educational intervention randomized trial in a sample of Puerto-Rican women. *Journal of Cultural Diversity, 16*(4), 171–177.

Ogden, J. (2003). Some problems with social cognition models: A pragmatic and conceptual analysis. *Health Psychology, 22*, 424–428.

Omran, S., & Ismail, A. A. (2010). Knowledge and beliefs of Jordanians toward colorectal cancer screening. *Cancer Nursing, 33*(2), 141–148.

Orensky, I. A., & Holdford, D. A. (2005). Predictors of noncompliance with warfarin therapy in an outpatient anticoagulation clinic. *Pharmacotherapy, 25*(12), 1801–1808.

Park, S., Chang, S., & Chung, C. (2005). Effects of a cognition-emotion focused program to increase public participation in Papanicolaou smear screening. *Public Health Nursing, 22*(4), 289–298.

Pielak, K. L., & Hilton, A. (2003). University students immunized and not immunized for measles: A comparison of beliefs, attitudes, and perceived barriers and benefits. *Canadian Journal of Public Health, 94*(3), 193–196.

Poss, J. E. (1999). Developing an instrument to study the tuberculosis screening behaviors of Mexican migrant farmworkers. *Journal of Transcultural Nursing, 10*(4), 306–319.

Rahmati-Najarkolaei, F., Tavafian, S. S., Gholami Fesharaki, M., & Jafari, M. R. (2015). Factors predicting nutrition and physical activity behaviors due to cardiovascular disease in Tehran University students: Application of health belief model. *Iran Red Crescent Medical Journal, 17*(3), e18879.

Rainey, R. C., & Harding, A. K. (2005). Acceptability of solar disinfection of drinking water treatment in Kathmandu Valley, Nepal. *International Journal of Environmental Health Research, 15*(5), 361–372.

Raz, A. E., Atar, M., Rodnay, M., Shoham-Vardi, I., & Carmi, R. (2003). Between acculturation and ambivalence: Knowledge of genetics and attitudes towards genetic testing in a consanguineous Bedouin community. *Community Genetics, 6*(2), 88–95.

Rodriguez-Reimann, D. I., Nicassio, P., Reimann, J. O., Gallegos, P. I., & Olmedo, E. L. (2004). Acculturation and health beliefs of Mexican Americans regarding tuberculosis prevention. *Journal of Immigrant Health, 6*(2), 51–62.

Rosenstock, I. M. (1974a). Historical origins of the health belief model. In M. H. Becker (Ed.), *The health belief model and personal health behavior* (pp. 1–8). Thorofare, NJ: Charles B. Slack.

Rosenstock, I. M. (1974b). The health belief model and preventive health behavior. In M. H. Becker (Ed.), *The health belief model and personal health behavior* (pp. 27–59). Thorofare, NJ: Charles B. Slack.

Rosenstock, I. M., Strecher, V. J., & Becker, M. H. (1988). Social learning theory and the health belief model. *Health Education Quarterly, 15*, 175–183.

Rotter, J. B. (1954). Social learning and clinical psychology. New York: Prentice-Hall.

Seo, M. A., & Min, S. K. (2005). Development of a structural model explaining medication compliance of persons with schizophrenia. *Yonsei Medical Journal, 46*(3), 331–340.

Shahnazi, H., Sabooteh, S., Sharifirad, G., Mirkarimi, K., & Hassanzadeh, A. (2015). The impact of education intervention on the health belief model constructs regarding anxiety of nulliparous pregnant women. *Journal of Education & Health Promotion, 4,* 27.

Sohler, N. L., Jerant, A., & Franks, P. (2015). Socio-psychological factors in the expanded health belief model and subsequent colorectal cancer screening. *Patient Education & Counseling, 98*(7), 901–907.

Tavafian, S. S., Hasani, L., Aghamolaei, T., Zare, S., & Gregory, D. (2009). Prediction of breast self-examination in a sample of Iranian women: An application of the Health Belief Model. *BMC Women's Health, 9,* 37.

Tolman, E. C. (1955). Principles of performance. *Psychological Review, 62,* 315–326.

Torbaghan, A. E., Farmanfarma, K. K., Moghaddam, A. A., & Zarei, Z. (2014). Improving breast cancer preventive behavior among female medical staff: The use of educational intervention based on health belief model. *The Malaysian Journal of Medical Sciences, 21*(5), 44–50.

Tyrrell, J., Poulet, C., Pe Pin, J. L., & Veale, D. (2006). A preliminary study of psychological factors affecting patients' acceptance of CPAP therapy for sleep apnoea syndrome. *Sleep Medicine, 7*(4), 375–379.

Unson, C. G., Fortinsky, R., Prestwood, K., & Reisine, S. (2005). Osteoporosis medications used by older African-American women: Effects of socioeconomic status and psychosocial factors. *Journal of Community Health, 30*(4), 281–297.

Vaitinadin, N. S., Rosen, B., Ying, J., Wilson, B, & Sharma, M. (2015). Using health-belief model to predict childhood obesity prevention behaviors among elementary school age children in India. Published abstract in the *Proceedings of the American Public Health Association Annual Meeting, 143, Session 4183.* (Abstract available from: https://apha.confex.com/apha/143am/webprogram/Paper331725.html.)

Van Horn, E. (2005). An exploration of recurrent injury prevention in patients with trauma. *Orthopaedic Nursing, 24*(4), 249–258.

Von Ah, D., Ebert, S., Ngamvitroj, A., Park, N., & Kang, D. H. (2004). Predictors of health behaviours in college students. *Journal of Advanced Nursing, 48*(5), 463–474.

Wai, C. T., Wong, M. L., Ng, S., Cheok, A., Tan, M. H., Chua, W., et al. (2005). Utility of the health belief model in predicting compliance of screening in patients with chronic hepatitis B. *Alimentary Pharmacology and Therapeutics, 21*(10), 1255–1262.

Welch, J. L., Bennett, S. J., Delp, R. L., & Agarwal, R. (2006). Benefits of and barriers to dietary sodium adherence. *Western Journal of Nursing Research, 28*(2), 162–180.

Werner, P. (2003). Factors influencing intentions to seek a cognitive status examination: A study based on the health belief model. *International Journal of Geriatric Psychiatry, 18*(9), 787–794.

Wong, C. Y., & Tang, C. S. (2005). Practice of habitual and volitional health behaviors to prevent severe acute respiratory syndrome among Chinese adolescents in Hong Kong. *Journal of Adolescent Health, 36*(3), 193–200.

Yue, Z., Li, C., Weilin, Q., & Bin, W. (2015). Application of the health belief model to improve the understanding of antihypertensive medication adherence among Chinese patients. *Patient Education & Counseling, 98*(5), 669–673.

Zagumny, M. J., & Brady, D. B. (1998). Development of the AIDS Health Belief Scale (AHBS). *AIDS Education and Prevention, 10*(2), 173–179.

THE TRANSTHEORETICAL MODEL

Chapter 4

KEY CONCEPTS

- action stage
- consciousness raising
- contemplation stage
- counterconditioning
- decisional balance
- dramatic relief
- environmental reevaluation
- helping relationships
- levels of change
- maintenance stage
- precontemplation stage
- preparation stage
- reinforcement management
- self-efficacy
- self-liberation
- self-reevaluation
- social liberation
- stages of change
- stimulus control
- temptation
- transtheoretical model

AFTER READING THIS CHAPTER YOU SHOULD BE ABLE TO

- Describe the historical genesis of the transtheoretical model
- List 10 processes of the transtheoretical model
- Summarize the applications of the transtheoretical model in health education and health promotion
- Identify educational methods for modifying each process from the transtheoretical model
- Apply the transtheoretical model in changing a health behavior of your choice

The **transtheoretical model (TTM)** has had various names over the years and has been tested and expanded in accordance with various theories. It is currently one of the most popular models in the field of behavior change. This model focuses on explaining behavior change, whereas many other models focus just on the behavior. The TTM is unique in that it specifies a time dimension in behavior change. It proposes that people move through various stages while making a behavior change and that the whole process can take anywhere from 6 months to 5 years. Due to its emphasis on stages, the model is also known as the stages of change (SOC) model. More than 1,000 publications have cited this model since its origin in the late 1970s.

This chapter begins with a discussion of the historical aspects of the genesis of this model. Next we describe the various constructs or processes that make up the model. Applications of the TTM in behavioral research, primary prevention, and secondary prevention are discussed next. Finally, we discuss the limitations of the model and present a skill-building application using the TTM.

HISTORICAL PERSPECTIVE

In the late 1970s, James Prochaska from the University of Rhode Island undertook to review the various theories of psychotherapy. In this process he laid the foundations for the transtheoretical model (Prochaska, 1979). Prochaska is currently the director of the Cancer Prevention Research Consortium and professor of clinical and health psychology at the University of Rhode Island. He completed his doctorate in clinical psychology in 1969 at Wayne State University. He has won several awards, including the Top Five Most Cited Authors in Psychology award from the American Psychology Society. In his book *Systems of Psychotherapy: A Transtheoretical Analysis*, published in 1979, Prochaska reviewed 18 theories of psychotherapy, among them Adlerian therapy (Adler, 1929), behavior therapy (Wolpe, 1973), emotional flooding therapies (Olsen, 1976), existential analysis (Binswanger, 1958), Freud's psychoanalysis (1959), gestalt therapy (Perls, 1969), rational emotive therapy (Ellis, 1973), Rogers's client-centered therapy (1951), and transactional analysis (Berne, 1966). Although these psychotherapies were quite different from each other, Prochaska saw that they shared certain commonalities in how they looked at the process of change (Prochaska, 1999). During the same time he teamed with Carlo DiClemente, who did his doctoral work at the University of Rhode Island and is now a professor of psychology at the University of Maryland, to develop and refine the TTM (Prochaska & DiClemente, 1983).

TTM has been a major force in helping the field progress to more inclusive approaches to research and practice that complement old paradigms with new ones. It does not put old paradigms to rest, but rather complements these with more comprehensive approaches.

—James O. Prochaska
(2006, p. 772)

In the 1980s, the University of Rhode Island Change Assessment (URICA) scale was developed for problems leading individuals to psychotherapy (McConnaughy, DiClemente, Prochaska, & Velicer, 1989). This is a 32-item self-report using the TTM that measures attitudes toward behavior change for different problems. A version of URICA for alcohol use has also been developed called URICA-A (Migneault, Velicer, Prochaska, & Stevenson, 1999).

In the 1990s, two scales were developed using the TTM. The first is the Readiness to Change Questionnaire (RCQ), developed by Rollnick, Heather, Gold, and Hall (1992). The RCQ consists of three 4-item scales: precontemplation, contemplation, and action. Items pertaining to maintenance were included in the original scale, but the factor was not found to be empirically valid and was later excluded. The second scale is the Stages of Change Readiness and Treatment Eagerness Scale (SOCRATES), which was developed by Miller and Tonigan (1996). Originally this was a 40-item instrument, but it has now been reduced to 19 items. In the 2000s, the TTM was applied to a variety of applications and was found to be effective for behavior change as described later in this chapter. In the 2010s, the TTM has been extended to health coaching (Holden, Davidson, & O'Halloran, 2014; Hudlicka, 2013; Nelson et al., 2012) and online applications (Hudlicka, 2013; Partridge et al., 2015). The TTM at present enjoys the status of being the most popular model. Studies using this model continue to be reported every year.

CONSTRUCTS OF THE TRANSTHEORETICAL MODEL

The first construct of the TTM is **stages of change**. The stages of change are depicted in **Figure 4-1**. The construct of stages provides a temporal or time dimension and implies that change occurs over time (Prochaska, 2000). The construct also offers a middle level of abstraction between psychological states and personality traits. Stages are dynamic like psychological states and yet have stable characteristics like personality traits. This enables a person to move from one stage to another while making a behavior change. A person transits through five stages when considering changing a behavior (**Table 4-1**).

The first stage is the **precontemplation stage**, when a person is not considering change in the foreseeable future, usually defined as the next 6 months. There are two categories of people in this stage. First are uninformed or less informed people who are unaware of the consequences of their behavior. Second are people who have experimented with change but have failed in the past so that they are no longer seeking to change. Usually this second category is resistant or unmotivated to change.

The second stage is the **contemplation stage**, when one is considering change in the foreseeable future but not immediately, usually defined as between 1 and 6 months. These people have considered the benefits (or pros) and costs (or cons) of changing their behavior. The third stage is the **preparation stage**, when one is planning for change in the immediate future, usually defined as in the next month. The people in this stage have taken some significant steps, such as going to a recovery group, buying some exercise equipment, consulting a counselor, buying self-help materials, and so on.

The fourth stage is the **action stage**, in which the person has made meaningful change in the past 6 months. Behaviors are actions, and the new actions can be observed clearly in this stage. The person is making conscious efforts to perform the new actions. The fifth stage is the **maintenance stage**, in which the person has maintained the change for a period of time, usually considered as 6 or more months. Prochaska (2000) estimates that the maintenance stage can range in duration from 6 months to up to 5 years. When changing negative habits, the term **termination** is used

FIGURE 4-1 Stages of change in the transtheoretical model. The progression through the stages is not linear but cyclical or spiral; one might progress from precontemplation to action and then regress to contemplation and then again progress to action and so on.

Table 4-1	Stages of Behavior Change in the Transtheoretical Model
Precontemplation	One is not considering change in the foreseeable future, usually defined as the next 6 months.
Contemplation	One is considering change in the foreseeable future but not immediately, usually defined as between 1 and 6 months.
Preparation	One is planning for change in the immediate future, usually defined as in the next month.
Action	One has made meaningful change in the past 6 months.
Maintenance	One has maintained change for a period of time, usually considered as 6 or more months.

when the person has completely quit the habit, has no temptation to relapse, and is fully self-efficacious to continue with the change.

The progression through these stages is not linear but cyclical or spiral; one might progress from precontemplation to action and then regress to contemplation, and then again progress to action, and so on (Prochaska, DiClemente, & Norcross, 1992).

The second construct of the TTM pertains to the 10 processes of change, summarized in **Table 4-2**. The first process of change, which is borrowed from the Freudian school of psychotherapy (Freud, 1960), is the process of **consciousness raising**. Consciousness raising is an experiential process that entails raising awareness about the causes, consequences, and cures for a particular problem. This can be achieved by arranging for observation sessions, confronting the participants on the issue, providing interpretations from the literature, providing feedback to the participants, or giving an informational lecture or talk. This process is important in the precontemplation and contemplation stages in helping people move forward.

The second process of change is **dramatic relief**, which is an experiential process that enhances emotional arousal about one's behavior and emphasizes the relief that can come from changing it. This can be facilitated through methods such as enacting a psychodrama, having the participants partake in a role play, sharing personal testimony from people in similar situations, or allowing the participants to grieve over their situation so that their emotions are brought forward. This process is important in the precontemplation and contemplation stages in helping people move forward.

The third process of change is **environmental reevaluation**, which is the experiential process that involves both affective and cognitive components regarding how the behavior affects one's environment and how changing the behavior would influence the environment. It can be influenced by empathy training, values clarification, or family or network interventions. It is also important in the precontemplation and contemplation stages.

The fourth process of change is **self-reevaluation**, an experiential process that involves both affective and cognitive components and includes a person's assessment of his or her self-image with the new behavior. The self-image can be changed by using imagery, healthier role models, and values clarification. Self-reevaluation is important in the contemplation and preparation stages.

The fifth process of change is **self-liberation**, a behavioral process that entails belief that one can change and a commitment and recommitment to act on that change. It can be facilitated by

Table 4-2	Key Processes of the Transtheoretical Model	
Construct	**Definition**	**How to Modify?**
Consciousness raising	Experiential process that entails raising awareness about causes and cures for a particular problem	• Discussion sharing observations • Discussion with confrontations • Discussion sharing interpretations • Discussion with feedback • Lecture
Dramatic relief	Experiential process that enhances emotional arousal about one's behavior and the relief that can come from changing it	• Psychodrama • Role playing • Personal testimony • Grieving
Environmental reevaluation	Experiential process that involves both affective and cognitive components on how the behavior affects one's environment and how changing the behavior would influence the environment	• Empathy training • Discussion with value clarification • Family or network interventions
Self-reevaluation	Experiential process that involves both affective and cognitive components and includes one's assessment of self-image with the new behavior	• Imagery • Healthier role models • Discussion with values clarification
Self-liberation	Behavioral process that entails belief that one can change and a commitment and recommitment to act on that change	• Making public commitments • Making resolutions • Providing multiple alternatives to choose from
Counterconditioning	Behavioral process that requires learning new, healthier behavior to replace old, unhealthy behavior	• Desensitization • Assertion • Practicing relaxation • Cognitive counters to irrational self-statements
Reinforcement management (contingency management)	Behavioral process that utilizes reinforcements and punishments for taking steps in a particular direction	• Self-reinforcements • Contracting • Group recognition

(continues)

Table 4-2	Key Processes of the Transtheoretical Model (*continued*)	
Construct	**Definition**	**How to Modify?**
Stimulus control	Behavioral process that involves modifying the environment to increase cues for healthy behavior and decrease cues for unhealthy behavior	• Avoidance • Environmental reengineering by removing cues for unhealthy behavior • Self-help groups that provide cues for healthier behavior
Helping relationships	Behavioral process that entails developing caring, open, trusting, and accepting relationships to adhere to the healthy behavior	• Rapport building • Health educator calls • Buddy systems • Self-help groups
Social liberation	Experiential process that results in an increase in social opportunities or alternatives	• Advocacy • Empowerment methods • Policies

making public commitments as opposed to private commitments, making resolutions, or having multiple alternatives to choose from. Prochaska (2000) noted that whenever possible we should try to provide people with the three best possible choices. Having fewer than or more than three choices is less effective. This process is important in the preparation and action stages and helps to confirm the person's commitment toward behavior change.

The sixth process of change is **counterconditioning**, which refers to a behavioral process that requires learning a new, healthier behavior to replace the unhealthy behavior. Methods such as desensitization, assertion, practicing relaxation, or using cognitive counters to irrational self-statements can be utilized to facilitate this process. This process is important in the action stage.

The seventh process of change is borrowed from the Skinnerian tradition (Skinner, 1953) and is called **contingency management** or **reinforcement management**. This is a behavioral process that utilizes reinforcements and punishments for taking steps in a particular direction. The process can be fostered by developing self-reinforcements, using contracts, and providing group recognition for achievements with regard to behavior acquisition. This process is important in the action and maintenance stages.

The eighth process of change is **stimulus control**, a behavioral process that involves modifying the environment to increase cues for healthy behavior and decrease cues for unhealthy behavior. Behavior can be modified by avoidance of the cues for unhealthy behavior, environmental reengineering that removes cues for unhealthy behaviors, and participation in self-help groups that provide cues for healthy behaviors. This process is important in the action and maintenance stages.

The ninth process of change is borrowed from the Rogerian school of psychotherapy (Rogers, 1961) and is called **helping relationships**. This is a behavioral process that entails developing caring, open, trusting, and accepting relationships to help the person adhere to the healthy behavior. These can be developed through rapport building, health educator calls, formation of buddy systems, and participation in self-help groups. This process is important in the action and maintenance stages.

The final process of change is **social liberation**, which refers to an experiential process that increases social opportunities or alternatives. Social liberation can be enhanced through advocacy, empowerment-building methods, and policies that increase social opportunities. The relationship of this process to specific stages is unclear (Prochaska, Redding, & Evers, 2008), but it probably helps in the preparation and action stages.

The third construct of the TTM is **decisional balance**, or pros and cons. This construct has been taken from the work of Janis and Mann (1977) with decision making. It addresses the relative importance placed by an individual on the advantages (pros) of behavior change as opposed to the disadvantages (cons). According to this model, behavior change occurs when the pros of the behavior change are viewed as more important than the cons of change. Hence, educators must make an attempt to enhance the pros while reducing the cons. This construct is especially important in the precontemplation and contemplation stages of change.

The fourth construct of the TTM is **self-efficacy**. This construct, taken from Bandura's social cognitive theory (1986), refers to the confidence that a person has in his or her ability to pursue a given behavior. It is specific to the behavior and is in the present. It is not about the past or future. Self-efficacy is discussed in Chapter 3 in connection with the health belief model and is discussed in detail in Chapter 7.

The fifth construct of the TTM, which goes hand in hand with self-efficacy, is **temptation**. Temptation refers to the urge to engage in unhealthy behavior when confronted with a difficult situation (Prochaska et al., 2008). It is, in essence, the converse of self-efficacy. In research, the same set of items using different response formats is used to measure both self-efficacy and temptation. Temptation is represented by three factors that denote the most common types of tempting situations: negative affect or emotional distress, positive social situations, and craving.

> While research results to date are encouraging, much still needs to be done to advance the Transtheoretical Model. Research should explore relationships of TTM variables with constructs from other established health behavior theories including perceived risk, subjective norms, and problem severity.
>
> —Prochaska, Redding, and Evers (2008, p. 115)

The sixth construct of the TTM that is usually considered in psychotherapy is **levels of change** (Prochaska, 1995). These are usually used in interventions in clinical psychological settings. Five distinct but interrelated levels of psychological problems can be addressed in psychotherapy: symptom/situational problems, maladaptive cognitions, current interpersonal conflicts, family/system conflicts, and intrapersonal conflicts. These levels have limited utility for designing health behavior change interventions and have been included in this chapter mainly to provide a sense of completeness. **Figure 4-2** depicts the relationship of the constructs and processes of the TTM to stages of change.

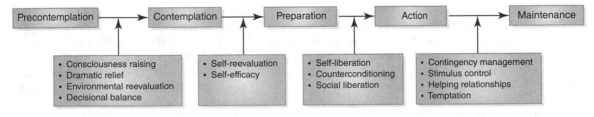

FIGURE 4-2 Relationship of the constructs and processes of the transtheoretical model to stages of change.

PHASES OF INTERVENTIONS BASED ON THE TRANSTHEORETICAL MODEL

Prochaska (1999) identified five phases for planning interventions based on the TTM:

1. Recruitment
2. Retention
3. Progress
4. Process
5. Outcomes

The strong principle of progress holds that to progress from precontemplation to effective action, the pros of changing must increase 1 standard deviation.

The weak principle of progress holds that to progress from contemplation to effective action, the cons of changing must decrease ½ standard deviation.

—James O. Prochaska (2000, p. 117)

In the *recruitment phase*, measures are taken to persuade a large number of people to join the program. In this phase professionals must proactively reach out to the target population. With regard to the stage of change people are in for any given behavior to be changed, DiClemente and Prochaska (1998) suggest a thumb rule of 40, 40, 20. That is, 40% of the target population are in the precontemplation stage, 40% in the contemplation stage, and 20% in the preparation stage.

In the *retention phase*, efforts must be taken to retain people who join the program. This can be done by matching the processes of change with the stage of change a person is in today. In the *progress phase*, efforts must be taken to help people progress during and after the intervention. In the *process phase*, efforts must be made to help participants move from one stage to another, and processes of change must be applied. The pros for changing must be underscored in precontemplation. The cons must be decreased during contemplation to progress to action. Processes of change must be matched with the stage. In the *outcomes phase*, the end results are measured.

APPLICATIONS OF THE TRANSTHEORETICAL MODEL

Some examples of behavioral research in which the TTM has been used are studying gender differences in intimate partner violence (Babcock, Canady, Senior, & Eckhardt, 2005; Burke, Mahoney, Gielen, McDonnell, & O'Campo, 2009), impact of poor sleep quality on health behaviors (Hui & Grandner, 2015), modeling to remedy alcohol abuse among patients with mental illness (Zhang, Harmon, Werkner, & McCormick, 2006), studying patients' participation in medical decision making (Arora, Ayanian, & Guadagnoli, 2005), predicting physician behavior to recommend colonoscopy (Honda & Gorin, 2006), predictive modeling for bicycle helmet use (Weiss, Okun, & Quay, 2004), predictive modeling for chlamydia and gonorrhea (Chacko et al., 2006), predictive modeling for physical activity (Dishman et al., 2009; Rhodes & Plotnikoff, 2006), predictive modeling in ethnically diverse women at risk for HIV (Gazabon, Morokoff, Harlow, Ward, & Quina, 2006), evaluating a processes of change scale for alcohol misuse (Freyer et al., 2006), profiling youth who do not use drugs (J. L. Johnson et al., 2006), developing a scale for mammography on processes of change (Pruitt et al., 2010), developing a scale for osteoporosis prevention behaviors

Table 4-3	Applications of the Transtheoretical Model in Behavioral Research

Gender differences in intimate partner violence

Impact of poor sleep quality on health behaviors

Modeling to remedy alcohol abuse among patients with mental illness

Patients' participation in medical decision making

Predicting physician behavior to recommend colonoscopy

Predictive modeling for bicycle helmet use

Predictive modeling for chlamydia and gonorrhea

Predictive modeling for physical activity

Predictive modeling in ethnically diverse women at risk for HIV

Processes of change scale for alcohol misuse

Profiling youth who do not use drugs

Scale for mammography on processes of change

Scale for osteoporosis prevention behaviors in older adults

Staging of adults experiencing hearing difficulties

in older adults (Popa, 2005), and staging of adults with hearing difficulties (Manchaia, Rönnberg, Andersson, & Lunner, 2015). **Table 4-3** summarizes these applications.

Some examples in which the TTM has been used for primary prevention are for increasing acceptance of contraceptives in men (Ha, Jayasuriya, & Owen, 2005); changing sun protection behaviors (Falk & Anderson, 2008; Kristjansson, Ullen, & Helgason, 2004); health coaching for mindfulness meditation training (Hudlicka, 2013); HIV, sexually transmitted disease (STD), and pregnancy prevention in adolescents (Hacker, Brown, Cabral, & Dodds, 2005); increasing fruit and vegetable consumption (Henry, Reimer, Smith, & Reicks, 2006); overweight and obesity reduction in primary care (Logue et al., 2005); promoting physical activity (Fahrenwald, Atwood, Walker, Johnson, & Berg, 2004; Fahrenwald & Shangreaux, 2006; Fahrenwald & Sharma, 2002; Mostafavi, Ghofranipour, Feizi, & Pirzadeh, 2015); preventing dental caries (Wu & Switzer-Nadasdi, 2014); training lay health advisors (Kobetz, Vatalaro, Moore, & Earp, 2005); tobacco cessation counseling by dental hygienists (Monson & Engeswick, 2005); promoting use of a food thermometer when cooking meat (Takeuchi, Edlefsen, McCurdy, & Hillers, 2006); promoting use of hearing protection devices by workers (Raymond & Lusk, 2006); and weight management (Partridge et al., 2015). **Table 4-4** summarizes these applications.

Some examples in which the TTM has been used for secondary and tertiary prevention are adherence to activity recommendations in chronic low back pain (Basler, Bertalanffy, Quint, Wilke, & Wolf, 2007), adherence to antiretroviral therapy in AIDS (Highstein, Willey, & Mundy, 2006), adherence to lipid-lowering drugs (S. S. Johnson et al., 2006), adherence to medication for treatment of multiple sclerosis (Berger, Liang, & Hudmon, 2005), cardiac rehabilitation intervention (Beckie, 2006; Paradis, Cossette, Frasure-Smith, Heppell, & Guertin, 2010), cervical cancer screening (Abdullah & Su, 2013; Tung, 2010; Tung, Nguyen, & Tran, 2008), colorectal cancer screening (Zimmerman, Tabbarah, Trauth, Nowalk, & Ricci, 2006), adherence to continuous positive airway pressure treatment in sleep apnea (Stepnowsky, Marler, Palau, & Annette Brooks, 2006), diabetes self-management (Kim & Seo, 2014), dietary fat modification in breast

Table 4-4	Applications of the Transtheoretical Model in Primary Prevention
Acceptance of contraceptives in men	
Changing sun protection behaviors	
Health coaching for mindfulness meditation training	
HIV, STD, and pregnancy prevention in adolescents	
Increasing fruit and vegetable consumption	
Overweight and obesity reduction in primary care	
Physical activity promotion	
Prevention of dental caries	
Training lay health advisors	
Tobacco cessation counseling by dental hygienists	
Use of food thermometer when cooking meat	
Use of hearing protection devices by workers	
Weight management	

cancer survivors (Politi, Rabin, & Pinto, 2006), health coaching for child asthma care (Nelson et al., 2012), health coaching in low back pain (Holden, Davidson, & O'Halloran, 2014), hypercholes-terolemia education classes (Kotani, Saiga, Sakane, & Kurozawa, 2005), mammography participation (Hur, Kim, & Park, 2005; Lin & Wang 2009), a physical activity program for prostate cancer patients (Taylor et al., 2006), STD screening (Chacko et al., 2010), smoking cessation (Aveyard et al., 2006; Roig et al., 2010; Schumann, John, Rumpf, Hapke, & Meyer, 2006), and Web-based physical activity promotion in persons with disabilities (Kosma, Cardinal, & McCubbin, 2005). **Table 4–5** summarizes these applications.

Table 4-5	Applications of the Transtheoretical Model in Secondary and Tertiary Prevention
Adherence to activity recommendations in chronic low back pain	
Adherence to antiretroviral therapy in AIDS	
Adherence to lipid-lowering drugs	
Adherence to medication for treatment of multiple sclerosis	
Cardiac rehabilitation intervention	
Cervical cancer screening	
Colorectal cancer screening	
Continuous positive airway pressure treatment adherence in sleep apnea	
Diabetes self-management	
Dietary fat modification in breast cancer survivors	
Health coaching for child asthma care	

Table 4-5	Applications of the Transtheoretical Model in Secondary and Tertiary Prevention (*continued*)
Health coaching for low back pain	
Hypercholesterolemia education classes	
Mammography participation	
Physical activity program for prostate cancer patients	
STD screening	
Smoking cessation	
Web-based physical activity promotion in persons with disabilities	

LIMITATIONS OF THE TRANSTHEORETICAL MODEL

Despite the great popularity enjoyed by the TTM, there have been several criticisms of this model. Some critics have even argued that the model should be completely abandoned (West, 2005). Many critics (Bandura, 1997; Davidson, 1992; Littell & Girvin, 2002; Sutton, 1996; West, 2005) have argued that the stages in the model are arbitrary and that classifying a population into different stages has little utility. They see change as a continuous process that cannot be categorized. Whitelaw, Baldwin, Bunton, and Flynn (2000) noted that classifying people in stages has several problems. First, people can move through the stages of the model in minutes. Second, the validity of self-reported behavior with regard to stage is questionable. Third, a significant number of people cannot be assigned to recognized stages. Herzog (2005, p. 1040) noted "that there has never been a peer-reviewed account of the developmental research that led to the creation of the stages of change algorithm." Littell and Girvin (2002) noted that there is little empirical evidence regarding sequential transition between the stages and that no single study has documented movement through the entire spectrum of stages. Etter (2005) pointed out that classifying people in stages such as precontemplation means lumping different categories together, and people who have never thought of changing their behavior may be grouped with people who have relapsed after making successful behavior change.

In rejoinder, Prochaska (2006) has clarified that stage of change is a discrete variable that some people mistakenly consider a theory, which leads to confusion. Migneault, Adams, and Read (2005) also noted that most applications of the TTM in the area of substance abuse have focused on the construct of stages of change and very few have focused on other constructs such as processes, decisional balance, and self-efficacy. More constructs of the model need to be used.

Another limitation of the TTM that has been pointed out in the literature is its lack of predictive potential (West, 2005). Migneault, Adams, and Read (2005) noted that application of the TTM to substance abuse behaviors has yielded mixed results and that the model is descriptive rather than predictive. There is definitive need to make the model robust in its predictive potential.

Another limitation of the model is that theories aim for parsimony, or use of few constructs to predict the phenomenon, and the TTM is not parsimonious (West, 2006). Salient constructs that account for the majority of the variance need to be identified to make the TTM parsimonious so that it can be of more practical utility.

In a systematic review to gauge the effectiveness of dietary and physical activity interventions for weight loss in overweight and obese adults based on the TTM, Mastellos and colleagues (2014) concluded that the TTM provided "very low quality evidence that it might lead to better dietary and physical activity habits." Although there are definite limitations to this model, just like all other models and theories, there is no need to completely abandon its use as some of its critics have suggested. What is needed is better measurement of the constructs of the model, particularly the processes of change; better and more rigorous reification of its constructs; and further refinement of the model.

APPLICATION EXERCISE

In this chapter you have been given examples of applications of the transtheoretical model in behavioral research, in primary prevention, and in secondary and tertiary prevention. Choose an area of application that you like and locate the full-text article of the example in that area. Critically examine how the model has been used in that application.

One such example is the development of a physical activity intervention, "Moms on the Move," for mothers in the Women, Infants, and Children (WIC) program (Fahrenwald, Atwood, Walker, Johnson, & Berg, 2004; Fahrenwald & Sharma, 2002). The intervention was designed for women in the contemplation and preparation stages of physical activity behavior change. The constructs used in the intervention were decisional balance, self-efficacy for physical activity, three behavioral processes (self-liberation, helping relationships, and counterconditioning), and an experiential process (environmental reevaluation). The primary delivery mode was provider-delivered counseling supplemented with an interactive brochure and four biweekly provider-delivered telephone contacts. Using an experimental design the authors were able to demonstrate statistically significant changes in the TTM constructs and physical activity behavior.

Read these two articles and prepare a 250-word critique. In your critique pay attention to appropriateness of selection of constructs, adequate operationalization of constructs in the instrument and intervention, validity and reliability of instruments, appropriateness of statistical analyses, appropriateness of conclusions, and ability to generalize the results.

SKILL-BUILDING ACTIVITY

Let us see how we can apply the transtheoretical model to the issue of smoking cessation. Let us assume that most of the members in the group of smokers are in the precontemplation stage of change. The TTM is an extensive model and is difficult to fully operationalize. Thus, we will choose a few constructs that would be important to move the participants from precontemplation to action: decisional balance, consciousness raising, dramatic relief, self-liberation, and self-efficacy. The scheme is depicted diagrammatically in **Figure 4-3**.

To modify the construct of decisional balance, the educational process of discussion can be used. In the discussion, the pros of abstaining from smoking must be underscored, and alternatives to smoking should be highlighted. The cons or costs of quitting must be reduced through the discussion. Discussion can be used to modify the construct of consciousness raising for quitting smoking and exploring alternatives to smoking. In the discussion, specific techniques of confrontation about the unhealthy behavior and feedback regarding healthy behaviors need to be used. The construct of dramatic relief can be modified through a role play in which a smoker goes through various kinds of problems because of the habit of smoking. The construct of self-liberation can be

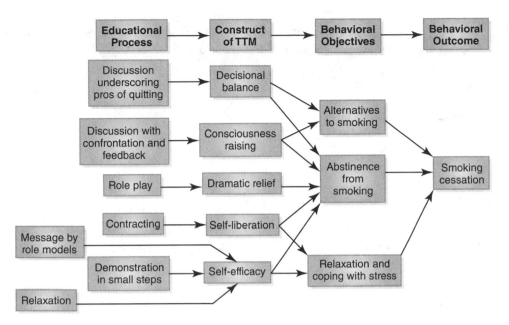

FIGURE 4-3 Application of the transtheoretical model for a smoking cessation program.

modified through use of the method of contracting, in which each participant creates a contract about quitting smoking and agrees to adhere to it. Finally, to modify the construct of self–efficacy, small steps to use for quitting smoking could be outlined and relaxation as an alternative for coping with stress could be demonstrated. Role models can be used to emphasize the message.

Using this approach, you can apply the TTM to a health behavior issue of your choice for any given target population. **Table 4–6** provides a set of questions to assist you in choosing an educational method that corresponds to various constructs of the TTM.

Table 4-6	Choosing the Educational Method for Planning a Health Education Program Using the Transtheoretical Model

1. What is the best approach to determine the stage of change?
   - Self-report survey
   - Group discussion
   - Individual interview
   - Other

2. What is the best educational method to facilitate decisional balance?
   - Lecture
   - Discussion
   - Brainstorming
   - Role play
   - Simulation
   - Other

(continues)

Table 4-6	Choosing the Educational Method for Planning a Health Education Program Using the Transtheoretical Model (*continued*)

3. What is the best educational method to facilitate self-efficacy?
   - Demonstration
   - Role play
   - Video with a credible role model
   - Stress reduction techniques
     - Progressive muscle relaxation
     - Visual imagery
     - Autogenic training
     - Yoga
     - Other
   - Other

4. What is the best educational method to facilitate overcoming temptations?
   - Demonstration
   - Role play
   - Psychodrama
   - Stress reduction techniques
     - Progressive muscle relaxation
     - Visual imagery
     - Autogenic training
     - Yoga
     - Other
   - Other

5. What is the best educational method to facilitate consciousness raising?
   - Discussion with confrontation
   - Discussion with feedback
   - Discussion with interpretations
   - Lecture
   - Other

6. What is the best educational method to facilitate dramatic relief?
   - Psychodrama
   - Role play
   - Opportunity to grieve
   - Personal testimonies
   - Other

7. What is the best educational method to facilitate self-reevaluation?
   - Discussion about values
   - Use of healthy role models
   - Imagery
   - Other

| Table 4-6 | Choosing the Educational Method for Planning a Health Education Program Using the Transtheoretical Model (*continued*) |

8. What is the best educational method to facilitate environmental reevaluation?
   - Discussion with empathy
   - Screening documentaries
   - Lecture
   - Other

9. What is the best educational method to facilitate self-liberation?
   - Contracting
   - Making resolutions
   - Giving public testimony
   - Brainstorming
   - Other

10. What is the best educational method to facilitate helping relationships?
    - Alliance with health educator
    - Buddy system
    - Self-help group
    - Other

11. What is the best educational method to facilitate counterconditioning?
    - Stress reduction techniques
      - Progressive muscle relaxation
      - Visual imagery
      - Autogenic training
      - Yoga
      - Other
    - Assertion
    - Positive self-statements
    - Other

12. What is the best educational method to facilitate reinforcement management?
    - Contracting
    - Discussion
    - Group recognition
    - Other

13. What is the best health promotion method to facilitate stimulus control?
    - Environmental engineering
    - Avoidance of stimuli
    - Self-help groups
    - Other

14. What is the best health promotion method to facilitate social liberation?
    - Advocacy
    - Empowerment training
    - Changing policies
    - Other

SUMMARY

The transtheoretical model (TTM) or stages of change (SOC) model, which originated from the field of psychotherapy, is at present the most popular model in research and practice related to health education. The TTM is a model of behavior change that posits that people move through five stages of change, from precontemplation (not thinking about change) to contemplation (thinking about change over the next 6 months) to preparation (thinking about change in the next month) to action (having made but not completed meaningful change in the past 6 months) and finally to maintenance (acquisition of the healthy behavior for 6 or more months).

The TTM identifies 10 processes of change and the constructs of decisional balance, self-efficacy, and overcoming temptations, which aid the behavior change. Decisional balance is the construct of the TTM that addresses the relative importance placed by an individual on the advantages (pros) of behavior change as opposed to the disadvantages (cons). Self-efficacy is the confidence that a person has in his or her ability to pursue a given behavior. Temptation refers to the urge to engage in unhealthy behavior when confronted with a difficult situation.

The processes of change are categorized as either experiential or behavioral in nature. Experiential processes include consciousness raising, dramatic relief, environmental reevaluation, social liberation, and self-reevaluation. Behavioral processes include stimulus control, counterconditioning, helping relationships, reinforcement management, and self-liberation. The TTM has been widely used in behavioral research, primary prevention, and secondary prevention. Some critics have raised objections to the robustness of TTM, but it continues to be a popular model.

IMPORTANT TERMS

action stage
consciousness raising
contemplation stage
contingency management
counterconditioning
decisional balance
dramatic relief
environmental reevaluation
helping relationships
levels of change
maintenance stage
precontemplation stage

preparation stage
reinforcement management
self-efficacy
self-liberation
self-reevaluation
social liberation
stages of change
stimulus control
temptation
termination
transtheoretical model (TTM)

REVIEW QUESTIONS

1. Describe the historical genesis of the transtheoretical model.
2. Discuss the five stages of behavior change in the TTM.

3. List and define the 10 key processes of change in the TTM.
4. How can stimulus control be modified?
5. Differentiate between self-liberation and social liberation.
6. Describe the five phases for planning interventions based on the TTM.
7. Discuss the limitations of the TTM.
8. Apply the TTM for promoting leisure-time physical activity in a group of African American women.

WEBSITES TO EXPLORE

Applying The TTM to Family Practice

www.aafp.org/afp/2000/0301/p1409.html

This website presents an interesting application of the TTM to family physicians; namely how a family physician can help patients change their health behaviors. Two tools have been introduced in this article: the Readiness to Change Ruler and the Agenda-Setting Chart. *Read this article. Evaluate the usefulness of the tools. Do you think family physicians can change patients' behaviors or do we need health education specialists? Why or why not?*

Applying the TTM to Substance Abuse

www.addictioneducation.co.uk/transtheoretical2001.pdf

This website presents an article that reviews applications of the TTM to substance abuse. The applications to smoking cessation and alcohol and drug abuse have been presented and critiqued. *Read this article. What can you say about the effectiveness of the TTM for changing substance abuse–related behaviors? Prepare a short paper on your position.*

Boston University: Webcast by Dr. James Prochaska

http://cpr.bu.edu/resources/webcast/stages-of-change

This website, sponsored by the Center for Psychiatric Rehabilitation at Boston University, includes a 2001 webcast featuring Dr. James Prochaska, who discusses the TTM. You will have to complete a free registration in order to see the webcast. The title of his talk is "Helping Populations Progress through Stages of Change." *Visit this website and view the webcast. Summarize your reaction to the presentation.*

Cancer Prevention Research Center (CPRC): Transtheoretical Model

http://web.uri.edu/cprc/

The originator of the TTM, Dr. James Prochaska, is the director of this center. The website provides a summary of the TTM with a link to retrieve a detailed version of the model. The other links pertain to stages of change, processes of change, decisional balance, self-efficacy, the CPRC, and several measures related to TTM. *Visit the link with the measures and review one instrument in an area of your choice. Discuss its strengths and weaknesses.*

Transtheoretical Model: Pro-Change

www.prochange.com/transtheoretical-model-of-behavior-change

This website provides a description of the transtheoretical model by Pro-Change Behavior Systems, a behavior change company that partners with wellness companies and institutions to produce programs to reduce health risk behaviors. *Read the description and see how the TTM has evolved from the 1980s to the 2010s. Prepare an application of the TTM to a behavior of your choice using the directions provided on the website.*

University of Maryland: HABITS—Health and Addictive Behaviors: Investigating Transtheoretical Solutions

www.umbc.edu/psyc/habits/

This website was developed by Dr. Carlo DiClemente and his team at the University of Maryland. It summarizes the publications, assessment tools, presentations of team members, and many other things. *Visit this website and review some of the assessment tools. Discuss the strengths and weaknesses of any one tool of your choice.*

REFERENCES

Abdullah, F., & Su, T. T. (2013). Applying the transtheoretical model to evaluate the effect of a call-recall program in enhancing Pap smear practice: A cluster randomized trial. *Preventive Medicine, 57*(Suppl.), S83–S86.

Adler, A. (1929). *Problems of neurosis.* London: Kegan Paul.

Arora, N. K., Ayanian, J. Z., & Guadagnoli, E. (2005). Examining the relationship of patients' attitudes and beliefs with their self-reported level of participation in medical decision-making. *Medical Care, 43*(9), 865–872.

Aveyard, P., Lawrence, T., Cheng, K. K., Griffin, C., Croghan, E., & Johnson, C. (2006). A randomized controlled trial of smoking cessation for pregnant women to test the effect of a transtheoretical model-based intervention on movement in stage and interaction with baseline stage. *British Journal of Health Psychology, 11*(Pt. 2), 263–278.

Babcock, J. C., Canady, B. E., Senior, A., & Eckhardt, C. I. (2005). Applying the transtheoretical model to female and male perpetrators of intimate partner violence: Gender differences in stages and processes of change. *Violence and Victims, 20*(2), 235–250.

Bandura, A. (1986). *The social foundations of thought and action: A social cognitive theory.* Upper Saddle River, NJ: Prentice-Hall.

Bandura, A. (1997). *Self-efficacy: The exercise of control.* New York: W. H. Freeman.

Basler, H. D., Bertalanffy, H., Quint, S., Wilke, A., & Wolf, U. (2007). TTM-based counselling in physiotherapy does not contribute to an increase of adherence to activity recommendations in older adults with chronic low back pain—a randomised controlled trial. *European Journal of Pain, 11*(1), 31–37.

Beckie, T. M. (2006). A behavior change intervention for women in cardiac rehabilitation. *Journal of Cardiovascular Nursing, 21*(2), 146–153.

Berger, B. A., Liang, H., & Hudmon, K. S. (2005). Evaluation of software-based telephone counseling to enhance medication persistency among patients with multiple sclerosis. *Journal of the American Pharmacists Association, 45*(4), 466–472.

Berne, E. (1966). *Principles of group treatment.* New York: Oxford University Press.

Binswanger, L. (1958). The existential analysis school of thought. In R. May, E. Angel, & H. Ellenberger (Eds.), *Existence.* New York: Basic Books.

Burke, J. G., Mahoney, P., Gielen, A., McDonnell, K. A., & O'Campo, P. (2009). Defining appropriate stages of change for intimate partner violence survivors. *Violence and Victims, 24*(1), 36–51.

Chacko, M. R., Wiemann, C. M., Kozinetz, C. A., Diclemente, R. J., Smith, P. B., Velasquez, M. M., et al. (2006). New sexual partners and readiness to seek screening for chlamydia and gonorrhoea: Predictors among minority young women. *Sexually Transmitted Infections, 82*(1), 75–79.

Chacko, M. R., Wiemann, C. M., Kozinetz, C. A., von Sternberg, K., Velasquez, M. M., Smith, P. B., et al. (2010). Efficacy of a motivational behavioral intervention to promote chlamydia and gonorrhea screening in young women: A randomized controlled trial. *Journal of Adolescent Health, 46*(2), 152–161.

Davidson, R. (1992). Prochaska and DiClemente's model of change: A case study? *British Journal of Addiction, 87*, 821–822.

DiClemente, C. C., & Prochaska, J. O. (1998). Toward a comprehensive, transtheoretical model of change. Stages of change and addictive behaviors. In W. R. Miller & N. Heather (Eds.), *Treating addictive behaviors* (2nd ed., pp. 3–24). New York: Plenum Press.

Dishman, R. K., Thom, N. J., Rooks, C. R., Motl, R. W., Horwath, C., & Nigg, C. R. (2009). Failure of post-action stages of the transtheoretical model to predict change in regular physical activity: A multiethnic cohort study. *Annals of Behavioral Medicine, 37*(3), 280–293.

Ellis, A. (1973). *Humanistic psychotherapy: The rational emotive approach.* New York: McGraw-Hill.

Etter, J. (2005). Theoretical tools for the industrial era in smoking cessation counselling: A comment on West (2005). *Addiction, 100*, 1041–1042.

Fahrenwald, N. L., Atwood, J. R., Walker, S. N., Johnson, D. R., & Berg, K. (2004). A randomized pilot test of "Moms on the Move": A physical activity intervention for WIC mothers. *Annals of Behavioral Medicine, 27*(2), 82–90.

Fahrenwald, N. L., & Shangreaux, P. (2006). Physical activity behavior of American Indian mothers. *Orthopaedic Nursing, 25*(1), 22–29.

Fahrenwald, N. L., & Sharma, M. (2002). Development and expert evaluation of "Moms on the Move": A physical activity intervention for WIC mothers. *Public Health Nursing, 19*(6), 423–439.

Falk, M., & Anderson, C. (2008). Prevention of skin cancer in primary healthcare: An evaluation of three different prevention effort levels and the applicability of a phototest. *European Journal of General Practice, 14*(2), 68–75.

Freud, S. (1959). The question of lay analysis. In J. Strachey (Ed.), *The standard edition of the complete psychological works of Sigmund Freud.* London: Hogarth Press.

Freud, S. (1960). *The ego and the id.* New York: Norton. (Original work published 1923)

Freyer, J., Bott, K., Riedel, J., Wedler, B., Meyer, C., Rumpf, H. J., et al. (2006). Psychometric properties of the "Processes of Change" scale for alcohol misuse and its short form (POC-20). *Addictive Behaviors, 31*, 821–832.

Gazabon, S. A., Morokoff, P. J., Harlow, L. L., Ward, R. M., & Quina, K. (2006). Applying the transtheoretical model to ethnically diverse women at risk for HIV. *Health Education and Behavior, 34*(2), 297–314.

Ha, B. T., Jayasuriya, R., & Owen, N. (2005). Predictors of men's acceptance of modern contraceptive practice: Study in rural Vietnam. *Health Education and Behavior, 32*(6), 738–750.

Hacker, K., Brown, E., Cabral, H., & Dodds, D. (2005). Applying a transtheoretical behavioral change model to HIV/STD and pregnancy prevention in adolescent clinics. *Journal of Adolescent Health, 37*(3 Suppl.), S80–S93.

Henry, H., Reimer, K., Smith, C., & Reicks, M. (2006). Associations of decisional balance, processes of change, and self-efficacy with stages of change for increased fruit and vegetable intake among low-income, African-American mothers. *Journal of American Dietetic Association, 106*(6), 841–849.

Herzog, T. A. (2005). When popularity outstrips the evidence: Comments on West (2005). *Addiction, 100*, 1040–1041.

Highstein, G. R., Willey, C., & Mundy, L. M. (2006). Development of stage of readiness and decisional balance instruments: Tools to enhance clinical decision-making for adherence to antiretroviral therapy. *AIDS and Behavior, 10*(5), 563–573.

Holden, J, Davidson, M., O'Halloran, P. D. (2014). Health coaching for low back pain: A systematic review of the literature. *International Journal of Clinical Practice, 68*(8), 950–962.

Honda, K., & Gorin, S. S. (2006). A model of stage of change to recommend colonoscopy among urban primary care physicians. *Health Psychology, 25*(1), 65–73.

Hudlicka, E. (2013). Virtual training and coaching of health behavior: Example from mindfulness meditation training. *Patient Education and Counseling, 92*(2), 160–166.

Hui, S. K., & Grandner, M. A. (2015). Associations between poor sleep quality and stages of change of multiple health behaviors among participants of employee wellness program. *Preventive Medicine Reports, 2*, 292–299.

Hur, H. K., Kim, G. Y., & Park, S. M. (2005). Predictors of mammography participation among rural Korean women age 40 and over. *Taehan Kanho Hakhoe Chi, 35*, 1443–1450.

Janis, I. L., & Mann, L. (1977). *Decision making: A psychological analysis of conflict, choice, and commitment.* New York: Free Press.

Johnson, J. L., Evers, K. E., Paiva, A. L., Van Marter, D. F., Prochaska, J. O., Prochaska, J. M., et al. (2006). Prevention profiles: Understanding youth who do not use substances. *Addictive Behaviors, 31*(9), 1593–1606.

Johnson, S. S., Driskell, M. M., Johnson, J. L., Dyment, S. J., Prochaska, J. O., Prochaska, J. M., et al. (2006). Transtheoretical model intervention for adherence to lipid-lowering drugs. *Disease Management, 9*(2), 102–114.

Kim, H. H., & Seo, H. J. (2014). HealthTWITTER initiative: Design of a social networking service based tailored application for diabetes self-management. *Health Informatics Research, 20*(3), 226–230.

Kobetz, E., Vatalaro, K., Moore, A., & Earp, J. A. (2005). Taking the transtheoretical model into the field: A curriculum for lay health advisors. *Health Promotion Practice, 6*(3), 329–337.

Kosma, M., Cardinal, B. J., & McCubbin, J. A. (2005). A pilot study of a Web-based physical activity motivational program for adults with physical disabilities. *Disability and Rehabilitation, 27*, 1435–1442.

Kotani, K., Saiga, K., Sakane, N., & Kurozawa, Y. (2005). The effects of interval length between sessions in a hypercholesterolemia education class. *Acta Medica Okayama, 59*(6), 271–277.

Kristjansson, S., Ullen, H., & Helgason, A. R. (2004). The importance of assessing the readiness to change sun-protection behaviours: A population-based study. *European Journal of Cancer, 40*, 2773–2780.

Lin, Z. C., & Wang, S. F. (2009). A tailored Web-based intervention to promote women's perceptions of and intentions for mammography. *Journal of Nursing Research, 17*(4), 249–260.

Littell, J. H., & Girvin, H. (2002). Stages of change. A critique. *Behavior Modification, 26*, 223–273.

Logue, E., Sutton, K., Jarjoura, D., Smucker, W., Baughman, K., & Capers, C. (2005). Transtheoretical model-chronic disease care for obesity in primary care: A randomized trial. *Obesity Research, 13*, 917–927.

Manchaiah, V., Rönnberg, J., Andersson, G., & Lunner, T. (2015). Stages of change profiles among adults experiencing hearing difficulties who have not taken any action: A cross-sectional study. *PLoS One, 10*(6), e0129107.

Mastellos, N., Gunn, L. H., Felix, L. M., Car, J., & Majeed, A. (2014). Transtheoretical model stages of change for dietary and physical exercise modification in weight loss management for overweight and obese adults. *Cochrane Database Systematic Review, 2*, CD008066.

McConnaughy, E. A., DiClemente, C. C., Prochaska, J. O., & Velicer, W. F. (1989). Stages of change in psychotherapy: A follow-up report. *Psychotherapy, 4*, 494–503.

Migneault, J. P., Adams, T. B., & Read, J. P. (2005). Application of the transtheoretical model to substance abuse: Historical development and future directions. *Drug and Alcohol Review, 24*, 437–448.

Migneault, J. P., Velicer, W. F., Prochaska, J. O., & Stevenson, J. F. (1999). Decisional balance for immoderate drinking in college students. *Substance Use and Misuse, 34*, 1325–1346.

Miller, W. R., & Tonigan, J. S. (1996). Assessing drinkers' motivations for change: The Stages of Readiness and Treatment Eagerness Scale (SOCRATES). *Psychology of Addictive Behaviors, 10*, 81–89.

Monson, A. L., & Engeswick, L. M. (2005). Promotion of tobacco cessation through dental hygiene education: A pilot study. *Journal of Dental Education, 69*, 901–911.

Mostafavi, F., Ghofranipour, F., Feizi, A., & Pirzadeh, A. (2015). Improving physical activity and metabolic syndrome indicators in women: A transtheoretical model-based intervention. *International Journal of Preventive Medicine, 6*, 28.

Nelson, K. A., Highstein, G., Garbutt, J., Trinkaus, K., Smith, S. R., & Strunk, R. C. (2012). Factors associated with attaining coaching goals during an intervention to improve child asthma care. *Contemporary Clinical Trials*, *33*(5), 912–919.

Olsen, P. (1976). *Emotional flooding*. New York: Human Sciences Press.

Paradis, V., Cossette, S., Frasure-Smith, N., Heppell, S., & Guertin, M. C. (2010). The efficacy of a motivational nursing intervention based on the stages of change on self-care in heart failure patients. *Journal of Cardiovascular Nursing*, *25*(2), 130–141.

Partridge, S. R., McGeechan, K., Hebden, L., Balestracci, K., Wong, A. T., Denney-Wilson, E., et al. (2015). Effectiveness of a mHealth lifestyle program with telephone support (TXT2BFiT) to prevent unhealthy weight gain in young adults: Randomized controlled trial. *JMIR mHealth and uHealth*, *3*(2), e66.

Perls, F. (1969). *Gestalt therapy verbatim*. Lafayette, CA: Real People Press.

Politi, M. C., Rabin, C., & Pinto, B. (2006). Biologically based complementary and alternative medicine use among breast cancer survivors: Relationship to dietary fat consumption and exercise. *Support Care Cancer*, *14*(10), 1064–1069.

Popa, M. A. (2005). Stages of change for osteoporosis preventive behaviors: A construct validation study. *Journal of Aging and Health*, *17*, 336–350.

Prochaska, J. O. (1979). *Systems of psychotherapy: A transtheoretical analysis*. Homewood, IL: Dorsey Press.

Prochaska, J. O. (1995). An eclectic and integrative approach: Transtheoretical therapy. In A. S. Gurman & S. B. Messer (Eds.), *Essential psychotherapies: Theory and practice* (pp. 403–440). New York: Guilford Press.

Prochaska, J. O. (1999). How do people change, and how can we change to help many more people? In M. A. Hubble, B. L. Duncan, & S. D. Miller (Eds.), *The heart and soul of change: What works in therapy* (pp. 227–255). Washington, DC: American Psychological Association.

Prochaska, J. O. (2000). Change at differing stages. In C. R. Snyder & R. E. Ingram (Eds.), *Handbook of psychological change: Psychotherapy processes and practices for the 21st century* (pp. 109–127). New York: Wiley.

Prochaska, J. O. (2006). Moving beyond the transtheoretical model. *Addiction*, *101*, 768–774.

Prochaska, J. O., & DiClemente, C. C. (1983). Stages and processes of self change in smoking: Toward an integrative model of change. *Journal of Consulting and Clinical Psychology*, *5*, 390–395.

Prochaska, J. O., DiClemente, C. C., & Norcross, J. C. (1992). In search of how people change: Applications to addictive behaviors. *American Psychologist*, *47*, 1102–1114.

Prochaska, J. O., Redding, C. A., & Evers, K. E. (2008). The transtheoretical model and stages of change. In K. Glanz, B. K. Rimer, & K. Viswanath (Eds.), *Health behavior and health education: Theory, research, and practice* (4th ed., pp. 97–121). San Francisco: Jossey-Bass.

Pruitt, S. L., McQueen, A., Tiro, J. A., Rakowski, W., Diclemente, C. C., & Vernon, S. W. (2010). Construct validity of a mammography processes of change scale and invariance by stage of change. *Journal of Health Psychology*, *15*(1), 64–74.

Raymond, D. M., 3rd, & Lusk, S. L. (2006). Staging workers' use of hearing protection devices: Application of the transtheoretical model. *AAOHN Journal*, *54*(4), 165–172.

Rhodes, R. E., & Plotnikoff, R. C. (2006). Understanding action control: Predicting physical activity intention-behavior profiles across 6 months in a Canadian sample. *Health Psychology*, *25*(3), 292–299.

Rogers, C. (1951). *Client-centered therapy*. Boston: Houghton Mifflin.

Rogers, C. R. (1961). *On becoming a person*. Boston: Houghton Mifflin.

Roig, L., Perez, S., Prieto, G., Martin, C., Advani, M., Armengol, A., et al. (2010). Cluster randomized trial in smoking cessation with intensive advice in diabetic patients in primary care. ITADI Study. *BMC Public Health*, *10*, 58.

Rollnick, S., Heather N., Gold, R., & Hall, W. (1992). Development of a short readiness to change questionnaire for use in brief opportunistic interventions among excessive drinkers. *British Journal of Addiction*, *87*, 743–754.

Schumann, A., John, U., Rumpf, H. J., Hapke, U., & Meyer, C. (2006). Changes in the "stages of change" as outcome measures of a smoking cessation intervention: A randomized controlled trial. *Preventive Medicine*, *43*(2), 101–106.

Skinner, B. F. (1953). *Science and human behavior.* New York: Macmillan.

Stepnowsky, C. J., Marler, M. R., Palau, J., & Annette Brooks, J. (2006). Social-cognitive correlates of CPAP adherence in experienced users. *Sleep Medicine, 7*(4), 350–356.

Sutton, S. (1996). Can stages of change provide guidance in the treatment of addictions? A critical examination of Prochaska and DiClemente's model. In G. Edwards & C. Dare (Eds.), *Psychotherapy, psychological treatments and the addictions* (pp. 189–205). Cambridge, UK: Cambridge University Press.

Takeuchi, M. T., Edlefsen, M., McCurdy, S. M., & Hillers, V. N. (2006). Development and validation of stages-of-change questions to assess consumers' readiness to use a food thermometer when cooking small cuts of meat. *Journal of American Dietetic Association, 106*(2), 262–266.

Taylor, C. L., Demoor, C., Smith, M. A., Dunn, A. L., Basen-Engquist, K., Nielsen, I., et al. (2006). Active for life after cancer: A randomized trial examining a lifestyle physical activity program for prostate cancer patients. *Psycho-oncology, 15*(10), 847–862.

Tung, W. C. (2010). Benefits and barriers of pap smear screening: Differences in perceptions of Vietnamese American women by stage. *Journal of Community Health Nursing, 27*(1), 12–22.

Tung, W. C., Nguyen, D. H., & Tran, D. N. (2008). Applying the transtheoretical model to cervical cancer screening in Vietnamese-American women. *International Nursing Review, 55*(1), 73–80.

Weiss, J., Okun, M., & Quay, N. (2004). Predicting bicycle helmet stage-of-change among middle school, high school, and college cyclists from demographic, cognitive, and motivational variables. *Journal of Pediatrics, 145,* 360–364.

West, R. (2005). Time for a change: Putting the transtheoretical (stages of change) model to rest [Editorial]. *Addiction, 100,* 1036–1039.

West, R. (2006). The transtheoretical model of behavior change and the scientific method. *Addiction, 101,* 774–778.

Whitelaw, S., Baldwin, S., Bunton, R., & Flynn, D. (2000). The status of evidence and outcomes in stages of change research. *Health Education Research, 15,* 707–718.

Wolpe, J. (1973). *The practice of behavior therapy* (2nd ed.). New York: Pergamon Press.

Wu, A., & Switzer-Nadasdi, R. (2014). The role of health behavior in preventing dental caries in resource-poor adults: A pilot intervention. *Journal of the Tennessee Dental Association, 94*(2), 17–21.

Zhang, A. Y., Harmon, J. A., Werkner, J., & McCormick, R. A. (2006). The long-term relationships between the motivation for change and alcohol use severity among patients with severe and persistent mental illness. *Journal of Addictive Diseases, 25*(1), 121–128.

Zimmerman, R. K., Tabbarah, M., Trauth, J., Nowalk, M. P., & Ricci, E. M. (2006). Predictors of lower endoscopy use among patients at three inner-city neighborhood health centers. *Journal of Urban Health, 83*(2), 221–230.

THEORY OF REASONED ACTION AND THEORY OF PLANNED BEHAVIOR

KEY CONCEPTS

- attitude toward the behavior
- behavior
- behavioral beliefs
- behavioral intention
- control beliefs
- motivation to comply
- normative beliefs
- outcome evaluations
- perceived behavioral control
- perceived power
- subjective norm
- theory of planned behavior
- theory of reasoned action

AFTER READING THIS CHAPTER YOU SHOULD BE ABLE TO

- Describe the historical genesis of the theory of reasoned action (TRA) and the theory of planned behavior (TPB)
- List the constructs of the TRA and TPB
- Summarize the applications of the TRA and TPB in health education and health promotion
- Identify educational methods and match these to modify each construct from the TRA and TPB
- Apply the TRA and TPB in changing a health behavior of your choice

This chapter discusses the **theory of reasoned action (TRA)** and its newer, more evolved version, the **theory of planned behavior (TPB)**. The salient feature of both theories is their claim that behavioral intention is the most important determinant of behavior. Both theories contend that people consider the implications of their actions before deciding to engage in or refrain from any given behavior. Freudian theory and others view behavior as being controlled by unconscious motives or desires. These two theories emphasize the role of thought in decision making about engaging in behaviors. The TRA states that a person's intention is determined by two antecedents, one comprising personal factors and the other social influence. However, it is not assumed that these beliefs and attitudes are necessarily reasonable or correct, which is why it is not called the theory of *reasonable* action. The TPB adds a third predictor, that of control over the behavior. These theories also provide strong guidance with regard to construct measurement, which is invaluable for both practitioners and researchers.

> Theory of Reasoned Action is designed to explain virtually any human behavior, whether we want to understand why a person bought a new car, voted against a school bond issue, was absent from work, or engaged in premarital sexual intercourse.
>
> —Ajzen and Fishbein (1980, p. 4)

This chapter begins with a description of the historical genesis of these theories. Next we describe the various constructs that make up the theories. Then we discuss the applications of the TRA and TPB in health education and health promotion. Finally, we discuss the limitations of the TRA and TPB and present a skill-building application.

HISTORICAL PERSPECTIVE

In the mid- to late 1960s, Martin Fishbein (1965, 1967), a social psychologist at the University of Illinois at Urbana, examined the relationship between beliefs and attitudes. He defined *attitudes* as learned predispositions to respond to an object or class of objects in a favorable or unfavorable way. He defined *beliefs* as hypotheses concerning the nature of objects. He differentiated between beliefs and attitudes and also talked about the distinction between "belief in" an object and "belief about" an object. "Belief in" an object refers to the existence of an object, whereas "belief about" an object deals with the nature of that object. He also differentiated between attitudes toward objects and attitudes toward behaviors. For example, a health educator working with women seeking a Pap test may look at attitudes regarding cervical cancer (object) or at attitudes regarding getting a Pap test (behavior). Emphasis on the latter aspect, attitude toward behavior, served as the origin of the present-day TRA.

In the 1970s, Fishbein teamed up with Icek Ajzen of the University of Massachusetts at Amherst to write *Belief, Attitude, Intention and Behavior: An Introduction to Theory and Research* (Fishbein & Ajzen, 1975), which formed the basis of the TRA. The theory linked beliefs to attitudes, which in turn were linked to intentions, which led to behaviors. In coming up with this theory, they reviewed several then-existing theories, such as learning theories (Hull, 1943; Spence, 1956), value expectancy theories (Atkinson, 1957; Rotter, 1954; Tolman, 1955), consistency theories such as the balance theory (Heider, 1946), the congruity principle (Osgood & Tannenbaum, 1955), Festinger's (1957) theory of cognitive dissonance, and attribution theories (Bem, 1965; Kelley, 1971). Learning theories describe when a given response is associated with a given stimulus. Value expectancy theories postulate that a behavior depends on the value placed by an individual on an outcome (value) and the individual's estimate of the likelihood that a given action will result in that outcome (expectancy).

Consistency theories deal with the effects of inconsistencies among beliefs, attitudes, intentions, and behaviors. Attribution theories purport to explain how people make causal explanations and how they answer questions beginning with "why."

In 1980, Ajzen and Fishbein published a second book, *Understanding Attitudes and Predicting Social Behavior*, which simplified the TRA and made it more accessible for use in a variety of fields. The theory was popular among researchers and practitioners throughout the early 1980s. Sheppard, Hartwick, and Warshaw (1988) performed a meta-analysis and found that the TRA had strong predictive utility. Still, some researchers, including Professor Ajzen, felt that the theory was deficient in explaining behavior, especially the behavior of people who have little power or feel they have little power over their behaviors. As a result, he added the construct of perceived behavioral control to the TRA (Ajzen, 1991). His new thinking was based on Rotter's (1966) locus of control theory, Atkinson's (1964) theory of achievement motivation, and Bandura's (1986) social cognitive theory. The addition of this construct resulted in the theory of planned behavior (TPB).

> **The centrality of the attitude concept remains unchallenged and, if anything, its importance has increased.**
>
> —Fishbein and Ajzen
> (1975, p. v)

In 2004, Francis and colleagues developed a manual for health service researchers to construct questionnaires based on the TPB. Martin Fishbein died in November 2009, causing a setback in the further development of these theories. However, today both theories continue to be among the popular theories in health education and health promotion, and researchers and practitioners continue to use them in various applications.

CONSTRUCTS OF THE THEORY OF REASONED ACTION AND THEORY OF PLANNED BEHAVIOR

Figure 5-1 represents the TRA and TPB diagrammatically. The first construct is **behavior**. Usually this is a single action performed by an individual that is observable. In health education and health promotion, we are interested in many such behaviors, such as condom use, eating five servings of vegetables and fruits, and so on. Ajzen and Fishbein (1980) also talk about behavioral categories that involve sets of actions rather than a single action, which are not easily observable. In health education and health promotion, we are interested in many such behaviors, such as being physically active every day, healthy eating, and so on. The behavior should be defined in terms of its target, action, context, and time (TACT). For example, let us consider the behavior of helping sedentary African American women practice 30 minutes of aerobic dancing at a local church. Here the target is the African American women, the action is aerobic dancing, the context is the sedentary nature of the women, and the time is 30 minutes. In the TRA and TPB, defining and measuring the behavior accurately is very important. Often the behavior is measured by self-reports.

The second construct in the TRA and TPB is **behavioral intention**. This is the thought to perform the behavior, which is an immediate determinant of the given behavior. This construct is the hallmark of this model, which was the first to posit that intention is a proximal measure of behavior. The intention also has the components of TACT. It is usually measured on a 7-point bipolar scale that includes the categories of extremely probable (+3), quite probable (+2), slightly probable (+1), neither probable nor improbable (0), slightly improbable (−1), quite improbable (−2),

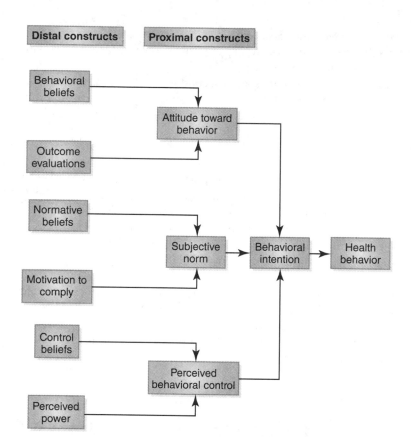

FIGURE 5-1 The upper portion including proximal constructs of attitude toward behavior and subjective norm constitute the theory of reasoned action; all three proximal constructs together constitute the theory of planned behavior.

and extremely improbable (−3). There should be a high degree of correspondence between intention and behavior. Intentions change over time, so the intention must be measured as close to the occurrence of the behavior as possible. The advantage of measuring behavioral intention is that if actual behavior cannot be easily measured in an intervention, then the behavioral intention serves as a useful indicator.

The third construct in the TRA and TPB is **attitude toward the behavior**, which refers to the overall feeling of like or dislike toward any given behavior. The more favorable a person's attitude is toward a behavior, the more likely it is that he or she will intend to perform the behavior; conversely, the more unfavorable a person's attitude is toward the behavior, the more likely it is that he or she will intend not to perform the behavior. Attitude is measured on a 7-point semantic differential scale ranging from favorable to unfavorable or from good to bad. The attitude toward a behavior is shaped by the fourth and fifth constructs of the TRA and TPB, namely, behavioral beliefs and outcome evaluations.

The fourth construct of the TRA and TPB, which is a determinant of attitude toward behavior, is **behavioral beliefs**. Behavioral beliefs are beliefs that performing a given behavior will lead to certain outcomes. The fifth construct is **outcome evaluations**, or the value a person places on each outcome resulting from performance of the behavior. Together, the behavioral beliefs and outcome evaluations determine the attitude toward the behavior. Behavioral beliefs are measured on a 7-point unipolar scale such as extremely unlikely (1) to extremely likely (7). Outcome evaluations are measured on a 7-point bipolar scale such as extremely good (+3), quite good (+2), slightly good (+1), neither good nor bad (0), slightly bad (−1), quite bad (−2), and extremely bad (−3).

A multiplicative score between the behavioral beliefs and the outcome evaluations is derived to assess attitudes toward a behavior. For example, let us look at the behavior of exercising. A person may think of exercising and say that it makes him or her sweaty and thus rate exercise as extremely unlikely (1) to occur and as quite bad (−2). Such a person would have an attitude score of −2, or a negative attitude toward exercise. Another person might think of exercising and say it gives him or her a feeling of high energy and thus rate it as extremely likely (7) to occur and as quite good (+2). Such a person would have an attitude score of +14, or a positive attitude toward exercise. Behavioral beliefs can be modified by brainstorming all possible outcomes in an educational session. To modify outcome evaluations, a discussion on positive outcomes needs to be undertaken.

The sixth construct in the TRA and TPB is **subjective norm**, which refers to a person's belief that most of the significant others in his or her life think the person should or should not perform the behavior. For example, a person might think, "If I exercise, my spouse will be proud of me." This is the second predictor of behavioral intention. In forming a subjective norm, people consider the normative expectations of others in their environment. It is usually measured on a 7-point unipolar scale with a range of strongly agree (7) to strongly disagree (1). The subjective norm is shaped by two constructs—normative beliefs and motivation to comply—which form the seventh and eighth constructs of the TRA and TPB.

The seventh construct of the TRA and TPB is **normative beliefs**, which refer to how a person thinks others who are significant in his or her life would like him or her to behave. For example, a person might think that his or her spouse, parents, and friends believe exercise is good and approve of people who exercise. Normative beliefs are measured on a 7-point bipolar scale with a range of strongly agree (+3), moderately agree (+2), slightly agree (+1), neither agree nor disagree (0), slightly disagree (−1), moderately disagree (−2), and strongly disagree (−3). In educational settings normative beliefs can be influenced by using a role play or psychodrama that helps the person become cognizant of how others may think about him or her. Discussion or arranging a panel discussion can help the person think more critically about the perception of significant others in his or her life.

The eighth construct of the TRA and TPB is **motivation to comply**, which refers to the degree to which a person wants to act in accordance with the perceived wishes of those significant in his or her life. For example, a person might think that what his or her spouse, parents, and friends think about that person's plans for exercise matters a lot. Motivation to comply is usually measured on a 7-point unipolar scale with a range of extremely likely (7) to extremely unlikely (1). To influence motivation to comply, educational techniques such as role play, psychodrama, or discussion can be used, whereby people may become cognizant of their motivations to comply. With these eight constructs, the TRA is complete. **Table 5-1** summarizes these constructs and describes how to modify each one.

In subsequent research, Ajzen added the following three constructs to create the TPB. The ninth construct in the TPB is **perceived behavioral control**, which refers to how much a person feels he or she is in command of enacting the given behavior. It is dependent on the constructs of control belief and perceived power (Montano & Kasprzyk, 2008). Perceived behavioral control is

Table 5-1	Key Constructs of the Theory of Reasoned Action	
Construct	**Definition**	**How to Modify?**
Behavior	Single, observable action performed by an individual, or a category of actions with a specific target, action, context, and time (TACT)	By influencing a behavioral intention, which is dependent on attitude toward the behavior and subjective norms
Behavioral intention	The thought to perform the behavior, which is an immediate determinant of the given behavior	By influencing attitude toward the behavior and subjective norms
Attitude toward the behavior	Overall feeling of like or dislike toward any given behavior	By influencing behavioral beliefs and outcome evaluations
Behavioral beliefs	Beliefs that performing a given behavior leads to certain outcomes	Brainstorming all possible outcomes
Outcome evaluations	Value a person places on each outcome resulting from performance of the behavior	Discussion about positive outcomes
Subjective norm	One's belief that most of the significant others in one's life think one should or should not perform the behavior	By influencing normative beliefs and motivation to comply
Normative beliefs	How a person thinks that other people who are significant in his or her life would like him or her to behave	• Role play • Psychodrama • Panel discussion • Discussion
Motivation to comply	Degree to which a person wants to act in accordance with the perceived wishes of those significant in his or her life	• Role play • Psychodrama • Discussion

measured on a 7-point unipolar scale with a range of strongly agree (7) to strongly disagree (1). Perceived behavioral control is a proxy measure of actual behavioral control and is hypothesized to be directly linked in predicting or explaining the behavior. Perceived behavioral control is a good assessment of actual control over the behavior, especially when volitional control is not high (Montano & Kasprzyk, 2008).

The tenth construct in the TPB is **control beliefs**, which are beliefs about internal and external factors that may inhibit or facilitate the performance of the behavior. For example, a person may believe that he or she can exercise at any time, whereas another person may believe that he or she can exercise only during the times when the gym is open. These are measured on a 7-point scale with unipolar adjectives ranging from unlikely (1) to likely (7). To modify control beliefs, one can use discussion about factors that facilitate behavior, provide incentives, and reduce inhibiting factors.

The eleventh, and final, construct in the TPB is **perceived power**, which refers to a person's perception of how easy or difficult it is to perform the behavior in each condition identified in that person's control beliefs. For example, a control belief may be that a person is able to exercise

Table 5-2	Additional Constructs of the Theory of Planned Behavior	
Construct	**Definition**	**How to Modify?**
Perceived behavioral control	How much a person feels he or she is in command of enacting the given behavior	By influencing control beliefs and perceived power
Control beliefs	Beliefs about internal and external factors that may inhibit or facilitate the performance of the behavior	• Discussion about factors that facilitate behavior • Incentives • Reduction of inhibiting factors
Perceived power	Perception about how easy or difficult it is to perform the behavior in each condition identified in the control beliefs	• Having role models model the behavior • Removing barriers • Breaking down the behavior into small steps

only during the times when the gym is open. Perceived power would explore how easy or how difficult it would be for the person to exercise when the gym is open. It is usually measured on a 7-point scale with bipolar adjectives ranging from extremely difficult (−3), moderately difficult (−2), slightly difficult (−1), neither difficult nor easy (0), slightly easy (+1), and moderately easy (+2), to extremely easy (+3). To modify perceived power, educational methods such as having role models model the desired behavior, removing barriers, and breaking down the behavior into small steps could be used. **Table 5-2** summarizes these additional constructs and how to modify them.

APPLICATIONS OF THE THEORY OF REASONED ACTION AND THEORY OF PLANNED BEHAVIOR

Some examples in which the TRA has been used in health education and health promotion are for acceptance of the diagnosis of depression (Van Voorhees et al., 2005), attitudes about genetically modified foods (Silk, Weiner, & Parrott, 2005), colorectal cancer screening (Zimmerman, Tabbarah, Trauth, Nowalk, & Ricci, 2006), condom use (Fife-Schaw, & Abraham, 2009), a developmental care training program for neonatal nurses (Milette, Richard, & Martel, 2005), exercise/physical activity (Downs, Graham, Yang, Bargainnier, & Vasil, 2006; Wang, Worsley, & Cunningham, 2009), health coaching in a community pharmacy disease management program (Luder, Frede, Kirby, King, & Heaton, 2015), an HIV prevention program in adolescent mothers (Koniak-Griffin & Stein, 2006), mammography behavior and intention (Ham, 2006), modeling alcohol use (Zamboanga, Schwartz, Ham, Jarvis, & Olthuis, 2009), modeling intention to choose normal vaginal delivery (Kanani, Allahverdipour, & Asghari Jafarabad, 2015), osteoporosis prevention (Tussing & Chapman-Novakofski, 2005), patient compliance during orthodontic treatment (Bos, Hoogstraten, &

> It is possible to distinguish between beliefs, attitude, intentions, and behaviors, obtain valid and reliable measures for these, and to show that these are systematically related.
>
> —Fishbein and Ajzen (1975, p. 16)

Prahl-Andersen, 2005), physician intention to prescribe emergency contraception (Sable, Schwartz, Kelly, Lisbon, & Hall, 2006), predicting alcohol-impaired driving (Espada, Griffin, Gonzálvez, & Orgilés, 2015), predicting pneumococcal vaccination (Zimmerman et al., 2005), promoting healthy diet (Peng, 2009), promoting milk with 1% or less fat (Booth-Butterfield & Reger, 2004), prostate cancer genetic screening (Doukas, Localio, & Li, 2004), school-based intervention for HIV/AIDS prevention (Kinsler, Sneed, Morisky, & Ang, 2004), sunscreen use behavior (Abroms, Jorgensen, Southwell, Geller, & Emmons, 2003), testicular self-examination taught by nurse practitioners (Kleier, 2004), and violence prevention (Meyer, Roberto, Boster, & Roberto, 2004). **Table 5-3** summarizes these applications.

Table 5-3	Applications of the Theory of Reasoned Action in Health Education and Health Promotion
Acceptance of a diagnosis of depression	
Attitudes about genetically modified foods	
Colorectal cancer screening	
Condom use	
Developmental care training program for neonatal nurses	
Exercise/physical activity behavior	
Health coaching in a community pharmacy disease management program	
HIV prevention program in adolescent mothers	
Mammography behavior and intention	
Modeling alcohol use	
Modeling intention to choose normal vaginal delivery	
Osteoporosis prevention	
Patient compliance during orthodontic treatment	
Physician intention to prescribe emergency contraception	
Predicting alcohol-impaired driving	
Predicting pneumococcal vaccination	
Promoting healthy diet	
Promoting milk with 1% or less fat	
Prostate cancer genetic screening	
School-based intervention for HIV/AIDS prevention	
Sunscreen use behavior	
Testicular self-examination taught by nurse practitioners	
Violence prevention	

Some examples in which the TPB has been used in health education and health promotion are for condom use (Boer & Mashamba, 2005), controlling preschoolers' sugar snacking (Astrom & Kiwanuka, 2006), exercise/physical activity behavior (Hagger et al., 2009; Marsh, Papaioannou, & Theodorakis, 2006; Rhodes, Warburton, & Bredin, 2009), hand washing in health care workers (Whitby, McLaws, & Ross, 2006), health coaching for physical activity (Jacobs, Hagger, Streukens, De Bourdeaudhuij, & Claes, 2011), healthy eating behaviors (Fila & Smith, 2006), hoist usage for moving a dependent patient among health care workers (Rickett, Orbell, & Sheeran, 2006), hypoglycemic medication among type 2 diabetics (Farmer, Kinmonth, & Sutton, 2006), mammography (O'Neill et al., 2008; Tolma, Reininger, Evans, & Ureda, 2006), medical tourism intentions (Ramamonjiarivelo, Martin, & Martin, 2015), mental health problems among prison inmates (Skogstad, Deane, & Spicer, 2006), multivitamin use among women (Pawlak, Connell, Brown, Meyer, & Yadrick, 2005), organ donation (Park, Smith, & Yun, 2009), predicting alcohol use (Park, Klein, Smith, & Martell, 2009; Quinlan, Jaccard, & Blanton, 2006), predicting binge drinking behavior (Norman & Conner, 2006), predicting fruit consumption (Brug, de Vet, de Nooijer, & Verplanken, 2006; de Bruijn, Brug, & Van Lenthe, 2009), predicting smoking among adolescents (van den Eijnden, Spijkerman, & Engels, 2006; Van De Ven, Engels, Otten, & Van Den Eijnden, 2007), predicting substance abuse behavior (Vederhus, Zemore, Rise, Clausen, & Høie, 2015), school-based intervention to promote physical activity (Angelopoulos, Milionis, Grammatikaki, Moschonis, & Manios, 2009; Tsorbatzoudis, 2005), self-management of rheumatoid arthritis (Strating, van Schuur, & Suurmeijer, 2006), sexual and reproductive health in early adolescence (Aaro et al., 2006), small business owners' health and safety intentions (Brosseau & Li, 2005), smoking cessation (Bledsoe, 2005; Kim, 2008), use of assistive devices by home nurses (Roelands, Van Oost, Depoorter, Buysse, & Stevens, 2006), and vaccination against influenza (Gallagher & Povey, 2006). **Table 5-4** summarizes these applications.

> **We have long been convinced to demonstrate the utility of a theory in applied settings as well as in laboratory settings. This has led us to investigate such diverse problems as voting behavior, family planning, consumer behavior, occupational choice, and weight reduction.**
>
> —Ajzen and Fishbein (1980, p. 97)

LIMITATIONS OF THE THEORY OF REASONED ACTION AND THEORY OF PLANNED BEHAVIOR

Both the TRA and TPB predict behavioral intention and behavior but do not necessarily explain behavior change, which is the primary concern in health education and health promotion programs. Hence, they do not provide detailed and specific guidance for behavior modification. Another limitation of the TRA and TPB is that they do not consider personality-related factors, cultural factors, and demographic variables, which also shape behavior. In his later work, Fishbein (2008) suggested adding an integrative model (IM) of behavioral prediction to the TRA to account for environmental and other factors that moderate the intention–behavior relationship. Also, the TPB assumes that perceived behavioral control predicts actual behavioral control, which may not always happen. Finally, these theories focus only on rational thoughts and do not account for irrational thoughts or fears, which health educators often encounter.

Jane Ogden (2003) noted that the TRA and TPB are pragmatic theories, but she criticized their conceptual bases and discussed several limitations of these theories. First, based on a literature

Table 5-4	Applications of the Theory of Planned Behavior in Health Education and Health Promotion
Condom use
Controlling preschoolers' sugar snacking
Exercise/physical activity behavior
Hand washing in health care workers
Health coaching for physical activity
Healthy eating behaviors
Hoist usage for moving a dependent patient among health care workers
Hypoglycemic medication among type 2 diabetics
Mammography
Medical tourism intentions
Mental health problems among prison inmates
Multivitamin use among women
Organ donation
Predicting alcohol use
Predicting binge drinking behavior
Predicting fruit consumption
Predicting smoking among adolescents
Predicting substance abuse behavior
School-based intervention to promote physical activity
Self-management of rheumatoid arthritis
Sexual and reproductive health in early adolescence
Small business owners' health and safety intentions
Smoking cessation
Use of assistive devices by home nurses
Vaccination against influenza

review, Ogden observed that some studies of TPB reported no role for subjective norms, others showed no predictive role for perceived behavioral control, and some showed no role for attitudes. She contended that these theories may not be predictive or account for low variance, but often investigators rationalize this by arguing that the variables were not adequately operationalized rather than questioning the predictive potential of these theories. Ogden questioned the testability of these theories. Ajzen and Fishbein (2004), in a rejoinder, clarified that the relative importance of attitudes, subjective norms, and perceptions of behavioral control for the prediction of intentions is expected to vary from behavior to behavior and from population to population. They argued that of the three theoretical antecedents, sometimes only one or two may be necessary in a given situation.

Ogden (2003) also talked about two types of truth in the philosophy of science: synthetic truth, which can be known through exploration and testing, and analytic truth, which is known by definition. She contended that the TRA and TPB focus on analytic truth, whereby the conclusions are not supported by observation. She also noted that behavior is mostly measured by self-reports rather than objective measures. In their rejoinder, Ajzen and Fishbein (2004) presented evidence from structural equation modeling that supported the path mentioned in the theories. They also defended self-reports because it is virtually impossible to obtain objective measurement of some behaviors (such as condom use) and extremely expensive and time consuming for others (such as exercise).

Finally, Ogden (2003) noted that answering questions about an individual's cognition in the operationalization of these theories may change and create an individual's thinking rather than tap into how that person thought to begin with. Ajzen and Fishbein (2004) noted that this concern is universal to all behavioral science research.

APPLICATION EXERCISE

In this chapter we have presented several examples of applications of the TRA and TPB in health education and health promotion. Choose one application in which you are interested and locate the full-text article for that application. Review and critique that example.

One example is the study by O'Neill and colleagues (2008) that examined behavioral intentions for adherence to mammography using the TPB. In addition to the constructs of the TPB, they included previous barriers, previous mammography maintenance, and age as potential predictors. A cross-sectional survey design was utilized and administered to 2,062 currently adherent women who were due for their mammograms in 3 to 4 months. All TPB variables significantly predicted (p < 0.05) behavioral intention except subjective norms.

Locate the full-text article of this study and in a critique of 250 words comment on how the TPB was used. In your critique pay attention to how the constructs were reified. Were they operationalized adequately? Was validity and reliability of the instrument established? Were the statistical analyses appropriate? Were the conclusions accurate? Can the results be generalized?

SKILL-BUILDING ACTIVITY

Let us see how we can apply the TPB to the behavior of condom use. (Application of the TRA is a subset of the application of the TPB.) This application is depicted in **Figure 5-2**.

Let us first define the target as college students; the action, which is condom use; the context, which is while having sex; and the time, which is every time an individual had sex. According to the TPB, the behavioral intention precedes the behavior. The proximal predictive constructs of intention include attitude toward condom use, subjective norm, and perceived behavioral control. To influence the construct of attitude toward condom use, the constructs of behavioral beliefs and outcome evaluations need to be modified. To modify behavioral beliefs, a brainstorming session can be organized in which the participants share their perceived outcomes about condom use.

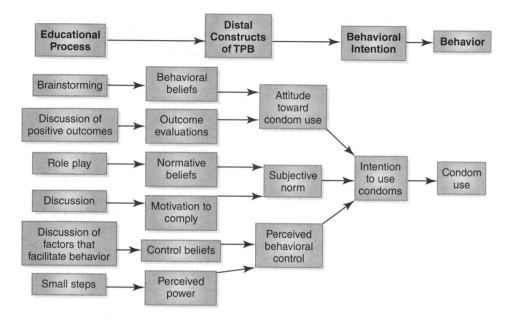

FIGURE 5-2 How the theory of planned behavior can be used for promoting condom use behavior.

Instead of brainstorming, elicitation interviews with 15 to 20 members of the target audience could be organized. To modify outcome evaluations, a discussion on the positive outcomes of condom use, such as prevention of diseases and prevention of pregnancy, can be organized that would help all participants develop their outlook about positive effects.

To modify subjective norms, we would need to modify normative beliefs and motivation to comply. Normative beliefs can be modified by use of a role play that depicts the most significant others in a family situation approving of the behavior of condom use. The participants would then perhaps be able to apply that observation to their own lives and make a deduction that significant others in their lives would also approve of the behavior. To modify motivation to comply, a discussion can be organized that would try to sway the participants' belief that parents, friends, teachers, and all significant others consider using condoms important and that each person must use condoms.

To modify perceived behavioral control, the constructs of control beliefs and perceived power must be modified. To modify control beliefs, we can organize a discussion about factors that facilitate condom use behavior, such as keeping condoms readily accessible, having a prior discussion with one's partner, and so on. To modify perceived power, condom use can be demonstrated in small steps, and role models can demonstrate the behavior of condom use. Using this approach, you can apply the TRA or TPB to any health behavior for a target group of your choice. **Table 5-5** provides a set of questions to assist you in choosing an educational method that corresponds to different constructs.

Table 5-5	Choosing the Educational Method for Health Education Program Planning Using the TRA and TPB

1. How will you define the behavior and behavioral intention?
   - Target: _____
   - Action: _____
   - Context: _____
   - Time: _____

2. What is the best educational method to facilitate behavioral beliefs?
   - Brainstorming
   - Discussion
   - Elicitation interviews
   - Other

3. What is the best educational method to facilitate outcome evaluations?
   - Discussion on positive outcomes
   - Lecture
   - Video with a credible role model
   - Other

4. What is the best educational method to facilitate normative beliefs?
   - Discussion
   - Role play
   - Psychodrama
   - Panel discussion
   - Simulation
   - Other

5. What is the best educational method to facilitate motivation to comply?
   - Discussion
   - Role play
   - Psychodrama
   - Simulation
   - Other

6. What is the best educational method to facilitate control beliefs?
   - Discussion about factors that facilitate behavior
   - Incentives
   - Reduction of inhibiting factors
   - Other

7. What is the best educational method to facilitate perceived power?
   - Demonstration of behavior in small steps
   - Having a role model model the behavior
   - Removing barriers
   - Other

SUMMARY

In the late 1960s and early 1970s, Martin Fishbein and Icek Ajzen propounded the theory of reasoned action (TRA). The theory claims that behavioral intention precedes behavior and is determined by attitude toward the behavior and subjective norm. Attitude toward the behavior is the individual's overall like or dislike of any given behavior and is determined by behavioral beliefs (beliefs that performing a given behavior leads to certain outcomes) and outcome evaluations (the value a person places on each outcome resulting from performance of a given behavior). Subjective norm is one's belief that most of the significant others in one's life think one should or should not perform the behavior and is determined by normative beliefs (a person's beliefs about how other people who are significant in his or her life would like him or her to behave) and motivation to comply (the degree to which a person wants to act in accordance with the perceived wishes of those significant in his or her life).

In the late 1980s and early 1990s, Ajzen added the construct of perceived behavioral control (how much a person feels that he or she is in command of enacting the given behavior) and created the theory of planned behavior (TPB). The construct of perceived behavioral control is dependent on control beliefs (beliefs about internal and external factors that may inhibit or facilitate the performance of the behavior) and perceived power (perception about how easy or difficult it is to perform the behavior in each condition identified in the control beliefs).

Both the TRA and TPB have been used widely in health education and health promotion and continue to be applied. Lack of focus on behavior change, not considering all predictors, the gap between perceived behavioral control and actual behavioral control, exclusive focus on rational thoughts, variations in predictive constructs, reliance on self-reports, and influences from measuring questionnaires are some identified limitations of the TRA and TPB.

IMPORTANT TERMS

attitude toward the behavior

behavior

behavioral beliefs

behavioral intention

control beliefs

motivation to comply

normative beliefs

outcome evaluations

perceived behavioral control

perceived power

subjective norm

theory of planned behavior (TPB)

theory of reasoned action (TRA)

REVIEW QUESTIONS

1. Discuss the historical genesis of the theory of reasoned action (TRA) and the theory of planned behavior (TPB).
2. List and define the constructs of the TRA.

3. List and define the constructs of the TPB.
4. Differentiate between subjective norms and normative beliefs.
5. Discuss the limitations of the TRA and TPB.
6. Apply the TPB to the promotion of condom use in college students.

WEBSITES TO EXPLORE

Applying the TPB for Obesity Prevention

https://etd.ohiolink.edu/ap/10?0::NO:10:P10_ACCESSION_NUM:ucin1282055620

This website provides access to the dissertation of Dr. Melinda Ickes who developed predictive models on obesity-related behaviors in middle school students. *Download her dissertation. See how a dissertation is written and then look at her instrument provided in the appendix. Write a short critique on her instrument.*

Constructing Questionnaires on the TRA and TPB

http://openaccess.city.ac.uk/1735/1/TPB%20Manual%20FINAL%20May2004.pdf

This is a manual developed by Francis and colleagues on how to develop questionnaires based on the TPB. It presents all the steps needed with examples in developing and managing a TPB questionnaire. *Take time to read this manual. Develop a TPB questionnaire for a health behavior and target population of your choice. Obtain feedback from your instructor on your questionnaire.*

Professor Icek Aizen (Ajzen)

www.people.umass.edu/aizen/

The website of Professor Icek Ajzen contains his contact information, professional background, teaching interests, research interests, a list of publications, and information on the TPB. The link to the TPB provides a depiction and bibliography of the model, tips on constructing a questionnaire based on the TPB, tips on designing an intervention based on the TPB, and frequently asked questions. *Read the frequently asked questions. Summarize what new things you learned.*

Resource Center for Adolescent Pregnancy Prevention (RECAPP)

http://recapp.etr.org/recapp/

On the RECAPP website, click on "Theories & Approaches" (on the left side). It will take you to a page that has a link which summarizes the TRA, discusses its key concepts, explains how the TRA was developed, includes two research study summaries, discusses how the TRA can be applied, discusses challenges, and lists resources. *Review one of the research study summaries and comment on its strengths and weaknesses.*

University of Twente: TPB & TRA

www.tcw.utwente.nl/theorieenoverzicht/Theory%20clusters/Health%20Communication/theory_planned_behavior.doc/

This website from the University of Twente in the Netherlands summarizes the TRA and TPB. Included in the presentation are history, core assumptions and statements, favorite methods, scope and application, and references. *Review this website and locate an account of an application of this theory. Discuss its strengths and weaknesses.*

YouTube: Theory of Planned Behavior

https://www.youtube.com/watch?v=C49o3OccS5c

This is a short video by Erin Long-Crowell that explains the TPB. The definition, examples, and usefulness of this theory are explained in this video. *Watch this video. Summarize your learning and reaction to this video in a one-page paper.*

REFERENCES

Aaro, L. E., Flisher, A. J., Kaaya, S., Onya, H., Fuglesang, M., Klepp, K. I., et al. (2006). Promoting sexual and reproductive health in early adolescence in South Africa and Tanzania: Development of a theory- and evidence-based intervention programme. *Scandinavian Journal of Public Health, 34*(2), 150–158.

Abroms, L., Jorgensen, C. M., Southwell, B. G., Geller, A. C., & Emmons, K. M. (2003). Gender differences in young adults' beliefs about sunscreen use. *Health Education and Behavior, 30*(1), 29–43.

Ajzen, I. (1991). The theory of planned behavior. *Organizational Behavior and Human Decision Process, 50*, 179–211.

Ajzen, I., & Fishbein, M. (1980). *Understanding attitudes and predicting social behavior.* Englewood Cliffs, NJ: Prentice-Hall.

Ajzen, I., & Fishbein, M. (2004). Questions raised by a reasoned action approach: Comment on Ogden (2003). *Health Psychology, 23*, 431–434.

Angelopoulos, P. D., Milionis, H. J., Grammatikaki, E., Moschonis, G., & Manios, Y. (2009). Changes in BMI and blood pressure after a school based intervention: The CHILDREN study. *European Journal of Public Health, 19*(3), 319–325.

Astrom, A. N., & Kiwanuka, S. N. (2006). Examining intention to control preschool children's sugar snacking: A study of carers in Uganda. *International Journal of Paediatric Dentistry, 16*(1), 10–18.

Atkinson, J. W. (1957). Motivational determinants of risk taking behavior. *Psychological Review, 64*, 359–372.

Atkinson, J. W. (1964). *An introduction to motivation.* Princeton, NJ: Van Nostrand.

Bandura, A. (1986). *Social foundations of thought and action: A social cognitive theory.* Englewood Cliffs, NJ: Prentice-Hall.

Bem, D. J. (1965). An experimental analysis of self persuasion. *Journal of Experimental Social Psychology, 1*, 199–218.

Bledsoe, L. K. (2005). Smoking cessation: An application of theory of planned behavior to understanding progress through stages of change. *Addictive Behaviors, 31*(7), 1271–1276.

Boer, H., & Mashamba, M. T. (2005). Psychosocial correlates of HIV protection motivation among black adolescents in Venda, South Africa. *AIDS Education and Prevention, 17*(6), 590–602.

Booth-Butterfield, S., & Reger, B. (2004). The message changes belief and the rest is theory: The "1% or less" milk campaign and reasoned action. *Preventive Medicine, 39*(3), 581–588.

Bos, A., Hoogstraten, J., & Prahl-Andersen, B. (2005). The theory of reasoned action and patient compliance during orthodontic treatment. *Community Dentistry and Oral Epidemiology, 33*(6), 419–426.

Brosseau, L. M., & Li, S. Y. (2005). Small business owners' health and safety intentions: A cross-sectional survey. *Environmental Health, 4*, 23.

Brug, J., de Vet, E., de Nooijer, J., & Verplanken, B. (2006). Predicting fruit consumption: Cognitions, intention, and habits. *Journal of Nutrition Education and Behavior, 38*(2), 73–81.

de Bruijn, G. J., Brug, J., & Van Lenthe, F. J. (2009). Neuroticism, conscientiousness and fruit consumption: Exploring mediator and moderator effects in the theory of planned behaviour. *Psychology & Health*, *24*(9), 1051–1069.

Doukas, D. J., Localio, A. R., & Li, Y. (2004). Attitudes and beliefs concerning prostate cancer genetic screening. *Clinical Genetics*, *66*(5), 445–451.

Downs, D. S., Graham, G. M., Yang, S., Bargainnier, S., & Vasil, J. (2006). Youth exercise intention and past exercise behavior: Examining the moderating influences of sex and meeting exercise recommendations. *Research Quarterly for Exercise and Sport*, *77*(1), 91–99.

Espada, J. P., Griffin, K. W., Gonzálvez, M. T., & Orgilés, M. (2015). Predicting alcohol-impaired driving among Spanish youth with the theory of reasoned action. *Spanish Journal of Psychology*, *18*, E43. doi: 10.1017/sjp.2015.44.

Farmer, A., Kinmonth, A. L., & Sutton, S. (2006). Measuring beliefs about taking hypoglycaemic medication among people with type 2 diabetes. *Diabetic Medicine*, *23*(3), 265–270.

Festinger, L. (1957). *A theory of cognitive dissonance*. Evanston, IL: Row, Peterson.

Fife-Schaw, C., & Abraham, C. (2009). How much behaviour change should we expect from health promotion campaigns targeting cognitions? An approach to pre-intervention assessment. *Psychology & Health*, *24*(7), 763–776.

Fila, S., & Smith, C. (2006). Applying the theory of planned behavior to healthy eating behaviors in urban Native American youth. *International Journal of Behavioral Nutrition and Physical Activity*, *3*(1), 11.

Fishbein, M. (1965). A consideration of beliefs, attitudes, and their relationship. In I. D. Steiner & M. Fishbein (Eds.), *Current studies in social psychology* (pp. 107–120). New York: Holt Rinehart and Winston.

Fishbein, M. (1967). Attitude and the prediction of behavior. In M. Fishbein (Ed.), *Readings in attitude theory and measurement* (pp. 477–492). New York: Wiley.

Fishbein, M. (2008). A reasoned action approach to health promotion. *Medical Decision Making*, *28*(6), 834–844.

Fishbein, M., & Ajzen, I. (1975). *Belief, attitude, intention and behavior: An introduction to theory and research*. Reading, MA: Addison-Wesley.

Francis, J. J., Eccles, M. P., Johnston, M., Walker, A., Grimshaw, J., Foy, R., et al. (2004). *Constructing questionnaires based on the theory of planned behaviour*. Newcastle upon Tyne, UK: Centre for Health Services Research, University of Newcastle.

Gallagher, S., & Povey, R. (2006). Determinants of older adults' intentions to vaccinate against influenza: A theoretical application. *Journal of Public Health*, *28*(2), 139–144.

Hagger, M., Chatzisarantis, N. L., Hein, V., Soos, I., Karsai, I., Lintunen, T., et al. (2009). Teacher, peer and parent autonomy support in physical education and leisure-time physical activity: A trans-contextual model of motivation in four nations. *Psychology & Health*, *24*(6), 689–711.

Ham, O. K. (2006). Factors affecting mammography behavior and intention among Korean women. *Oncology Nursing Forum*, *33*(1), 113–119.

Heider, F. (1946). Attitudes and cognitive organization. *Journal of Psychology*, *21*, 107–112.

Hull, C. L. (1943). *The principles of behavior*. New York: Appleton-Century-Crofts.

Jacobs, N., Hagger, M. S., Streukens, S., De Bourdeaudhuij, I., & Claes, N. (2011). Testing an integrated model of the theory of planned behaviour and self-determination theory for different energy balance-related behaviours and intervention intensities. *British Journal of Health Psychology*, *16*(Pt 1), 113–134. doi: 10.1348/135910710X519305.

Kanani, S., Allahverdipour, H., & Asghari Jafarabadi, M. (2015). Modeling the intention to choose natural vaginal delivery: Using reasoned action and social cognitive theories. *Health Promotion Perspectives*, *5*(1), 24–33. doi: 10.15171/hpp.2015.004.

Kelley, H. H. (1971). *Attribution in social interaction*. New York: General Learning Press.

Kim, S. S. (2008). Predictors of short-term smoking cessation among Korean American men. *Public Health Nursing*, *25*(6), 516–525.

Kinsler, J., Sneed, C. D., Morisky, D. E., & Ang, A. (2004). Evaluation of a school-based intervention for HIV/AIDS prevention among Belizean adolescents. *Health Education Research*, *19*(6), 730–738.

Kleier, J. A. (2004). Nurse practitioners' behavior regarding teaching testicular self-examination. *Journal of the American Academy of Nurse Practitioners, 16*(5), 206–208, 210, 212.

Koniak-Griffin, D., & Stein, J. A. (2006). Predictors of sexual risk behaviors among adolescent mothers in a human immunodeficiency virus prevention program. *Journal of Adolescent Health, 38*(3), 297.e1–11.

Luder, H., Frede, S., Kirby, J., King, K., & Heaton, P. (2015). Health beliefs describing patients enrolling in community pharmacy disease management programs. *Journal of Pharmacy Practice*, [EPub], *pii*: 0897190014566311.

Marsh, H. W., Papaioannou, A., & Theodorakis, Y. (2006). Causal ordering of physical self-concept and exercise behavior: Reciprocal effects model and the influence of physical education teachers. *Health Psychology, 25*(3), 316–328.

Meyer, G., Roberto, A. J., Boster, F. J., & Roberto, H. L. (2004). Assessing the Get Real About Violence curriculum: Process and outcome evaluation results and implications. *Health Communication, 16*(4), 451–474.

Milette, I. H., Richard, L., & Martel, M. J. (2005). Evaluation of a developmental care training programme for neonatal nurses. *Journal of Child Health Care, 9*(2), 94–109.

Montano, D. E., & Kasprzyk, D. (2008). The theory of reasoned action and the theory of planned behavior. In K. Glanz, B. Rimer, & K. Viswanath (Eds.), *Health behavior and health education: Theory, research and practice* (4th ed., pp. 67–96). San Francisco: Jossey-Bass.

Norman, P., & Conner, M. (2006). The theory of planned behaviour and binge drinking: Assessing the moderating role of past behaviour within the theory of planned behaviour. *British Journal of Health Psychology, 11*(Pt. 1), 55–70.

Ogden, J. (2003). Some problems with social cognition models: A pragmatic and conceptual analysis. *Health Psychology, 22*, 424–428.

O'Neill, S. C., Bowling, J. M., Brewer, N. T., Lipkus, I. M., Skinner, C. S., Strigo, T. S., et al. (2008). Intentions to maintain adherence to mammography. *Journal of Women's Health, 17*(7), 1133–1141.

Osgood, C. E., & Tannenbaum, P. H. (1955). The principle of congruity in the prediction of attitude change. *Psychological Review, 62*, 42–55.

Park, H. S., Klein, K. A., Smith, S., & Martell, D. (2009). Separating subjective norms, university descriptive and injunctive norms, and U. S. descriptive and injunctive norms for drinking behavior intentions. *Health Communication, 24*(8), 746–751.

Park, H. S., Smith, S. W., & Yun, D. (2009). Ethnic differences in intention to enroll in a state organ donor registry and intention to talk with family about organ donation. *Health Communication, 24*(7), 647–659.

Pawlak, R., Connell, C., Brown, D., Meyer, M. K., & Yadrick, K. (2005). Predictors of multivitamin supplement use among African-American female students: A prospective study utilizing the theory of planned behavior. *Ethnicity and Disease, 15*(4), 540–547.

Peng, W. (2009). Design and evaluation of a computer game to promote a healthy diet for young adults. *Health Communication, 24*(2), 115–127.

Quinlan, S. L., Jaccard, J., & Blanton, H. (2006). A decision theoretic and prototype conceptualization of possible selves: Implications for the prediction of risk behavior. *Journal of Personality, 74*(2), 599–630.

Ramamonjiarivelo, Z., Martin, D. S., & Martin, W. S. (2015). The determinants of medical tourism intentions: Applying the theory of planned behavior. *Health Marketing Quarterly, 32*(2), 165–179. doi: 10.1080/07359683.2015.1033934.

Rhodes, R. E., Warburton, D. E., & Bredin, S. S. (2009). Predicting the effect of interactive video bikes on exercise adherence: An efficacy trial. *Psychology, Health & Medicine, 14*(6), 631–640.

Rickett, B., Orbell, S., & Sheeran, P. (2006). Social-cognitive determinants of hoist usage among health care workers. *Journal of Occupational Health Psychology, 11*(2), 182–196.

Roelands, M., Van Oost, P., Depoorter, A. M., Buysse, A., & Stevens, V. (2006). Introduction of assistive devices: Home nurses' practices and beliefs. *Journal of Advanced Nursing, 54*(2), 180–188.

Rotter, J. B. (1954). *Social learning and clinical psychology.* New York: Prentice-Hall.

Rotter, J. B. (1966). Generalized expectancies for internal versus external control of reinforcement. *Psychological Monographs, 80*(1, No. 609).

Sable, M. R., Schwartz, L. R., Kelly, P. J., Lisbon, E., & Hall, M. A. (2006). Using the theory of reasoned action to explain physician intention to prescribe emergency contraception. *Perspectives on Sexual and Reproductive Health, 38*(1), 20–27.

Sheppard, B. H., Hartwick, J., & Warshaw, P. R. (1988). The theory of reasoned action: A meta-analysis of past research with recommendations for modifications and future research. *Journal of Consumer Research, 15,* 325–343.

Silk, K. J., Weiner, J., & Parrott, R. L. (2005). Gene cuisine or Frankenfood? The theory of reasoned action as an audience segmentation strategy for messages about genetically modified foods. *Journal of Health Communication, 10,* 751–767.

Skogstad, P., Deane, F. P., & Spicer, J. (2006). Social-cognitive determinants of help-seeking for mental health problems among prison inmates. *Criminal Behavior and Mental Health, 16*(1), 43–59.

Spence, K. W. (1956). *Behavior theory and conditioning.* New Haven, CT: Yale University Press.

Strating, M. M., van Schuur, W. H., & Suurmeijer, T. P. (2006). Contribution of partner support in self-management of rheumatoid arthritis patients. An application of the theory of planned behavior. *Journal of Behavioral Medicine, 29*(1), 51–60.

Tolma, E. L., Reininger, B. M., Evans, A., & Ureda, J. (2006). Examining the theory of planned behavior and the construct of self-efficacy to predict mammography intention. *Health Education and Behavior, 33*(2), 233–251.

Tolman, E. C. (1955). Principles of performance. *Psychological Review, 62,* 315–326.

Tsorbatzoudis, H. (2005). Evaluation of a school-based intervention programme to promote physical activity: An application of the theory of planned behavior. *Perceptual and Motor Skills, 101*(3), 787–802.

Tussing, L., & Chapman-Novakofski, K. (2005). Osteoporosis prevention education: Behavior theories and calcium intake. *Journal of American Dietetic Association, 105,* 92–97.

van den Eijnden, R. J., Spijkerman, R., & Engels, R. C. (2006). Relative contribution of smoker prototypes in predicting smoking among adolescents: A comparison with factors from the theory of planned behavior. *European Addiction Research, 12*(3), 113–120.

Van De Ven, M. O., Engels, R. C., Otten, R., & Van Den Eijnden, R. J. (2007). A longitudinal test of the theory of planned behavior predicting smoking onset among asthmatic and non-asthmatic adolescents. *Journal of Behavioral Medicine, 30*(5), 435–445.

Van Voorhees, B. W., Fogel, J., Houston, T. K., Cooper, L. A., Wang, N. Y., & Ford, D. E. (2005). Beliefs and attitudes associated with the intention to not accept the diagnosis of depression among young adults. *Annals of Family Medicine, 3*(1), 38–46.

Vederhus, J. K., Zemore, S. E., Rise, J., Clausen, T., & Høie, M. (2015). Predicting patient post-detoxification engagement in 12-step groups with an extended version of the theory of planned behavior. *Addiction Science & Clinical Practice, 10*(1), 15. doi: 10.1186/s13722-015-0036-3.

Wang, W. C., Worsley, A., & Cunningham, E. G. (2009). Social ideological influences on food consumption, physical activity and BMI. *Appetite, 53*(3), 288–296.

Whitby, M., McLaws, M. L., & Ross, M. W. (2006). Why healthcare workers don't wash their hands: A behavioral explanation. *Infection Control and Hospital Epidemiology, 27*(5), 484–492.

Zamboanga, B. L., Schwartz, S. J., Ham, L. S., Jarvis, L. H., & Olthuis, J. V. (2009). Do alcohol expectancy outcomes and valuations mediate peer influences and lifetime alcohol use among early adolescents? *Journal of Genetic Psychology, 170*(4), 359–376.

Zimmerman, R. K., Tabbarah, M., Nowalk, M. P., Raymund, M., Jewell, I. K., Block, B., et al. (2005). Predictors of pneumococcal polysaccharide vaccination among patients at three inner-city neighborhood health centers. *American Journal of Geriatric Pharmacotherapy, 3*(3), 149–159.

Zimmerman, R. K., Tabbarah, M., Trauth, J., Nowalk, M. P., & Ricci, E. M. (2006). Predictors of lower endoscopy use among patients at three inner-city neighborhood health centers. *Journal of Urban Health, 83*(2), 221–230.

THEORIES OF STRESS AND COPING

Chapter 6

KEY CONCEPTS

- challenge
- chronic strains
- chronic stressors
- commitment
- community-wide strains
- comprehensibility
- control
- coping
- daily hassles
- emotion-focused coping
- event-based models
- general adaptation syndrome
- hardiness
- life events or life change events
- manageability
- meaningfulness

- nonevents
- optimism
- persistent life difficulties
- problem-focused coping
- recent life events
- remote life events
- response-based models
- role strains
- sense of coherence
- social network
- social support
- stress
- stressors
- transactional model
- type A personality
- type B personality

AFTER READING THIS CHAPTER YOU SHOULD BE ABLE TO

- Describe the historical genesis of theories of stress and coping
- List the constructs of the expanded transactional model, the theory of hardiness, and the theory of sense of coherence

- Describe the role of social networks, social support, and optimism on stress and coping
- Summarize the applications of theories of stress and coping in health education and health promotion
- Identify educational methods and match these to modify each construct from theories of stress and coping
- Apply the theories of stress and coping in reducing stress

This chapter discusses theories of stress and coping. Stress is an integral part of any behavior change. People experience some amount of stress when changing any given behavior. If this stress is very high, new behavior cannot be acquired. Stress can be produced by a variety of external and internal events other than acquiring a new behavior. Often this stress is harmful and causes negative sequelae. Various theories, models, and constructs have been developed to explain the stress process. Some of these theories and models focus on the effects of stress, some on the causes of stress, others on personality characteristics, and some on coping responses. This chapter integrates the understanding of stress across these various models and theories. In health education and health promotion, we are interested in understanding the stress process as well as in finding ways to reduce negative stress, so the emphasis is on modifying those constructs that can be altered.

It is not the stressor but your perception of the stress that is important.

—Romas and Sharma (2010, p. 1)

The chapter begins by describing the historical aspects of the genesis of these theories. Next we describe the various constructs that make up these theories and discuss the applications of theories of stress and coping in health education and health promotion. We then discuss the limitations of the theories of stress and coping and present a skill-building application.

HISTORICAL PERSPECTIVE

The concept of **stress** was unknown in physiology and psychology prior to 1932. The term had been used mainly in physical sciences to denote cracks in the structure of buildings that were caused by pressure. Walter Cannon (1932), a physiologist, first defined stress as a "fight or flight" syndrome. He stated that when an organism is presented with a stressful stimulus, it responds by either fighting with it or running away from it. This was the origin of **response-based models** of stress.

The response-based concept was further elaborated by the work of Swedish physiologist Hans Selye (1936, 1974a, 1974b, 1982), who described the **general adaptation syndrome**. While trying to isolate a new sex hormone in rats, Selye observed that exposing rats to events such as cold, heat, injury, infection, loss of blood, pain, and other noxious stimuli resulted in their adrenal glands secreting corticoid hormones (a steroid) and their bodies going through three stages that he called the general adaptation syndrome (**Figure 6-1**). He labeled the first stage the *alarm reaction*, in which a living organism's homeostasis, or balance, is disrupted by the noxious stimuli. In this phase the endocrine glands (ductless glands that pour their secretions directly into the blood), especially the adrenal glands, begin secreting hormones (corticosteroids) that help to supply more energy to the body. This is accompanied by a shrinkage of lymphatic structures, a decrease in blood volume, and development of ulcers in the stomach. The second stage is *resistance*, in which the body tries to resist the noxious stimuli. In this stage the adaptation energy continues to be depleted. The third and final stage of the general adaptation syndrome is *exhaustion*. Exhaustion causes permanent damage

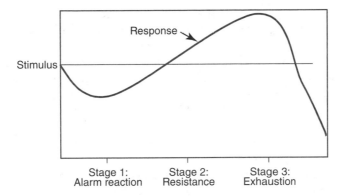

Stimulus

Response

Stage 1:
Alarm reaction

Stage 2:
Resistance

Stage 3:
Exhaustion

FIGURE 6-1 Stages of the general adaptation syndrome.

to the system; if the noxious agent is not removed, the organism's energy becomes depleted, and death may follow.

The response-based modeling of stress that originated from the work of physiologists and discussed hormonal and physiological responses remained the major model of stress until the 1960s, when event-based models and the concept of coping began to be understood in psychology. Thomas Holmes and Richard Rahe (1967) developed the Social Readjustment Rating Scale, which listed 43 life events, each with a predetermined weight, and asked a person to identify events he or she had experienced in the past year. They empirically found that the higher a person's score was on the scale, the greater the chances of that individual developing sickness in the subsequent year. The **event-based models** changed the paradigm from the effect (response) to the cause (stressor).

Alongside the event-based models, the concept of **coping** also developed, which led to establishment of the transactional model of coping. The term *coping* can be traced back to the concept of **defense mechanisms** described in the psychoanalytical model by the famous Austrian neurologist Sigmund Freud (1923). In the 1920s, Freud described the mechanisms of defense that a person's mind uses to protect itself. These included methods such as introjection, isolation, projection reversal, reaction formation, regression, repression, sublimation, turning against the self, and undoing. According to Freud, defense mechanisms were the devices that the mind used to alter the individual's perception of situations that disturbed the internal milieu or mental balance. He applied this concept in identifying sources of anxiety using a free association technique on patients.

In the 1930s one of Freud's associates, Austrian-born physician Alfred Adler, differed from Freud and argued that defense mechanisms were protective against external threats or challenges (Sharma, 2003). Sigmund Freud's daughter and renowned psychologist, Anna Freud (1937), included both these viewpoints and underscored the role of defense mechanisms as being protective against both internal and external threats. She also extended the repertoire of defense mechanisms to include denial, intellectualization, ego restriction, and identifying with the aggressor. Therefore, it appears that the concept of defense mechanisms is very similar to that of coping, which it preceded. However, in the 1970s, psychologist Norma Haan (1977) distinguished defense mechanisms from coping. She explained that coping is purposeful and involves choices, whereas defense mechanisms are rigid and set. Coping, according to Haan, is focused on the present, whereas defense mechanisms are premised on the past and distort the present.

Using the concept of coping, Richard Lazarus (1966, 1984), a professor of psychology at the University of California–Berkley, developed the **transactional model**. According to this model, all stressful experiences, including chronic illnesses, are perceived as person–environment transactions. In these transactions, the person undertakes a four-stage assessment known as *appraisal* (Lazarus & Folkman, 1984). When confronted with any stressor, the first stage is the *primary appraisal* of the event. In this stage, the person internally determines the severity of the stressor and whether he or she is in trouble. If the stressor is perceived to be severe or threatening, has caused harm or loss in the past, or has affected someone known to the person, then the stage of *secondary appraisal* occurs. If, on the other hand, the stressor is judged to be irrelevant or poses minimal threat, then stress does not develop any further, and no further coping occurs. The secondary appraisal determines how much control the person has over the stressor. Based on this understanding, the individual ascertains what means of control are available to him or her. This is the stage known as *coping*. According to the transactional model, there are two broad categories of coping: problem-focused coping and emotion-focused coping. Finally, the fourth stage is *reappraisal*, during which the person determines whether the effects of the stressor have been effectively negated.

In the 1970s Suzanne Kobasa (1979a, 1979b) conducted an eight-year study of executives undergoing the major stress of losing their jobs or being reassigned and found that individuals who displayed a certain set of personality characteristics remained healthier and happier during the crisis. She labeled such personality traits **hardiness**. Friedman and Rosenman (1974) classified people into type A and type B personalities. The **type A personality** was characterized by hurrying, exercising control over people and things, a sense of urgency, and a challenging nature. The **type B personality** was more laid back and had a more relaxed disposition. It was found that people with type B personalities had less stress than those with type A personalities. In the late 1970s and 1980s, a medical sociologist, Aaron Antonovsky (1979, 1987), proposed the theory of **sense of coherence**, which postulated that people who possess a higher sense of coherence tend to cope with life better. In the 1980s another construct that moderates the influence of stressors was discovered, namely, social support. Scheier and Carver (1985) also suggested the construct of optimism as having a beneficial effect on coping.

> The nature and severity of the stress disorder could depend on at least three factors: (1) the formal characteristics of the environmental demands, (2) the quality of the emotional response generated by the demands, or in particular individuals facing these demands, and (3) the process of coping mobilized by the stressful commerce.
>
> —Lazarus (1974, p. 327)

CONSTRUCTS OF THEORIES OF STRESS AND COPING

A model incorporating theories of stress and coping is depicted in **Figure 6-2**. The primary construct of theories of stress and coping is that of **stressors**, which are demands from the internal or external environment that an individual perceives as being harmful or threatening (Lazarus & Folkman, 1984). These are divided into three general classes: discrete, major life events; ongoing, everyday chronic stressors; and the absence of major happenings, or nonevents (Romas & Sharma, 2010).

Life events, or **life change events**, are discrete, observable, and objectively reportable events that require some social or psychological adjustment, or both, on the part of the individual

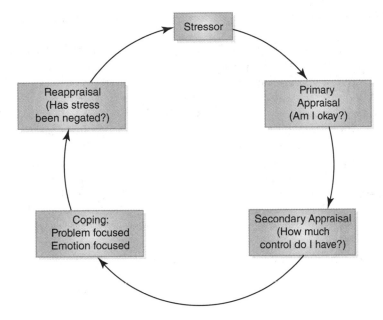

FIGURE 6-2 Model of stress and coping.

(Wheaton, 1994). Examples of such events are the death of a family member, starting a new job, and buying a new home. If these happened in the recent past (within the last year), they are called **recent life events**; if they occurred further in the past (such as childhood events) and are bothersome as memories, they are called **remote life events**.

McLean and Link (1994) classified **chronic stressors** into five types:

1. **Persistent life difficulties**: Life events lasting longer than six months, such as long-term disability.
2. **Role strains**: Strain from either performing a specific role (such as parenting, working, or being in a relationship) or performing a multiplicity of roles at the same time.
3. **Chronic strains**: Responses of one social group to another, such as overt or covert, intentional or unintentional discriminatory behavior due to race, ethnicity, and so on.
4. **Daily hassles**: Everyday problems, such as getting stuck in traffic.
5. **Community-wide strains**: Stressors that operate at an ecological level, such as residing in a high-crime neighborhood.

Nonevents are of three kinds: (1) when desired or anticipated events do not occur (e.g., wanting to graduate but not having enough credits), (2) when desired events do not occur even though their occurrence is normative for people of a certain group (e.g., a person does not get married when most people of his or her age are married), and (3) not having anything to do (e.g., being bored).

Most of the time stressors cannot be modified and have to be endured. However, a person's perception of the stressors can be changed. Some stressors can be changed by modifying the environment. For example, if one is stressed about taking a class from a certain instructor and that class is also offered by another instructor, signing up for the class with the second instructor can alleviate the stress.

The second construct of the theories of stress and coping is that of **primary appraisal**, in which the person determines the severity of the stressor and makes an assessment regarding whether he or she is in trouble. To modify this construct in an educational program, participants could be asked to keep a stress diary, participate in a brainstorming session to identify the stressors affecting them at any given time, or participate in a discussion of the stressors and their severity.

In **secondary appraisal**, the person determines how much control he or she has over the stressor. If control is high, no stress develops; if control is low, stress develops. To modify secondary appraisal in an educational program, stress diaries, brainstorming, or discussion can be helpful.

The construct of **problem-focused coping** is based on a person's capability to think and to alter the environmental event or situation. Examples of this strategy at the thought process level include utilization of problem-solving skills, interpersonal conflict resolution, advice seeking, time management, goal setting, and gathering more information about what is causing the stress. Problem solving requires thinking through various alternatives, evaluating the pros and cons of different solutions, and then implementing a solution that seems most advantageous to reduce the stress. Examples of this strategy at the behavioral or action level include activities such as joining a smoking cessation program, compliance with a prescribed medical treatment, adherence to a diabetic diet plan, and scheduling and prioritizing tasks for managing time.

In the construct of **emotion-focused coping**, the focus is on altering the way one thinks or feels about a situation or an event. Examples of this strategy at the thought process level include denying the existence of the stressful situation, freely expressing emotions, avoiding the stressful situation, making social comparisons, and looking at the bright side of things. Examples of this strategy at the behavioral or action level include seeking social support to negate the influence of the stressful situation; use of exercise, relaxation, or meditation; joining support groups; and practicing religious rituals. Negative examples include escaping through the use of alcohol and drugs.

The final construct of the theories of stress and coping is **reappraisal**, which is the feedback loop by which the person determines whether the effects of the stressor have been effectively negated. To modify this construct, techniques such as stress diaries, brainstorming, or discussion can again be helpful. **Table 6-1** summarizes the constructs.

HARDINESS

> The mechanism whereby stressful life events produce illness is presumably physiological. Whatever this physiological response is, the personality characteristics of hardiness may cut into it, decreasing the likelihood of breakdown into illness.
>
> —Kobasa (1985, p. 187)

As we have seen, the theory of hardiness also originated in the 1970s. Hardiness has three constructs (Taylor & Aspinwall, 1996): control, commitment, and challenge (**Table 6-2**). **Control** refers to a person's belief that he or she causes the events of his or her life and can influence the environment. The greater a person's belief in his or her control, the better that person is able to endure the adverse effects of stress. Control can be modified in an educational program by conducting a discussion on this topic or by having participants role play situations in which they experience control and relate it to their lives.

Commitment refers to a person's tendency to become involved in whatever he or she encounters or to a feeling of deep involvement in the activities of life. The higher a person's commitment, the higher that

Table 6-1	Key Constructs of Theories of Stress and Coping	
Construct	**Definition**	**How to Modify?**
Stressors	Demands from the internal or external environment that one perceives as being harmful or threatening. These are of three kinds: life events, chronic stressors, and nonevents.	Most stressors cannot be modified and must be endured. What can be modified is the person's perception of the stressors. Some stressors can be modified by environmental engineering.
Primary appraisal	Person determines the severity of the stressor and makes an assessment regarding whether he or she is in trouble.	• Stress diary • Brainstorming • Discussion
Secondary appraisal	Person determines how much control he or she has over the stressor.	• Stress diary • Brainstorming • Discussion
Problem-focused coping	Method of dealing with a given stressor that focuses on the ability to think about and alter the environmental event or situation.	• Problem-solving skills • Interpersonal conflict resolution • Advice seeking • Time management • Goal setting • Discussion to gather more information about what is causing the stress
Emotion-focused coping	Method of dealing with a stressor in which the focus is on altering the way one thinks or feels about a situation or an event.	• Exercise • Relaxation • Meditation • Joining support groups
Reappraisal	Feedback loop in which the person determines whether the effects of the stressor have been effectively negated.	• Stress diary • Brainstorming • Discussion

Table 6-2	Key Constructs of the Theory of Hardiness	
Construct	**Definition**	**How to Modify?**
Control	Belief that one causes the events of one's life and can influence the environment.	• Discussion • Role play
Commitment	Tendency to involve oneself in whatever one encounters, or a feeling of deep involvement in the activities of life.	• Discussion • Role play
Challenge	Willingness to undertake change, confront new activities, and obtain opportunities for growth.	• Goal setting

person's ability to cope with stress. To modify commitment in an educational program, the educator can facilitate a discussion on the topic, or the effects of commitment can be portrayed in a role play.

Challenge refers to a person's willingness to undertake change, confront new activities, and obtain opportunities for growth. The greater a sense of challenge a person has, the easier he or she is able to cope with stress. To modify the construct of challenge, one can use goal setting, whereby participants set incrementally challenging goals for themselves.

SENSE OF COHERENCE

Another theory that originated in the 1970s was that of the sense of coherence (Antonovsky, 1979, 1987). The three constructs of the sense of coherence are comprehensibility, manageability, and meaningfulness (**Table 6-3**). **Comprehensibility** refers to the extent to which the individual perceives that the stressors he or she confronts make cognitive sense, which implies that there is some set structure, consistency, order, clarity, and predictability. To modify comprehensibility in an educational program, a discussion session that clarifies the stressors and interprets them can provide clarity and predictability.

Manageability refers to the extent to which a person feels that the resources under his or her control are adequate to meet the demands posed by the stressors. To modify this construct in educational sessions, the educator can facilitate a brainstorming session in which all the potential resources can be enlisted. A support group that is able to provide additional resources can be built into the educational program.

Meaningfulness refers to the extent to which the person feels that life makes sense emotionally and that at least some of the stressors in life are worth investing energy in and are worthy of commitment and engagement. It entails looking at challenges in life as something welcome rather than burdensome. It can be modified in an educational session by organizing a discussion about changing one's perspective regarding stressors.

Table 6-3	Key Constructs of the Theory of Sense of Coherence	
Construct	**Definition**	**How to Modify?**
Comprehensibility	The extent to which one perceives that the stressors that confront one make cognitive sense, implying that there is some set structure, consistency, order, clarity, and predictability.	Clarify the stressors and interpret them such that they have clarity and predictability.
Manageability	The extent to which one feels that the resources under one's control are adequate to meet the demands posed by the stressors.	• Brainstorming to identify all resources • Support group to increase resources
Meaningfulness	The extent to which one feels that life makes sense emotionally and that at least some of the stressors in life are worth investing energy in and are worthy of commitment and engagement.	• Discussion about perspective toward stressors

SOCIAL NETWORKS AND SOCIAL SUPPORT

A **social network** consists of all the relationships that an individual has in his or her life. Social networks serve many functions. Practically speaking, nothing can be accomplished without them. All the daily activities that we perform require assistance from our social networks. In other words, no human being can be an island in himself or herself. Some of the functions of social networks have been given names. For example, sometimes our thinking and behaviors are changed by others. This is called *social influence* (Heaney & Israel, 2008). Sometimes we share leisure-time and other activities with others. This is called *companionship* (Heaney & Israel, 2008). Likewise some of these relationships are helpful to us and are called **social support**. The construct of social support has been found to moderate the negative effects of stressors (Heaney & Israel, 2008). Social support is not only helpful in moderating the negative effects of stress but also in other walks of life including assistance with health behavior change. We have seen in Chapter 4 that one of the processes of change was "helping relationships," which is nothing else but social support. We saw that this construct was crucial in the action and maintenance stages of behavior change.

House (1981) classified social support into four types: (1) emotional support, which entails providing understanding, love, caring, and reliance; (2) informational support, which entails providing information, guidance, and counsel; (3) instrumental support, which entails providing concrete assistance and support; and (4) appraisal support, which entails providing evaluative assistance. Social support can be naturally occurring, in the form of parents, spouse, other family members, and friends, or it can be created artificially by the health education specialist, health coach, nursing educator, dietitian, or other health care provider. Social support buffers the effects of stressors and shields a person from negative consequences.

These days social media is also an important means to build and use social support. Many people rely on friends from social media such as Facebook to discuss and find solutions to everyday issues and problems. Social media is being used in health promotion programs (Balatsoukas, Kennedy, Buchan, Powell, & Ainsworth, 2015). Approaches utilizing social media have the potential to increase the efficiency and effectiveness of many public health campaigns. On the other hand, there could be unintended and even harmful consequences of erroneous or misleading health information being transmitted through these media. So, one has to be cautious in the use of social media as an approach for health promotion. This work is in its infancy, and more systematic research needs to be undertaken to conclusively say whether these approaches are beneficial.

OPTIMISM

A final construct that has been linked to resistance to stress is **optimism** (Scheier & Carver, 1985), which is the tendency to expect the best possible outcome or to think about the most hopeful aspects of any situation. Several studies have linked optimism to better coping and health. Optimism acts through several pathways to ensure better health. First, optimism affects a person's efforts to avoid illness by increasing attention to information about potential health threats. Second, optimism directly improves coping. Third, optimism acts through its influence on the maintenance of positive mood. Martin Seligman has talked about the modifiability of this construct in his books *Learned Optimism* (1990) and *What You Can Change and What You Can't* (1994). To modify the construct of optimism in an educational program, the educator can facilitate a lecture or discussion on its value.

APPLICATIONS OF THE THEORIES OF STRESS AND COPING

Theories of stress and coping have been used in a variety of health education and promotion applications, including for cardiac rehabilitation following myocardial infarction (Macinnes, 2005), coping following traumatic brain injury (Anson & Ponsford, 2006; Matarazzo et al., 2014; Moore et al., 2014; Strom & Kosciulek, 2007), coping in breast cancer survivors (Lebel, Rosberger, Edgar, & Devins, 2008; Wonghongkul, Dechaprom, Phumivichuvate, & Losawatkul, 2006), coping with elderly health conditions (Poderico, Ruggiero, Iachini, & Iavarone, 2006), coping with arthritis (Rosenzweig et al., 2010; Tak, 2006), coping in head and neck cancer patients (Vidhubala, Latha, Ravikannan, Mani, & Karthikesh, 2006), coping in newly incarcerated adolescents (Brown & Ireland, 2006), coping in old-age psychosis (Berry, Barrowclough, Byrne, & Purandare, 2006), coping in Parkinson's disease (Ghielen et al., 2015; Pickut et al., 2015), coping in siblings with sickle cell disease (Gold, Treadwell, Weissman, & Vichinsky, 2008), coping in survivors of domestic violence (Lewis et al., 2006; Watlington & Murphy, 2006), coping with diabetes mellitus (Gåfvels, Rane, Wajngot, & Wändell, 2014; Samuel-Hodge, Watkins, Rowell, & Hooten, 2008; Thoolen, Ridder, Bensing, Gorter, & Rutten, 2009), coping with exacerbation of psoriasis and eczema (Wahl, Mork, Hanestad, & Helland, 2006), health coaching after cancer (Wagland, Fenlon, Tarrant, Howard-Jones, & Richardson, 2015), health coaching for mindfulness (Robins, Kiken, Holt, & McCain, 2014), prevention of atherosclerosis (Jedryka-Goral et al., 2006), prevention of recurrent depression (Bockting et al., 2006), quality-of-life assessment for stroke caregivers (Van Puymbroeck & Rittman, 2005), smoking cessation (Friis, Forouzesh, Chhim, Monga, & Sze, 2006), and a worksite stress management program (Shimazu, Umanodan, & Schaufeli, 2006). **Table 6-4** summarizes these applications.

The theory of hardiness has been used in a variety of health education and promotion applications, including for adaptation in families of young children with chronic asthma (Svavarsdottir, Rayens, & McCubbin, 2005), family-level intervention for parents of children with cancer (Svavarsdottir & Sigurdardottir, 2005, 2006), military training of soldiers (Cacioppo et al., 2015; Eid & Morgan, 2006), modeling coping in spousal caregivers of persons with dementia (DiBartolo & Soeken, 2003), modeling emotional regulation in irritable bowel syndrome (Mazaheri, Nikneshan, Daghaghzadeh, & Afshar, 2015), modeling for mental health among mothers of adult children with intellectual disability (Ben-Zur, Duvdevany, & Lury, 2005), modeling health in women who have experienced physical and sexual abuse (Heckman & Clay, 2005), modeling psychological status and physical function in osteoarthritis patients (Kee, 2003), modeling substance abuse behavior (Abdollahi & Abu Talib, 2015), modeling well-being in older women (Smith, Young, & Lee, 2004), modeling work stress and job satisfaction (Lambert, Lambert, Petrini, Li, & Zhang, 2007; McCalister, Dolbier, Webster, Mallon, & Steinhardt, 2006), organizational and psychological adjustment in managers (Ghorbani & Watson, 2005), psychological distress in police officers (Andrew et al., 2008; Andrew et al., 2013), a qualitative study of adults aging with HIV (Vance & Woodley, 2005), a qualitative study of hardiness in intensive care unit nurses (Hurst & Koplin-Baucum, 2005; Whitmer, Hurst, & Prins, 2009), a qualitative study of women with paraplegia (Kinder, 2005), and workplace stress reduction (Lambert, Lambert, & Yamase, 2003). **Table 6-5** summarizes these applications.

Table 6-4	Applications of Theories of Stress and Coping in Health Education and Health Promotion

Cardiac rehabilitation following myocardial infarction

Coping following traumatic brain injury

Coping in breast cancer survivors

Coping with elderly health conditions

Coping with arthritis

Coping in head and neck cancer patients

Coping in newly incarcerated adolescents

Coping in old-age psychosis

Coping in Parkinson's disease

Coping in siblings with sickle cell disease

Coping in survivors of domestic violence

Coping with diabetes mellitus

Coping with exacerbation of psoriasis and eczema

Health coaching after cancer

Health coaching for mindfulness

Prevention of atherosclerosis

Prevention of recurrent depression

Quality-of-life assessment for stroke caregivers

Smoking cessation

Worksite stress management program

The theory of sense of coherence has been used in a variety of health education and promotion applications, including for an addiction recovery program (Chen, 2006), associations with quality of life among women with systemic lupus erythematosus (Abu-Shakra et al., 2006), coping in the next of kin of cancer patients who are in palliative home care (Milberg & Strang, 2003), coping with inflammatory bowel disease (Freitas et al., 2015), coping with serious accidental injury (Hepp, Moergeli, Buchi, Wittmann, & Schnyder, 2005), couple therapy aimed at reducing marital distress and psychiatric symptoms (Lundblad & Hansson, 2005), determinants of mental health (Malinauskiene, Leisyte, & Malinauskas, 2009), an educational program after breast cancer surgery (Koinberg, Langius-Eklof, Holmberg, & Fridlund, 2006), health coaching for attention deficit hyperactivity disorder (ADHD) (Wentz, Nydén, & Krevers, 2012), health coaching for chronic diseases (Sahlen, Johansson, Nyström, & Lindholm, 2013), modeling sick leave

Table 6-5	Applications of the Theory of Hardiness in Health Education and Health Promotion
Adaptation in families of young children with chronic asthma	
Family-level intervention for parents of children with cancer	
Military training of soldiers	
Modeling coping in spousal caregivers of persons with dementia	
Modeling emotional regulation in irritable bowel syndrome	
Modeling for mental health among mothers of adult children with intellectual disability	
Modeling health in women who have experienced physical and sexual abuse	
Modeling psychological status and physical function in osteoarthritis patients	
Modeling substance abuse behavior	
Modeling well-being in older women	
Modeling work stress and job satisfaction	
Organizational and psychological adjustment in managers	
Psychological distress in police officers	
Qualitative study of adults aging with HIV	
Qualitative study of hardiness in intensive care unit nurses	
Qualitative study of women with paraplegia	
Workplace stress reduction	

Each person must find a way to relieve his pent-up energy without creating conflicts with his fellow men. Such an approach not only insures peace of mind but also earns goodwill, respect, and even love of our neighbors, the highest degree of security and the noblest status symbol to which the human being can aspire.

—Selye (1985, p. 28)

absence in parents of children with Down syndrome (Hedov, Wikblad, & Anneren, 2006), pain management in spinal cord injury patients (Kennedy, Lude, Elfström, & Smithson, 2010; Norrbrink Budh, Kowalski, & Lundeberg, 2006), predicting depression in mass-evacuated adults from Kosovo (Roth & Ekblad, 2006), predicting oral and general health behaviors (Savolainen et al., 2009), predicting quality of life among spouses of stroke patients (Larson et al., 2005), quality of life in older people (Borglin, Jakobsson, Edberg, & Hallberg, 2006; Volanen et al., 2010), relationship with stress in parents of children with developmental disabilities (Oelofsen & Richardson, 2006), and relationship with tobacco use (El-Shahawy, Sun, Tsai, Rohrbach, & Sussman, 2015; Glanz, Maskarinec, & Carlin, 2005). **Table 6–6** summarizes these applications.

Social support has been used in health education and health promotion in a variety of applications. Some of these are association with depression (Grav, Hellzèn, Romild, & Stordal, 2012), association with quality of life in diabetes (Cassarino-Perez & Dell'Aglio, 2015), coping with breast

Table 6-6	Applications of the Theory of Sense of Coherence in Health Education and Health Promotion

Addiction recovery program

Associations with quality of life among women with systemic lupus erythematosus

Coping in the next of kin of cancer patients who are in palliative home care

Coping with inflammatory bowel disease

Coping with serious accidental injury

Couple therapy aimed at reducing marital distress and psychiatric symptoms

Determinants of mental health

Educational program after breast cancer surgery

Health coaching for attention deficit hyperactivity disorder (ADHD)

Health coaching for chronic disease

Modeling sick leave absence in parents of children with Down syndrome

Pain management in spinal cord injury patients

Predicting depression in mass-evacuated adults from Kosovo

Predicting oral and general health behaviors

Predicting quality of life among spouses of stroke patients

Quality of life in older people

Relationship with stress in parents of children with developmental disabilities

Relationship with tobacco use

cancer (Saita, Acquati, & Kayser, 2015), coping with cervical cancer (Wenzel et al., 2015), ensuring fruit and vegetable consumption (Rugel & Carpiano, 2015), physical activity maintenance in older adults (Floegel et al., 2015), reducing post–partum depression (Kim, Connolly, & Tamim, 2014), and relationship with caregiver burden among caregivers of patients with cancer (Kahriman & Zaybak, 2015). **Table 6-7** summarizes these applications.

The construct of optimism has also been used in health education and health promotion. Some of the applications of optimism are association with depression in breast cancer patients (Levkovich, Cohen, Pollack, Drumea, & Fried, 2014), association with mood, coping, and immune change (Segerstrom, Taylor, Kemeny, & Fahey, 1998), as a contributor to resilience in cancer patients (Rosenberg, Yi-Frazier, Wharton, Gordon, & Jones, 2014), in conjunction with laughter yoga therapy for hemodialysis patients (Bennett et al., 2015), psychological intervention after physical traumas (Skogstad, Hem, Sandvik, & Ekeberg, 2015), rehabilitation patients of poisoning (Feng, Li, & Chen, 2015), and relationship with meaning in life for HIV patients (Audet, Wagner, & Wallston, 2015). **Table 6-8** summarizes these applications.

Table 6-7	Applications of Social Support in Health Education and Health Promotion
Association with depression	
Association with quality of life in diabetes	
Coping with breast cancer	
Coping with cervical cancer	
Ensuring fruit and vegetable consumption	
Physical activity maintenance in older adults	
Reducing post-partum depression	
Relationship with caregiver burden among caregivers of patients with cancer	

Table 6-8	Applications of the Construct of Optimism in Health Education and Health Promotion
Association with depression in breast cancer patients	
Association with mood, coping, and immune change	
Contributor to resilience in cancer patients	
In conjunction with laughter yoga therapy for hemodialysis patients	
Psychological intervention after physical traumas	
Rehabilitation patients of poisoning	
Relationship with meaning in life for HIV patients	

LIMITATIONS OF THE THEORIES OF STRESS AND COPING

We have seen that there are three major kinds of theories of stress and coping. The strength of response-based models is that they explicate the physiological relationships involved in stress, but some of the limitations of this model are the nonspecificity of stimuli, the lack of accounting for individual variations, the lack of accounting for differences in stressors, and lack of attention to cognitive processing of stressors. Event-based models are strong in terms of clarifying stressors, introducing the notion of coping, and explaining the differences in stressors but have the limitations of not covering physiological mechanisms and not distinguishing between cause and effect (e.g., disease is an event that produces stress as well as being an outcome of stress).

The strengths of the transactional model of stress are that it explains coping in steps; underscores the importance of thinking, perception, and determination of controllability; emphasizes the role of chronic stressors or daily hassles as being more important than once-in-a-while life events; takes into account the interaction between the individual and the environment; and has a feedback

Table 6-9	Comparison of Response-Based, Event-Based, and Transactional Models of Stress and Coping	
Model	**Strengths**	**Weaknesses**
Response-based models	Explicates the physiological mechanisms	• Nonspecificity of stimuli/ stressors • Does not account for individual variations • Multiplicity of stressors not addressed • No attention to the cognitive processing of the stressor(s)
Event-based models	• Clarifies stressors • Introduces the notion of coping (or dealing with environmental events) • Explains a multiplicity of stressors	• Does not cover physiological mechanisms • Does not distinguish between cause and effect (e.g., disease is considered an event that produces stress as well as an outcome of stress)
Transactional model	• Explains coping in steps • Underscores the importance of thinking, perception, and determination of controllability • Emphasizes the role of chronic stressors or daily hassles as being more important than once-in-a-while life events • Takes into account the communication process or interaction between the individual and the environment, including other people • Existence of a feedback mechanism, or "closed loop" system, in this model (reappraisal)	• Lack of objective measurement of coping • Does not consider personality characteristics • Does not cover physiological mechanisms

mechanism or "closed loop" system in the form of reappraisal. The chief limitations of this model are that coping is not measured objectively, does not cover personality characteristics, and does not cover physiological mechanisms. **Table 6–9** summarizes the strengths and weaknesses of the three major models of stress and coping.

APPLICATION EXERCISE

In this chapter we have presented several applications of theories of stress and coping, hardiness, sense of coherence, social support, and optimism in health education and health promotion. Locate the full text of an article of any application that interests you and read and critique that article. One such article is from Japan in which Tomotsune and colleagues (2009) examined the association between sense of coherence and coping profile in Tsukuba Research Park City workers. They used the Sense of Coherence Scale and the Brief Scale for Coping Profile (BSCP) and mailed these surveys to 20,742 employees at educational and research institutions in Tsukuba Research Park City, Japan. They had a response rate of 57.9%, with 12,009 returned surveys. It was found that workers with higher sense of coherence scores utilized problem-focused coping, whereas workers with lower sense of coherence scores used emotion-focused coping.

Read and critique this article in 250 words. Pay attention to the operationalization of independent and dependent variables, instrumentation, response rate, data analysis, and data interpretation in writing your critique.

SKILL-BUILDING ACTIVITY

Let us see how we can apply the transactional model of stress and coping for developing healthy coping behavior in a group of college students. **Figure 6-3** depicts each of the constructs of the transactional model of coping and links these with the educational processes and behavioral objectives in this example.

The health education intervention would start with the primary appraisal, or stressor identification. This can be done by keeping a stress diary. Secondary appraisal can be modified through a brainstorming session. Problem-focused coping can be used to help students build problem-solving skills. A demonstration of how to apply the steps of problem solving to help participants think through many solutions and identify the pros and cons of each solution before choosing one solution will be used as an educational method. Emotion-focused coping would involve teaching the behavioral skill of relaxation to the students using the technique of progressive muscle relaxation. The final construct, reappraisal, can be facilitated through a discussion in which participants

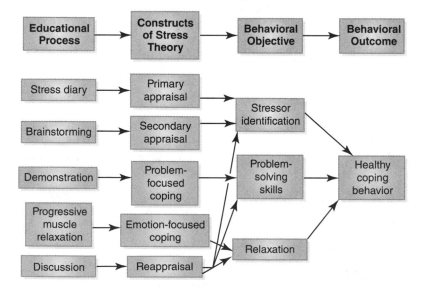

FIGURE 6-3 How the transactional model can be used to develop healthy coping.

think about how successful they have been in identifying stressors, using problem–solving skills, and learning relaxation. Using this approach, you can plan a coping intervention either as a stand-alone program such as the one discussed here or as one part of a larger behavior change program. **Table 6–10** provides a set of questions to help you define this program.

Table 6-10	**Choosing the Educational Methods for Health Education Program Planning Using Theories of Stress and Coping**

Make a decision on the best method for the following questions. Explain why you chose the method and why not the others.

1. What is the best method to facilitate primary appraisal?
   - Stress diary
   - Brainstorming
   - Discussion
   - Other

2. What is the best educational method to facilitate secondary appraisal?
   - Stress diary
   - Brainstorming
   - Discussion
   - Other

3. What is the best educational method to facilitate problem-focused coping?
   - Demonstration of problem-solving skills
   - Interpersonal conflict resolution
   - Advice seeking
   - Time management
   - Goal setting
   - Discussion
   - Other

4. What is the best educational method to facilitate emotion-focused coping?
   - Exercise
   - Relaxation
   - Meditation
   - Support groups
   - Other

5. What is the best educational method to facilitate reappraisal?
   - Stress diary
   - Brainstorming
   - Discussion
   - Other

6. What is the best educational method to facilitate control (theory of hardiness)?
   - Discussion
   - Role play
   - Simulation
   - Other

(continues)

Table 6-10	Choosing the Educational Methods for Health Education Program Planning Using Theories of Stress and Coping (*continued*)

7. What is the best educational method to facilitate commitment (theory of hardiness)?
    - Discussion
    - Role play
    - Simulation
    - Other

8. What is the best educational method to facilitate challenge (theory of hardiness)?
    - Discussion
    - Goal setting
    - Other

9. What is the best educational method to facilitate comprehensibility (sense of coherence)?
    - Discussion clarifying the stressors
    - Lecture
    - Other

10. What is the best educational method to facilitate manageability (sense of coherence)?
    - Brainstorming
    - Support groups
    - Other

11. What is the best educational method to facilitate meaningfulness (sense of coherence)?
    - Lecture
    - Discussion
    - Other

12. What is the best educational method to facilitate optimism?
    - Lecture
    - Discussion
    - Other

SUMMARY

In physiology and psychology, the concept of stress originated in the 1930s with the response-based models based on the work of Walter Cannon and Hans Selye. These models looked at myriad physiological effects of stress on the body. This conceptualization was followed by the event-based models, which looked at the role of life events or discrete stressors in the causation of stress. Between the 1960s and 1980s, Richard Lazarus proposed the transactional model of stress, in which a person interacts with the environment while going through four stages: primary appraisal, secondary appraisal, coping, and reappraisal.

In addition to these models, several sets of personality characteristics were identified as predictors of healthier coping. One such personality trait, identified by Suzanne Kobasa, is hardiness, which comprises three factors: commitment, control, and challenge. Similarly, Friedman and Rosenman classified personality into types A and B and found that type B personalities had less stress compared with type A. Aaron Antonovsky proposed a theory of the sense of coherence, which suggested that people who possess a higher sense of coherence tend to cope better in life. A sense of coherence comprises comprehensibility, manageability, and meaningfulness. Another construct is social support, which entails the help obtained through social relationships and interpersonal exchanges and is protective against negative effects arising from stressors. Finally, the construct of optimism (a personality disposition that refers to the tendency to expect the best possible outcome) has been found to have a beneficial effect on coping.

IMPORTANT TERMS

challenge
chronic strains
chronic stressors
commitment
community-wide strains
comprehensibility
control
coping
daily hassles
defense mechanisms
emotion-focused coping
event-based models
general adaptation syndrome
hardiness
life events (life change events)
manageability
meaningfulness
nonevents

optimism
persistent life difficulties
primary appraisal
problem-focused coping
reappraisal
recent life events
remote life events
response-based models
role strains
secondary appraisal
sense of coherence
social network
social support
stress
stressors
transactional model
type A personality
type B personality

REVIEW QUESTIONS

1. Differentiate between response-based and event-based models.
2. Describe the transactional model.
3. Discuss the general adaptation syndrome.
4. Define stressors. Provide a classification of stressors.
5. Describe the constructs of hardiness.
6. Describe the constructs of the sense of coherence.
7. Differentiate between problem-focused and emotion-focused coping.
8. Apply the transactional model of stress and coping to the development of healthy coping behavior in a group of college students.

WEBSITES TO EXPLORE

American Institute of Stress

www.stress.org/

This website provides information about the American Institute of Stress, a not-for-profit organization established in 1978 to serve as a clearinghouse for information on stress-related issues. *Use this website to explore the contributions of some of the well-known personalities in the stress field.*

Sense of Coherence and Food Selection

www.nutritionj.com/content/4/1/9

This website provides a link to an article published in *Nutrition Journal* by Lindmark and colleagues in 2005. The purpose of this study was to evaluate associations between dietary intake and sense of coherence (SOC) in adults. *Read this article and comment on the association between SOC and dietary intake.*

Sense of Coherence Scale

http://jech.bmjjournals.com/cgi/content/abstract/59/6/460

This website provides the abstract and link to an article published in the *Journal of Epidemiology and Community Health* in 2005 by Monica Eriksson and Bengt Lindstrom that systematically reviews and analyzes the psychometric properties of Antonovsky's Sense of Coherence (SOC) Scale. *Read and comment on the various types of reliability and validity of the SOC scale reported in the article.*

Stress and Disease: Contributions of Hans Selye

http://home.cc.umanitoba.ca/~berczii/hans-selye/my-teacher-hans-selye-and-his-legacy.html

This website from the University of Manitoba summarizes the contributions of Hans Selye. It also provides links to the Canadian Institute of Stress, several books, and sites related to neuroimmunobiology. *Review this website and summarize the contributions of Hans Selye to the stress field.*

Stress Free Network

www.stressfree.com/

Review the graphic model of stress provided as a link on this website. *Check the featured item and write a brief summary of what was featured.*

Transactional Model of Stress and Coping: University of Twente

www.utwente.nl/cw/theorieenoverzicht/Theory%20Clusters/Health%20Communication/transactional_model_of_stress_and_coping/

This website from the University of Twente, Netherlands, summarizes the transactional model of stress and coping. Its history, assumptions, conceptual model, favorite methods, scope and application, and examples are presented. *Review the website and determine which constructs were discussed in the chapter and which were new.*

REFERENCES

Abdollahi, A., & Abu Talib, M. (2015). Hardiness, spirituality, and suicidal ideation among individuals with substance abuse: The moderating role of gender and marital status. *Journal of Dual Diagnosis, 11*(1), 12–21. doi: 10.1080/15504263.2014.988558.

Abu-Shakra, M., Keren, A., Livshitz, I., Delbar, V., Bolotin, A., Sukenik, S., et al. (2006). Sense of coherence and its impact on quality of life of patients with systemic lupus erythematosus. *Lupus, 15*(1), 32–37.

Andrew, M. E., McCanlies, E. C., Burchfiel, C. M., Charles, L. E., Hartley, T. A., Fekedulegn, D., et al. (2008). Hardiness and psychological distress in a cohort of police officers. *International Journal of Emergency Mental Health, 10*(2), 137–147.

Andrew, M. E., Mnatsakanova, A., Howsare, J. L., Hartley, T. A., Charles, L. E., Burchfiel, C.M., et al. (2013). Associations between protective factors and psychological distress vary by gender: The Buffalo Cardio-Metabolic Occupational Police Stress Study. *International Journal of Emergency Mental Health, 15*(4), 277–288.

Anson, K., & Ponsford, J. (2006). Coping and emotional adjustment following traumatic brain injury. *Journal of Head Trauma Rehabilitation, 21*(3), 248–259.

Antonovsky, A. (1979). *Health, stress, and coping.* San Francisco: Jossey-Bass.

Antonovsky, A. (1987). *Unraveling the mystery of health: How people manage stress and stay well.* San Francisco: Jossey-Bass.

Audet, C. M., Wagner, L. J., & Wallston, K. A. (2015). Finding meaning in life while living with HIV: Validation of a novel HIV meaningfulness scale among HIV-infected participants living in Tennessee. *BMC Psychology, 3*(1), 15. doi: 10.1186/s40359-015-0070-7.

Balatsoukas, P., Kennedy, C. M., Buchan, I., Powell, J., & Ainsworth, J. (2015). The role of social network technologies in online health promotion: A narrative review of theoretical and empirical factors influencing intervention effectiveness. *Journal of Medical Internet Research, 17*(6), e141. doi: 10.2196/jmir.3662.

Bennett, P. N., Parsons, T., Ben-Moshe, R., Neal, M., Weinberg, M. K., Gilbert, K., et al. (2015). Intradialytic laughter yoga therapy for haemodialysis patients: A pre-post intervention feasibility study. *BMC Complementary and Alternative Medicine, 15*, 176. doi: 10.1186/s12906-015-0705-5.

Ben-Zur, H., Duvdevany, I., & Lury, L. (2005). Associations of social support and hardiness with mental health among mothers of adult children with intellectual disability. *Journal of Intellectual Disability Research, 49*(Pt. 1), 54–62.

Berry, K., Barrowclough, C., Byrne, J., & Purandare, N. (2006). Coping strategies and social support in old age psychosis. *Social Psychiatry and Psychiatric Epidemiology, 41*(4), 280–284.

Bockting, C. L., Spinhoven, P., Koeter, M. W., Wouters, L. F., Visser, I., & Schene, A. H. (2006). Differential predictors of response to preventive cognitive therapy in recurrent depression: A 2-year prospective study. *Psychotherapy and Psychosomatics, 75*(4), 229–236.

Borglin, G., Jakobsson, U., Edberg, A. K., & Hallberg, I. R. (2006). Older people in Sweden with various degrees of present quality of life: Their health, social support, everyday activities and sense of coherence. *Health and Social Care in the Community, 14*(2), 136–146.

Brown, S. L., & Ireland, C. A. (2006). Coping style and distress in newly incarcerated male adolescents. *Journal of Adolescent Health, 38*(6), 656–661.

Cacioppo, J. T., Adler, A. B., Lester, P. B., McGurk, D., Thomas, J. L., Chen, H. Y., & Cacioppo, S. (2015). Building social resilience in soldiers: A double dissociative randomized controlled study. *Journal of Personality & Social Psychology, 109*(1):90–105. doi: 10.1037/pspi0000022.

Cannon, W. B. (1932). *The wisdom of the body.* New York: Norton.

Cassarino-Perez, L., & Dell'Aglio, D. D. (2015). Health-related quality of life and social support in adolescents with type 1 diabetes. *Spanish Journal of Psychology, 17*, E108. doi: 10.1017/sjp.2014.101.

Chen, G. (2006). Social support, spiritual program, and addiction recovery. *International Journal of Offender Therapy and Comparative Criminology, 50*(3), 306–323.

DiBartolo, M. C., & Soeken, K. L. (2003). Appraisal, coping, hardiness, and self-perceived health in community-dwelling spouse caregivers of persons with dementia. *Research in Nursing and Health, 26*(6), 445–458.

Eid, J., & Morgan, C. A., III. (2006). Dissociation, hardiness, and performance in military cadets participating in survival training. *Military Medicine, 171*(5), 436–442.

El-Shahawy, O., Sun, P., Tsai, J. Y., Rohrbach, L. A., & Sussman, S. (2015). Sense of coherence and tobacco use myths among adolescents as predictors of at-risk youth cigarette use. *Substance Use & Misuse, 50*(1), 8–14. doi: 10.3109/10826084.2014.957767.

Feng, J., Li, S., & Chen, H. (2015). Impacts of stress, self-efficacy, and optimism on suicide ideation among rehabilitation patients with acute pesticide poisoning. *PLoS One, 10*(2), e0118011. doi: 10.1371/journal.pone.0118011.

Floegel, T. A., Giacobbi, P. R. Jr, Dzierzewski, J. M., Aiken-Morgan, A. T., Roberts, B., McCrae, C. S., et al. (2015). Intervention markers of physical activity maintenance in older adults. *American Journal of Health Behavior, 39*(4), 487–499. doi: 10.5993/AJHB.39.4.5.

Freitas, T. H., Andreoulakis, E., Alves, G. S., Miranda, H. L., Braga, L. L., Hyphantis, T., & Carvalho, A. F. (2015). Associations of sense of coherence with psychological distress and quality of life in inflammatory bowel disease. *World Journal of Gastroenterology, 21*(21), 6713–6727. doi: 10.3748/wjg.v21.i21.6713.

Freud, A. (1937). *The ego and mechanism of defense.* London: Hogarth Press.

Freud, S. (1923). *The ego and the id.* New York: Norton.

Friedman, M., & Rosenman, R. H. (1974). *Type A behavior and your heart.* New York: Fawcett Crest.

Friis, R. H., Forouzesh, M., Chhim, H. S., Monga, S., & Sze, D. (2006). Sociocultural determinants of tobacco use among Cambodian Americans. *Health Education Research, 21*(3), 355–365.

Gåfvels, C., Rane, K., Wajngot, A., & Wändell, P. E. (2014). Follow-up two years after diagnosis of diabetes in patients with psychosocial problems receiving an intervention by a medical social worker. *Social Work in Health Care, 53*(6), 584–600. doi: 10.1080/00981389.2014.909916.

Ghielen, I., van den Heuvel, O. A., de Goede, C. J., Houniet-de Gier, M., Collette, E. H., Burgers-Bots. I. A., et al. (2015). BEWARE: Body awareness training in the treatment of wearing-off related anxiety in patients with Parkinson's disease: Study protocol for a randomized controlled trial. *Trials, 16*(1), 283.

Ghorbani, N., & Watson, P. J. (2005). Hardiness scales in Iranian managers: Evidence of incremental validity in relationships with the five factor model and with organizational and psychological adjustment. *Psychological Reports, 96*(3 Pt. 1), 775–781.

Glanz, K., Maskarinec, G., & Carlin, L. (2005). Ethnicity, sense of coherence, and tobacco use among adolescents. *Annals of Behavioral Medicine, 29*(3), 192–199.

Gold, J. I., Treadwell, M., Weissman, L., & Vichinsky, E. (2008). An expanded transactional stress and coping model for siblings of children with sickle cell disease: Family functioning and sibling coping, self-efficacy and perceived social support. *Child: Care, Health, & Development, 34*(4), 491–502.

Grav, S., Hellzèn, O., Romild, U., & Stordal, E. (2012). Association between social support and depression in the general population: The HUNT study, a cross-sectional survey. *Journal of Clinical Nursing, 21*(1–2), 111–120. doi: 10.1111/j.1365-2702.2011.03868.x.

Haan, N. (1977). *Coping and defending: Processes of self-environment organization.* New York: Academic Press.

Heaney, C. A., & Israel, B. A. (2008). Social networks and social support. In K. Glanz, B. K. Rimer, & K. Viswanath (Eds.), *Health behavior and health education: Theory, research and practice* (4th ed., pp. 189–210). San Francisco: Jossey-Bass.

Heckman, C. J., & Clay, D. L. (2005). Hardiness, history of abuse and women's health. *Journal of Health Psychology, 10*(6), 767–777.

Hedov, G., Wikblad, K., & Anneren, G. (2006). Sickness absence in Swedish parents of children with Down's syndrome: Relation to self-perceived health, stress and sense of coherence. *Journal of Intellectual Disability Research, 50*(7), 546–552.

Hepp, U., Moergeli, H., Buchi, S., Wittmann, L., & Schnyder, U. (2005). Coping with serious accidental injury: A one-year follow-up study. *Psychotherapy and Psychosomatics, 74*(6), 379–386.

Holmes, T. H., & Rahe, R. H. (1967). The Social Readjustment Rating Scale. *Journal of Psychosomatic Research*, *11*, 213–218.

House, J. S. (1981). *Work stress and social support*. Reading, MA: Addison-Wesley.

Hurst, S., & Koplin-Baucum, S. (2005). A pilot qualitative study relating to hardiness in ICU nurses: Hardiness in ICU nurses. *Dimensions of Critical Care Nursing*, *24*(2), 97–100.

Jedryka-Goral, A., Pasierski, T., Zabek, J., Widerszal-Bazyl, M., Radkiewicz, P., Szulczyk, G. A., et al. (2006). Risk factors for atherosclerosis in healthy employees—a multidisciplinary approach. *European Journal of Internal Medicine*, *17*(4), 247–253.

Kahriman, F., & Zaybak, A. (2015). Caregiver burden and perceived social support among caregivers of patients with cancer. *Asian Pacific Journal of Cancer Prevention*, *16*(8), 3313–3317.

Kee, C. C. (2003). Older adults with osteoarthritis. Psychological status and physical function. *Journal of Gerontological Nursing*, *29*(12), 26–34.

Kennedy, P., Lude, P., Elfström, M. L., & Smithson, E. (2010). Sense of coherence and psychological outcomes in people with spinal cord injury: appraisals and behavioural responses. *British Journal of Health Psychology*, *15*(Pt 3), 611–621. doi: 10.1348/135910709X478222.

Kim, T. H., Connolly, J. A., & Tamim, H. (2014). The effect of social support around pregnancy on postpartum depression among Canadian teen mothers and adult mothers in the maternity experiences survey. *BMC Pregnancy and Childbirth*, *14*, 162. doi: 10.1186/1471-2393-14-162.

Kinder, R. A. (2005). Psychological hardiness in women with paraplegia. *Rehabilitation Nursing*, *30*(2), 68–72.

Kobasa, S. C. (1979a). Personality and resistance to illness. *American Journal of Community Psychology*, *7*, 413–423.

Kobasa, S. C. (1979b). Stressful life events, personality, and health: An inquiry into hardiness. *Journal of Personality and Social Psychology*, *37*, 1–11.

Kobasa, S. C. (1985). Stressful life events, personality, and health: An inquiry into hardiness. In A. Monat & R. S. Lazarus (Eds.), *Stress and coping: An anthology* (pp. 174–188). New York: Columbia University Press.

Koinberg, I., Langius-Eklof, A., Holmberg, L., & Fridlund, B. (2006). The usefulness of a multidisciplinary educational program after breast cancer surgery: A prospective and comparative study. *European Journal of Oncology Nursing*, *10*(4), 273–282.

Lambert, V. A., Lambert, C. E., Petrini, M., Li, X. M., & Zhang, Y. J. (2007). Workplace and personal factors associated with physical and mental health in hospital nurses in China. *Nursing and Health Sciences*, *9*(2), 120–126.

Lambert, V. A., Lambert, C. E., & Yamase, H. (2003). Psychological hardiness, workplace stress and related stress reduction strategies. *Nursing and Health Sciences*, *5*(2), 181–184.

Larson, J., Franzen-Dahlin, A., Billing, E., Arbin, M., Murray, V., & Wredling, R. (2005). Predictors of quality of life among spouses of stroke patients during the first year after the stroke event. *Scandinavian Journal of Caring Science*, *19*(4), 439–445.

Lazarus, R. S. (1966). *Psychological stress and the coping process*. New York: McGraw-Hill.

Lazarus, R. S. (1974). Psychological stress and coping in adaptation and illness. *International Journal of Psychiatry in Medicine*, *5*, 321–333.

Lazarus, R. S. (1984). Puzzles in the study of daily hassles. *Journal of Behavioral Medicine*, *7*, 375–389.

Lazarus, R. S., & Folkman, S. (1984). *Stress, appraisal, and coping*. New York: Springer.

Lebel, S., Rosberger, Z., Edgar, L., & Devins, G. M. (2008). Predicting stress-related problems in long-term breast cancer survivors. *Journal of Psychosomatic Research*, *65*(6), 513–523.

Levkovich, I., Cohen, M., Pollack, S., Drumea, K., & Fried, G. (2014). Cancer-related fatigue and depression in breast cancer patients postchemotherapy: Different associations with optimism and stress appraisals. *Palliative and Supportive Care*, 1–11 Retrieved from http://dx.doi.org/10.1017/S147895151400087X

Lewis, C. S., Griffing, S., Chu, M., Jospitre, T., Sage, R. E., Madry, L., & Primm, B. J. (2006). Coping and violence exposure as predictors of psychological functioning in domestic violence survivors. *Violence Against Women*, *12*(4), 340–354.

Lundblad, A. M., & Hansson, K. (2005). Outcomes in couple therapy: Reduced psychiatric symptoms and improved sense of coherence. *Nordic Journal of Psychiatry*, *59*(5), 374–380.

MacInnes, J. D. (2005). The illness perceptions of women following acute myocardial infarction: Implications for behaviour change and attendance at cardiac rehabilitation. *Women and Health, 42*(4), 105–121.

Malinauskiene, V., Leisyte, P., & Malinauskas, R. (2009). Psychosocial job characteristics, social support, and sense of coherence as determinants of mental health among nurses. *Medicina, 45*(11), 910–917.

Matarazzo, B. B., Hoffberg, A. S., Clemans, T. A., Signoracci, G. M., Simpson, G. K., & Brenner, L. A. (2014). Cross-cultural adaptation of the Window to Hope: A psychological intervention to reduce hopelessness among U.S. veterans with traumatic brain injury. *Brain Injury, 28*(10), 1238–1247. doi: 10.3109/02699052.2014.916419.

Mazaheri, M., Nikneshan, S., Daghaghzadeh, H., & Afshar, H. (2015). The role of positive personality traits in emotion regulation of patients with irritable bowel syndrome (IBS). *Iranian Journal of Public Health, 44*(4), 561–569.

McCalister, K. T., Dolbier, C. L., Webster, J. A., Mallon, M. W., & Steinhardt, M. A. (2006). Hardiness and support at work as predictors of work stress and job satisfaction. *American Journal of Health Promotion, 20*(3), 183–191.

McLean, D. E., & Link, B. G. (1994). Unraveling complexity: Strategies to refine concepts, measures, and research designs in the study of life events and mental health. In W. R. Avison & I. H. Gotlib (Eds.), *Stress and mental health: Contemporary issues and prospects for the future* (pp. 15–42). New York: Plenum Press.

Milberg, A., & Strang, P. (2003). Meaningfulness in palliative home care: An interview study of dying cancer patients' next of kin. *Palliative and Supportive Care, 1*(2), 171–180.

Moore, M., Winkelman, A., Kwong, S., Segal, S. P., Manley, G. T., & Shumway, M. (2014). The emergency department social work intervention for mild traumatic brain injury (SWIFT-Acute): A pilot study. *Brain Injury, 28*(4), 448–455. doi: 10.3109/02699052.2014.890746.

Norrbrink Budh, C., Kowalski, J., & Lundeberg, T. (2006). A comprehensive pain management programme comprising educational, cognitive and behavioural interventions for neuropathic pain following spinal cord injury. *Journal of Rehabilitation Medicine, 38*(3), 172–180.

Oelofsen, N., & Richardson, P. (2006). Sense of coherence and parenting stress in mothers and fathers of preschool children with developmental disability. *Journal of Intellectual and Developmental Disability, 31*(1), 1–12.

Pickut, B., Vanneste, S., Hirsch, M. A., Van Hecke, W., Kerckhofs, E., Mariën. P., et al. (2015). Mindfulness training among individuals with Parkinson's disease: Neurobehavioral effects. *Parkinson's Disease, 2015*, 816404. doi: 10.1155/2015/816404.

Poderico, C., Ruggiero, G., Iachini, T., & Iavarone, A. (2006). Coping strategies and cognitive functioning in elderly people from a rural community in Italy. *Psychological Reports, 98*(1), 159–168.

Robins, J. L., Kiken, L., Holt, M., & McCain, N. L. (2014). Mindfulness: An effective coaching tool for improving physical and mental health. *Journal of the American Association of the Nurse Practitioners, 26*(9), 511–518. doi: 10.1002/2327-6924.12086.

Romas, J. A., & Sharma, M. (2010). *Practical stress management. A comprehensive workbook for managing change and promoting health* (5th ed.). San Francisco: Benjamin Cummings.

Rosenberg, A. R., Yi-Frazier, J. P., Wharton, C., Gordon, K., & Jones, B. (2014). Contributors and inhibitors of resilience among adolescents and young adults with cancer. *Journal of Adolescent and Young Adult Oncology, 3*(4), 185–193.

Rosenzweig, S., Greeson, J. M., Reibel, D. K., Green, J. S., Jasser, S. A., & Beasley, D. (2010). Mindfulness-based stress reduction for chronic pain conditions: Variation in treatment outcomes and role of home meditation practice. *Journal of Psychosomatic Research, 68*(1), 29–36.

Roth, G., & Ekblad, S. (2006). A longitudinal perspective on depression and sense of coherence in a sample of mass-evacuated adults from Kosovo. *Journal of Nervous and Mental Disease, 194*(5), 378–381.

Rugel, E. J., & Carpiano, R. M. (2015). Gender differences in the roles for social support in ensuring adequate fruit and vegetable consumption among older adult Canadians. *Appetite, 92*, 102–109. doi: 10.1016/j.appet.2015.05.011.

Sahlen, K. G., Johansson, H., Nyström, L., & Lindholm, L. (2013). Health coaching to promote healthier lifestyle among older people at moderate risk for cardiovascular diseases, diabetes and depression: A study protocol for a randomized controlled trial in Sweden. *BMC Public Health, 13*, 199. doi: 10.1186/1471-2458-13-199.

Saita, E., Acquati, C., & Kayser, K. (2015). Coping with early stage breast cancer: examining the influence of personality traits and interpersonal closeness. *Frontiers in Psychology*, *6*, 88. doi: 10.3389/fpsyg.2015.00088.

Samuel-Hodge, C. D., Watkins, D. C., Rowell, K. L., & Hooten, E. G. (2008). Coping styles, well-being, and self-care behaviors among African Americans with type 2 diabetes. *Diabetes Educator*, *34*(3), 501–510.

Savolainen, J., Suominen-Taipale, A., Uutela, A., Aromaa, A., Härkänen, T., & Knuuttila, M. (2009). Sense of coherence associates with oral and general health behaviours. *Community Dental Health*, *26*(4), 197–203.

Scheier, M. F., & Carver, C. S. (1985). Optimism, coping, and health: Assessment and implications of generalized outcome expectancies. *Health Psychology*, *4*, 219–247.

Segerstrom, S. C., Taylor, S. E., Kemeny, M. E., & Fahey, J. L. (1998). Optimism is associated with mood, coping, and immune change in response to stress. *Journal of Personality and Social Psychology*, *74*(6), 1646–1655.

Seligman, M.E.P. (1990). *Learned optimism*. New York: Pocket Books.

Seligman, M.E.P. (1994). *What you can change and what you can't: The complete guide to self improvement*. New York: Alfred A. Knopf.

Selye, H. (1936). A syndrome produced by diverse nocuous agents. *Nature*, *138*, 32.

Selye, H. (1974a). *Stress without distress*. Philadelphia: Lippincott.

Selye, H. (1974b). *The stress of life*. New York: McGraw-Hill.

Selye, H. (1982). History and present status of stress concept. In L. Goldberger & S. Breznitz (Eds.), *Handbook of stress: Theoretical and clinical aspects* (pp. 7–17). New York: Free Press.

Selye, H. (1985). History and present status of the stress concept. In A. Monat & R. S. Lazarus (Eds.), *Stress and coping: An anthology* (pp. 17–29). New York: Columbia University Press.

Skogstad, L., Hem, E., Sandvik, L., & Ekeberg, O. (2015). Nurse-led psychological intervention after physical traumas: A randomized controlled trial. *Journal of Clinical Medicine Research*, *7*(5), 339–347. doi: 10.14740/jocmr2082w.

Sharma, M. (2003). Coping: Strategies. In N. A. Pitrowski (Ed.), *Magill's encyclopedia of social science: Psychology* (pp. 442–446). Pasadena, CA: Salem Press.

Shimazu, A., Umanodan, R., & Schaufeli, W. B. (2006). Effects of a brief worksite stress management program on coping skills, psychological distress and physical complaints: A controlled trial. *International Archives of Occupational and Environmental Health*, *80*(1), 60–69.

Smith, N., Young, A., & Lee, C. (2004). Optimism, health-related hardiness and well-being among older Australian women. *Journal of Health Psychology*, *9*(6), 741–752.

Strom, T. Q., & Kosciulek, J. (2007). Stress, appraisal and coping following mild traumatic brain injury. *Brain Injury*, *21*(11), 1137–1145.

Svavarsdottir, E. K., Rayens, M. K., & McCubbin, M. (2005). Predictors of adaptation in Icelandic and American families of young children with chronic asthma. *Family and Community Health*, *28*(4), 338–350.

Svavarsdottir, E. K., & Sigurdardottir, A. O. (2005). The feasibility of offering a family level intervention to parents of children with cancer. *Scandinavian Journal of Caring Sciences*, *19*(4), 368–372.

Svavarsdottir, E. K., & Sigurdardottir, A. O. (2006). Developing a family-level intervention for families of children with cancer. *Oncology Nursing Forum*, *33*(5), 983–990.

Tak, S. H. (2006). An insider perspective of daily stress and coping in elders with arthritis. *Orthopaedic Nursing*, *25*(2), 127–132.

Taylor, S. E., & Aspinwall, L. G. (1996). Mediating and moderating processes in psychosocial stress. Appraisal, coping, resistance, and vulnerability. In H. B. Kaplan (Ed.), *Psychosocial stress: Perspectives on structure, theory, life course and methods* (pp. 71–110). San Diego: Academic Press.

Thoolen, B. J., Ridder, D., Bensing, J., Gorter, K., & Rutten, G. (2009). Beyond good intentions: The role of proactive coping in achieving sustained behavioural change in the context of diabetes management. *Psychology & Health*, *24*(3), 237–254.

Tomotsune, Y., Sasahara, S., Umeda, T., Hayashi, M., Usami, K., Yoshino, S., et al. (2009). The association of sense of coherence and coping profile with stress among Research Park City workers in Japan. *Industrial Health*, *47*(6), 664–672.

Vance, D. E., & Woodley, R. A. (2005). Strengths and distress in adults who are aging with HIV: A pilot study. *Psychological Reports*, *96*(2), 383–386.

Van Puymbroeck, M., & Rittman, M. R. (2005). Quality-of-life predictors for caregivers at 1 and 6 months poststroke: Results of path analyses. *Journal of Rehabilitation Research and Development*, *42*(6), 747–760.

Vidhubala, E., Latha, Ravikannan, R., Mani, C. S., & Karthikesh, M. (2006). Coping preferences of head and neck cancer patients—Indian context. *Indian Journal of Cancer*, *43*(1), 6–11.

Volanen, S. M., Suominen, S., Lahelma, E., Koskenvuo, K., Koskenvuo, M., & Silventoinen, K. (2010). Sense of coherence and intentions to retire early among Finnish women and men. *BMC Public Health*, *10*, 22.

Wagland, R., Fenlon, D., Tarrant, R., Howard-Jones, G., & Richardson, A. (2015). Rebuilding self-confidence after cancer: A feasibility study of life-coaching. *Support Care in Cancer*, *23*(3), 651–659. doi: 10.1007/s00520-014-2399-5.

Wahl, A. K., Mork, C., Hanestad, B. R., & Helland, S. (2006). Coping with exacerbation in psoriasis and eczema prior to admission in a dermatological ward. *European Journal of Dermatology*, *16*(3), 271–275.

Watlington, C. G., & Murphy, C. M. (2006). The roles of religion and spirituality among African American survivors of domestic violence. *Journal of Clinical Psychology*, *62*(7), 837–857.

Wentz, E., Nydén, A., & Krevers, B. (2012). Development of an internet-based support and coaching model for adolescents and young adults with ADHD and autism spectrum disorders: A pilot study. *European Child and Adolescent Psychiatry*, *21*(11), 611–622. doi: 10.1007/s00787-012-0297-2.

Wenzel, L., Osann, K., Hsieh, S., Tucker, J. A., Monk, B. J., & Nelson. E. L. (2015). Psychosocial telephone counseling for survivors of cervical cancer: Results of a randomized biobehavioral trial. *Journal of Clinical Oncology*, *33*(10), 1171–1179. doi: 10.1200/JCO.2014.57.4079.

Wheaton, B. (1994). Sampling the stress universe. In W. R. Avison & I. H. Gotlib (Eds.), *Stress and mental health: Contemporary issues and prospects for the future* (pp. 15–42). New York: Plenum Press.

Whitmer, M., Hurst, S., & Prins, M. (2009). Intergenerational views of hardiness in critical care nurses. *Dimensions of Critical Care Nursing*, *28*(5), 214–220.

Wonghongkul, T., Dechaprom, N., Phumivichuvate, L., & Losawatkul, S. (2006). Uncertainty appraisal coping and quality of life in breast cancer survivors. *Cancer Nursing*, *29*(3), 250–257.

SOCIAL COGNITIVE THEORY

Chapter 7

KEY CONCEPTS

- emotional coping
- environment
- forethought capability
- goal setting or self-control
- knowledge
- outcome expectancies
- outcome expectations
- reciprocal determinism
- self-efficacy

- self-efficacy in overcoming impediments
- self-reflective capability
- self-regulatory capability
- situational perception
- social cognitive theory
- social learning theory
- symbolizing capability
- vicarious capability

AFTER READING THIS CHAPTER YOU SHOULD BE ABLE TO

- Identify the five basic human capabilities according to social cognitive theory
- List the constructs of social cognitive theory
- Summarize the applications of social cognitive theory in health education and health promotion
- Identify educational methods and match these to modify each construct from social cognitive theory
- Apply social cognitive theory for changing a health behavior of your choice

This chapter discusses **social cognitive theory (SCT)**, which was earlier known as social learning theory (SLT). The word *social* refers to the social origins of thought and action. *Cognitive* refers to the influential causal contributions of thought processes to human motivation, affect, and action. The word *theory* alludes to the fact that this model has been empirically tested and can explain, describe, predict, or control behavior.

Social cognitive theory posits that human behavior can be explained by a triadic reciprocal causation. One angle of the tripod consists of the behavior. The second angle consists of environmental factors, and the third angle consists of personal factors such as cognitions, affect, and biological events. The unique interaction among these three dimensions results in behavior change. Hence, all three dimensions—personal factors, behavioral factors, and environmental factors—must be targeted in designing health education and health promotion interventions. This is known as **reciprocal determinism**. Over the past three decades many research studies, articles, and books by Albert Bandura and other research workers have substantiated the application of this theory in predicting, explaining, and changing behavior in a variety of settings. Some examples are clinical psychology for the treatment of phobias, counseling for parenting, career development, educational programs, and health education and health promotion.

> A theory that denies that thoughts can regulate actions does not lend itself readily to the explanation of complex human behavior.
>
> —Bandura (1986)

This chapter begins with a description of the historical aspects of the genesis of social cognitive theory. Next we describe the underpinnings of SCT and the various constructs that make up this theory and discuss the applications of SCT in health education and health promotion. Finally, we discuss the limitations of SCT and provide a skill-building application.

HISTORICAL PERSPECTIVE

Historically, social cognitive theory superseded several earlier theories developed to explain behavior. In the early part of the 20th century, the psychodynamic theory developed by Sigmund Freud (1923/1960) proposed that behavior was shaped by a dynamic interplay of subconscious and unconscious needs, drives, impulses, and instincts. However, this theory lacked predictive value, was difficult to test, and entailed no social dimension, thereby offering limited utility. Another early behavior theory was Gordon Allport's (1937) trait theory, which emphasized determination of behavior through broad, enduring dispositions. Weak empirical support and inconsistency of behavior across situations and over time did not provide much credence to this line of thought.

Learning theories were also popular in psychology, such as those by Dollard and Miller (1950), Rotter (1954), and Skinner (1953). A major limitation of these theories was that they were tested either on animal models or on human subjects in one-person situations and therefore did not consider the social aspects of learning.

In 1963 Albert Bandura at Stanford University, in collaboration with Richard Walters of the University of Waterloo, Ontario, proposed **social learning theory** (Bandura & Walters, 1963), which described the existence of three important influences on learning. The first is the role of *imitation*. Imitation provides three possible effects that contribute to learning: (1) a modeling effect, whereby the person directly copies the behavior; (2) an inhibitory or disinhibitory effect, whereby there is an increase or decrease in the behavior as a result of the observation; and (3) an eliciting effect, whereby imitation serves as a cue for releasing similar responses in the observer.

The second important influence in learning, according to Bandura and Walters (1963), is that of *reinforcement patterns*. Positive reinforcement, in the form of verbal approval or material rewards, tends to reinforce the occurrence of the behavior. Negative reinforcement, in the form of verbal or physical punishment by an authority figure, inhibits aggression as long as the punitive agent is present; however, children who receive a great deal of negative reinforcement display aggression toward objects other than the punitive agent.

The third important influence in learning is that of *self-control*. There are three forms of self-controlling behavior: (1) resistance to deviation, (2) regulation of self-administered rewarding resources, and (3) postponement of immediate reinforcements in lieu of some more valued reward in the future. Self-control is acquired and maintained by direct reinforcement that takes the form of disciplinary interventions, both negative and positive.

In 1969 Bandura wrote the *Principles of Behavior Modification*, which explained how social learning theory could be applied to a variety of behaviors. This approach was used in designing the Stanford three-community study, which began in 1972 in three northern California communities (Farquhar, 1978; Farquhar et al., 1977). The intervention targeted three risk factors: smoking, high serum cholesterol, and high blood pressure. The primary objectives of the intervention were to compare a mass media campaign alone in one community; a mass media campaign with high-risk screening and face-to-face instruction for high-risk individuals in the second community; and no health education with regard to knowledge and behavior related to cardiovascular disease, and measurement of various physiological indicators in the third community. The health education approach of this project had three distinct features: (1) mass media materials focused on teaching specific behavioral skills and affecting attitudes and motivation, (2) traditional behavior and self-control training, and (3) assessment of the knowledge deficits and media consumption patterns of intended audiences before the intervention. The study was able to demonstrate that mass media campaigns can increase knowledge and change habits, and that the approach is cost effective.

By 1977 Bandura had refined his approach, which he presented in his book *Social Learning Theory*. This refined approach formed the basis of the Stanford five-city project, which began in 1978 (Farquhar et al., 1985; Young, Haskell, Jatulis, & Fortmann, 1993). This intervention was implemented in northern California for six years in two treatment cities and two control cities, and in one city for surveillance only. The use of social learning theory in these two trials popularized this theory in health education and health promotion. In the 1980s, it was used in the Minnesota Heart Health Program (Luepker et al., 1994) and the Pawtucket Heart Health Program (Carleton, Lasater, Assaf, Feldman, & McKinlay, 1995), among other applications.

In 1986, Bandura renamed the theory social cognitive theory in his book *Social Foundations of Thought and Action*. Social cognitive theory continues to be popular today. In 1995, Bandura published *Self-Efficacy in Changing Societies*, which underscored the role of self-efficacy in behavior change. Self-efficacy is the behavior-specific confidence that a person has regarding pursuing or changing the behavior and is a unique contribution of this theory that has been borrowed by the health belief model, the transtheoretical model, and the theory of planned behavior (as perceived behavioral control). This construct accounts for the largest proportion of variance in work with this theory. In his works in the late 1990s and 2000s (1997, 2001a, 2001b, 2002, 2004, 2005), Bandura emphasized an agentic perspective; that is, the role of the person as an agent shaping and controlling his or her own life. In 2002, he was awarded the Healthtrac

> **Self-efficacy is the belief in one's capabilities to organize and execute the sources of action required to manage prospective situations.**
>
> —Bandura (1986)

Award. He delivered a lecture at the convention of the Society for Public Health Education that focused mainly on the theory's applications in health education and promotion (Bandura, 2004). Albert Bandura is among the most influential living psychologists of our times. At the time of writing this edition, Albert Bandura was 89 years old and was David Starr Jordan Professor Emeritus of Social Science in Psychology at Stanford University but not actively contributing to the literature.

UNDERPINNINGS OF SOCIAL COGNITIVE THEORY

One of the distinctive features of SCT is the importance it places on the potential of human beings. According to this theory, five basic human capabilities or competencies describe human beings. These are depicted in **Figure 7-1**. The first such capability is the **symbolizing capability**, which refers to the use of symbols in attributing meaning to experiences. It is an important tool for understanding, creating, and managing one's environment. Most environmental events are interpreted cognitively rather than directly. By using symbols, people give structure, meaning, and continuity to their experiences. The symbolizing capability also helps in communicating with others at any distance in time and space. For example, when you are reading this textbook it is due to the symbolizing capability that I am able to compose the message and you are able to read and comprehend.

The **vicarious capability** refers to the ability to learn from observing other people's behavior and the consequences they face. This ability is important because it enables people to generate and regulate behavior without tedious trial and error. Some complex skills can be mastered only through modeling. Modeling is not simply a process of response mimicry but entails creativity and innovativeness as well. For example, when you see another student being rewarded by a pleasing remark from your instructor in response to answering a question you learn that answering questions may give you the same consequence, and you want to try it next time.

Forethought capability refers to the fact that most behavior is purposive and regulated by prior thoughts. People motivate themselves and plan their actions using their forethought capability. Although future events do not have actual existence, they can be imagined and can serve as motivators in the present. Usually the course of action that is likely to bring positive rewards is easily adopted, whereas the course that is likely to produce negative outcomes is not adopted. For example, the fact that you are reading this book is not random. You thought about buying the book, planned time for reading it, and are now reading it—all because of forethought capability.

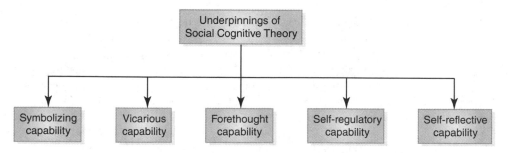

FIGURE 7-1 Underpinnings of social cognitive theory.

Self-regulatory capability refers to setting internal standards and self-evaluative reactions for one's behavior. Self-satisfaction is gained from meeting desirable standards, and dissatisfaction results from below-standard performance. People are proactive and constantly set challenging goals for themselves, which also plays an important role in self-regulation. For example, based on the grade you desired and the grade you got on your mid-term exam you are adjusting the effort that you are putting in for this course. This is self-regulatory capability.

The final capability is **self-reflective capability**, which is the analysis of experiences and examination of one's own thought processes. People are not just agents of action but also self-examine and critique their own actions. They generate ideas, act on them based on an anticipated outcome, and then in retrospect judge the accuracy and value of the outcomes, finally modifying their thinking as needed. According to Bandura (2001a), verification of one's thought processes happens in four ways: (1) enactive verification, in which one looks at the closeness between one's thoughts and the results of one's action; (2) vicarious verification, in which one looks at other people's actions and compares that with one's thinking; (3) persuasive verification, in which one evaluates one's beliefs against what others believe; and (4) logical verification, in which one compares one's thinking against knowledge that is known. For example, on the basis of the courses you have taken and the interactions you have had with your instructors and other students you reflect on the career that you want to choose. This is self-reflective capability.

> **People are not only agents of action but self-examiners of their own functioning.**
>
> —Bandura (2001a, p. 10)

CONSTRUCTS OF SOCIAL COGNITIVE THEORY

The constructs of Bandura's theory have been described in the literature in several ways. This chapter uses the depiction elaborated by Bandura in his presentation regarding the application of SCT in health promotion (Bandura, 2004). The constructs, their definitions, and ways to modify each construct are summarized in **Table 7-1** and depicted in **Figure 7-2**.

The first construct of SCT is *knowledge*, which is learning facts and gaining insights related to an action, idea, object, person, or situation. In simple words, knowledge is information and facts on a topic. Knowledge is an essential component for any behavior change. It is a necessary precondition for change, but often is not sufficient for making the behavior change. In the context of health education and health promotion, knowledge of the risks and benefits of different health practices is required for behavior change interventions. To modify knowledge, the health educator can provide information in the form of a lecture, a demonstration, or fact sheets on the topic.

The second construct of SCT is **outcome expectations**, which is the anticipation of the probable outcomes that would ensue as a result of engaging in the behavior under discussion. In simple words, outcome expectations are the expected results. Bandura (2004) identifies three types of outcomes or results: (1) physical outcomes, which include positive and negative consequences of the behavior; (2) the outcome of social approval or disapproval of engaging or disengaging in the behavior; and (3) positive and negative self-evaluations. For example, some possible outcome expectations for a person being motivated to be physically active may be losing weight, looking attractive, being able to make more friends, having less chance of acquiring heart disease, and improving his or her self-image. The higher the expectations, the greater the likelihood of acquiring the behavior.

Table 7-1	Key Constructs of Social Cognitive Theory	
Construct	Definition	How to Modify?
Knowledge	Learning facts and gaining insights related to an action, idea, object, person, or situation (Information and facts on a topic)	• Lecture • Informational talk • Providing fact sheets
Outcome expectations	Anticipation of the probable outcomes that would ensue as a result of engaging in the behavior under discussion (Expected results)	• Discussion of benefits • Brainstorming • Role play
Outcome expectancies	Value a person places on the probable outcomes that would result from performing a behavior (Importance of expected results)	• Discussion of values • Brainstorming • Role play
Situational perception	How one perceives and interprets the environment around oneself (Awareness around the behavior and environment)	• Rectify misperceptions
Environment	Physical or social circumstances or conditions that surround a person (Physical and social surroundings)	• Provide opportunities to overcome personal and situational impediments • Provide access to the health system • Build social support around the person
Self-efficacy	Confidence in one's ability to pursue a behavior (Behavioral confidence)	• Practice in small steps (e.g., breaking down the complex behavior of physical activity into doable small steps) • Have a role model demonstrate (e.g., a video of a well-known movie star with whom the target audience can associate performing the same behaviors) • Use persuasion and reinforcement (e.g., tell participants that they have what it takes to perform the behavior, and attribute past failures to external reasons) • Reduce stress associated with implementing a new behavior (e.g., have women take a relaxing shower before doing a breast self-examination)
Self-efficacy in overcoming impediments	Confidence that a person has in overcoming barriers while performing a given behavior (Behavioral confidence in counteracting difficulties)	• Practice overcoming barriers in small steps • Have a role model demonstrate overcoming barriers • Use persuasion and reinforcement in overcoming barriers • Reduce stress while overcoming barriers

Table 7-1	Key Constructs of Social Cognitive Theory (*continued*)	
Construct	**Definition**	**How to Modify?**
Goal setting or self-control	Setting goals and developing plans to accomplish chosen behaviors (Establishing goals)	• Provide opportunities for setting goals • Self-monitoring • Provide personal rewards to reinforce accomplishment of goals
Emotional coping	Techniques employed by the person to control the emotional and physiological states associated with acquisition of a new behavior (Managing emotions)	• Progressive muscle relaxation • Yoga/meditation • Autogenic training • Visual imagery • Other stress management techniques

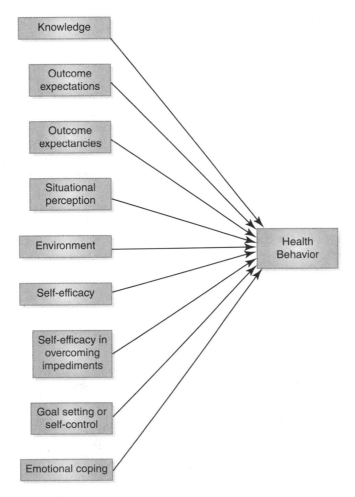

FIGURE 7-2 Constructs of social cognitive theory.

To modify outcome expectations, the health educator can facilitate a discussion on the possible outcomes from engaging in the desired behavior. Other methods could be brainstorming or a role play that depicts the effects of the behavior on a person.

The construct of SCT that goes hand-in-hand with outcome expectations is **outcome expectancies**, which refers to the value a person places on the probable outcomes that would result from performing a behavior. In simple words, the outcome expectancies are about the importance of expected results. The higher the expectancies, the greater the chance that the individual will perform the behavior. For example, in motivating students, possible outcomes of getting an A grade could be to graduate early, to have more friends, to learn more about the subject, and so on. If students value these outcomes, they are likely to work harder to get an A in the course. Students who do not value these associated outcomes are likely to put in less effort. Likert scales are often used to measure outcome expectations and outcome expectancies. The expectations are multiplied with corresponding expectancies and then summed to arrive at a score of expectations (outcome expectations plus outcome expectancies). To modify expectancies, a discussion or brainstorming session on values associated with outcomes can be organized. Expectancies also can be influenced by a psychodrama or a role play.

The fourth construct of SCT is **situational perception**, which refers to how one perceives and interprets the environment (McAlister, Perry, & Parcel, 2008). In simple words, situational perception is the awareness around the behavior and environment. Any misperceptions hinder the behavior change. Thus efforts must be made to remove misperceptions and to promote social norms that are healthy. For example, in a teen pregnancy program, a large number of teens may believe it is normative for most teens to be sexually active, but the statistical evidence does not support this belief. Providing correct information and explaining it would rectify the situational perception. To modify situational perception, misperceptions can be modified in either a discussion or a lecture.

The fifth construct of SCT, **environment**, refers to the physical or social circumstances or conditions that surround a person. In simple words, environment consists of physical and social surroundings. Whereas situational perception involves a person's interpretation of his or her surroundings, environment consists of the actual conditions. Some effective means of modifying this construct are creating opportunities to overcome personal and situational impediments, providing access to the health system, and building social support around the person. Example applications of this construct are creating facilities for physical activity in the community (physical environment) and creating learning experiences for eliciting and maintaining social support from friends to maintain exercise behavior (social environment).

The sixth construct of SCT is **self-efficacy**, which is the confidence a person has in his or her ability to pursue a behavior or in simple words behavioral confidence. Self-efficacy is behavior specific and is in the present. It is not about the past or future. Self-efficacy plays a central role in behavior change. Bandura (2004) notes that unless people believe that they can produce the desired changes by their own efforts, there will be very little incentive to put in that effort. Four strategies can be used in building self-efficacy:

1. *Break down the complex behavior into practical and doable small steps.* For example, instead of simply telling people to read food labels, the educator may teach participants how to find the title and then how to find information on serving size, total calories, calories from fat, the constitution of different food groups, and so on, using small steps.

2. *Use a demonstration from credible role models.* For example, in facilitating an educational program about obesity prevention, having a movie star who has successfully gone through the process of losing weight share his or her story would help in enhancing the self-efficacy of the participants.

3. *Use persuasion and reassurance.* If a person has failed in the past to make a behavior change, those failures can be attributed to external reasons. If the person has succeeded in related fields, those successes can be compared with the behavior the person is trying to change. For example, in a quitting alcohol program, the health educator could ask participants to identify one instance when they were successful in changing a negative behavior or in acquiring a positive behavior and then could state that they can do the same thing with the alcohol behavior.

4. *Reduce stress.* Any behavior change is associated with some amount of stress, which hinders the change process. Reducing stress is an effective means of building self-efficacy. For example, if children find giving up watching television to be stressful, they can be instructed in how to relax either by listening to music or by practicing progressive muscle relaxation.

The seventh construct is **self-efficacy in overcoming impediments**, which refers to the confidence that a person has in overcoming barriers while performing a given behavior. In simple words, this means behavioral confidence in counteracting difficulties. This construct is related to self-efficacy in that it is situation specific, pertains to the present, and represents a level of confidence. Sometimes considered as a subset of self-efficacy, it is better to think of it as a separate construct. For example, to become more physically active, one must overcome several barriers, such as being tired, feeling depressed, feeling anxious, encountering bad weather, and having other interesting things to do. To modify the construct of self-efficacy in overcoming impediments, helpful techniques include practicing to overcome each barrier in small steps, having role models demonstrate success, using persuasion, and reducing stress.

The eighth construct is **goal setting** or **self-control**, which refers to setting goals and developing plans to accomplish chosen behaviors. When one sets goals and develops concrete plans, behavior change becomes easier. Goals are proximal (near) and distal (far off). Proximal goals are immediate accomplishments, whereas distal goals set the course of making change. To modify the construct of goal setting or self-control, educators need to provide opportunities for setting goals, show individuals how to monitor their progress, and provide personal rewards to reinforce the attainment of goals.

> Social cognitive theory acknowledges the influential role of evolved factors in human adaptation and change, but it rejects one-sided evolutionism in which evolved biology shapes behavior but the selection pressures of social and technological innovations on biological evolutions get ignored.
>
> —Bandura (2001a, p. 20)

The final construct in SCT is **emotional coping**, which refers to the techniques employed by the person to control the emotional and physiological states associated with acquisition of a new behavior. In simple words, this is management of emotions. This construct is often reified in association with self-efficacy. To modify emotional coping, stress management techniques such as progressive muscle relaxation, yoga, autogenic training, and visual imagery are useful. For example, a program that teaches aerobics to a group of sedentary employees at a worksite may also need to utilize stress management techniques that reduce the anxiety associated with learning a new skill.

APPLICATIONS OF SOCIAL COGNITIVE THEORY

Some examples of behavior research in which SCT has been used include analysis of online social networks to understand information-sharing behaviors (Yoon & Tourassi, 2014), assessing medication adherence (Dilorio et al., 2009; Kalichman et al., 2005), defining correlates of physical activity in fibromyalgia patients (Oliver & Cronan, 2005), defining predictors of exercise participation (Gu, Zhang, & Smith, 2015; Kaewthummanukul, Brown, Weaver, & Thomas, 2006), identifying perceptions of whole-grain foods and the factors influencing their intake by children (Burgess-Champoux, Marquart, Vickers, & Reicks, 2006), modeling adolescents' sexual behavior on exposure to sexual content on television (Martino, Collins, Kanouse, Elliott, & Berry, 2005), modeling father–son communication about sex (Dilorio, McCarty, & Denzmore, 2006), nutritional correlates of childhood obesity (Knowlden & Sharma, 2015), predicting bullying and victimization (Mouttapa, Valente, Gallaher, Rohrbach, & Unger, 2004), predicting condom use among university students (Mashegoane, Moalusi, Peltzer, & Ngoepe, 2004), predicting fruit and vegetable intake in children (Bere & Klepp, 2005), predicting heavy drinking in college students (Gilles, Turk, & Fresco, 2006), predicting obesity prevention behaviors (Sharma, Mehan, & Surabhi, 2008–2009; Sharma, Wagner, & Wilkerson, 2005–2006), predicting physical activity behavior (Rhodes & Plotnikoff, 2005; Tavares, Plotnikoff, & Loucaides, 2009), predicting physician behavior to recommend colonoscopy (Honda & Gorin, 2006), predicting reproductive health behavioral intention in adolescent women with diabetes (Wang, Charron-Prochownik, Sereika, Siminerio, & Kim, 2006), predicting sexually risky behaviors among adolescent mothers (Koniak-Griffin & Stein, 2006), and profiling community-based rehabilitation volunteers (Sharma & Deepak, 2003). **Table 7-2** summarizes these applications.

Some examples in which SCT has been used for primary prevention include an active ergonomics training program in computer users (Greene, DeJoy, & Olejnik, 2005), comic books for childhood obesity prevention (Branscum, Sharma, Wang, Wilson, & Rojas-Guyler, 2013), family planning decision making (Ha, Jayasuriya, & Owen, 2005), health coaching in individuals with intellectual disabilities (Elinder, Bergström, Hagberg, Wihlman, & Hagströmer, 2010), health coaching with pre-diabetes patients (Cha et al., 2014), HIV prevention programs (Boutin-Foster et al., 2010; Dilorio et al., 2006; Li et al., 2014), nutrition education programs (Powers, Struempler, Guarino, & Parmer, 2005; Shilts, Lamp, Horowitz, & Townsend, 2009), a poison prevention education program (Schwartz, Howland, Mercurio-Zappala, & Hoffman, 2003), prevention and reduction of aggressive behavior (Orpinas & Horne, 2004), prevention of childhood obesity (Canavera, Sharma, & Murnan, 2008–2009; Safdie, Cargo, Richard, & Lévesque, 2014), problem-solving skills (Coates, Malouff, & Rooke, 2008; Sharma, Petosa, & Heaney, 1999; Shimazu, Kawakami, Irimajiri, Sakamoto, & Amano, 2005), a self-help physical activity intervention at the workplace (Griffin-Blake & DeJoy, 2006), a self-help weight management intervention (Tufano & Karras, 2005), self-regulation of driving among high-risk older drivers (Stalvey & Owsley, 2003), a sun protection intervention in preschoolers (Gritz et al., 2006), a smoking cessation program (Patten et al., 2009; Ramelson, Friedman, & Ockene, 1999), smoking prevention programs (Langlois, Petosa, & Hallam, 1999), using a smart phone to promote physical activity

> The field of health is changing from a disease model to a health model. It is just as meaningful to speak of levels of vitality and healthfulness as of degrees of impairment and debility. Health promotion should begin with goals not means. If health is the goal, biomedical interventions are not the only means to it.
>
> —Bandura (2004, p. 143)

Table 7-2	Applications of Social Cognitive Theory in Behavioral Research
Analysis of online social networks to understand information-sharing behaviors	
Assessing medication adherence	
Defining correlates of physical activity in fibromyalgia patients	
Defining predictors of exercise participation	
Identifying perceptions of whole-grain foods and the factors influencing their intake by children	
Modeling adolescents' sexual behavior on exposure to sexual content on television	
Modeling father–son communication about sex	
Nutritional correlates of childhood obesity	
Predicting bullying and victimization	
Predicting condom use among university students	
Predicting fruit and vegetable intake in children	
Predicting heavy drinking in college students	
Predicting obesity prevention behaviors	
Predicting physical activity behavior	
Predicting physician behavior to recommend colonoscopy	
Predicting reproductive health behavioral intention in adolescent women with diabetes	
Predicting sexually risky behaviors among adolescent mothers	
Profiling community-based rehabilitation volunteers	

(Lubans, Smith, Skinner, & Morgan, 2014), a walking program (Rovniak, Hovell, Wojcik, Winett, & Martinez-Donate, 2005), and Web-assisted instruction for physical activity (Suminski & Petosa, 2006). **Table 7-3** summarizes these applications.

Some examples in which SCT has been used for secondary and tertiary prevention are for adherence to continuous positive airway pressure (CPAP) treatment for sleep apnea (Stepnowsky, Marler, Palau, & Annette Brooks, 2006), behavior change intervention after knee replacement (Harnirattisai & Johnson, 2005), cancer screening in women with mobility impairments (Peterson, Suzuki, Walsh, Buckley, & Krahn, 2012), a childhood asthma management program (McGhan, Wells, & Befus, 1998), diabetes education programs (Chapman-Novakofski & Karduck, 2005; Rosal et al., 2014), dietary approaches to reducing hypertension (Rankins, Sampson, Brown, & Jenkins-Salley, 2005), HIV risk reduction intervention among HIV-positive individuals (Poudel, Buchanan, & Poudel-Tandukar, 2015), intervention to improve the quality of life for women with breast cancer (Blacklock, Rhodes, Blanchard, & Gaul, 2010; Graves, Carter, Anderson, & Winett, 2003), a lifestyle program for leg ulcer patients (Heinen, Bartholomew, Wensing, Kerkhof, & Achterberg, 2006), mammography screening among American Indian women (Dignan et al., 2005), medication self-management among people with epilepsy (Dilorio et al., 2005; Dilorio et al., 2009), a physical activity program for prostate cancer patients (Taylor et al., 2006), promotion of female condom use

Table 7-3	Applications of Social Cognitive Theory in Primary Prevention
Active ergonomics training program in computer users	
Comic books for childhood obesity prevention	
Family planning decision making	
Health coaching in individuals with intellectual disabilities	
Health coaching with pre-diabetes patients	
HIV prevention programs	
Nutrition education programs	
Poison prevention education program	
Prevention and reduction of aggressive behavior	
Prevention of childhood obesity	
Problem-solving skills	
Self-help physical activity intervention at the workplace	
Self-help weight management intervention	
Self-regulation of driving among high-risk older drivers	
Smoking cessation program	
Smoking prevention programs	
Sun protection intervention in preschoolers	
Using a smart phone to promote physical activity	
Walking program	
Web-assisted instruction for physical activity	

in a sexually transmitted disease clinic (Artz et al., 2005), rehabilitation following myocardial infarction and coronary artery bypass grafting (Hiltunen et al., 2005), skin self-examination by patients at high risk for melanoma (Hay et al., 2006), and weight loss in overweight and obese women (Annesi, 2010; Klohe-Lehman et al., 2006). **Table 7-4** summarizes these applications.

LIMITATIONS OF SOCIAL COGNITIVE THEORY

Social cognitive theory is a robust behavioral theory, and its biggest advantage is that it can be applied easily. The other important dimension of this theory is that social structural factors are integrated with personal determinants, which is often not the case with other theories of behavior. However, like all theories, this theory has some limitations. Some critics have noted that the theory is about learning and is, therefore, more applicable for children. The theory is not specifically designed for changing behavior. For example, the transtheoretical model is specific about changing

Table 7-4	Applications of Social Cognitive Theory in Secondary and Tertiary Prevention
Adherence to continuous positive airway pressure (CPAP) treatment for sleep apnea
Behavior change intervention after knee replacement
Cancer screening in women with mobility impairments
Childhood asthma management program
Diabetes education program
Dietary approaches to reducing hypertension
HIV risk reduction intervention among HIV-positive individuals
Intervention to improve the quality of life for women with breast cancer
Lifestyle program for leg ulcer patients
Mammography screening among American Indian women
Medication self-management among people with epilepsy
Physical activity program for prostate cancer patients
Promotion of female condom use in a sexually transmitted disease clinic
Rehabilitation following myocardial infarction and coronary artery bypass grafting
Skin self-examination by patients at high risk for melanoma
Weight loss in overweight and obese women

behaviors and provides indications of the different stages through which a person moves. SCT provides no such guidance.

The theory has many constructs, and often it is not possible to reify all these constructs, which tends to limit the theory's usage. Ideally, a theory should be parsimonious. Also, the single most important predictor of the theory is identified as self-efficacy. Often, the items that measure self-efficacy are very similar to the items that measure the behavior, thus adding to measurement bias. Further, questions meant to measure an individual's cognition in SCT often change and create the responder's thinking rather than tapping into how exactly that individual thinks to begin with. Prochaska (2006) has criticized SCT as lacking arrangement of constructs in mathematical relationships. As a result, different practitioners use different sets of constructs in different combinations. Finally, Prochaska (2006) notes that SCT-based interventions mainly target those who are prepared to change a behavior; in the process, such interventions miss a large majority of the population. A theory should provide guidance for change for people with varying levels of readiness.

APPLICATION EXERCISE

In this chapter we have presented several applications of social cognitive theory in behavioral research, in primary, secondary, and tertiary prevention. Choose an area of interest to you from these applications and read the full-text article to see how the theory was used in that context. One such example is the study done by Sharma, Wagner, and Wilkerson (2005–2006) in the area of obesity prevention behaviors among children. They chose four obesity prevention behaviors: limiting television viewing, encouraging daily physical activity, increasing fruit and vegetable intake, and increasing water consumption. They chose selected constructs of social cognitive theory: expectations (multiplicative score of outcome expectations and outcome expectancies) for each of the four behaviors, self-efficacy for each of the four behaviors, and self-control for each of the four behaviors. They developed a 52-item valid and reliable scale that was administered to 159 fifth-grade students. Minutes of physical activity were predicted by self-efficacy to exercise and number of times taught at school ($R^2 = 0.072$). Hours of TV watching were predicted by number of times taught about healthy eating at school and self-control through goal setting ($R^2 = 0.055$). Glasses of water consumed were predicted by expectations for drinking water ($R^2 = 0.091$). Servings of fruits and vegetables consumed were predicted by self-efficacy of eating fruits and vegetables ($R^2 = 0.137$). This is a useful study that demonstrates how social cognitive theory has been used.

Locate the full-text article for this study and prepare a 250-word critique on its methodology. Pay attention to the study sample, selection of behaviors, instrumentation, reliability and validity of the instrument used, data analysis, and data interpretation, including the threats to internal and external validity.

SKILL-BUILDING ACTIVITY

Let us see how we can apply SCT to the issue of developing problem-solving skills in upper elementary school children. **Figure 7-3** depicts each of the constructs from SCT and links these with educational processes and behavioral objectives to develop problem-solving skills.

We need to be parsimonious in our selection of constructs from the theory, so let's choose six constructs. The health education intervention would start by modifying the construct of situational perception by brainstorming about potential stressors that would require problem solving by the children. A lecture to build knowledge about stressors and the steps of problem solving can be given. To modify outcome expectations, a discussion on the benefits of problem-solving skills can be organized. Some examples of these benefits could include increased popularity with friends, faster learning, better grades, more fun with family, and more fun at school. To modify outcome expectancies, the relevance of the anticipated outcomes to the students' personal lives can be discussed.

To modify self-efficacy, the steps of problem solving can be broken down into small steps. These steps could be as follows: (1) identify the stressor, (2) think of many ways to deal with each stressor, (3) think of all the good points about each way, (4) think of all the bad points about each way, and (5) choose one solution after looking at the good and bad points for several possible solutions. Messages that role models use these steps of problem solving can be used to reinforce self-efficacy. Stress management techniques can be practiced while applying the steps of problem solving, which also reinforces self-efficacy. Finally, to modify self-control, the children can be instructed to write goals for applying problem-solving skills and then reward themselves when they accomplish their goals.

Using this approach, plan a health education program for a behavior issue of your choice. **Table 7-5** provides a set of questions to assist you in choosing educational methods that correspond to different constructs of social cognitive theory.

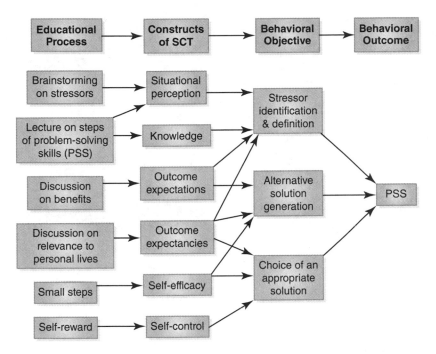

FIGURE 7-3 How social cognitive theory (SCT) has been used to modify problem-solving skills.

Table 7-5	Choosing the Educational Methods for Health Education Program Planning Using Social Cognitive Theory

1. What is the best educational method to facilitate knowledge?
    - Lecture
    - Informational talk
    - Fact sheets
    - Other

2. What is the best educational method to facilitate outcome expectations?
    - Discussion
    - Brainstorming
    - Role play
    - Simulation
    - Other

3. What is the best educational method to facilitate outcome expectancies?
    - Discussion
    - Brainstorming
    - Role play
    - Simulation
    - Other

(continues)

Table 7-5	Choosing the Educational Methods for Health Education Program Planning Using Social Cognitive Theory (*continued*)

4. What is the best educational method to facilitate situational perception?
   - Discussion
   - Brainstorming
   - Role play
   - Simulation
   - Other

5. What is the best educational method to facilitate changes in environment?
   - Making physical changes in the environment
   - Building social support
   - Providing access to health care
   - Other

6. What is the best educational method to facilitate self-efficacy?
   - Demonstration
   - Role play
   - Video with a credible role model
   - Stress reduction techniques
     - Progressive muscle relaxation
     - Visual imagery
     - Autogenic training
     - Yoga/meditation
     - Other
   - Other

7. What is the best educational method to facilitate self-efficacy in overcoming impediments?
   - Demonstration
   - Role play
   - Video with a credible role model
   - Stress reduction techniques
   - Progressive muscle relaxation
     - Visual imagery
     - Autogenic training
     - Yoga/meditation
     - Other
   - Other

8. What is the best educational method to facilitate self-control?
   - Group formation
   - Coalition building
   - Registration of not-for-profit organization
   - Other

9. What is the best educational method to facilitate emotional coping?
   - Progressive muscle relaxation
   - Autogenic training
   - Yoga/meditation
   - Visual imagery
   - Other

SUMMARY

Albert Bandura, a professor of psychology at Stanford University, is the originator of social cognitive theory (previously called social learning theory). This theory explains human behavior as a triadic reciprocal causation among behavior, environment, and personal factors (such as cognitions, affect, and biological events). Five basic human capabilities describe human beings according to this theory: symbolizing capability (use of symbols in attributing meaning to experiences), vicarious capability (learning from observing other people's behavior and the consequences they face), forethought capability (most behavior is purposive and regulated by prior thoughts), self-regulatory capability (setting internal standards and self-evaluative reactions for one's behavior), and self-reflective capability (analysis of experiences and thinking about one's own thought processes).

The constructs of the theory include knowledge (learning facts and gaining insights related to an action, idea, object, person, or situation), outcome expectations (anticipation of the probable outcomes that would ensue as a result of engaging in the behavior), outcome expectancies (the value a person places on the probable outcomes that would result from performing a behavior), situational perception (how a person perceives and interprets the environment around him- or herself), environment (physical or social circumstances or conditions that surround a person), self-efficacy (the confidence that a person has in his or her ability to pursue a behavior), self-efficacy in overcoming impediments (the confidence that a person has in overcoming barriers while performing a given behavior), goal setting or self-control (setting goals and developing plans to accomplish chosen behaviors), and emotional coping (techniques employed by the person to control the emotional and physiological states associated with acquisition of a new behavior). The constructs are amenable to modification by different educational methods. Social cognitive theory has been applied over the past 30 years in a variety of areas within health promotion and education.

IMPORTANT TERMS

emotional coping
environment
forethought capability
goal setting
outcome expectancies
outcome expectations
reciprocal determinism
self-control
self-efficacy

self-efficacy in overcoming impediments
self-reflective capability
self-regulatory capability
situational perception
social cognitive theory (SCT)
social learning theory
symbolizing capability
vicarious capability

REVIEW QUESTIONS

1. Describe the historical genesis of social cognitive theory.
2. Discuss reciprocal determinism.
3. Discuss the underpinnings of social cognitive theory.
4. What is self-efficacy and how can it be built?
5. Describe the constructs of social cognitive theory.
6. Discuss the limitations of social cognitive theory.
7. Apply social cognitive theory in changing a behavior of your choice for a target population of your choice.

WEBSITES TO EXPLORE

Albert Bandura: Biographical Sketch

http://stanford.edu/dept/psychology/bandura/

This website was originally developed in 2004 and maintained by Frank Pajares at Emory University, but it is now maintained by Stanford University. The website provides a detailed biography of Albert Bandura along with links to various important events and accomplishments in his life. *Read the biography of Albert Bandura and prepare a reaction paper explaining what impressed you most about him.*

Albert Bandura

www.ship.edu/~cgboeree/bandura.html

This website, developed and maintained by George Boeree of Shippensburg University in Pennsylvania, provides a brief biography of Bandura and an interesting account of social learning theory. *Review this website and describe how social learning theory is used in therapy.*

IDEA: Social Cognitive Theory Compared with Constructivism and Cooperative Learning

http://i-d-e-a.org/page109.html

This website presents an overview of social cognitive theory and compares it with the theories of constructivism and cooperative learning. As we have seen, in social cognitive theory self-efficacy, self-control, outcome expectations, and outcome expectancies are important factors related to behavior development. In constructivism, the learner actively constructs new ideas and interprets concepts based on current and past knowledge. In cooperative learning, the learner is actively engaged in the learning process. *Review this website and compare and contrast the three theoretical approaches.*

Overview of Self-Efficacy

http://p20motivationlab.org

This is the website for P20 Motivation and Learning Lab, which is directed by Dr. Ellen Usher from the University of Kentucky. This website explores academic motivation in a variety of contexts and describes practices that best promote and sustain the motivation students need to acquire skills essential for success and well-being in present times. Search for the term *self-efficacy* on this website. You will get several results. *Read about self-efficacy, sources of self-efficacy, and teacher self-efficacy. Summarize your readings in a brief paper.*

Social Cognitive Theory: Brief Video

www.youtube.com/watch?v=S4N5J9jFW5U

This website features a 4-minute video on social cognitive theory. Watch the Bobo doll experiment and the account of snake phobia therapy. *Share one important implication you discovered about SCT by watching this video.*

REFERENCES

Allport, G. W. (1937). *Personality: A psychological interpretation*. New York: Holt.

Annesi, J. J. (2009). Dose-response and self-efficacy effects of an exercise program on vigor change in obese women. *American Journal of the Medical Sciences, 339*(2), 127–132.

Artz, L., Macaluso, M., Kelaghan, J., Austin, H., Fleenor, M., Robey, L., et al. (2005). An intervention to promote the female condom to sexually transmitted disease clinic patients. *Behavior Modification, 29*(2), 318–369.

Bandura, A. (1969). *Principles of behavior modification*. New York: Prentice-Hall.

Bandura, A. (1977). *Social learning theory*. Englewood Cliffs, NJ: Prentice-Hall.

Bandura, A. (1986). *Social foundations of thought and action*. Englewood Cliffs, NJ: Prentice-Hall.

Bandura, A. (Ed.). (1995). *Self-efficacy in changing societies*. New York: Cambridge University Press.

Bandura, A. (1997). *Self-efficacy: The exercise of control*. New York: W. H. Freeman.

Bandura, A. (2001a). Social cognitive theory: An agentic perspective. *Annual Review of Psychology, 52*, 1–26.

Bandura, A. (2001b). Social cognitive theory of mass communication. *Mediapsychology, 3*, 265–299.

Bandura, A. (2002). Social cognitive theory in cultural context. *Applied Psychology: An International Review, 51*(2), 269–290.

Bandura, A. (2004). Health promotion by social cognitive means. *Health Education and Behavior, 31*, 143–164.

Bandura, A. (2005). The primacy of self-regulation in health promotion. *Applied Psychology: An International Review, 54*(2), 245–254.

Bandura, A., & Walters, R. H. (1963). *Social learning and personality development*. New York: Holt, Rinehart and Winston.

Bere, E., & Klepp, K. I. (2005). Changes in accessibility and preferences predict children's future fruit and vegetable intake. *International Journal of Behavioral Nutrition and Physical Activity, 2*, 15.

Blacklock, R., Rhodes, R., Blanchard, C., & Gaul, C. (2010). Effects of exercise intensity and self-efficacy on state anxiety with breast cancer survivors. *Oncology Nursing Forum, 37*(2), 206–212.

Boutin-Foster, C., McLaughlin, N., Gray, A., Ogedegbe, A., Hageman, I., Knowlton, C., et al. (2010). Reducing HIV and AIDS through Prevention (RHAP): A theoretically based approach for teaching HIV prevention to adolescents through an exploration of popular music. *Journal of Urban Health*, Epub ahead of print. PMID: 20195778.

Branscum, P., Sharma, M., Wang, L. L., Wilson, B. R., & Rojas-Guyler, L. (2013). A true challenge for any superhero: An evaluation of a comic book obesity prevention program. *Family & Community Health, 36*(1), 63–76. doi: 10.1097/FCH.0b013e31826d7607.

Burgess-Champoux, T., Marquart, L., Vickers, Z., & Reicks, M. (2006). Perceptions of children, parents, and teachers regarding whole-grain foods, and implications for a school-based intervention. *Journal of Nutrition Education and Behavior, 38*(4), 230–237.

Canavera, M., Sharma, M., & Murnan, J. (2008–2009). Development and pilot testing a social cognitive theory-based intervention to prevent childhood obesity among elementary students in rural Kentucky. *International Quarterly of Community Health Education, 29*(1), 57–70.

Carleton, R. A., Lasater, T. M., Assaf, A. R., Feldman, H. A., & McKinlay, S. (1995). The Pawtucket Heart Health Program: Community changes in cardiovascular risk factors and projected disease risk. *American Journal of Public Health, 85*, 777–785.

Cha, E., Kim, K. H., Umpierrez, G., Dawkins, C. R., Bello, M. K., Lerner, H. M., et al. (2014). A feasibility study to develop a diabetes prevention program for young adults with prediabetes by using digital platforms and a handheld device. *Diabetes Educator, 40*(5), 626–637. doi: 10.1177/0145721714539736.

Chapman-Novakofski, K., & Karduck, J. (2005). Improvement in knowledge, social cognitive theory variables, and movement through stages of change after a community-based diabetes education program. *Journal of the American Dietetic Association, 105*(10), 1613–1616.

Coates, C., Malouff, J. M., & Rooke, S. E. (2008). Efficacy of written modeling and vicarious reinforcement in increasing use of problem-solving methods by distressed individuals. *Journal of Psychology, 142*(4), 413–425.

Dignan, M. B., Burhansstipanov, L., Hariton, J., Harjo, L., Rattler, T., Lee, R., et al. (2005). A comparison of two Native American Navigator formats: Face-to-face and telephone. *Cancer Control, 12*(Suppl. 2), 28–33.

Dilorio, C., Escoffery, C., Yeager, K. A., McCarty, F., Henry, T. R., Koganti, A., et al. (2009). WebEase: Development of a Web-based epilepsy self-management intervention. *Preventing Chronic Disease, 6*(1), A28.

Dilorio, C., McCarty, F., & Denzmore, P. (2006). An exploration of social cognitive theory mediators of father-son communication about sex. *Journal of Pediatric Psychology, 31*(9), 917–927.

Dilorio, C., McCarty, F., Depadilla, L., Resnicow, K., Holstad, M. M., Yeager, K., et al. (2009). Adherence to antiretroviral medication regimens: A test of a psychosocial model. *AIDS and Behavior, 13*(1), 10–22.

Dilorio, C., Resnicow, K., McCarty, F., De, A. K., Dudley, W. N., Wang, D. T., et al. (2006). Keepin' it R.E.A.L.! Results of a mother-adolescent HIV prevention program. *Nursing Research, 55*(1), 43–51.

Dilorio, C., Shafer, P. O., Letz, R., Henry, T. R., Schomer, D. L., Yeager, K., et al. (2005). Project EASE: A study to test a psychosocial model of epilepsy medication management. *Epilepsy and Behavior, 5*(6), 926–936.

Dollard, J., & Miller, N. E. (1950). *Personality and psychotherapy.* New York: McGraw-Hill.

Elinder, L. S, Bergström, H., Hagberg, J., Wihlman, U., & Hagströmer, M. (2010). Promoting a healthy diet and physical activity in adults with intellectual disabilities living in community residences: Design and evaluation of a cluster-randomized intervention. *BMC Public Health, 10*, 761. doi: 10.1186/1471-2458-10-761.

Farquhar, J. W. (1978). The community-based model of lifestyle intervention trials. *American Journal of Epidemiology, 108*, 103–111.

Farquhar, J. W., Fortmann, S. P., Maccoby, N., Haskell, W. I., Williams, P., Flora, J., et al. (1985). The Stanford five-city project: Design and methods. *American Journal of Epidemiology, 122*(2), 323–334.

Farquhar, J. W., Maccoby, N., Wood, P. D., Alexander, J. K., Breitrose, H., Brown, B. W., Jr., et al. (1977). Community education for cardiovascular health. *Lancet, 1*, 1192–1195.

Freud, S. (1960). *The ego and the id.* New York: Norton. (Original work published 1923)

Gilles, D. M., Turk, C. L., & Fresco, D. M. (2006). Social anxiety, alcohol expectancies, and self-efficacy as predictors of heavy drinking in college students. *Addictive Behaviors, 31*(3), 388–398.

Graves, K. D., Carter, C. L., Anderson, E. S., & Winett, R. A. (2003). Quality of life pilot intervention for breast cancer patients: Use of social cognitive theory. *Palliative and Support Care, 1*(2), 121–134.

Greene, B. L., DeJoy, D. M., & Olejnik, S. (2005). Effects of an active ergonomics training program on risk exposure, worker beliefs, and symptoms in computer users. *Work, 24*(1), 41–52.

Griffin-Blake, C. S., & DeJoy, D. M. (2006). Evaluation of social-cognitive versus stage-matched, self-help physical activity interventions at the workplace. *American Journal of Health Promotion, 20*(3), 200–209.

Gritz, E. R., Tripp, M. K., James, A. S., Harris, R. B., Mueller, N. H., Chamberlain, R. M., et al. (2006). Effects of a preschool staff intervention on children's sun protection: Outcomes of Sun Protection Is Fun! *Health Education and Behavior*, Epub. PMID: 16740505.

Gu, X., Zhang, T., & Smith, K. (2015). Psychosocial predictors of female college students' motivational responses: A prospective analysis. *Perceptual and Motor Skills, 120*(3), 700–713. doi: 10.2466/06.PMS.120v19x0.

Ha, B. T., Jayasuriya, R., & Owen, N. (2005). Increasing male involvement in family planning decision making: Trial of a social-cognitive intervention in rural Vietnam. *Health Education Research, 20*(5), 548–556.

Harnirattisai, T., & Johnson, R. A. (2005). Effectiveness of a behavioral change intervention in Thai elders after knee replacement. *Nursing Research, 54*(2), 97–107.

Hay, J. L., Oliveria, S. A., Dusza, S. W., Phelan, D. L., Ostroff, J. S., & Halpern, A. C. (2006). Psychosocial mediators of a nurse intervention to increase skin self-examination in patients at high risk for melanoma. *Cancer Epidemiology Biomarkers and Prevention, 15*(6), 1212–1216.

Heinen, M. M., Bartholomew, L. K., Wensing, M., Kerkhof, P., & Achterberg, T. (2006). Supporting adherence and healthy lifestyles in leg ulcer patients: Systematic development of the Lively Legs program for dermatology outpatient clinics. *Patient Education and Counseling, 61*(2), 279–291.

Hiltunen, E. F., Winder, P. A., Rait, M. A., Buselli, E. F., Carroll, D. L., & Rankin, S. H. (2005). Implementation of efficacy enhancement nursing interventions with cardiac elders. *Rehabilitation Nursing, 30*(6), 221–229.

Honda, K., & Gorin, S. S. (2006). A model of stage of change to recommend colonoscopy among urban primary care physicians. *Health Psychology, 25*(1), 65–73.

Kaewthummanukul, T., Brown, K. C., Weaver, M. T., & Thomas, R. R. (2006). Predictors of exercise participation in female hospital nurses. *Journal of Advanced Nursing, 54*(6), 663–675.

Kalichman, S. C., Cain, D., Fuhrel, A., Eaton, L., Di Fonzo, K., & Ertl, T. (2005). Assessing medication adherence self-efficacy among low-literacy patients: Development of a pictographic visual analogue scale. *Health Education Research, 20*(1), 24–35.

Klohe-Lehman, D. M., Freeland-Graves, J., Anderson, E. R., McDowell, T., Clarke, K. K., Hanss-Nuss, H., et al. (2006). Nutrition knowledge is associated with greater weight loss in obese and overweight low-income mothers. *Journal of American Dietetic Association, 106*(1), 65–75.

Knowlden, A. P., & Sharma, M. (2015). Social cognitive maternal-mediated nutritional correlates of childhood obesity. *International Quarterly of Community Health Education, 35*(2), 177–191. doi: 10.1177/0272684X15569678.

Koniak-Griffin, D., & Stein, J. A. (2006). Predictors of sexual risk behaviors among adolescent mothers in a human immunodeficiency virus prevention program. *Journal of Adolescent Health, 38*(3), 297.e1–11.

Langlois, M. A., Petosa, R., & Hallam, J. S. (1999). Why do effective smoking prevention programs work? Student changes in social cognitive theory constructs. *Journal of School Health, 69*(8), 326–331.

Li, X., Lin, D., Wang, B., Du, H., Tam, C. C., & Stanton, B. (2014). Efficacy of theory-based HIV behavioral prevention among rural-to-urban migrants in China: A randomized controlled trial. *AIDS Education & Prevention, 26*(4), 296–316. doi: 10.1521/aeap.2014.26.4.296.

Lubans, D. R., Smith, J. J., Skinner, G., & Morgan, P. J. (2014). Development and implementation of a smartphone application to promote physical activity and reduce screen-time in adolescent boys. *Frontiers in Public Health, 2*, 42. doi: 10.3389/fpubh.2014.00042.

Luepker, R. V., Murray, D. M., Jacobs, D. R., Mittelmark, M. B., Bracht, N., Carlaw, R., et al. (1994). Community education for cardiovascular disease prevention: Risk factor changes in the Minnesota Heart Health Program. *American Journal of Public Health, 84*, 1383–1393.

Martino, S. C., Collins, R. L., Kanouse, D. E., Elliott, M., & Berry, S. H. (2005). Social cognitive processes mediating the relationship between exposure to television's sexual content and adolescents' sexual behavior. *Journal of Personality and Social Psychology, 89*(6), 914–924.

Mashegoane, S., Moalusi, K. P., Peltzer, K., & Ngoepe, M. A. (2004). The prediction of condom use intention among South African university students. *Psychological Reports, 95*(2), 407–417.

McAlister, A. L., Perry, C. L., & Parcel, G. S. (2008). How individuals, environments, and health behavior interact. Social cognitive theory. In K. Glanz, B. K. Rimer, & K. Viswanath (Eds.), *Health behavior and health education: Theory, research, and practice* (4th ed., pp. 169–188). San Francisco: Jossey-Bass.

McGhan, S. L., Wells, H. M., & Befus, A. D. (1998). The "Roaring Adventures of Puff": A childhood asthma education program. *Journal of Pediatric Health Care, 12*(4), 191–195.

Mouttapa, M., Valente, T., Gallaher, P., Rohrbach, L. A., & Unger, J. B. (2004). Social network predictors of bullying and victimization. *Adolescence, 39*(154), 315–335.

Oliver, K., & Cronan, T. A. (2005). Correlates of physical activity among women with fibromyalgia syndrome. *Annals of Behavioral Medicine, 29*(1), 44–53.

Orpinas, P., & Horne, A. M. (2004). A teacher-focused approach to prevent and reduce students' aggressive behavior: The GREAT Teacher Program. *American Journal of Preventive Medicine, 26*(Suppl. 1), 29–38.

Patten, C. A., Petersen, L. R., Hughes, C. A., Ebbert, J. O., Morgenthaler Bonnema, S., Brockman, T. A., et al. (2009). Feasibility of a telephone-based intervention for support persons to help smokers quit: A pilot study. *Nicotine & Tobacco Research, 11*(4), 427–432.

Peterson, J. J., Suzuki, R., Walsh, E. S., Buckley, D. I., & Krahn, G. L. (2012). Improving cancer screening among women with mobility impairments: Randomized controlled trial of a participatory workshop intervention. *American Journal of Health Promotion, 26*(4), 212–216. doi: 10.4278/ajhp.100701-ARB-226.

Poudel, K. C., Buchanan, D. R., & Poudel-Tandukar, K. (2015). Effects of a community-based HIV risk reduction intervention among HIV-positive individuals: Results of a quasi-experimental study in Nepal. *AIDS Education & Prevention, 27*(3), 240-256. doi: 10.1521/aeap.2015.27.3.240.

Powers, A. R., Struempler, B. J., Guarino, A., & Parmer, S. M. (2005). Effects of a nutrition education program on the dietary behavior and nutrition knowledge of second-grade and third-grade students. *Journal of School Health, 75*(4), 129–133.

Prochaska, J. O. (2006). Is social cognitive theory becoming a transtheoretical model? A comment on Dijkstra et al. (2006). *Addiction, 101*, 916–917.

Ramelson, H. Z., Friedman, R. H., & Ockene, J. K. (1999). An automated telephone-based smoking cessation education and counseling system. *Patient Education and Counseling, 36*(2), 131–144.

Rankins, J., Sampson, W., Brown, B., & Jenkins-Salley, T. (2005). Dietary Approaches to Stop Hypertension (DASH) intervention reduces blood pressure among hypertensive African American patients in a neighborhood health care center. *Journal of Nutrition Education and Behavior, 37*(5), 259–264.

Rhodes, R. E., & Plotnikoff, R. C. (2005). Can current physical activity act as a reasonable proxy measure of future physical activity? Evaluating cross-sectional and passive prospective designs with the use of social cognition models. *Preventive Medicine, 40*(5), 547–555.

Rosal, M. C., Heyden, R., Mejilla, R., Capelson, R., Chalmers, K. A., Rizzo DePaoli, M., et al. (2014). A virtual world versus face-to-face intervention format to promote diabetes self-management among African American women: A pilot randomized clinical trial. *JMIR Research Protocols, 3*(4), e54. doi: 10.2196/resprot.3412.

Rotter, J. B. (1954). *Social learning and clinical psychology.* Englewood Cliffs, NJ: Prentice-Hall.

Rovniak, L. S., Hovell, M. F., Wojcik, J. R., Winett, R. A., & Martinez-Donate, A. P. (2005). Enhancing theoretical fidelity: An e-mail-based walking program demonstration. *American Journal of Health Promotion, 20*(2), 85–95.

Safdie, M., Cargo, M., Richard, L., & Lévesque, L. (2014). An ecological and theoretical deconstruction of a school-based obesity prevention program in Mexico. *International Journal of Behavioral Nutrition & Physical Activity, 11*, 103. doi: 10.1186/s12966-014-0103-2.

Schwartz, L., Howland, M. A., Mercurio-Zappala, M., & Hoffman, R. S. (2003). The use of focus groups to plan poison prevention education programs for low-income populations. *Health Promotion Practice, 4*(3), 340–346.

Sharma, M., & Deepak, S. (2003). An intercountry study of expectations, roles, attitudes and behaviors of community-based rehabilitation volunteers. *Asia Pacific Disability Rehabilitation Journal, 14*, 179–190.

Sharma, M., Mehan, M. B., & Surabhi, S. (2008–2009). Using social cognitive theory to predict obesity prevention behaviors among preadolescents in India. *International Quarterly of Community Health Education, 29*(4), 351–361.

Sharma, M., Petosa, R., & Heaney, C. A. (1999). Evaluation of a brief intervention based on social cognitive theory to develop problem solving skills among sixth grade children. *Health Education and Behavior, 26*, 465–477.

Sharma, M., Wagner, D. I., & Wilkerson, J. (2005–2006). Predicting childhood obesity prevention behaviors using social cognitive theory. *International Quarterly of Community Health Education, 24*(3), 191–203.

Shilts, M. K., Lamp, C., Horowitz, M., & Townsend, M. S. (2009). Pilot study: EatFit impacts sixth graders' academic performance on achievement of mathematics and English education standards. *Journal of Nutrition Education & Behavior, 41*(2), 127–131.

Shimazu, A., Kawakami, N., Irimajiri, H., Sakamoto, M., & Amano, S. (2005). Effects of Web-based psychoeducation on self-efficacy, problem solving behavior, stress responses and job satisfaction among workers: A controlled clinical trial. *Journal of Occupational Health, 47*(5), 405–413.

Skinner, B. F. (1953). *Science and human behavior.* New York: Macmillan.

Stalvey, B. T., & Owsley, C. (2003). The development and efficacy of a theory-based educational curriculum to promote self-regulation among high-risk older drivers. *Health Promotion Practice, 4*(2), 109–119.

Stepnowsky, C. J., Marler, M. R., Palau, J., & Annette Brooks, J. (2006). Social-cognitive correlates of CPAP adherence in experienced users. *Sleep Medicine, 7*(4), 350–356.

Suminski, R. R., & Petosa, R. (2006). Web-assisted instruction for changing social cognitive variables related to physical activity. *Journal of American College Health, 54*(4), 219–225.

Tavares, L. S., Plotnikoff, R. C., & Loucaides, C. (2009). Social-cognitive theories for predicting physical activity behaviours of employed women with and without young children. *Psychology, Health, & Medicine, 14*(2), 129–142.

Taylor, C. L., Demoor, C., Smith, M. A., Dunn, A. L., Basen-Engquist, K., Nielsen, I., et al. (2006). Active for Life After Cancer: A randomized trial examining a lifestyle physical activity program for prostate cancer patients. *Psychooncology, 15*(10), 847–862.

Tufano, J. T., & Karras, B. T. (2005). Mobile eHealth interventions for obesity: A timely opportunity to leverage convergence trends. *Journal of Medical Internet Research, 7*(5), e58.

Wang, S. L., Charron-Prochownik, D., Sereika, S. M., Siminerio, L., & Kim, Y. (2006). Comparing three theories in predicting reproductive health behavioral intention in adolescent women with diabetes. *Pediatric Diabetes, 7*(2), 108–115.

Yoon, H. J., & Tourassi. G. (2014). Analysis of online social networks to understand information sharing behaviors through social cognitive theory. *Annual ORNL Biomedical Science and Engineering Center Conference*, 2014. doi: 10.1109/BSEC.2014.6867744.

Young, D. R., Haskell, W. L., Jatulis, D. E., & Fortmann, S. P. (1993). Associations between changes in physical activity and risk factors for coronary heart disease in a community-based sample of men and women: The Stanford five-city project. *American Journal of Epidemiology, 138*, 205–216.

SOCIAL MARKETING

Chapter 8

KEY CONCEPTS

- audience segmentation
- exchange theory
- marketing mix
- partnership
- place
- policy
- price
- product
- promotion
- publics
- purse strings
- social marketing

AFTER READING THIS CHAPTER YOU SHOULD BE ABLE TO

- Describe the historical genesis of social marketing
- List the constructs of social marketing
- Differentiate between commercial marketing and social marketing
- Summarize the applications of social marketing in health education and health promotion
- Identify key constructs from the social marketing model
- Apply the social marketing model to influence a health behavior of your choice

This chapter discusses the social marketing model. **Social marketing** is the use of commercial marketing techniques to help a target population acquire a beneficial health behavior (Weinreich, 2011). Social marketing has become a popular choice for influencing behavior in both the government and not-for-profit sectors in the United States and in many other countries around the world. In the field of health, some important applications of social marketing include family planning, recruiting blood donors, reducing infant mortality through oral rehydration, promoting dental sealants, campaigns against skin cancer, promoting insecticide-treated nets in Africa, and preventing smoking in adolescents (Andreasen & Kotler, 2008). The foundational pillar of the marketing concept is a "customer-centered mindset" that forces planners to identify and satisfy the needs and wants of the target audiences (Lee & Kotler, 2015). The primary difference between social marketing and commercial marketing is in their objectives. In social marketing, the primary purpose is to benefit the target audience and change behaviors that have social implications.

This chapter begins by describing the historical aspects of the genesis of social marketing. Next, we delineate the differences between commercial marketing and social marketing and describe the social marketing approach and the various constructs that make up this model. We then discuss applications of social marketing in health education and health promotion. Finally, we outline the limitations of social marketing and present a skill-building application.

HISTORICAL PERSPECTIVE

Social marketing had its origins in India, where it was used in the 1960s to promote a family planning program, particularly the use of condoms (Harvey, 1999). The process entailed subsidizing condoms and supplying them through existing commercial distribution networks, using the mass media, and using other retail marketing techniques (Thapa, Prasad, Rao, Severy, & Rao, 1994). Partnerships were formed with corporations such as Unilever and Brooke Bond Tea Company to market the Nirodh brand of condoms. Under the program, condoms sales exceeded one billion by the mid-1990s, a multifold increase from the initial years of the program. This continues to be one of the largest applications of social marketing in the world, and the program has been expanded to include other products such as oral contraceptives, oral rehydration solution, iron folate, and female condoms.

> Social marketing is the application of commercial marketing techniques to the analysis, planning, execution, and evaluation of programs designed to influence the voluntary behavior of target audiences in order to improve their personal welfare and that of their society.
>
> —Andreasen (1995, p. 7)

In the 1950s, U.S. sociologist G. D. Wiebe (1951–1952) first suggested that marketing might be applied to "selling brotherhood" and other social ideas. This suggestion was incorporated in the work of Philip Kotler in the late 1960s. Kotler and Levy (1969) suggested that marketing was a pervasive societal activity that included all transactions. Kotler and Zaltman (1971) first defined social marketing as "the design, implementation, and control of programs calculated to influence the acceptability of social ideas and involving considerations of product planning, pricing, communication, distribution, and marketing research" (p. 5). However, interest in social marketing was lukewarm throughout the 1970s and most of the 1980s (Andreasen, 2003). The main type of social marketing that occurred was marketing of contraceptives, in which the product was just like a product in commercial marketing and a nominal price was involved. Not much marketing of ideas was done.

Social marketing made major advancements in the late 1980s and throughout the 1990s. In 1989, the first textbook on social marketing was published by Kotler and Roberto. They defined social marketing as a "social change technology involving the design, implementation, and control of programs aimed at increasing the acceptability of a social idea or practice in one or more groups of target adopters" (p. 24), thus placing social marketing in synchrony with health education and health promotion. In 1988 in Australia, an antitobacco campaign ("Quit") and a campaign against skin cancer ("Sun Smart") based on social marketing were launched (Elliott, 1991). In 1995, Andreasen defined social marketing as "the application of commercial marketing techniques to the analysis, planning, execution, and evaluation of programs designed to influence the voluntary behavior of target audiences in order to improve their personal welfare and that of their society" (p. 7). This definition brought the idea closer to health education and health promotion, where the purpose is also behavior change.

In 1994, the journal *Social Marketing Quarterly* was founded, and the Social Marketing Institute was founded in Washington, D.C., in 1999. The mission of the institute was to advance the science and art of social marketing. Some of the major social marketing initiatives in the 1990s were the U.S. Department of Agriculture's 5-a-Day campaign; the Centers for Disease Control and Prevention's campaign to inform health care professionals and the public that stomach ulcers were caused by the bacterium *Helicobacter pylori* and could be cured with antibiotics; North Carolina's statewide seat belt enforcement campaign, the "Click It or Ticket" program, which is still in use in other states; and a national breast-feeding promotional campaign through the Women, Infants, and Children (WIC) program (Social Marketing Institute, 2006).

In *Social Marketing in the 21st Century* Alan Andreasen (2006) laments that at present social marketing is in danger of being "pigeonholed as a downstream approach." He believes that most social marketing applications are geared toward rectifying bad behaviors, such as smoking, neglecting prenatal care, and so on. As a result, opportunities to use social marketing to foster positive behaviors are being lost. In any case, the social marketing approach is quite strong, as is evidenced by the growing number of publications and diverse applications using this model. The latest trends in social marketing involve use of the Internet including online surveys and social media.

> **Social marketing consists of a voluntary exchange between two or more parties, in which each is trying to further its own perceived self-interest while recognizing the need to accommodate the perceived self-interest of the other to achieve its own ends.**
>
> —Rothschild (1999)

DIFFERENCES BETWEEN COMMERCIAL MARKETING AND SOCIAL MARKETING

The primary difference between social marketing and commercial marketing is in their objectives. In social marketing, the primary purpose is to benefit the target audience and change behaviors that have social implications. Andreasen and Kotler (2008) have identified additional differences between commercial marketing and social marketing (**Table 8-1**). The expectations in social

Table 8-1	Differences Between Commercial Marketing and Social Marketing	
Attribute	**Commercial Marketing**	**Social Marketing**
Purpose	Making profits	Making behavior change for social causes
Expectations	Modest	Demanding, such as complete eradication of a problem or universal adoption of a behavior
Scrutiny	Usually done in the private sector	Done from a variety of sources: government, public, and funders
Novelty	Usually selling a known product	Sometimes selling an idea that is totally new (e.g., bacteria cause ulcers)
Education level	Variable and includes different sections	Usually vulnerable sections of audiences with low literacy
Distasteful behaviors	Usually caters to what public likes	Often has to address what people do not want to change (e.g., wearing a seat belt)
Involvement between marketer and public	Little	Often very high
Benefits	Clear in profits	Often invisible
Third parties	Direct benefits to people using the product	Often the benefits are to third parties, such as poor people
Self-rewards	Usually the rewards are external (e.g., discount better product)	Usually the rewards offered are internal or self-rewards (e.g., weight loss)
Budgets	Generous	Limited
Funding	Usually private	Usually government or not-for-profit foundations
Choices of products	Numerous	Limited

marketing are more demanding, the scrutiny is done from a variety of sources, the idea that is sold is often totally new, and the educational level of the target audience is usually low. Social marketing often has to address what people do not want to change, has a high level of involvement between the marketer and the public, and often has invisible benefits or benefits that go to third parties. The rewards offered for making the recommended change are usually self-rewards, and budgets and the choice of products are limited.

APPROACH AND CONSTRUCTS OF SOCIAL MARKETING

A core concept in marketing is developed in **exchange theory** (Thackeray & Brown, 2005). Exchange theory implies the transfer or transaction of something valuable between two individuals or groups (Flora, Schooler, & Pierseon, 1997). In social marketing, this transaction is voluntary and must be of benefit to the consumer (Lefebvre & Flora, 1988). The target audience must view the benefits as outweighing the costs for making the behavior change. For example, in a health promotion program that encourages participants to engage in physical activity, the costs to individuals would be loss of free time, loss of time to watch television, and so on. The benefits the social marketer offers must be more appealing than these losses, such as more energy to do things, the ability to lose weight, and so on.

There is no universal consensus regarding the social marketing model among social marketing professionals. Various authors have described different steps in social marketing. For example, Andreasen (1995) has defined six stages:

1. *Listening stage.* Background analysis and listening to the target audience.
2. *Planning stage.* The marketing mission, objectives, goals, and strategy are defined.
3. *Structuring stage.* A marketing organization, procedures, benchmarks, and feedback mechanisms are established.
4. *Pretesting stage.* Key program elements are tested.
5. *Implementing stage.* The strategy is put into effect.
6. *Monitoring stage.* Program progress is tracked.

Andreasen notes that the movement across these six stages is not linear but is an upward spiral process. The target audience is central in this planning process.

The National Cancer Institute (2005) has suggested four steps in a wheel of planning for social marketing: (1) planning and strategy development; (2) developing and pretesting concepts, messages, and materials; (3) implementing the program; and (4) assessing effectiveness and making refinements. The wheel of planning signifies that it is a cyclical process whereby assessment of effectiveness feeds right back into the planning and strategy development step to constantly improve the social marketing campaign.

Weinreich (2011) has described a somewhat similar sequence of five steps: (1) planning, (2) message and material development, (3) pretesting, (4) implementation, and (5) evaluation. The first step, planning, entails four components: formative research, analysis, segmenting the target audience, and strategy development. **Formative research** involves collecting quantitative and qualitative data about the problem, its context, the attitudes and behaviors of the target audience, ways to reach the target audience, and existing messages and materials. In the analysis component, the problem, environment, and resources available for the program are analyzed. In **audience segmentation**, distinct groups of people who are similar to each other in particular characteristics and are thus likely to respond to messages in a similar way are identified. Segments may be based on such factors as geography, demography, medical history, personality characteristics, attitudes, behaviors, and so on. After identifying the segments, data about the target audience's knowledge, attitudes, and behavior is collected. Qualitative methods such as focus groups, in-depth interviews, and case studies or quantitative methods such as surveys are used in this component. These days, online surveys using Survey Monkey or Qualtrics and others are becoming popular in formative research. Survey Monkey, for example, is a survey builder tool that helps one develop simple or sophisticated surveys for online administration (mobile, Web, or social media) and data collection. The survey questions can be multiple choice, rating scales, comments/essay box questions, demographic questions, and other types. The results are easy to obtain and have presentation-ready charts and reports. One can also buy respondents of different target groups from their pool of respondents. You can develop and administer a brief survey for free at www.surveymonkey.com or subscribe for more elaborate surveys. Another survey builder is Qualtrics, which can be accessed at www.qualtrics.com/. The fourth component in the first step is *strategy development*, in which the goals and objectives are set and the social marketing mix is chosen. In marketing, the four Ps that define the **marketing mix** are product, price, place, and promotion. Weinreich (1999) has defined four additional Ps for social marketing: publics, partnership, policy, and purse strings.

The first P is **product**. In social marketing, the product is the behavior or offering that is intended to be adopted by the target audience. The product can be a physical product, such as condoms; a service, such as mammography; a practice, such as eating five or more servings of fruits and vegetables a day; or an intangible idea, such as environmental protection. The product must be able to fill a need felt by people and must be appealing and attractive. It is important to link potential benefits and subsequent benefits to the product, thereby making it attractive to the target audience. It is also important to find out about competing ideas (products) and to explain why the target audience would prefer the product being socially marketed. For example, if one were marketing physical activity, the competition would be from sedentary activities such as watching television or surfing the Internet. Knowing the competition allows one to plan counterarguments.

Price refers to the tangible and intangible things that the target audience has to give up in order to adopt the new idea (product). The price could be money, which is tangible, but often it is an intangible cost such as time, effort, or giving up an old way of life. Formative research should discover what the target audience considers to be the price for adopting the new behavior. This research should include an assessment of all barriers that confront the target population. Ways to minimize the costs and remove barriers must be considered in designing the strategy.

In commercial marketing, **place** refers to the distribution channels, or where and how customers will get the product. In social marketing, place refers to where the target audience will be exposed to messages about the behavior. For example, if we were advocating physical activity, we would need to determine whether the message would be delivered at the home of the person by a television spot, a newspaper article, or through the Internet. The message could also be given at the workplace, either on a bulletin board or by e-mail. The message could be given in community forums, such as the grocery store, local church, community center, or doctor's office. Messages need to be targeted to a particular place to be effective. Along with the messages, the product (idea or behavior) should be made available at that particular place. For example, if physical activity is to be done at home, then a stationary bike or treadmill should be available so the person can exercise while watching television. Distribution channels, or who will deliver the message, need to be decided. For example, if we want to promote physical activity, we could use a peer-to-peer network or counseling sessions through phone calls from the doctor's office.

Promotion is the mechanism by which one gets the message across to the target audience. Various techniques are used. Examples are advertisements, such as public service announcements (PSAs); public relations, such as writing letters to the editor or creating press releases; promotions, such as having a contest; media advocacy, such as holding a press event for policy change; personal selling, such as having a counseling session; special events, such as organizing a health fair; and entertainment, such as organizing a psychodrama.

The fifth P, **publics**, refers to both the primary and secondary audiences involved in the program. The primary audience is the target audience to whom the behavior change is targeted. In making their decisions, the members of the primary target audience may depend on other people. For example, in a smoking prevention program for adolescents, their parents, peers, and teachers would all be secondary audiences who need to provide the same messages. Policy makers are another secondary group that influences any decision and needs to be involved.

Partnership refers to collaborating with multiple individuals or organizations who work on the same issue. No single organization has sufficient resources to significantly influence the huge outcome usually expected in social marketing. As a result, it makes sense for different organizations to form a coalition around the issue and then target it from different angles. Such collaborations can occur if two organizations either share the same goal or share the same target population.

Policy refers to creating the environmental supports needed to sustain the behavior change. For example, for promoting five or more servings of fruits and vegetables policies must be in place that allow vending machines to dispense such items and that make fruits and vegetables available at affordable rates. Some effective approaches for modifying policies are techniques such as advocacy, media advocacy, lobbying, and working with policy makers or legislators.

The final P is the **purse strings**, which refers to the amount of money available for the campaign. In social marketing, there is no profit to sustain the efforts. All efforts in social marketing depend on resources in the form of donations or grants; therefore, grant writing is an important aspect of running a social marketing campaign. Other sources of funding, including selling a tangible product, also must be considered. **Table 8-2** summarizes the eight Ps of social marketing, and **Figure 8-1** illustrates the social marketing model.

The second step in social marketing is *message and materials development*. This step has three components: identifying appropriate channels, developing effective messages, and developing creative strategy. Identifying appropriate channels entails identifying where the target population will be performing the behavior (place) and then matching the channels. For example, if physical activity is to be performed at community centers, then the channels of health fairs at the community center, community center newsletter announcements, billboard announcements, and so on need to be organized. The step of developing effective messages needs to use some of the behavioral theories elaborated in this book, such as the health belief model, transtheoretical model, theory of reasoned action, theory of planned behavior, social cognitive theory, and the diffusion of innovations model. Developing creative strategy entails being creative in packaging the set of messages and materials.

The third step in social marketing is *pretesting*. Some of the aspects that need to be checked while pretesting the materials are their acceptability by the target audience, attractiveness to the target population, comprehension by the target population, completeness, and appropriateness for the target population. Techniques such as focus groups, nominal groups, central location interviews, questionnaires, and expert review can be used.

Table 8-2	Key Constructs of Social Marketing	
Construct	**Definition**	**How to Modify?**
Product	Behavior or offering that is intended for the target audience to adopt	• Match with a need felt by the target audience • Make it appealing and attractive • Link potential benefits and subsequent benefits to the product • Find out about the competing ideas (products) and why the target audience would prefer the product being socially marketed
Price	Tangible and intangible things that the target audience has to give up in order to adopt the new idea (product)	• Find ways to minimize the costs • Find ways to eliminate barriers
Place	Where the target audience will perform the behavior	• Target messages at the particular place where the behavior will be performed • Make the product (idea or behavior) available at that particular place • Choose appropriate distribution channels or who will deliver the message
Promotion	Mechanism by which one gets the message across to the target audience	• Advertising • Public relations • Promotions • Media advocacy • Personal selling • Special events • Entertainment
Publics	Primary and secondary audiences involved in the program	• Involve primary audiences • Involve secondary audiences
Partnership	Establish collaboration with multiple individuals or organizations who work on the same issue	• Build coalitions
Policy	Create the environmental supports needed to sustain the behavior change	• Advocate, lobby, and create policies regarding the issue
Purse strings	Amount of money available for the campaign	• Write grants • Sell a tangible product

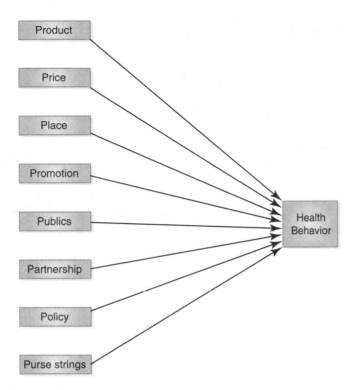

FIGURE 8-1 The social marketing model.

The fourth step in social marketing is *implementation*, in which the strategy is put into action. All the logistic arrangements are put into test during this stage. The logistics include the costs of the program, the human resources involved in the program, and all the materials needed for the program. Usual costs in social marketing campaigns include costs associated with advertising of the program, such as through television, newspaper, radio, billboards, social media, road signs, signage at institutions, operation of toll-free lines, and so on. The human resources include both the paid staff and volunteers. The human resources need to be constantly monitored during the social marketing campaign, and assistance/support must be provided to them.

The final stage is *evaluation*. A variety of designs and methods can be used in the evaluation step, such as a posttest-only design, a single-group pretest/posttest design, a quasi-experimental design, or an experimental design with a randomized control group. In terms of methods for data collection, self-reports as well as observational methods can be effective.

> **Social Marketing is a larger idea than social promotion and advertising. We need to highlight the importance of the other three Ps, product, price, and place, in determining whether a social marketing campaign will be successful. We must add the idea that client behavior analysis, segmentation, and positioning are critical concepts in developing our social marketing approach.**
>
> —Kotler (2005, p. 147)

APPLICATIONS OF SOCIAL MARKETING

Social marketing has been used in a variety of applications in health education and health promotion. These applications include antitobacco campaigns (Fallin, Neilands, Jordan, Hong, & Ling, 2015, Lin, & Hullman, 2005; Perusco et al., 2010), a campaign to improve antibiotic use (Goossens et al., 2006), campaigns to reduce the stigma of mental illness (Corrigan & Gelb, 2006; Evans-Lacko et al., 2013), a community-wide physical activity campaign (Reger-Nash et al., 2006; Rissel et al., 2010), designing a cancer prevention program (Miner, White, Lubenow, & Palmer, 2005; Sinclair & Foley, 2009), diabetes prevention programs (Bachar et al., 2006; HEALTHY study group et al., 2009), an educational program aimed at improving prescribing for hypertension (Horn et al., 2006), family health advocacy for pregnant and parenting women (Baffour, Jones, & Contreras, 2006), health coaching in a worksite wellness program (LeCheminant & Merrill, 2102), increasing cervical cancer screening (Bethune & Lewis, 2009; Millett, Zelenyanszki, Furlong, & Binysh, 2005), increasing condom use (Farris, Aquilino, Batra, Marshall, & Losch, 2015; Meekers, Agha, & Klein, 2005; Piot et al., 2010), increasing female condom use (Bull et al., 2008; Meekers & Richter, 2005), increasing syphilis awareness (Stephens, Bernstein, McCright, & Klausner, 2010; Vega & Roland, 2005), increasing use of bicycle helmets (Ludwig, Buchholz, & Clarke, 2005), iron-folic acid supplementation in Cambodian women (Crape et al., 2005), leprosy elimination in Sri Lanka (Williams, Dewapura, Gunawardene, & Settinayake, 1998), nutrition education in preschoolers (Young, Anderson, Beckstrom, Bellows, & Johnson, 2004), physical activity promotion in adolescent girls (Staten, Birnbaum, Jobe, & Elder, 2006), promoting human papillomavirus (HPV) vaccination (Cates & Coyne-Beasley, 2015), promoting insecticide-treated nets in Africa (De Allegri et al., 2010; Maxwell, Rwegoshora, Magesa, & Curtis, 2006), promoting iron nutrition for at-risk infants (Verrall, Napash, Leclerc, Mercure, & Gray-Donald, 2006), promoting preconceptional use of folic acid (Quinn, Hauser, Bell-Ellison, Rodriguez, & Frias, 2006), recruiting men who have sex with men for HIV research (Silvestre et al., 2006), reducing adolescent dating violence (Lambert, Bishop, Guetig, & Frew, 2014), reducing marijuana and alcohol use among adolescents (Slater et al., 2006), a self-help weight management intervention (Tufano & Karras, 2005), and a tractor rollover protection structure (ROPS) campaign (Sorensen, Jenkins, Bayes, Clark, & May, 2010). **Table 8-3** summarizes these applications.

> **For decades the health sector has watched as big companies have used marketing to wreak havoc on public health. Social marketing enables us to fight fire with fire.**
>
> —Hastings and McDermott (2006, p. 1212)

LIMITATIONS OF SOCIAL MARKETING

Social marketing is a useful model that is still being refined. There are definite advantages to this approach, such as extensive formative research, pretesting of the components before implementation, and the use of the marketing mix. However, like all other models and theories, social marketing has some limitations. First, in public health, the goal is to reach as many people as possible; however, in social marketing, audience segmentation and the use of tailored messages filter out

Table 8-3	Applications of the Social Marketing Model in Health Education and Health Promotion
Antitobacco campaigns	
Campaign to improve antibiotic use	
Campaign to reduce the stigma of mental illness	
Community-wide physical activity campaign	
Designing cancer prevention programs	
Diabetes prevention program	
Educational program aimed at improving prescribing for hypertension	
Family health advocacy for pregnant and parenting women	
Health coaching in a worksite wellness program	
Increasing cervical cancer screening	
Increasing condom use	
Increasing female condom use	
Increasing syphilis awareness	
Increasing use of bicycle helmets	
Iron-folic acid supplementation in Cambodian women	
Leprosy elimination in Sri Lanka	
Nutrition education in preschoolers	
Physical activity promotion in adolescent girls	
Promoting human papillomavirus (HPV) vaccination	
Promoting insecticide-treated nets in Africa	
Promoting iron nutrition for at-risk infants	
Promoting preconception use of folic acid	
Recruiting men who have sex with men for HIV research	
Reducing adolescent dating violence	
Reducing marijuana and alcohol use among adolescents	
Self-help weight management intervention	
Tractor rollover protection structure (ROPS) campaign	

many people who may be in need of the services or behavior change. Second, social marketing requires a lot of lead time for extensive formative research and pretesting (Marshall, Bryant, Keller, & Fridinger, 2006). Often the program planners do not have that much time and need to implement the intervention faster; they also often do not have the resources to expend on preplanning.

Social marketing has been labeled "motivational manipulation," especially by thinkers from third world countries (Banerji, 1986). Delivery of health education programs as social marketing campaigns that rely on technomanagerial approaches often drains resources that could be used to build the basic infrastructure in developing countries. Sometimes the solutions advocated by social marketing in these situations are Band-Aid solutions that do not address the root causes and do not involve community participation. Almost always, the social marketer decides what behaviors will constitute improvement; community members do not have much say. This unequal playing field between marketers and the public poses ethical dilemmas as well (Grier & Bryant, 2005).

> Social marketing needs to be marketed to major social action groups, both governmental and nongovernmental, so that these groups will seek more social marketing consultants and offer more funding for social marketing campaigns. This will convince marketing students and marketing professionals that they can find a challenging and remunerative career in social marketing.
>
> —Kotler (2005, p. 147)

Andreasen (2006) noted that social marketing as an approach to social change lacks clarity. There are multiple definitions, the field is not well differentiated and lacks academic stature, and there is a lack of appreciation of social marketing at top levels. These observations are based on empirical research from more than 300 personal interviews, 100 field questionnaires, and two focus groups conducted by Social Marketing Institute researchers.

Social marketing is more effective for behaviors that need to be changed once or only a few times, but is less effective for behaviors that must be repeated and maintained over a period of time (Evans, 2006). Finally, Peattie and Peattie (2003) noted that social marketing depends too much on commercial marketing for its theoretical underpinnings and must formulate its own theoretical basis. They suggested that the four Ps be renamed as follows: social proposition (product), costs (price), accessibility (place), and communication (promotion).

APPLICATION EXERCISE

In this chapter we have provided several examples of applications of the social marketing model. Choose an area that interests you and locate the full-text article of that application. You will be able to see how social marketing has been applied in that application. One such example is the study by Rissel and colleagues (2010), who developed, implemented, and evaluated the Cycling Connecting Communities (CCC) project in Sydney, Australia. The project was based on the social marketing model. It utilized various techniques such as organizing bike rides and related events, teaching courses for cycling skills, distributing cycling maps of the area to residents, and covering cycling events in the local press. For evaluation they employed a quasi-experimental design. Pre- and postintervention telephone surveys with an interval of 24 months were administered to experimental group residents in Fairfield and Liverpool and to a demographically similar comparison group in Bankstown. The results demonstrated statistically significant ($p \leq 0.05$) awareness levels of the Cycling Connecting Communities project in the experimental group (13.5%) as compared to the comparison group (8.0%). The rates of cycling in the experimental group (32.9%) were also significantly higher than those in the comparison group (9.7%). The bicycle paths were used more by the experimental group (28.3%) than by the comparison group (16.2%), which was also statistically significant (p ≤0.05). This study shows how a project based on the social marketing model can successfully influence health behaviors.

Locate the full-text article of this study and prepare a critique of 250 words. Pay attention to the steps of social marketing—which steps were implemented and to what extent. Look at the evaluation step more closely. What design was used, what methods were used for data collection, and what methods were used for data analysis? Examine the threats to internal and external validity in data interpretation.

SKILL-BUILDING ACTIVITY

Let us see how we can apply the social marketing model to the issue of promoting physical activity among middle-aged women. Let us assume that formative research and audience segmentation have identified the target audience as African American women. **Figure 8-2** provides a diagrammatic depiction of the application of social marketing to this example.

The first construct that needs to be determined is product. We need to articulate a specific behavior, which could be defined as 30 minutes of moderate-intensity physical activity on at least five days a week (preferably all days). Some activities that might appeal to this audience are brisk walking, doing yard work, swimming, riding a bicycle, and dancing. A brief message that could appeal is "Work out for 30 minutes a day." The message would need to be pretested and refined with the members of the target audience.

The second construct that needs to be reified is price. Modification of costs and barriers needs to be done. Some potential costs are time, child care, health club dues, discomfort, and missing a favorite TV show. These could be countered by emphasizing that the activity takes only 30 minutes, initially reimbursing child care costs, offering a subsidized fee for health clubs or finding activities that can be done at home, clarifying that discomfort disappears with regular activity, and designing activities around the TV. Some potential barriers include lack of motivation, lack of skills, having no one to exercise with, and unsafe neighborhoods. These could be countered by having self-rewards, providing free lessons, having participants exercise in pairs or with a peer or a spouse, and stressing that participants should exercise at times when and places where it is safe.

The place for giving out the message could be at home through television, newspapers, or the Internet. Or it could be at the workplace through a bulletin board, e-mail, or a supervisor's memo. It could also be community outlets such as a grocery store, shopping mall, church, community center, or doctor's office. Community outlets, especially churches or community centers, are generally good choices for this target audience.

Promotion can be done through a billboard campaign in the community that shows the message "Work out for 30 minutes a day" and the image of an African American woman engaged in physical activity. Additional promotion can be done through a press release for all community outlets, such as newspapers, television channels, and radio shows. In addition, a walking club can be formed and promoted in the community. A community-based event such as a health fair can be used to launch the walking club.

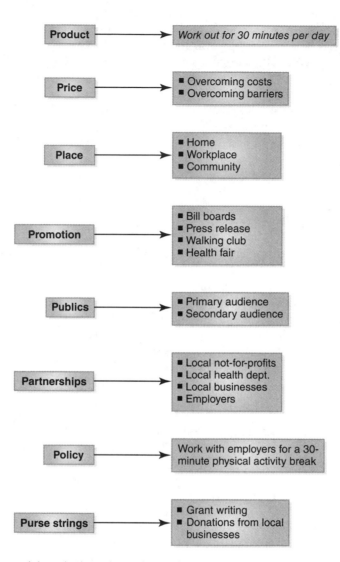

FIGURE 8-2 How the social marketing mix can be used to promote physical activity.

The fifth construct is publics. The primary audience for this campaign would be African American women, who would be targeted with the message. The secondary audience would be peers and spouses, who would need to be mobilized to help participants adhere to the physical activity routine.

To modify the construct of partnership, the organization initiating this program would need to work with local nonprofit agencies, such as the American Heart Association, American Cancer Society, local health department, local businesses, employers, and local gyms. Ideally, a coalition could be formed to which everyone could contribute systematically.

To modify policy, if feasible, the organization can work with employers to allow time for being physically active while at work. For example, a break of 30 minutes can be given to women for walking while they are at the office. The final construct is purse strings, which would involve the organization writing a grant to obtain funding. In-kind donations from local businesses can also be obtained.

Using this approach, you can plan to work on designing a social marketing–based campaign for a health behavior issue in a target audience of your choice. **Table 8-4** provides a set of questions to assist you in shaping the constructs of the social marketing mix.

Table 8-4	Shaping the Constructs of the Social Marketing Mix for Health Education Program Planning

1. What should be considered while developing the product?
   - One-time behavior or continuing behavior
   - Low-involvement behavior or high-involvement behavior
   - Individual decision involved in behavior or group decision involved in behavior
   - Creativity of the message
   - Appeal of the message
   - Attractiveness of the message

2. What should be considered while developing the price?
   - Costs
   - Ways to counteract costs
   - Barriers
   - Ways to counteract barriers

3. What should be considered while developing the place?
   - Home avenues
     - Television
     - Newspaper
     - Mail
     - Internet
   - Community avenues
     - Supermarkets
     - Shopping malls
     - Community centers
     - Churches
   - Workplace avenues
     - Bulletin boards
     - E-mail
     - Memos
   - Other avenues

(continues)

Table 8-4	Shaping the Constructs of the Social Marketing Mix for Health Education Program Planning (*continued*)

4. What should be considered while developing the promotion?
   - Advertising options
   - Public relations opportunities
   - Promotional avenues
   - Media advocacy opportunities
   - Personal selling options
   - Special events
   - Entertainment events

5. What should be considered while developing the publics?
   - Primary audience delineation
   - Secondary audience delineation

6. What should be considered while developing the partnerships?
   - Local health department
   - Local not-for-profit organizations working on same or similar topics
   - Local not-for-profit organizations working with same target audience
   - Local businesses
   - Other

7. What should be considered while developing the policy?
   - Agenda framing
   - Identifying policy makers
   - Opportunities to meet policy makers and legislators
   - Other

8. What should be considered while developing the purse strings?
   - Grant writing
   - Donations from local businesses
   - Selling tangible products
   - Other

 **SUMMARY**

Social marketing is the use of commercial marketing techniques to help a target population acquire a beneficial health behavior. Social marketing had its origins in India in the 1960s for promoting the family planning program by marketing condoms. In the United States the approach began to be used in the 1970s; it is at present a useful technique for behavior change.

Social marketing differs from commercial marketing in that social marketing is more demanding, the scrutiny is done from a variety of sources, the idea that is sold is often totally new, and the educational level of the target audience is usually low. Also, social marketing often has to address what people do not want to change, has high involvement between the marketer and the public, and often has invisible benefits or benefits that go to third parties. The rewards offered for making the recommended change are self-rewards, and budgets and the choice of products are limited. A salient concept in social marketing is that of exchange theory, which implies the voluntary transfer or transaction of something valuable between two parties. The benefits to the consumer must be underscored.

Social marketing goes through five steps: (1) planning, (2) message and material development, (3) pretesting, (4) implementation, and (5) evaluation. In planning, audience segmentation and marketing mix are important. In audience segmentation, distinct groups of people who are similar to each other in particular characteristics and are thus likely to respond to messages in a similar way are identified. In marketing mix, the product (behavior), price (costs and barriers), place, and promotion are considered. Social marketing adds a further four Ps: publics, partnership, policy, and purse strings. The social marketing model has been widely applied in health education and health promotion programs.

IMPORTANT TERMS

audience segmentation	price
exchange theory	product
formative research	promotion
marketing mix	publics
partnership	purse strings
place	social marketing
policy	

REVIEW QUESTIONS

1. Describe the historical genesis of social marketing.
2. Differentiate between social marketing and commercial marketing.
3. Define audience segmentation.
4. Describe the constructs of the social marketing model.
5. Apply the social marketing model to influence a health behavior of your choice.
6. Discuss the limitations of the social marketing model.

WEBSITES TO EXPLORE

Centers for Disease Control & Prevention (CDC): Health Information Campaigns

www.cdc.gov/healthmarketing/

This is the website of the Centers for Disease Control and Prevention (CDC), which documents several health communication campaigns, including the Act Against AIDS campaign for

HIV/AIDS prevention; the Get Smart campaign for appropriate antibiotic use; the One Test Two Lives campaign for testing for HIV in pregnancy; the Prevention Is Care campaign for preventing transmission by HIV-infected persons; the Choose Your Cover campaign, a skin cancer prevention and education campaign; and many others. *Read at least two accounts and comment on the extent of the application of the social marketing model.*

How Social Marketing Works in Health Care

www.ncbi.nlm.nih.gov/pmc/articles/PMC1463924/

This website presents a 2006 article on how social marketing works in health care written by W. Douglas Evans for the *British Medical Journal*. *Read this article and summarize what you learned in a one-page paper.*

Social Marketing.com

www.social-marketing.com/

This website was developed and is maintained by Nedra Kline Weinreich, the author of *Hands-On Social Marketing: A Step-by-Step Guide to Designing Change for Good*. The website links to workshops she conducts, her book, several articles about social marketing, other social marketing and health websites, and her contact information. *Review this website and explore the links mentioned here. Document at least two new ideas you learned about social marketing.*

Social Marketing for Leprosy

www.novartisfoundation.org

The website maintained by the Novartis Foundation for Sustainable Development discusses various issues and applications related to social marketing. In the website's search engine, type "social marketing" and read several articles including those about interrupting leprosy transmission in Asia, Africa, and Latin America and the "Let's talk about hypertension" campaign in low- and middle-income countries. *Summarize how social marketing was able to interrupt leprosy transmission.*

Social Marketing Listserv

listproc@listproc.georgetown.edu

This listserv is maintained at Georgetown University by Dr. Alan Andreasen for people with an interest in social marketing. *If you are interested in sharing information, asking questions, or offering comments on social marketing, please feel free to send them to this group.*

Social Marketing and Public Health

www.youtube.com/watch?v=QtBTVE7ewVA

This is a 14-minute video that talks about social marketing in public health using PowerPoint slides by Ashley Johnston. It reinforces some of the concepts presented in this book. *Watch this video. Summarize the uses of social marketing and social media in public health.*

REFERENCES

Andreasen, A. A. (1995). *Marketing social change: Changing behavior to promote health, social development, and the environment*. San Francisco: Jossey-Bass.

Andreasen, A. A. (2003). The life trajectory of social marketing. Some implications. *Marketing Theory, 3*(3), 293–303.

Andreasen, A. A. (2006). *Social marketing in the 21st century*. Thousand Oaks, CA: Sage.

Andreasen, A. R., & Kotler, P. (2008). *Strategic marketing for non-profit organizations* (7th ed.). Upper Saddle River, NJ: Prentice-Hall.

Bachar, J. J., Lefler, L. J., Reed, L., McCoy, T., Bailey, R., & Bell, R. (2006). Cherokee Choices: A diabetes prevention program for American Indians. *Preventing Chronic Disease, 3*(3), A103.

Baffour, T. D., Jones, M. A., & Contreras, L. K. (2006). Family health advocacy: An empowerment model for pregnant and parenting African American women in rural communities. *Family and Community Health, 29*(3), 221–228.

Banerji, D. (1986). *Social sciences and health service development in India: Sociology of formation of an alternative paradigm*. New Delhi, India: Lok Paksh.

Bethune, G. R., & Lewis, H. J. (2009). Let's talk about smear tests: Social marketing for the National Cervical Screening Programme. *Public Health, 123*(Suppl. 1), e17–22.

Bull, S. S., Posner, S. F., Ortiz, C., Beaty, B., Benton, K., Lin, L., et al. (2008). POWER for reproductive health: Results from a social marketing campaign promoting female and male condoms. *Journal of Adolescent Health, 43*(1), 71–78.

Cates, J. R., & Coyne-Beasley, T. (2015). Social marketing to promote HPV vaccination in pre-teenage children: Talk about a sexually transmitted infection. *Human Vaccines & Immunotherapeutics, 11*(2), 347–349. doi: 10.4161/21645515.2014.994458.

Corrigan, P., & Gelb, B. (2006). Three programs that use mass approaches to challenge the stigma of mental illness. *Psychiatric Services, 57*(3), 393–398.

Crape, B. L., Kenefick, E., Cavalli-Sforza, T., Busch-Hallen, J., Milani, S., & Kanal, K. (2005). Positive impact of a weekly iron-folic acid supplement delivered with social marketing to Cambodian women: Compliance, participation, and hemoglobin levels increase with higher socio-economic status. *Nutrition Reviews, 63*(12, Pt. 2), S134–S138.

De Allegri, M., Marschall, P., Flessa, S., Tiendrebéogo, J., Kouyaté, B., Jahn, A., et al. (2010). Comparative cost analysis of insecticide-treated net delivery strategies: Sales supported by social marketing and free distribution through antenatal care. *Health Policy & Planning, 25*(1), 28–38.

Elliott, B. J. (1991). *A re-examination of the social marketing concept*. Sydney: Elliott & Shanahan Research.

Evans, W. D. (2006). How social marketing works in health care. *British Medical Journal, 332*, 1207–1210.

Evans-Lacko, S., Malcolm, E., West, K., Rose, D., London, J., Rüsch, N., et al. (2013). Influence of Time to Change's social marketing interventions on stigma in England 2009–2011. *British Journal of Psychiatry, 55* (Suppl. 2013), s77–s88. doi: 10.1192/bjp.bp.113.126672.

Fallin, A., Neilands, T. B., Jordan, J. W., Hong, J. S., & Ling, P. M. (2015). Wreaking "havoc" on smoking: Social branding to reach young adult "partiers" in Oklahoma. *American Journal of Preventive Medicine, 48*(1 Suppl 1), S78–S85. doi: 10.1016/j.amepre.2014.09.008.

Farris, K. B., Aquilino, M. L., Batra, P., Marshall, V., & Losch, M. E. (2015). Impact of a passive social marketing intervention in community pharmacies on oral contraceptive and condom sales: A quasi-experimental study. *BMC Public Health, 15*, 143. doi: 10.1186/s12889-015-1495-x.

Flora, J. A., Schooler, C., & Pierseon, R. M. (1997). Effective health promotion among communities of color: The potential of social marketing. In M. E. Goldberg, M. Fishbein, & S. E. Middlestadt (Eds.), *Social marketing: Theoretical and practical perspectives* (pp. 353–373). Mahwah, NJ: Lawrence Erlbaum.

Goossens, H., Guillemot, D., Ferech, M., Schlemmer, B., Costers, M., van Breda, M., et al. (2006). National campaigns to improve antibiotic use. *European Journal of Clinical Pharmacology, 62*(5), 373–379.

Grier, S., & Bryant, C. A. (2005). Social marketing in public health. *Annual Review of Public Health, 26*, 319–339.

Harvey, P. D. (1999). *Let every child be wanted: How social marketing is revolutionizing contraceptive use around the world.* Westport, CT: Auburn House.

Hastings, G., & McDermott, L. M. (2006). Putting social marketing into practice. *British Medical Journal, 332*, 1210–1212.

HEALTHY study group, Hirst, K., Baranowski, T., DeBar, L., Foster, G. D., Kaufman, F., et al. (2009). HEALTHY study rationale, design and methods: Moderating risk of type 2 diabetes in multi-ethnic middle school students. *International Journal of Obesity, 33*(Suppl. 4), S4–S20.

Horn, F. E., Mandryk, J. A., Mackson, J. M., Wutzke, S. E., Weekes, L. M., & Hyndman, R. J. (2006). Measurement of changes in antihypertensive drug utilization following primary care educational interventions. *Pharmacoepidemiology and Drug Safety.* Epub PMID: 16634120

Kotler, P. (2005). *According to Kotler: The world's foremost authority on marketing answers your questions.* New York: American Management Association.

Kotler, P., & Levy, S. J. (1969). Broadening the concept of marketing. *Journal of Marketing, 33*, 10–15.

Kotler, P., & Roberto, E. (1989). *Social marketing: Strategies for changing public behavior.* New York: Free Press.

Kotler, P., & Zaltman, G. (1971). Social marketing: An approach to planned social change. *Journal of Marketing, 35*, 3–12.

Lambert, D. N., Bishop, L. E., Guetig, S., & Frew, P. M. (2014). A formative evaluation of social media campaign to reduce adolescent dating violence. *JMIR Research Protocols, 3*(4), e64. doi: 10.2196/resprot.3546.

LeCheminant, J. D., & Merrill, R. M. (2012). Improved health behaviors persist over two years for employees in a worksite wellness program. *Population Health Management, 15*(5), 261–266. doi: 10.1089/pop.2011.0083.

Lee, N. R., & Kotler, P. A. (2015). *Social marketing: Changing behaviors for good* (5th ed.). Thousand Oaks, CA: Sage Publishers.

Lefebvre, R. C., & Flora, J. A. (1988). Social marketing and public health intervention. *Health Education Quarterly, 15*, 299–315.

Lin, C. A., & Hullman, G. A. (2005). Tobacco-prevention messages online: Social marketing via the Web. *Health Communication, 18*(2), 177–193.

Ludwig, T. D., Buchholz, C., & Clarke, S. W. (2005). Using social marketing to increase the use of helmets among bicyclists. *Journal of American College Health, 54*(1), 51–58.

Marshall, R. J., Bryant, C., Keller, H., & Fridinger, F. (2006). Marketing social marketing: Getting inside those "big dogs' heads" and other challenges. *Health Promotion Practice, 7*, 206–212.

Maxwell, C., Rwegoshora, R., Magesa, S., & Curtis, C. (2006). Comparison of coverage with insecticide-treated nets in a Tanzanian town and villages where nets and insecticide are either marketed or provided free of charge. *Malaria Journal, 5*(1), 44.

Meekers, D., Agha, S., & Klein, M. (2005). The impact on condom use of the "100% Jeune" social marketing program in Cameroon. *Journal of Adolescent Health, 36*(6), 530.

Meekers, D., & Richter, K. (2005). Factors associated with use of the female condom in Zimbabwe. *International Family Planning Perspectives, 31*(1), 30–37.

Millett, C., Zelenyanszki, C., Furlong, C., & Binysh, K. (2005). An evaluation of a social marketing campaign to reduce the number of London women who have never been screened for cervical cancer. *Journal of Medical Screening, 12*(4), 204–205.

Miner, J. W., White, A., Lubenow, A. E., & Palmer, S. (2005). Geocoding and social marketing in Alabama's cancer prevention programs. *Preventing Chronic Disease*, *2*, A17.

National Cancer Institute. (2005). *Theory at a glance: A guide for health promotion practice* (2nd ed.). Washington, DC: U.S. Department of Health and Human Services. Retrieved May 20, 2006, from http://www.nci.nih.gov /theory/pdf

Peattie, S., & Peattie, K. (2003). Ready to fly solo? Reducing social marketing's dependency on commercial marketing theory. *Marketing Theory*, *3*, 365–385.

Perusco, A., Poder, N., Mohsin, M., Rikard-Bell, G., Rissel, C., Williams, M., et al. (2010). Evaluation of a comprehensive tobacco control project targeting Arabic-speakers residing in south west Sydney, Australia. *Health Promotion International*. Epub ahead of print, PMID: 20189945

Piot, B., Mukherjee, A., Navin, D., Krishnan, N., Bhardwaj, A., Sharma, V., et al. (2010). Lot quality assurance sampling for monitoring coverage and quality of a targeted condom social marketing programme in traditional and non-traditional outlets in India. *Sexually Transmitted Infections*, *86*(Suppl. 1), i56–i61.

Quinn, G. P., Hauser, K., Bell-Ellison, B. A., Rodriguez, N. Y., & Frias, J. L. (2006). Promoting pre-conceptional use of folic acid to Hispanic women: A social marketing approach. *Maternal and Child Health Journal*, *10*(5), 403–412.

Reger-Nash, B., Fell, P., Spicer, D., Fisher, B. D., Cooper, L., Chey, T., et al. (2006). BC Walks: Replication of a communitywide physical activity campaign. *Preventing Chronic Disease*, *3*(3), A90.

Rissel, C. E., New, C., Wen, L. M., Merom, D., Bauman, A. E., & Garrard, J. (2010). The effectiveness of community-based cycling promotion: Findings from the Cycling Connecting Communities project in Sydney, Australia. *International Journal of Behavioral Nutrition and Physical Activity*, *7*(1), 8.

Rothschild, M. L. (1999). Carrots, sticks, and promises: A conceptual framework for the management of public health and social issue behaviors. *Journal of Marketing*, *63*, 24–37.

Silvestre, A. J., Hylton, J. B., Johnson, L. M., Houston, C., Witt, M., Jacobson, L., et al. (2006). Recruiting minority men who have sex with men for HIV research: Results from a 4-city campaign. *American Journal of Public Health*, *96*(6), 1020–1027.

Sinclair, C., & Foley, P. (2009). Skin cancer prevention in Australia. *British Journal of Dermatology*, *161*(Suppl. 3), 116–123.

Slater, M. D., Kelly, K. J., Edwards, R. W., Thurman, P. J., Plested, B. A., Keefe, T. J., et al. (2006). Combining in-school and community-based media efforts: Reducing marijuana and alcohol uptake among younger adolescents. *Health Education Research*, *21*(1), 157–167.

Social Marketing Institute. (2006). *Success stories*. Retrieved July 10, 2006, from http://www.social-marketing.org /success.html

Sorensen, J. A., Jenkins, P., Bayes, B., Clark, S., & May, J. J. (2010). Cost-effectiveness of a ROPS social marketing campaign. *Journal of Agricultural Safety and Health*, *16*(1), 31–40.

Staten, L. K., Birnbaum, A. S., Jobe, J. B., & Elder, J. P. (2006). A typology of middle school girls: Audience segmentation related to physical activity. *Health Education and Behavior*, *33*(1), 66–80.

Stephens, S. C., Bernstein, K. T., McCright, J. E., & Klausner, J. D. (2010). Dogs Are Talking: San Francisco's social marketing campaign to increase syphilis screening. *Sexually Transmitted Diseases*, *37*(3), 173–176.

Thackeray, R., & Brown, K. M. (2005). Social marketing's unique contributions to health promotion practice. *Health Promotion Practice*, *6*, 365–368.

Thapa, S., Prasad, C. V., Rao, P. H., Severy, L. J., & Rao, S. R. (1994). Social marketing of condoms in India. *Advances in Population: Psychosocial Perspective*, *2*, 171–204.

Tufano, J. T., & Karras, B. T. (2005). Mobile eHealth interventions for obesity: A timely opportunity to leverage convergence trends. *Journal of Medical Internet Research*, *7*(5), e58.

Vega, M. Y., & Roland, E. L. (2005). Social marketing techniques for public health communication: A review of syphilis awareness campaigns in 8 U.S. cities. *Sexually Transmitted Diseases*, *32*(Suppl. 10), S30–S36.

Verrall, T., Napash, L., Leclerc, L., Mercure, S., & Gray-Donald, K. (2006). Community-based communication strategies to promote infant iron nutrition in northern Canada. *International Journal of Circumpolar Health*, *65*(1), 65–78.

Weinreich, N. K. (2011). *Hands on social marketing: A step-by-step guide to designing change for good* (2nd ed.). Thousand Oaks, CA: Sage.

Wiebe, G. D. (1951-1952). Merchandising commodities and citizenship on television. *Public Opinion Quarterly*, *15*, 679–691.

Williams, P. G., Dewapura, D., Gunawardene, P., & Settinayake, S. (1998). Social marketing to eliminate leprosy in Sri Lanka. *Social Marketing Quarterly*, *4*(4), 27–31.

Young, L., Anderson, J., Beckstrom, L., Bellows, L., & Johnson, S. L. (2004). Using social marketing principles to guide the development of a nutrition education initiative for preschool-aged children. *Journal of Nutrition Education and Behavior*, *36*(5), 250–257.

DIFFUSION OF INNOVATIONS

Chapter 9

KEY CONCEPTS

- change agent
- clarity of results
- communication channels
- compatibility
- complexity
- costs
- demonstrability
- diffusion
- homophily

- innovation
- opinion leaders
- perceived relative advantage
- pervasiveness
- reinvention
- reversibility
- time
- social networks
- social system

AFTER READING THIS CHAPTER YOU SHOULD BE ABLE TO

- Describe the historical genesis of the diffusion of innovations theory
- List the constructs of the diffusion of innovations theory
- Summarize the applications of the diffusion of innovations theory in public health
- Identify methods to modify constructs from the diffusion of innovations theory
- Apply the diffusion of innovations theory for changing a health behavior of your choice

Communication is essential for social change. . . . Social change is the process by which alteration occurs in the structure and function of a social system. National revolution, invention of a new manufacturing technique, founding of a village improvement council, adoption of birth control methods by a family—all are examples of social change.

—Rogers and Shoemaker (1971, p. 7)

The diffusion of innovations theory is a model that has been thoroughly tested. The term **diffusion** refers to the process by which a new idea, object, or practice filters through various channels in a community over time (Rogers, 2003). It is a special form of communication in which the idea that is being conveyed is new. The term **innovations** refers to the new ideas, objects, or practices that are to be adopted. The hallmark of the diffusion of innovations theory is that it deals with the dissemination of new ideas and their adoption by people in a systematic manner. In addition, the diffusion of innovations theory is a tool for social change. Once a new idea is infused into a community, change becomes inevitable.

This chapter begins by describing the historical aspects of the genesis of the diffusion of innovations theory. We then describe the approach taken by the diffusion of innovations theory and the various constructs that make up this theory. We discuss the applications of the diffusion of innovations theory in public health and the limitations of the theory, and then present a skill-building application.

HISTORICAL PERSPECTIVE

The diffusion of innovations theory can be traced back to the early 1900s, when Gabriel Tarde, a French sociologist and legal scholar, wrote *The Laws of Imitation* (Tarde, 1903/1969), which looked at factors that helped innovations spread. He used the term *imitation*, which is similar to the present-day term *adoption* (Rogers, 2003), to describe how innovations were accepted. Georg Simmel, a German philosopher and sociologist who was a contemporary of Tarde, introduced the notion of a *stranger*, who is a member of a system but not strongly attached to it. This concept was used later on in the diffusion of innovations theory. Tarde's and Simmel's propositions were followed by the work of anthropologist Clark Wissler (1923), who studied the diffusion of horses from Spanish explorers to American Indian tribes in the Plains. Wissler found that the introduction of horses caused the peaceful Indian tribes to go to war with neighboring tribes.

Empirical work with the diffusion of innovations theory began with a hybrid seed corn study conducted by rural sociologists Bryce Ryan and Neal Gross at Iowa State University (Ryan & Gross, 1943; Valente & Rogers, 1995). Hybrid seeds were developed in 1928. Their use increases a harvest by more than 20%, yet only a small number of farmers initially adopted the hybrid corn. Full diffusion of this innovation took almost 12 years, with the average farmer taking 7 years to progress from initial awareness to full-scale adoption of planting the whole field with hybrid seed. The main dependent variable was innovativeness (the degree to which an individual adopts early as compared with others). The cumulative number of farmers adopting the hybrid corn plotted against time formed an S-shaped curve; when plotted on a frequency basis, it formed a normal bell-shaped curve. Mass media were found to be important in the awareness stage, whereas interpersonal communication was more important at the persuasion stage (Rogers & Singhal, 1996).

Throughout the 1940s and 1950s, the diffusion of innovations theory was popular in rural sociology. In the 1950s, Everett Rogers, while pursuing his doctoral studies in rural sociology at Iowa State, became interested in the diffusion theory and worked on his dissertation in that area. In 1962, he wrote *Diffusion of Innovations*; at that time there were 405 publications on this theory (Rogers, 2004). In 2003, when the fifth edition of this book was published, more than 5,200 applications of this theory had been published in various fields (Rogers, 2003). Interested readers may consult this book for detailed information on this theory. Everett Rogers is the foremost authority on this theory and teaches at the University of New Mexico.

The applications of the diffusion of innovations theory in public health, health promotion, and health education began with immunization campaigns and family planning programs. From the 1960s onward, the diffusion of innovations theory was used to speed up the adoption of family planning methods in Latin America, Africa, and Asia. Recent impetus for applying the diffusion of innovations theory in public health has come from the HIV/AIDS epidemic. In the mid-1980s, the STOP AIDS intervention based on the diffusion of innovations theory was implemented and tested in San Francisco (Rogers & Shefner-Rogers, 1999). One of the components of this intervention was to identify opinion leaders who were bartenders at gay bars and train them in HIV prevention among gay men. This approach is now being evaluated in developing countries. In 2000, Malcolm Gladwell wrote *The Tipping Point: How Little Things Can Make a Big Difference*, in which he defined the "tipping point" as the moment when something unique becomes common. This is the purpose of the diffusion of innovations.

> **The diffusion model has now been around for a long time, almost 60 years. Is diffusion dead or dying? It is not declining. The number of diffusion publications completed per year continues to hold steady. Unlike most models of human behavior that begin to fade after some years of use, the diffusion model continues to attract strong interest from scholars.**
>
> —Rogers (2004, p. 19)

CONSTRUCTS OF THE DIFFUSION OF INNOVATIONS THEORY

An innovation refers to an idea, practice, or product (including services) that is perceived as new by an individual or other unit of adoption (Rogers, 2003). It does not matter how long this idea, practice, or product has been around. What matters is that the person who is adopting it *perceives* it as new. The newness of an innovation can be with regard to knowledge, persuasion, or the decision to adopt. Newness regarding knowledge refers to the situation in which the potential adopter was not previously aware of the product, practice, or idea. Newness regarding persuasion refers to the situation in which the potential adopter has not been previously contacted by anyone about the product, practice, or idea. Finally, newness regarding the decision to adopt pertains to the situation in which the potential adopter has not formed a positive or negative attitude about using the product, practice, or idea. Innovations are of three types: (1) *incremental innovations*, which reflect a relatively small improvement over previous products; (2) *distinctive innovations*, which represent significant improvement but do not entail any new technology or approach; and (3) *breakthrough innovations*, which are based on a new technology or approach (Schumann, Prestwood, Tong, & Vanston, 1994).

Innovations have several attributes (Frerichs, 1994; Greenhalgh, Robert, Bate, Macfarlane, & Kyriakidou, 2005; Rogers, 2003; Tornatzky & Klein, 1982). See **Table 9-1** for additional information on the attributes described here:

- **Perceived relative advantage**: Perception regarding how much better the new product, idea, or practice is than the one it will replace

Table 9-1	Key Attributes of Innovations	
Attribute	**Definition**	**How to Modify?**
Perceived relative advantage	The perception regarding how much better the new product, idea, or practice is than the one it will replace	Increase the perception that the innovation is advantageous in monetary terms, social terms, or in other respects.
Compatibility	The perception of the innovation's consistency with the values, past experiences, and needs of potential adopters	Make the idea consistent with the prevalent norms and values.
Complexity	The perception of the degree of difficulty in understanding and using the new idea, practice, or product	Simplify the idea, practice, or product.
Demonstrability	The degree to which an innovation may be experimented with on a limited basis	Provide an opportunity to try the idea, practice, or product either in small units or in total.
Clarity of results	The degree to which outcomes of an innovation are clearly visible	Disseminate information on the results of the innovation and make it more visible.
Costs	The tangible and intangible expenses incurred in the adoption of a new idea, practice, or product	Minimize costs as far as possible.
Reversibility	The ability and degree to which the status quo can be reinstated by ceasing to use the innovation	Make innovations reversible.
Pervasiveness	The degree to which an innovation requires changes or adjustments by other elements in the social system	Minimize changes in other parts.
Reinvention	The degree to which a potential adopter can adapt, refine, or modify the innovation to suit his or her needs	Allow for modification(s) by the user.

- **Compatibility**: Perception of the innovation's consistency with the values, past experiences, and needs of potential adopters
- **Complexity**: Perception of the degree of difficulty in understanding and using the new idea, practice, or product

- **Demonstrability**: The degree to which an innovation may be experimented with on a limited basis
- **Clarity of results**: The degree to which outcomes of an innovation are clearly visible
- **Costs**: The tangible and intangible expenses incurred in the adoption of a new idea, practice, or product
- **Reversibility**: The ability and degree to which the status quo can be reinstated by ceasing to use the innovation
- **Pervasiveness**: The degree to which an innovation requires changes or adjustments by other elements in the social system
- **Reinvention**: The degree to which a potential adopter can adapt, refine, or modify the innovation to suit his or her needs

These characteristics of innovations usually serve as independent variables in studies using this theory (Wolfe, 1994).

The second construct of the diffusion of innovations theory is **communication channels** (Rogers, 2003). These are the links between those who possess know-how regarding the innovation and those who have not yet adopted that innovation. They are the means by which messages are transferred between individuals. Communication channels are of three kinds: (1) *mass media channels*, such as television, radio, and newspapers; (2) *interpersonal channels*, which require face-to-face interaction between two or more individuals; and (3) *interactive communication channels*, such as the Internet. Mass media channels are the swiftest, reach a large number of people, and are especially advantageous in building awareness or knowledge about the innovation. Interpersonal channels are especially helpful in persuading a potential adopter. Therefore, in the initial stages of adoption one should use mass media channels, followed by interpersonal and interactive channels to reinforce the message and persuade the potential adopter.

The third construct of the diffusion of innovations theory is **time** (Rogers, 2003), which refers to the interval between becoming aware of an idea and adopting the idea. This can take from days to years, depending on the innovation. The time construct is involved with diffusion of innovations in three ways: (1) the innovation-decision process, (2) adopter categories, and (3) rate of adoption (Rogers, 2003). The *innovation-decision process* is a five-step process:

1. Gaining knowledge about the innovation
2. Being persuaded about the innovation
3. Deciding whether to adopt or reject the innovation
4. Implementing the innovation (putting it to use)
5. Confirming step: either reversing the decision or adopting the innovation

Adopter categories indicate people's willingness to adopt an innovation and have a bell-shaped distribution. The initial adopters are the innovators (2.5%), people who adopt quickly. Innovators by nature are adventurous, cosmopolitan, have geographically dispersed contacts, are high risk takers, and have a high tolerance for uncertainty and failure. The second category consists of the early adopters (13.5%). Early adopters are well-respected opinion leaders and well-integrated and judicious individuals. The early-majority category (34%) consists of people who are deliberate, highly connected within a peer system, and are ahead of the average. These adopters are followed by the late majority (34%). Late-majority adopters are skeptical, responsive to economic necessity, responsive

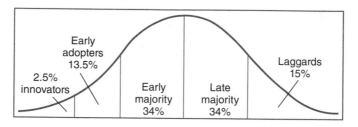

FIGURE 9-1 Distribution of adopter categories according to diffusion of innovations theory.

to social norms, have limited economic resources, and have a low tolerance for uncertainty. The final group are the laggards (16%). Laggards are more traditional in their disposition, are relatively isolated, have precarious economic situations, and are suspicious of change. **Figure 9–1** depicts the distribution of adopter categories on a normal curve. **Table 9–2** summarizes the characteristics of the five types of adopters and strategies that can be used to appeal to them.

The *rate of adoption* refers to the speed with which an innovation is adopted. If we plot the cumulative frequency against time, an S-shaped curve is obtained, which is the rate of adoption (**Figure 9–2**). The diffusion rate usually serves as the dependent variable in studies using the diffusion of innovations theory (Wolfe, 1994).

The fourth construct of the diffusion of innovations theory is the **social system** (Berwick, 2003; Rogers, 2003). A social system implies people in a society connected by a common goal and is composed of individuals, groups, organizations, or communities. An important aspect of the social system is how similar the group members are. Similarity among group members is called **homophily**. Innovations spread faster among homophilous groups (Cain & Mitman, 2002;

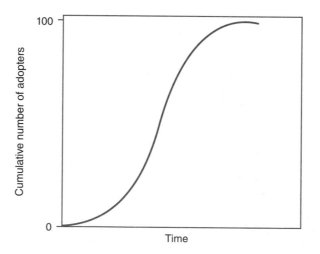

FIGURE 9-2 The S-shaped curve of diffusion.

Table 9-2	Characteristics of the Five Types of Adopters and Strategies to Appeal	
Type of Adopter	**Characteristics**	**Strategies to Appeal**
Innovators	• First to try the innovation • Venturesome • Interested in new ideas • Willing to take risks • Often the first to develop new ideas	• Just show the innovation/innovative behavior
Early adopters	• Represent opinion leaders • Enjoy leadership roles • Well integrated • Judicious • Embrace change opportunities • Already aware of the need to change • Very comfortable adopting new ideas	• How-to manuals • Information sheets on implementation
Early majority	• Adopt new ideas before the average person • Deliberate • Highly connected within a peer system • Need to see evidence that the innovation works before they are willing to adopt it	• Presentation of success stories • Evidence of the innovation's effectiveness
Late majority	• Skeptical of change • Responsive to economic necessity • Responsive to social norms • Have limited economic resources • Low tolerance for uncertainty • Only adopt an innovation after it has been tried by the majority	• Information on how many other people have tried the innovation and have adopted it successfully
Laggards	• Traditional in disposition • Conservative • Relatively isolated • Precarious economic situation • Suspicious of change	• Presentation of statistics • Presentation of fear appeals • Pressure from people in the other adopter groups

Rogers, 2003). Hence, to enhance the rate of diffusion of an innovation, identify the degree of homophily in the target audience and use homophilous agents to spread the message.

Another aspect of the social system is the use of **social networks**, which are person-centered webs of social relationships (Heaney & Israel, 2002) that provide friendship, advice, communication, and support (Valente, 1996). Social networks can be physical or virtual (i.e., in the cyberworld). The configuration of social networks through which innovations diffuse governs the pace and extent of diffusion. For example, in the 1960s, studies showed that diffusion of the practice of tetracycline prescription occurred faster among physicians with denser social networks than for isolated physicians (Cain & Mitman, 2002). To hasten diffusion, identify and utilize physical and virtual networks and create new networks.

The third aspect of the social system is the **change agent**, an individual who influences a potential adopter's decision about innovation in a favorable way (Haider & Kreps, 2004). An example of a change agent might be a health educator at a health department. The change agent must be used to favorably influence the decision. The fourth aspect of social systems is **opinion leaders**, individuals who are influential in a community and sway the beliefs and actions of their colleagues in either a positive or negative direction (Locock, Dopson, Chambers, & Gabbay, 2001). These are individuals who have greater exposure to new ideas through the media, have greater social participation, have higher social status, and are more innovative (Rogers & Shoemaker, 1971). To hasten diffusion, identify true opinion leaders and involve them in the campaign. Opinion leaders have been used in heart health trials, such as the Stanford five-city project (Farquhar et al., 1990) and the North Karelia project (Puska et al., 1986).

These characteristics of the social system usually serve as independent variables in studies using this theory (Wolfe, 1994). **Figure 9-3** depicts the constructs of the diffusion of innovations theory in a diagram. **Table 9-3** summarizes the key constructs of the diffusion of innovations theory, along with ways to modify them.

To apply these constructs of the diffusion of innovations theory for health programming, Dearing (2004) has suggested a nine-step process. The first step is selecting the topic, in which the area of concern with high societal need and fewer previous programs is selected. Next is identifying the program population, in which the target population is selected. The third step is deriving a sample of best practices, in which the best existing products pertaining to the topic are identified. The

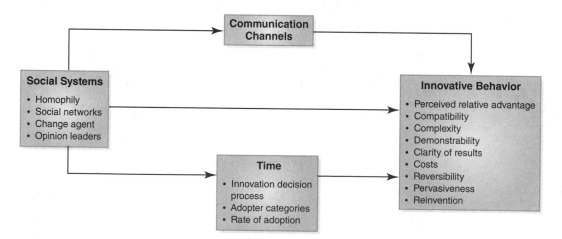

FIGURE 9-3 Depiction of the constructs of the diffusion of innovations theory.

Table 9-3	Key Constructs of the Diffusion of Innovations Theory	
Construct	**Definition**	**How to Modify?**
Innovation	An idea, practice, or product (including services) that is perceived as new by an individual or other unit of adoption	• Increase the perception that innovation is advantageous in monetary terms, social terms, or in other respects. • Make the idea consistent with the prevalent norms and values. • Simplify the idea, practice, or product. • Provide opportunity to try the idea, practice, or product either in small units or in total. • Disseminate information on results of the innovation and make it more visible. • Minimize costs as far as possible. • Make innovations reversible. • Minimize changes in other parts of the social system. • Allow for modification(s) by the user.
Communication channels	The link between those who have know-how regarding the innovation and those who have not yet adopted the innovation	• Use mass media for building awareness. • Use interpersonal channels for persuasion.
Time	The interval between becoming aware of an idea and adopting the idea	• Facilitate adoption over time.
Social system	People in a society connected by a common goal	• Facilitate adoption from person to person. • Use homophilous agents to spread the message. • Use social networks. • Use change agents. • Use opinion leaders.

fourth step is identifying intermediary networks. In this step, potential adopters are identified; there must be existing communication within this network. The fifth step is identifying opinion leaders in the intermediary network. Opinion leaders, as we have seen, are individuals who are influential in a community. They can be identified by sociometric questionnaires (in which respondents characterize their relations with others in the network), participant observation, expert interviews, or self-reports. Opinion leaders typically consist of 5% to 6% of the network membership. The sixth step is collecting pretest data, such as characteristics of members of the community and pretest opinions about the product. The next step is creation of a decision support tool, in which potential adopters can assess alternative best-practice products. The eighth step is to set up research design

Table 9-4	Steps for Applying the Diffusion of Innovations Theory for Health Programming
1.	Select the topic.
2.	Identify the program population.
3.	Derive a sample of best practices.
4.	Identify intermediary networks.
5.	Identify opinion leaders in the intermediary network.
6.	Collect pretest data.
7.	Create a decision support tool.
8.	Set up research design conditions.
9.	Measure the rate of adoption and participants' opinions post-test.

conditions, in which network members can be assigned to different conditions in which different variables are manipulated. The final step is post-test measurement, in which a post-test similar to the pretest can be administered and the rate of adoption in different conditions calculated. **Table 9-4** summarizes these steps.

> Improving the application of the Diffusion of Innovations model in the field of public health can lead to advances in health promotion and disease prevention on a global level.
>
> —Haider and Kreps (2004, p. 3)

A similar model for the diffusion of innovations theory in public health organizations, FOMENT, has been suggested by Muhiuddin Haider of George Washington University (Haider & Kreps, 2004). FOMENT is an acronym in which *F* stands for *focus* on a specific behavior change; *O* for *organization* of the behavior change program; *M* for *management*, which supports and approves the behavior change program; *E* for an *environment* that is conducive to behavior change; *N* for a *network* to diffuse innovations at the individual and organizational levels; and *T* for the *technology* available to diffuse innovations.

APPLICATIONS OF THE DIFFUSION OF INNOVATIONS THEORY

The diffusion of innovations theory has been used in a variety of applications in public health, health promotion, and health education. Most of the published studies on the diffusion of innovations theory use cross-sectional surveys of adopters done after they have adopted the innovation and pertain to a single innovation (Meyer, 2004). Some examples of the application of this theory for public health are adopting and implementing a picture archiving communication system (PACS) in hospitals (Pare & Trudel, 2007); adopting novel medication regimes for diabetes management (De Civita & Dasgupta, 2007; Pugh, Anderson, Pogach, & Berlowitz, 2003); adopting telemedicine in rural areas (Helitzer, Heath, Maltrud, Sullivan, & Alverson, 2003); designing Students Together Against Negative Decisions (STAND), a peer educator training curriculum for sexual risk reduction (Smith, Dane, Archer, Devereaux, & Katner, 2000; Smith & DiClemente, 2000); enriching a gerontology curriculum (Dorfman & Murty, 2005); health coaching for diabetes (Liddy, Johnston,

Nash, Ward, & Irving, 2014); impacting patient acceptance and use of consumer e-health innovations (Zhang, Yu, Yan, Ton & Spil, 2015); implementing change strategy for primary care treatment of depression (Dietrich et al., 2004); implementing computerized provider order entry (CPOE) in the outpatient setting (Ash et al., 2007); implementing family planning in developing countries (Murphy, 2004; Sharma & Sharma, 1996; Vaughan & Rogers, 2000); implementing a health counseling intervention in a cardiology outpatient clinic (Harting et al., 2005); implementing the National Quality Measurement and Reporting System (NQMRS) (McGlynn, 2003); implementing patient education in community pharmacies (Pronk, Blom, Jonkers, & Van Burg, 2001); implementing a sun protection program (Buller et al., 2005); implementing technology implementation systems to promote patient safety (Karsh, 2004); implementing telehomecare technology in community care (Hebert & Korabek, 2004); incorporating genomic medicine into primary care (Suther & Goodson, 2004); increasing Internet use by family physicians (Chew, Grant, & Tote, 2004); interpreting primary care physicians' attitudes regarding rotavirus immunization (Agyeman et al., 2009); predicting radon testing (Peterson & Howland, 1996); predicting smoking cessation (Deprey et al., 2009; Kuntsche & Gmel, 2005); recruiting in intervention trials (McMullen, Griffiths, Leber, & Greenhalgh, 2015); reducing the spread of sexually transmitted diseases and HIV infection (Backer & Rogers, 1998; Bertrand, 2004; Swendeman & Rotheram-Borus, 2010; Valente & Fosados, 2006); a social media-based health intervention (Young, Belin, Klausner, & Valente, 2015); translating research on diabetes self-management interventions into practice (Leeman, Jackson, & Sandelowski, 2006); using acetylcholinesterase inhibitors in Alzheimer's disease (Ruof, Mittendorf, Pirk, & von der Schulenburg, 2002); using decision support systems (DSS) by child welfare workers (Foster & Stiffman, 2009); using patient-driven computers in primary care services (Shakeshaft & Frankish, 2003); and using voodoo practitioners in Haiti to educate people about HIV/AIDS (Barker, 2004). **Table 9-5** summarizes these applications.

> **Examples of potentially constructive innovations in health care can be as simple as ensuring that an improved drug regimen published in a refereed journal article immediately becomes the norm in a practice group, or as complex as redesigning an entire scheduling system to better conform to sound principles from queuing theory.**
>
> —Berwick (2003, p. 1969)

LIMITATIONS OF THE DIFFUSION OF INNOVATIONS THEORY

The diffusion of innovations theory has been in existence for quite some time and has been tested empirically and refined. It offers several advantages in guiding the adoption of something that is novel or new. However, like all other models and theories, this approach has some limitations. In health promotion and education, there are few real innovations (Tornatzky & Fleischer, 1990). People often know about the issues and may have tried the behavior. For example, almost all smokers know that smoking is injurious to their health, and many have tried to quit. So quitting is not an innovation for them. Use of the diffusion of innovations theory is challenging in these circumstances.

Public health interventions are preventive in nature, whereby the individual has to adopt the new idea today to avoid the likelihood of a negative consequence occurring at a later date. For example, a smoker would need to quit smoking today to prevent development of lung cancer 20

Table 9-5	Applications of the Diffusion of Innovations Theory in Public Health
Adopting and implementing a picture archiving communication system (PACS) in hospitals
Adopting novel medication regimens for diabetes management
Adopting telemedicine in rural areas
Designing Students Together Against Negative Decisions (STAND), a peer educator training curriculum for sexual risk reduction
Enriching a gerontology curriculum
Health coaching for diabetes
Impacting patient acceptance and use of consumer e-health innovations
Implementing change strategy for primary care treatment of depression
Implementing computerized provider order entry (CPOE) in the outpatient setting
Implementing family planning in developing countries
Implementing health counseling intervention in the cardiology outpatient clinic
Implementing a National Quality Measurement and Reporting System (NQMRS)
Implementing patient education in community pharmacies
Implementing a sun protection program
Implementing technology implementation systems to promote patient safety
Implementing telehomecare technology in community care
Incorporating genomic medicine into primary care
Increasing Internet use by family physicians
Interpreting primary care physicians attitude regarding rotavirus immunization Predicting radon testing
Predicting smoking cessation
Recruiting in intervention trials
Reducing the spread of sexually transmitted diseases and HIV infection
Social media-based health intervention
Translating research on diabetes self-management interventions into practice
Using acetylcholinesterase inhibitors in Alzheimer's disease
Using decision support systems (DSS) by child welfare workers
Using patient-driven computers in primary care services
Using voodoo practitioners in Haiti to educate people about HIV/AIDS

or so years later. Such a long interval poses special challenges, and diffusion occurs more slowly (Rogers, 2002). It needs to be kept in mind that diffusion of innovations in health is a complex process that occurs at multiple levels, across many different settings, and utilizes different strategies (Oldenburg & Parcel, 2002; Parcel, Perry, & Taylor, 1990).

Oftentimes in health promotion and health education, the interventions are designed for lower socioeconomic groups, people with low literacy levels, and other vulnerable community members. The adoption and diffusion process is easier and smoother in the wealthier and more highly educated populations than in the vulnerable populations, which present a number of challenges and barriers. As a consequence, the gap between the haves and the have-nots widens even further.

> **Diffusion is a multifaceted perspective about social change. Scholars dating at least to Georg Simmel and Gabriel Tarde 100 years ago theorized about imitative behavior at the level of small groups and within communities, and the relation between these micro-level processes to macro-level social change in which sectors, networks, and cities change.**
>
> —Dearing (2004, p. 24)

Another issue with the diffusion of innovations theory is pro-innovation bias (Rogers, 2003). This refers to the preconception that an innovation should be diffused and adopted by all members of society in a rapid manner without rejection or reinvention. This is often not possible with many health promotion and education objectives. For example, it is virtually impossible at present to think that no one will smoke or that everyone will engage in 30 minutes of physical activity every day. Rogers (2003) suggested conducting research while the innovation is still being adopted rather than waiting for it to be completely adopted, studying unsuccessful innovations and examining the broader context in which an innovation diffuses.

Finally, Nutley, Davies, and Walter (2002) have talked about the limitations of focusing on linear-stage models of decision making with the diffusion of innovations theory. Seldom does the adoption of innovation follow a linear path as suggested in the theory. Often the path is uneven, and results that fit the S-shaped curve are not achieved (Chattoe & Gilbert, 1997; Mohr, 1987; Rosegger, 1996). Hence Nutley, Davies, and Walter (2002) advocate a nonlinear, dynamic process that pays more attention to systemic context and norms. In this regard, Westarp (2003) has suggested relational and structural models. Relational models analyze how direct contacts between participants in networks influence the decision to adopt or not adopt an innovation, whereas structural models focus on the pattern of all relationships and show how the structural characteristics of a social system determine the diffusion process.

APPLICATION EXERCISE

In this chapter, we have introduced several applications of the diffusion of innovations model in public health. Choose any area that interests you and locate the full-text article of that application to see how the model has been used. One such application is by Deprey and colleagues (2009), who have described the activities of the Oregon Tobacco Quit Line (OTQL). The *innovation* that the project had was the nicotine patch. They distributed a 2-week starter kit of this patch free of charge to their callers for 2.5 months (*time*). The *communication channels* they used were radio programs, word of mouth, e-mails, and letters to public and private sector partners. The social systems they tapped were health plans, local policy makers, media sources, and referral sources such as health care providers. Some of the outcomes of the intervention were increased media attention, a 12-times increase in calls to the program, and a reach to 1.3% of the smokers.

Read the full-text article and prepare a critique of 250 words on this application.

SKILL-BUILDING ACTIVITY

Let us see how we can apply the diffusion of innovations theory in health education and health promotion. Currently in the profession of health education and health promotion, the National Commission for Health Education Credentialing (NCHEC) provides a certification system. Other professions, such as physicians, nurses, and dietitians, are registered practitioners. Let us assume we want to start the innovation of "registered health educators."

In applying the diffusion of innovations theory, we would first look at the construct of innovation and its attributes. The first attribute is perceived relative advantage. For all existing and prospective health educators, this innovation should seem advantageous. Employers could be convinced to give a nominal raise to those who become registered health educators, thus providing a monetary advantage. The social status that comes with being a registered member of the profession would need to be underscored. The ability to write the credential RHEd with one's name would need to be marketed. The second attribute is compatibility. This innovation is in direct synchrony with the previous innovation of Certified Health Education Specialist (CHES) and should build on that to be successful. The third attribute is that of complexity. The process should be similar to that of becoming a CHES, and thus not very complex. The simpler the process, the better its chances of adoption. The fourth attribute, demonstrability, would not be possible with this innovation. The fifth attribute is that of clarity of results. The results of several years of success with CHES and with registration in other disciplines could be shared. The sixth attribute is costs, which would have to be kept at a nominal rate similar to that involved with CHES. The seventh attribute of reversibility would be easy: a person who does not want to be registered would simply abstain from paying the annual dues. The eighth attribute is that of pervasiveness. To influence this attribute, employers would need to make adjustments by endorsing the idea of registered health educators and mandating that only such individuals be hired in health education jobs. The ninth attribute, reinvention, does not apply to this innovation.

The second construct is that of communication channels. Mass mailing of information about the innovation (registration for health educators) would need to be sent to existing CHES practitioners, the 258 institutions of higher education that award degrees in health education, and all major employers who hire health educators (e.g., county health departments, state health departments, major hospitals, major school systems, and large companies with health and wellness units). Interpersonal communication using people who have adopted the innovation would also need to be done. A website detailing the innovation would need to be set up.

The third construct is that of time. The flow of time would involve the five-step process of providing knowledge about the innovation, persuading health educators about the innovation, helping health educators decide about the innovation, starting the first batch of registered health educators, and then confirming their continuation as registered health educators. A count of people adopting the innovation could be kept so that a rate of adoption curve could be plotted.

The fourth construct is that of the social system. The first aspect of the social system is homophily. Health educators comprise diverse groups. Thus the first task would be to decrease the diversity and make the innovation appeal to the common attributes of all health educators. The second aspect is social networks. Health educators who have adopted the innovation could be used to spread the message to other health educators. The electronic network of health educators (HEDIR) could also be used in this process. The third aspect of the social system is the change agent. The leadership at the National Commission for Health Education Credentialing should take up the task of coordinating and sending the necessary information and becoming change agents. The fourth aspect of the social system is opinion leaders, who would be composed of supervisors at workplaces and department chairs at the various institutions of higher education.

Using this approach, you can plan to work on spreading any innovation using the diffusion of innovations theory. **Table 9-6** provides a set of questions to consider when setting up your plan.

Table 9-6	**Shaping Constructs of the Diffusion of Innovations Theory for Health Education Program Planning**

1. What should be considered while developing the innovation?
   - Increase perceived relative advantage
   - Increase compatibility
   - Decrease complexity
   - Give opportunity for demonstrability
   - Show clarity of results
   - Minimize costs
   - Allow for reversibility
   - Work on factors affecting pervasiveness
   - Allow for reinvention

2. What should be considered while developing the communication channels?
   - Mass media
   - Interpersonal
   - Interactive

3. What should be considered while developing the time?
   - Innovation-decision process
   - Rate of adoption
   - Adopter categories

4. What should be considered while developing the social system?
   - Homophily
   - Social networks
   - Change agents
   - Opinion leaders

SUMMARY

The diffusion of innovations theory deals with the adoption of a new idea, practice, or object over a period of time. The origins of this theory are almost 100 years old, but the first empirical study was done by Bryce Ryan and Neal Gross at Iowa State University with hybrid corn seed in the 1940s. They studied the adoption process and the characteristics of the farmers who adopted the hybrid corn seed. Their work had implications not only in agriculture but also for a variety of disciplines, including health promotion and health education.

The four main constructs of the diffusion of innovations theory are innovation, communication channels, time, and social system. Several attributes of innovation are perceived relative advantage (perception about how much better the new product, idea, or practice is than the one it will replace), compatibility (the perception regarding the innovation's consistency with the values, past experiences, and needs of potential adopters), complexity (the perception of the degree of difficulty in understanding and using the new idea, practice, or product), demonstrability (the degree to which an innovation may be experimented with on a limited basis), clarity of results (the degree to which the outcomes of an innovation are clearly visible), costs (the tangible and intangible expenses incurred in the adoption of a new idea, practice, or product), reversibility (the ability and degree to which the status quo can be reinstated by ceasing to use the innovation), pervasiveness (the degree to which an innovation requires changes or adjustments by other elements in the social system), and reinvention (the degree to which a potential adopter can adapt, refine, or modify the innovation to suit his or her needs).

The communication channels are of three kinds: (1) mass media channels, such as television, radio, and newspapers; (2) interpersonal channels, which require face-to-face interaction between two or more individuals; and (3) interactive communication channels, such as the Internet.

The time construct is involved with the diffusion of innovations in three ways: (1) the innovation-decision process, (2) adopter categories, and (3) rate of adoption. The social system construct comprises homophily (similarity among group members), social networks (person-centered webs of social relationships), change agents (people who influence a potential adopter's decision about innovation in a favorable way), and opinion leaders (influential individuals in a community who sway the beliefs and actions of their colleagues in either a positive or negative direction). The diffusion of innovations theory has been widely applied in public health.

IMPORTANT TERMS

change agent	demonstrability
clarity of results	diffusion
communication channels	homophily
compatibility	innovation
complexity	opinion leaders
costs	perceived relative advantage

pervasiveness
reinvention
reversibility

social networks
social system
time

REVIEW QUESTIONS

1. Describe the historical genesis of the diffusion of innovations theory.
2. Discuss any five attributes of innovations.
3. What does the acronym FOMENT mean in the context of the diffusion of innovations?
4. Describe the four constructs of the diffusion of innovations theory.
5. Discuss the limitations of the diffusion of innovations theory.
6. Apply the diffusion of innovations theory for spreading any innovation of your choice.

WEBSITES TO EXPLORE

Core Diffusion of Innovations Initiative

www.coregroup.org/our-technical-work/initiatives/diffusion-of-innovations

This is the website of CORE Group, a membership association of international nongovernmental organizations (NGOs) that promotes and improves the health of children and women in developing countries through collaborative NGO action and learning. This website presents some applications of the diffusion of innovations theory, including a practical guide for Africa on vitamin A supplementation, a guide for community-based volunteer health educators, the partnership defined quality (PDQ) approach, a barrier analysis manual, a Census-Based, Impact-Oriented (CBIO) approach, and a safe motherhood program. *Review this website and read more about each of these six interventions. Which one interested you most and why?*

Diffusion of Innovations and Outreach

http://nnlm.gov/archive/pnr/eval/rogers.html

This website presents an article by Everett M. Rogers and Karyn L. Scott titled, "The Diffusion of Innovations Model and Outreach from the National Network of Libraries of Medicine to Native American Communities," which was written in 1997. The article summarizes lessons from 300 outreach projects. *Review this website and comment on outreach models and outreach strategies.*

Emergent Themes in the Sustainability of Primary Health Care Innovation

www.mja.com.au/public/issues/183_10_211105/sib10729_fm.html

This website synthesizes the findings of five studies of sustainability of primary health care innovation across six domains (political, institutional, financial, economic, client, and workforce). Three major themes emerge from their analysis. *Review these three themes. What can you say about generalization for diffusion of innovations from this review?*

Internet Use Among Doctors

www.stfm.org/fmhub/fm2004/October/Fiona645.pdf

This website presents a study by Chew and colleagues (2004) regarding the adoption of Internet use by family physicians using the diffusion of innovations theory. It summarizes the results of a survey of family physicians with regard to their Internet use and various strategies to increase the use. *Read this study and comment on how family physicians incorporate the Internet in their practices.*

National Aeronautics and Space Administration (NASA) Library

www.hq.nasa.gov/office/hqlibrary/ppm/ppm39.htm

The NASA headquarters library website summarizes articles and technical reports, books, and Internet sources on the diffusion of innovations theory. The website was organized in 2000. *Review this website and locate a source or Internet site. Read and summarize what you learned.*

National Center for the Study of Adult Learning and Literacy (NCSALL)

www.ncsall.net/?id=246

The National Center for the Study of Adult Learning and Literacy website summarizes the diffusion of innovations theory. NCSALL is a federally funded research and development center focusing on adult learning. *Read the account on the website and identify key components of the diffusion of innovations theory.*

Rogers on Diffusion of Innovations

www.youtube.com/watch?v=j1uc7yZH6eU

This is a 40-minute YouTube video in which Everett Rogers delivers a speech on the diffusion of innovations theory. *Watch this video and prepare a one-page reaction paper on the speech by the founder of the diffusion of innovations theory.*

REFERENCES

Agyeman, P., Desgrandchamps, D., Vaudaux, B., Berger, C., Diana, A., Heininger, U., et al. (2009). Interpretation of primary care physicians' attitude regarding rotavirus immunisation using diffusion of innovation theories. *Vaccine, 27*(35), 4771–4775.

Ash, J. S., Sittig, D. F., Dykstra, R. H., Guappone, K., Carpenter, J. D., & Seshadri, V. (2007). Categorizing the unintended sociotechnical consequences of computerized provider order entry. *International Journal of Medical Informatics, 76* (Suppl 1), S21–S27.

Backer, T. E., & Rogers, E. M. (1998). Diffusion of innovations theory and work-site AIDS programs. *Journal of Health Communication, 3*(1), 17–28.

Barker, K. (2004). Diffusion of innovations: A world tour. *Journal of Health Communication, 9*(Suppl. 1), 131–137.

Bertrand, J. T. (2004). Diffusion of innovations and HIV/AIDS. *Journal of Health Communication, 9*(Suppl. 1), 113–121.

Berwick, D. M. (2003). Disseminating innovations in health care. *Journal of the American Medical Association, 289,* 1969–1975.

Buller, D. B., Andersen, P. A., Walkosz, B. J., Scott, M. D., Cutter, G. R., Dignan, M. B., et al. (2005). Randomized trial testing a worksite sun protection program in an outdoor recreation industry. *Health Education and Behavior, 32*(4), 514–535.

Cain, M., & Mitman, R. (2002). *Diffusion of innovation in health care.* Oakland, CA: California Health Care Foundation. Retrieved July 20, 2006, from http://www.iftf.org/docs/SR-778_Diffusion_of_Innovation _in_HC.pdf.

Chattoe, E., & Gilbert, N. (1997). Modelling the adoption of AEMs as an innovation diffusion process. Retrieved July 20, 2006, from http://wwwlisc.clermont.cemagref.fr/ImagesProject/Results/ models/Diffusion%20Model /dolomieu.html.

Chew, F., Grant, W., & Tote, R. (2004). Doctors on-line: Using diffusion of innovations theory to understand Internet use. *Family Medicine, 36*(9), 645–650.

Dearing, J. W. (2004). Improving the state of health programming by using diffusion theory. *Journal of Health Communication, 9,* 21–36.

De Civita, M., & Dasgupta, K. (2007). Using diffusion of innovations theory to guide diabetes management program development: An illustrative example. *Journal of Public Health, 29*(3), 263–268.

Deprey, M., McAfee, T., Bush, T., McClure, J. B., Zbikowski, S., & Mahoney, L. (2009). Using free patches to improve reach of the Oregon Quit Line. *Journal of Public Health Management and Practice, 15*(5), 401–408.

Dietrich, A. J., Oxman, T. E., Williams, J. W., Jr., Kroenke, K., Schulberg, H. C., Bruce, M., et al. (2004). Going to scale: Re-engineering systems for primary care treatment of depression. *Annals of Family Medicine, 2*(4), 301–304.

Dorfman, L. T., & Murty, S. A. (2005). A diffusion of innovations approach to gerontological curriculum enrichment: Institutionalizing and sustaining curricula change. *Gerontology and Geriatrics Education, 26*(2), 35–50.

Farquhar, J. W., Fortmann, S. P., Flora, J. A., Taylor, C. B., Haskell, W. L., Williams, P. T., et al. (1990). Effects of a communitywide education on cardiovascular disease risk factors: The Stanford five-city project. *Journal of the American Medical Association, 264,* 359–365.

Foster, K. A., & Stiffman, A. R. (2009). Child welfare workers' adoption of decision support technology. *Journal of Technology in Human Services, 27*(2), 106–126.

Frerichs, G. R. (1994). The diffusion of innovations. In S. J. Levy, G. R. Frerichs, & H. L. Gordon (Eds.), *The Dartnell's marketing manager's handbook* (3rd ed., pp. 774–785). Chicago: Dartnell.

Gladwell, M. (2000). *The tipping point: How little things can make a big difference.* Boston: Little Brown.

Greenhalgh, T., Robert, G., Bate, P., Macfralane, F., & Kyriakidou, O. (2005). *Diffusion of innovations in health service organizations: A systematic literature review.* Malden, MA: Blackwell.

Haider, M., & Kreps, G. L. (2004). Forty years of diffusion of innovations: Utility and value in public health. *Journal of Health Communication, 9,* 3–11.

Harting, J., van Assema, P., Ruland, E., van Limpt, P., Gorgels, T., van Ree, J., et al. (2005). Implementation of an innovative health service: A "real-world" diffusion study. *American Journal of Preventive Medicine, 29*(2), 113–119.

Heaney, C. A., & Israel, B. A. (2002). Social networks and social support. In K. Glanz, B. K. Rimer, & F. M. Lewis (Eds.), *Health behavior and health education: Theory, research, and practice* (3rd ed., pp. 185–209). San Francisco: Jossey-Bass.

Hebert, M. A., & Korabek, B. (2004). Stakeholder readiness for telehomecare: Implications for implementation. *Telemedicine Journal and e-Health, 10*(1), 85–92.

Helitzer, D., Heath, D., Maltrud, K., Sullivan, E., & Alverson, D. (2003). Assessing or predicting adoption of telehealth using the diffusion of innovations theory: A practical example from a rural program in New Mexico. *Telemedicine Journal and e-Health, 9*(2), 179–187.

Karsh, B. T. (2004). Beyond usability: Designing effective technology implementation systems to promote patient safety. *Quality and Safety in Health Care, 13*(5), 388–394.

Kuntsche, S., & Gmel, G. (2005). The smoking epidemic in Switzerland: An empirical examination of the theory of diffusion of innovations. *Sozial und Praventivmedizin, 50*(6), 344–354.

Leeman, J., Jackson, B., & Sandelowski, M. (2006). An evaluation of how well research reports facilitate the use of findings in practice. *Journal of Nursing Scholarship, 38*(2), 171–177.

Liddy, C., Johnston, S., Nash, K., Ward, N., & Irving, H. (2014). Health coaching in primary care: A feasibility model for diabetes care. *BMC Family Practice, 15*, 60. doi: 10.1186/1471-2296-15-60.

Locock, L., Dopson, S., Chambers, D., & Gabbay, J. (2001). Understanding the role of opinion leaders in improving clinical effectiveness. *Social Science and Medicine, 53*, 745–757.

McGlynn, E. A. (2003). An evidence-based national quality measurement and reporting system. *Medical Care, 41*(Suppl. 1), I8–I15.

McMullen, H., Griffiths, C., Leber, W., & Greenhalgh, T. (2015). Explaining high and low performers in complex intervention trials: A new model based on diffusion of innovations theory. *Trials, 16*, 242. doi: 10.1186/s13063-015-0755-5.

Meyer, G. (2004). Diffusion methodology: Time to innovate. *Journal of Health Communication, 9*, 59–69.

Mohr, L. B. (1987). Innovation theory. In J. M. Pennings & A. Buitendam (Eds.), *New technology as organizational innovation* (pp. 13–31). Cambridge, MA: Ballinger.

Murphy, E. (2004). Diffusion of innovations: Family planning in developing countries. *Journal of Health Communication, 9*(Suppl. 1), 123–129.

Nutley, S., Davies, H., & Walter, I. (2002). Learning from the diffusion of innovations. Retrieved July 21, 2006, from http://www.st-andrews.ac.uk/~ruru/Learning%20from%20the%20Diffusion%20of%20Innovations.pdf

Oldenburg, B., & Parcel, G. S. (2002). Diffusion of innovations. In K. Glanz, B. K. Rimer, & F. M. Lewis (Eds.), *Health behavior and health education: Theory, research, and practice* (3rd ed., pp. 312–334). San Francisco: Jossey-Bass.

Parcel, G. S., Perry, C. L., & Taylor, W. C. (1990). Beyond demonstration: Diffusion of health promotion interventions. In N. Bracht (Ed.), *Health promotion at the community level*. Thousand Oaks, CA: Sage.

Pare, G., & Trudel, M. C. (2007). Knowledge barriers to PACS adoption and implementation in hospitals. *International Journal of Medical Informatics, 76*(1), 22–33.

Peterson, E. W., & Howland, J. (1996). Predicting radon testing among university employees. *Journal of Air and Waste Management Association, 46*(1), 2–11.

Pronk, M. C., Blom, A. T., Jonkers, R., & Van Burg, A. (2001). The diffusion process of patient education in Dutch community pharmacy: An exploration. *Patient Education and Counseling, 42*(2), 115–121.

Pugh, M. J., Anderson, J., Pogach, L. M., & Berlowitz, D. R. (2003). Differential adoption of pharmacotherapy recommendations for type 2 diabetes by generalists and specialists. *Medical Care Research and Review, 60*(2), 178–200.

Puska, P., Koskela, K., McAlister, A., Mayranen, H., Smolander, A., Moisio, S., et al. (1986). Use of lay opinion leaders to promote the diffusion of health innovations in a community programme: Lessons learned from the North Karelia project. *Bulletin of the World Health Organization, 64*(3), 437–446.

Rogers, E. M. (2002). Diffusion of preventive interventions. *Addictive Behaviors, 27*, 989–993.

Rogers, E. M. (2003). *Diffusion of innovations* (5th ed.). New York: Free Press.

Rogers, E. M. (2004). A prospective and retrospective look at the diffusion model. *Journal of Health Communication, 9*, 13–19.

Rogers, E. M., & Shefner-Rogers, C. L. (1999). Diffusion of innovations and HIV/AIDS prevention research. In W. N. Elwood (Ed.), *Power in the blood: A handbook on AIDS, politics, and communication* [electronic resource, pp. 405–414]. Mahwah, NJ: Lawrence Erlbaum.

Rogers, E. M., & Shoemaker, F. F. (1971). *Communication of innovations: A cross cultural approach* (2nd ed.). New York: Free Press.

Rogers, E. M., & Singhal, A. (1996). Diffusion of innovations. In M. B. Salwen & D. W. Stacks (Eds.), *An integrated approach to communication theory and research* (pp. 409–420). Mahwah, NJ: Lawrence Erlbaum.

Rosegger, G. (1996). *The economics of production and innovation: An industrial perspective* (3rd ed.). Oxford, UK: Butterworth Heinemann.

Ruof, J., Mittendorf, T., Pirk, O., & von der Schulenburg, J. M. (2002). Diffusion of innovations: Treatment of Alzheimer's disease in Germany. *Health Policy*, *60*(1), 59–66.

Ryan, B., & Gross, N. C. (1943). The diffusion of hybrid seed corn in two Iowa communities. *Rural Sociology*, *8*, 15–24.

Schumann, P. A., Prestwood, D. C. L., Tong, A. H., & Vanston, J. H. (1994). *Innovate! Straight path to quality, customer delight, and competitive advantage.* New York: McGraw-Hill.

Shakeshaft, A. P., & Frankish, C. J. (2003). Using patient-driven computers to provide cost-effective prevention in primary care: A conceptual framework. *Health Promotion International*, *18*(1), 67–77.

Sharma, V., & Sharma, A. (1996). Training of opinion leaders in family planning in India: Does it serve any purpose? *Revue d'épidémiologie et de santé publique*, *44*(2), 173–180.

Smith, M. U., Dane, F. C., Archer, M. E., Devereaux, R. S., & Katner, H. P. (2000). Students Together Against Negative Decisions (STAND): Evaluation of a school-based sexual risk reduction intervention in the rural South. *AIDS Education and Prevention*, *12*(1), 49–70.

Smith, M. U., & DiClemente, R. J. (2000). STAND: A peer educator training curriculum for sexual risk reduction in the rural South. Students Together Against Negative Decisions. *Preventive Medicine*, *30*(6), 441–449.

Suther, S. G., & Goodson, P. (2004). Texas physicians' perceptions of genomic medicine as an innovation. *Clinical Genetics*, *65*(5), 368–377.

Swendeman, D., & Rotheram-Borus, M. J. (2010). Innovation in sexually transmitted disease and HIV prevention: Internet and mobile phone delivery vehicles for global diffusion. *Current Opinion in Psychiatry*, *23*(2), 139–144.

Tarde, G. (1969). *The laws of imitation* (E. C. Parsons, Trans.). New York: Dover. (Original work published 1903)

Tornatzky, L. G., & Fleischer, M. (1990). *The process of technological innovation.* Lexington, MA: Lexington Books.

Tornatzky, L. G., & Klein, K. J. (1982). Innovation characteristics and innovation adoption-implementation: A meta-analysis of findings. IEEE *Transactions on Engineering Management*, *29*, 28–45.

Valente, T. W. (1996). Social network thresholds in the diffusion of innovations. *Social Networks*, *18*, 69–89.

Valente, T. W., & Fosados, R. (2006). Diffusion of innovations and network segmentation: The part played by people in promoting health. *Sexually Transmitted Diseases*, *33*(Suppl. 7), S23–S31.

Valente, T. W., & Rogers, E. M. (1995). The origins and development of the diffusion of innovations paradigm as an example of scientific growth. *Science Communication*, *16*, 242–273.

Vaughan, P. W., & Rogers, E. M. (2000). A staged model of communication effects: Evidence from an entertainment-education radio soap opera in Tanzania. *Journal of Health Communication*, *5*(3), 203–227.

Westarp, F. V. (2003). *Modeling software markets: Empirical analysis, network simulations, and marketing implications.* New York: Physica-Verlag.

Wissler, C. (1923). *Man and culture.* New York: Thomas Y. Crowell.

Wolfe, R. A. (1994). Organizational innovation: Review, critique, and suggested research directions. *Journal of Management Studies*, *31*, 407–431.

Young, S. D., Belin, T. R., Klausner, J. D., Valente, T. W. (2015). Methods for measuring diffusion of a social media-based health intervention. *Social Networking*, *4*(2), 41–46.

Zhang, X., Yu, P., Yan, J., Ton, A. M., & Spil, I. (2015). Using diffusion of innovation theory to understand the factors impacting patient acceptance and use of consumer e-health innovations: A case study in a primary care clinic. *BMC Health Services Research*, *15*, 71. doi: 10.1186/s12913-015-0726-2.

FREIRE'S MODEL OF ADULT EDUCATION

Chapter 10

KEY CONCEPTS

- codification
- conscientization
- critical consciousness
- dialogue
- informal education
- popular education

- praxis
- problematization or problem posing
- SHOWED model
- social reality
- transformation

AFTER READING THIS CHAPTER YOU SHOULD BE ABLE TO

- Describe Paulo Freire's contribution to adult education
- List the five constructs from Freire's adult education model
- Explain the application of Freire's model in health education
- Identify educational methods and match these to modify each construct from Freire's model to influence a health behavior
- Apply Freire's model to design an intervention to change a health behavior of your choice

Paulo Freire (1921–1997) was a Brazilian educator, philosopher, and political activist who worked in the area of adult literacy. His book *Pedagogy of the Oppressed* (Freire, 1970b) is currently one of the most cited books in education in Asia, Africa, and South America (Smith, 2005). It is popular in these continents because the prevailing conditions in these parts of the world are conducive to this approach. His model is also popular in the United States, where it has been used for community organization, health education, and social work in addition to adult education. His work is often compared with the work on experiential education by John Dewey (1938) in the United States. Freire's model is often employed by those who work with oppressed people and use informal education or popular education. **Informal education** is based on experiential learning (learning from one's experiences), uses simple conversation, and can take place in any setting. **Popular education** is similar to informal education; it is need based, does not have a hierarchical relationship between learners and facilitators, builds on community knowledge, and aims at political action (Hamilton & Cunningham, 1989). Freire's model is sometimes referred to as the *theory of liberation education* (Freire, 1985).

Freire believed that education was a means of freeing people from the "culture of silence" that is widely prevalent among the masses, especially in nonindustrialized countries (Freire, 1970b). The essence of Freire's teaching is **dialogue**, or becoming adept at two-way communication. He believed that the individual deprived of dialogue was oppressed. He looked at dialogue as the process and practice of liberation. Since dialogue is the essence of the Freirean approach, the latter is also called *participatory research* (Cornwall & Jewkes, 1995). The second hallmark of the Freirean methodology is the fundamental technique of **problematizing, or problem posing**. This approach is essentially the opposite of traditional education, which Freire labeled "banking education" (Freire, 1970b). Banking education provides ready-made answers or solutions to problems and does not allow people to think for themselves. The emphasis of the problem-posing approach lies in raising questions without providing any predetermined answers. The students reflect and arrive at the answers themselves.

> **Paulo Freire was a Brazilian educator whose book *Pedagogy of the Oppressed* is one of the most cited books in education in Asia, Africa, and South America.**
>
> —Smith, 2005

HISTORICAL PERSPECTIVE

Paulo Freire was born in 1921 in northeast Brazil in a well-to-do middle-class family that was severely affected by the Great Depression (1929–1939). His father died when Paulo was only 13 years old, and the family suffered from many difficulties during that period. With great efforts he attended the Recifé University and studied law, philosophy, and linguistics. Thereafter, he worked as a legal assessor in trade unions for a number of years but gradually drifted toward the field of education. In 1963, he became the director of the National Literacy Program in Brazil. This program led to political upheaval in its time because it overturned the traditional electoral base (in Brazil at the time, only the literate could vote).

Freire's work is considered to be an important example of education being used to bring about social change. In the 1970s, his book *Pedagogy of the Oppressed* (Freire, 1970b) and its reviews in Harvard publications established Freire as a radical, revolutionary pedagogue. Through his work as a consultant in the Office of Education of the World Council of Churches he became active in the struggles of several nonindustrialized countries, mostly in Africa. In the 1980s, he returned to Brazil, and with the help of the mayor of São Paulo, in 1989 he started a literacy program based on his theory of education that combined the church and the university. He was scheduled to teach at Harvard in September of 1997, but he died of a heart attack in May of that year at the age of 76.

> **Paulo Freire's work in literacy enabled illiterate people in Brazil to gain the right to vote, which is a great example of using education for political action.**

Some of Freire's other well-known books are *Cultural Action for Freedom* (1970a), *Education for Critical Consciousness* (1973), *Education: The Practice of Freedom* (1976), *The Politics of Education: Culture, Power and Liberation* (1985), *Pedagogy of Hope: Reviving Pedagogy of the Oppressed* (1995), and *Pedagogy of the Heart* (1997). In 2013, in Holyoke, Massachusetts, a group of educators received permission from the state to establish the Paolo Freire Social Justice Charter School (www.paulofreirecharterschool.org/). The school is based on the principles and teachings of Paulo Freire. Since then, another school has opened in Newark, New Jersey (www.thefreireschool.org).

APPROACH OF FREIRE'S MODEL

The Freirean model uses a three-phase process, which is summarized in **Table 10-1**. Although this approach appears to be simple, it is often difficult in practice because helping people reflect on their experiences requires a high degree of facilitation. The first phase in this approach is the *naming phase*, in which the facilitators and learners reflect on the question "What is the problem?" or "What is the question under discussion?" This has also been called the *listening stage*. It is conducted in equal partnership with the community members to identify problems and determine priorities (Gugushe, 1996). For example, when applying this theory with a group of overweight high school students, the group may identify their problem as being overweight or may identify the problem as spending too much time using computers and other media.

The second phase is the *reflection phase*, in which the facilitator poses the question "How do we explain this situation?" or "Why is this the case?" This phase is also called the *dialogue stage*. The discussion objects in this stage are often called **codes**, and the process itself **codification**. The codes are created to structure a discussion or problem-posing dialogue around the main issue or issues. A code is a physical representation of an identified community issue in any form. It could be a case study, role play, story, slide show, photograph, song, or so on. An effective code exemplifies a problematic situation with many facets so that participants can express their emotional and

Table 10-1	Three Phases of the Freirean Model
Phase	**Main Question for Reflection**
1: Naming (listening stage)	What is the problem?
2: Reflection (dialogue stage)	How do we explain this situation?
3: Action	What can be done to change this situation?

Table 10-2	SHOWED Model: A Practical Way to Apply the Freirean Model
What do we *see* here?	
What is really *happening*?	
How does the story relate to *our* lives?	
Why did the person acquire the problem?	
How is it possible for this person to become *empowered*?	
What can we *do* about it?	

social responses to it. The emphasis is on bringing out the inner emotions of participants as much as possible.

In some training programs, facilitators help in this reflection by using a five-step questioning strategy (debriefing) in which participants, after undergoing the codification process, are asked to (1) describe what they see and feel, (2) as a group define the many levels of the problem, (3) share similar experiences from their lives, (4) question why this problem exists, and (5) develop action plans to address the problem (Gugushe, 1996). For example, in a group of overweight high school students, the facilitators might implement a role play in which the various problems, such as being teased by fellow classmates, inability to participate in some activities in which they would like to participate, and not being comfortable with their body appearance, could be brought out to stir emotions in the participants. These emotions would then be used by the facilitator to initiate learning and to encourage participants to move to the next step, action.

The third phase is the *action phase*, characterized by the question "What can be done to change this situation?" or "What options do we have?" The unique feature of this pedagogical approach is that it is *process centered* as opposed to being outcome centered or product centered. It does not prescribe the attainment of any acceptable end product in the beginning; rather, it focuses on the approach that needs to be followed. In the example of working with a group of overweight high school students, the health educator needs to arrive at an action plan, but the specific content of that action plan is up to the group. The group might choose teasing about the problem of overweight as the most significant issue and develop a strategy of peer education, or the group might see physical inactivity as the major issue and develop an approach for becoming more physically active.

Another practical method for applying this model and remembering all the facilitation steps has been described by Wallerstein and Bernstein (1988). They applied Freire's ideas to alcohol and substance abuse prevention programs in youth and coined the acronym SHOWED. Their **SHOWED model** is depicted in **Table 10-2**.

CONSTRUCTS OF FREIRE'S MODEL

As discussed in earlier chapters, when using theories to design health education and health promotion programs, it is very important to organize the ideas from the theory into discrete constructs or building blocks that can be distinctly identified. This is particularly challenging with Freire's model because no source clearly identifies the constructs from his model. This chapter identifies five main concepts of Freire's theory that can be used by health education programs and presents these as key constructs (**Table 10–3**). These concepts are illustrated in **Figure 10–1**.

The first construct of Freire's model is *dialogue*, described as an authentic exchange between the learners and educators (or, for health education, between health educators and those in need of behavior change or their families). Dialogue entails real, concrete awareness of the context of facts (**social reality**). This reality or context must come from the perspective of the clients. This construct can be applied in health education settings by providing opportunities to have a two–way discussion between health educators and the people needing behavior change or their families. The discussion must explore the root causes of their behaviors. The techniques of brainstorming, small group discussion, large group discussion, and online discussion forums can be employed in this regard.

Evaluation of health education programs using the Freirean model is mostly done qualitatively (Sharma, 2001). However, quantitative measurement is also possible. To quantitatively evaluate the construct of dialogue, some of the dimensions that can be measured are the extent of two–way communication through self–reports, the extent of problem posing through an objective evaluation of the transcript or video of the discussions, and the extent of joint discovery of the social reality as

> **Dialogue cannot exist without humility.**
>
> —Paulo Freire (1970b)

Table 10-3	Key Constructs of Freire's Model	
Construct	**Definition**	**How to Modify?**
Dialogue	Two-way exchange between learners and educators	• Opportunity for two-way communication (e.g., open group discussion)
Conscientization	Identification of underlying systemic forces of oppression	• Identifying oppressive sources (e.g., brainstorming on root cause) • Working together as change agents (e.g., team-building activities) • Personalizing the issue (e.g., using role plays to generate emotions)
Praxis	Reflective action or active reflection	• Working on a specific project (e.g., a pilot project assignment)
Transformation	Relationship that identifies one as a political and social being	• Discussing political and social implications of chosen issues (e.g., use of case studies)
Critical consciousness	Political organization of those adversely affected	• Organizing those affected to take action (e.g., creation of a not-for-profit group)

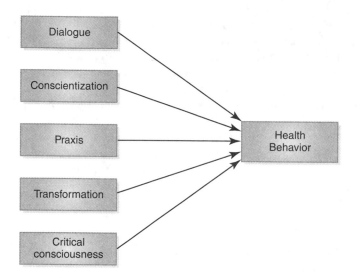

FIGURE 10-1 Constructs of Freire's model.

measured by either self-reports or analysis of the end products of dialogue. **Table 10-4** summarizes the quantitative indicators for different constructs of the Freirean model and their methods of measurement.

The second construct is **conscientization**, or efforts to identify and address the underlying systemic forces of oppression and inequality. Freire (1970b) calls conscientization a process of "humanization" or an effort to enlighten people about the obstacles preventing them from a clear perception of reality. For health education, it refers to identification of the root causes of unhealthy behaviors, which can be done by techniques such as brainstorming or reflecting on case studies. The second component of this construct is working together as change agents. This can be achieved by using team-building activities such as the broken squares game, team juggling game, and so on (Business Fundamentals, 2005). Finally, to influence this construct, the health educator needs to personalize the issue for the participants as much as possible. This can be done by using techniques such as role plays or simulations to generate emotions.

After implementation of this construct in community-based rehabilitation programs, the extent of identification of oppressive sources can be measured by self-report or by checking the transcripts or video recordings. The extent of working together as change agents can be evaluated by self-report or gauged by the products generated and tasks completed. Finally, the extent to which the key issue influences each participant at a personal level can be ascertained by a self-report questionnaire.

The third construct of Freire's model is **praxis**, which refers to what Freire (1985) calls "reflective action" or "active reflection." It is the method of tying together theory and practice. Often we find that a gap exists between preaching (theory) and practice. The purpose of this construct is to narrow that gap and possibly eliminate it. In technical terms, praxis is the linkage between

Table 10-4	Quantitative Indicators for Different Constructs of the Freirean Model and Their Methods of Measurement	
Construct	**Quantitative Indicators**	**Methods of Measurement**
Dialogue	• Extent of two-way communication • Extent of problem posing • Extent of joint discovery of social reality	• Self-reports • Evaluation of the transcript or video • Self-reports or analysis of the end products of dialogue
Conscientization	• Extent of identification of oppressive sources • Extent of working together as change agents • Extent to which the key issue influences each person at a personal level	• Self-reports or evaluation of transcript or video • Self-reports or evaluation of products generated and tasks completed • Self-reports
Praxis	• Extent of participation and reflection in project planning, implementation, and evaluation • Extent of perceived utility of the project	• Self-reports or assessment of actual products • Self-reports
Transformation	• Extent of focus on issue from the perspective of the people with the unhealthy behavior • Extent of unison on a collective viewpoint	• Self-reports • Self-reports
Critical consciousness	• Extent of cooperation among members; joint identification with the articulated issues, mission, and vision of the group • Extent of communication within the group • Extent of political organization of the group	• Self-reports • Self-reports or evaluation of video • Self-reports or analysis of the tasks completed

epistemology (source of knowledge) and ontology (reality). In health education interventions, it can be used when the participants work on a specific project and accomplish some tasks. An example could be joint creation of an action plan for behavior change and collective evaluation of it. Some of the researchable aspects that process and impact evaluation can assess for this construct include extent of participation in project planning, extent of reflection in project planning, extent of participation in project implementation, extent of reflection in project implementation, extent of participation in project evaluation, extent of reflection in project evaluation, and extent of perceived utility of the project. All of these can be gauged by self-reports or assessment of actual products.

The fourth construct of the Freirean model is **transformation**. Freire (1976) describes this as the process of changing *objects* (who have a naive consciousness of reality) into *subjects* (who see the theory behind the reality). It connotes independence, status, and integrity. It implies possession of "social consciousness," or being in a relationship that identifies one as a political and social being. In transformation, the solution is not to "integrate" people into the structure of oppression but to transform the structure so that they can become "beings for themselves" (Freire, 1970b). In simple terms, it means making people more aware of the political aspects of any issue.

This construct can be applied in health education by providing participants with opportunities for self-reflection followed by discussion. Educational techniques such as case studies are quite useful in influencing this construct. For example, a group of high school smokers could start to understand the profit-making motive of the tobacco industry through a case study in which they learn how the industry buys advertising on various media and lobbies legislators to get its products sanction, visibility, and coverage. Finally, they could become cognizant of how these issues influence smoking behaviors. Evaluators of health education programs can measure the extent of focus on the issue from the perspective of the people negatively affected by the unhealthy behavior, and the extent of unison on a collective viewpoint. These dimensions can be measured by self-reports.

> Education is never neutral. ... Either it conforms or it transforms.
>
> —Paulo Freire (1985)

The final construct of the Freirean model is **critical consciousness**. In essence, this refers to the political organization of those adversely affected. This can be applied in health education by building cooperation between health educators and persons with disabilities, fostering unity on issues, developing effective communication, and augmenting the process of political organization to change policies and legislation. In health education programs, it often leads to formation of a not-for-profit group. Evaluators of health education programs can measure the extent of cooperation among members; the extent of joint identification with the articulated issues, mission, and vision of the group; the extent of communication within the group; and the extent of political organization of the group. These dimensions can be measured by self-reports.

APPLICATIONS OF FREIRE'S MODEL IN HEALTH EDUCATION

The first application of Paulo Freire's work in health education and health promotion in the United States began in the 1980s in a study by Wallerstein and Bernstein (1988). They developed a youth-centered, intergenerational, experiential prevention program called the Adolescent Social Action Program (ASAP) in New Mexico. The program aimed at preventing substance abuse, particularly alcohol, in youth. The program was found to be useful in influencing several process variables, such as empathy, critical thinking, and belief in group action, and some impact variables, such as extent of participation in social action among the participants (Wallerstein & Sanchez-Merki, 1994). Over the years, the program, which started in one school, was successfully extended to several other schools utilizing the peer-to-peer model (Wallerstein, Sanchez-Merki, & Dow, 1997).

Since the initial application in the 1980s, the model has been used in a variety of applications in health education and promotion, both for individual-level behavior change and for community-level changes. Freire's model has been used in breast cancer control (Mishra et al., 1998), breast-feeding promotion (Daghio, Vezzani, & Ciardullo, 2003), building health literacy (Kickbusch, 2001; Nutbeam, 2000; Schillinger, 2001; Wang, 2000), community organization (Flick, Reese, Rogers, Fletcher, & Sonn, 1994; Minkler & Wallerstein, 1997), evaluation of coalitions (Sharma, 2002), evaluation of worker safety programs (Cole, 2002; McQuiston, 2000; Weinger & Lyons, 1992), health coaching (Irwin & Morrow, 2005), HIV/AIDS prevention (Campbell, 2004; Gil, 1998; Laver, van der Borne, & Kok, 2005–2006; Miranda & Barroso, 2007), improving decision making (Wittmann-Price, 2004), informing policy makers of the health situation in the community through community-taken photographs (Wang & Burris, 1994), intercultural health promotion (Ditton, 2005), malaria prevention and control (Geounuppakul, Butraporn, Kunstadter, Leemingsawat, & Pacheun, 2007), nutrition education (Krawinkel, Mahr, Wuestefeld, & ten Haaf, 2005), oral health promotion (Gugushe, 1996; Watt, 2002), participatory development of health education materials (Rudd & Comings, 1994), participatory program planning (Campbell & Jovchelovitch, 2000; Laverack & Labonte, 2000), participatory evaluation (Sharma & Deepak, 2001), patient education (Roter, 2000; Waters, 2000), a peer-to-peer approach for reproductive health (United Nations Educational, Scientific, and Cultural Organization, 2003), people with mental illness (Bellamy & Mowbray, 1998; Caragata, 2000; Rindner, 2004; Wells, Miranda, Bruce, Alegria, & Wallerstein, 2004), preparation of health educators (Helitzer & Wallerstein, 1999), preparation of nurse educators (Chalmers & Bramadat, 1996; Chiesa & Fracolli, 2007; Delia Rojo, Villela Bueno, & Silva, 2008; Hartrick, Lindsey, & Hills, 1994; Liimatainen, Poskiparta, Karhila, & Sjögren, 2001; Rush, 1997), reducing nutritional inequities (Travers, 1997), self-care education (Levin, 1999), education about sexually transmitted diseases (Dal Sasso, Pedrini, & Branco, 2004), training of health functionaries (Fonn & Xaba, 2001; Labonte, Feather, & Hills, 1999), understanding living with chronic illness (Plazas Mdel & Cameron, 2015), violence prevention (Monteiro et al., 2015), and work with abused women (Mann, 1987). **Table 10-5** summarizes these applications in health education and promotion.

The model has been applied with different racial and ethnic subgroups. For example, it has been used with African Americans (Waters, 2000), Native Americans (Davis & Reid, 1999), rural Chinese women (Wang & Burris, 1994), Hispanic girls (Gil, 1998), and South African health workers (Fonn & Xaba, 2001).

> **Education must begin with the solution of the teacher-student contradiction, by reconciling the poles of the contradiction so that both are simultaneously teachers and students.**
>
> Freire (1970b, p. 53)

LIMITATIONS OF FREIRE'S MODEL

Like all the models and theories discussed in this book, the Freirean model has some limitations. Freire has often been criticized for his contorted manner of writing and his obscurantism, which makes interpretation of concepts difficult and measurement complex. The terminology that has

Table 10-5	Applications of Freire's Model in Health Education and Health Promotion
Breast cancer control
Breast-feeding promotion
Building health literacy
Community organization
Evaluation of coalitions
Evaluation of worker safety programs
Health coaching
HIV/AIDS prevention
Improving decision making
Informing policy makers of the status of community health through community-taken photographs
Intercultural health promotion
Malaria prevention and control
Nutrition education
Oral health promotion
Participatory development of health education materials
Participatory program planning
Participatory evaluation
Patient education
Peer-to-peer approach for reproductive health
People with mental illness
Preparation of health educators
Preparation of nurse educators
Reducing nutritional inequities
Self-care education
Sexually transmitted diseases (STD) education
Training health functionaries
Understanding living with chronic illness
Violence prevention
Work with abused women

been used in this chapter is evidence that Freire's writing style is not very easy to follow and lends itself to multiple interpretations.

Freire's viewpoints are often considered too utopian or ideal. There is excessive idealism in the descriptions of knowing and of learners and educators participating as equals. Such participation is seldom achieved in real-world settings. It is often very difficult for a more educated person (educator) to shed his or her ego and begin to learn from the participants.

Freire presents a circular logic and demonstrates confusing repetitiveness in his writing style. As a consequence, it is difficult to differentiate the constructs of this model so that they are mutually exclusive. To use a theory, educators need all the ideas to be separate from each other so that they can be measured and evaluated distinctly.

The model has also been criticized for requiring social manipulation, which has been used to domesticate people rather than liberate them. Finally, the choice of codes (such as words and songs) in the dialogue step is purposively done so that there are no neutral words; instead, the codes challenge the social reality. This adds a bias to the scientific inquiry. In a way, the model is making people think and react in a predetermined fashion. Therefore, the political and social purpose inherent in the model can be challenged as being manipulative.

APPLICATION EXERCISE

In this chapter, we have introduced several applications of Freire's model in health education and health promotion. Choose an application in an area that interests you and locate the full-text article of that application. Analyze how the model was used in that context. One such application is by Geounuppakul and colleagues (2007) in the area of malaria prevention and control in Chiang Mai Province, Thailand. They used Freire's model to empower a women's group for prevention and control of malaria in an experimental community. Their sample included 45 women. The activities in the empowerment program included building self-esteem and self-confidence and utilization of insecticide-treated nets (ITN) to prevent and control malaria. A total of 10 participatory meetings were organized. The study collected qualitative data through focus-group discussions, observations, and in-depth interviews with women, their husbands, and youths at risk for malaria. Data were collected before the intervention and 3, 6, 9, and 12 months following the intervention from the experimental and a control community. It was found that in the experimental community malaria prevention behaviors, use of ITN, and self-esteem and self-confidence levels improved and were higher than in the control community. Definitive plans were made by the women in the experimental community that included protecting the family, giving malaria-related education, controlling mosquitoes, and using ITN. They also linked this activity to an income generation program.

Locate the full-text article of this application and prepare a critique of 250 words. Pay attention to the details provided regarding participatory meetings. How were they participatory? What methods have been described that make them stand out as "participatory"? Look at the evaluation design. How were the data collected and analyzed? What were the conclusions?

SKILL-BUILDING ACTIVITY

Let us see how we can apply Freire's model to the issue of unhealthy eating behaviors in high school students. **Figure 10-2** depicts each of the constructs from the Freirean model and links these with the educational processes and behavioral objectives in this example to modify the eating behavior of the students.

The health education intervention would start by modifying the construct of dialogue, which can be done through a discussion among students, their parents, school teachers, and administrators. The discussion could be organized outside of school hours, and the facilitator would need to ensure that it is conducted in an egalitarian manner. One or more sessions might be used to build initial rapport and then to identify problems regarding eating behaviors.

Brainstorming can be used to build conscientization and explore the root causes of eating problems and their consequences. Role plays on these aspects and team-building exercises can be used to further modify this construct. The construct of praxis can be modified by having participants implement a pilot project related to healthy eating. The specific nature of the pilot project needs to be decided by the participants, but an example could be reading food labels and researching the caloric information of all food products used in the school and finding low-fat alternatives for each high-fat product. To modify the transformation construct, political and social awareness needs to be increased, which can be done through a case study. For example, the reasons certain food products are included in school menus and others are excluded can be explored. Finally, to raise critical consciousness, the action group of students, teachers, administrators, parents, food

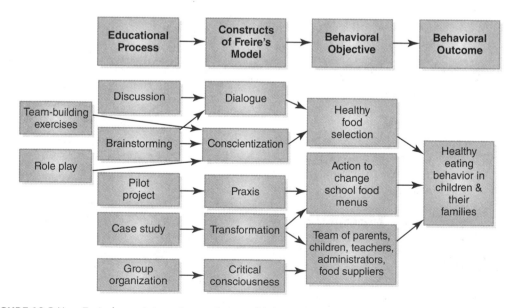

FIGURE 10-2 How Freire's model can be used to modify healthy eating behavior.

Table 10-6	Choosing the Educational Methods for Health Education Program Planning Using Freire's Model

1. What is the best educational method to facilitate dialogue?
   - Small group discussion
   - Large group discussion
   - Online discussion
   - Other

2. What is the best educational method to facilitate conscientization?
   - Discussion
   - Brainstorming
   - Role play
   - Simulation
   - Team-building exercises
   - Other

3. What is the best educational method to facilitate praxis?
   - Pilot project
   - Other

4. What is the best educational method to facilitate transformation?
   - Case study
   - Field visit
   - Other

5. What is the best educational method to facilitate critical consciousness?
   - Group formation
   - Coalition building
   - Registration of not-for-profit organization
   - Other

providers, and service personnel can form themselves into a regular unit to monitor healthy food products in the school.

Using Freire's model, work on a health behavior issue for a target group of your choice. **Table 10-6** provides a set of questions to assist you in choosing an educational method that corresponds to each of the different constructs.

SUMMARY

Paulo Freire (1921–1997), a Brazilian educator, is well known for his work using popular education to build adult literacy. In addition to adult education, his model has been used in community organization, development fields, social work, and health education. The three phases in his method are naming, reflection, and action.

The constructs of his theory are dialogue (two-way communication), conscientization (exploration of root causes of the problem), praxis (action and reflection), transformation (comprehension of political and social causes), and critical consciousness (formation of an organization). Dialogue can be facilitated through small group discussion, large group discussion, or online discussion. Conscientization can be facilitated by brainstorming, discussion, role play, simulation, and team-building exercises. Praxis can be facilitated by providing opportunities to develop action plans or implement pilot projects. Transformation can be facilitated by case studies, field visits, and so on. Critical consciousness can be developed by forming groups, building coalitions, and forming organizations.

IMPORTANT TERMS

codes

codification

conscientization

critical consciousness

dialogue

informal education

popular education

praxis

problematization (problem posing)

SHOWED model

social reality

transformation

REVIEW QUESTIONS

1. Discuss the three–phase approach of the Freirean model.
2. What does the acronym SHOWED mean in the context of the Freirean model?
3. Briefly describe the five constructs of Freire's model.
4. Differentiate between praxis and transformation.
5. How can critical consciousness be modified?
6. Using Freire's model, work to modify a health behavior issue for a target group of your choice.

WEBSITES TO EXPLORE

An Interview with Paulo Freire

http://aurora.icaap.org/talks/freire.html

This website presents an interview conducted with Paulo Freire in 1990. *Read this interview and discuss his views on conscientization.*

Informal Education

www.infed.org/

This website is an encyclopedia of informal education. Type "Paulo Freire" into the search engine and read the webpage that discusses Freire and informal education. It is called, "Paulo

Freire: Dialogue, praxis and education." *Read this account and reflect on the critique of Freire's work. To what extent do you agree or disagree with that critique?*

Paulo Freire Institute

www.paulofreire.org/

This is the bilingual website of the Paulo Freire Institute (PFI), which is an international not-for-profit organization consisting of a network of people and institutions from 24 countries. English version can be obtained in google chrome by clicking on 'translate page'. The institute conducts research; offers courses; consults with groups; produces, edits, and publishes works based on Freirian thought; and promotes events related to Freirian thought. *Explore this website and summarize the present activities of this institute.*

Paulo Freire Institute at the University of Central Lancashire

http://www.freire.org/

This is one of the organizations devoted to the advancement of Paulo Freire's work. The purpose of the institute is to advance Freire's pedagogy by bringing together scholars, activists, and teachers from around the world. *Explore this website and compare it to the eight other institutes on Paulo Freire from around the world. Write a summary of what you found out.*

Review of Paulo Freire's Books

http://fcis.oise.utoronto.ca/~daniel_schugurensky/freire/freirebooks.html

This website presents reviews of at least 20 books written by Paulo Freire. *Choose any one book by Freire from your library and read it. Then read the review of that book. To what extent do you agree with the reviewer?*

REFERENCES

Bellamy, C. D., & Mowbray, C. T. (1998). Supported education as an empowerment intervention for people with mental illness. *Journal of Community Psychology*, *26*, 401–413.

Business Fundamentals. (2005). *Team building activities*. Retrieved January 1, 2006, from http://www.businessfundamentals.com/TeamBuilding.htm.

Campbell, C. (2004). Creating environments that support peer education: Experiences from HIV/AIDS prevention in South Africa. *Health Education*, *104*, 197–200.

Campbell, C., & Jovchelovitch, S. (2000). Health, community and development: Towards a social psychology of participation. *Journal of Community and Applied Social Psychology*, *10*, 255–270.

Caragata, L. (2000). Using popular education groups: Can we develop a health promotions strategy for psychiatric consumers/survivors? *Canadian Journal of Community Mental Health*, *19*, 5–20.

Chalmers, K. I., & Bramadat, I. J. (1996). Community development: Theoretical and practical issues for community health nursing in Canada. *Journal of Advanced Nursing*, *24*, 719–726.

Chiesa, A. M., & Fracolli, L. A. (2007). An educational process to strengthen primary care nursing practices in São Paulo, Brazil. *International Nursing Review*, *54*(4), 398–404.

Cole, H. P. (2002). Cognitive-behavioral approaches to farm community safety education: A conceptual analysis. *Journal of Agricultural Safety and Health*, *8*, 145–159.

Cornwall, A., & Jewkes, R. (1995). What is participatory research? *Social Science and Medicine*, *41*, 1667–1676.

Daghio, M. M., Vezzani, M. D., & Ciardullo, A. V. (2003). Impact of an educational intervention on breastfeeding. *Birth, 30,* 214–215.

Dal Sasso, G. T. M., Pedrini, D., & Branco, I. (2004). *Interactive media of health education in sexually transmitted diseases (STDs).* Retrieved December 31, 2005, from http://cmbi.bjmu.edu.cn/news/report/2004/medinfo2004/pdffiles/papers/348_d040005155.pdf

Davis, S. M., & Reid, R. (1999). Practicing participatory research in American Indian communities. *American Journal of Clinical Nutrition, 69,* 755S–759S.

Delia Rojo, M., Villela Bueno, S. M., & Silva, E. C. (2008). Conceptions of nursing students on health promotion related to psychoactive substances. *Revista Latino Americana de Enfermagem, 16,* 627–633.

Dewey, J. (1938). *Experience & education.* New York: Kappa Delta Pi.

Ditton, M. (2005). *Research plan for intercultural health promotion education.* Retrieved December 31, 2005, from http://conference.herdsa.org.au/2005/pdf/non_refereed/075.pdf

Flick, L. H., Reese, C. G., Rogers, G., Fletcher, P., & Sonn, J. (1994). Building community for health: Lessons from a seven-year-old neighborhood/university partnership. *Health Education Quarterly, 21,* 369–380.

Fonn, S., & Xaba, M. (2001). Health workers for change: Developing the initiative. *Health Policy and Planning, 16*(Suppl. 1), 13–18.

Freire, P. (1970a). *Cultural action for freedom.* Cambridge, MA: Harvard Educational Review and Center for the Study of Development and Social Change.

Freire, P. (1970b). *Pedagogy of the oppressed.* New York: Continuum.

Freire, P. (1973). *Education for critical consciousness.* New York: Continuum.

Freire, P. (1976). *Education: The practice of freedom.* London: Writers and Readers Cooperative.

Freire, P. (1985). *The politics of education: Culture, power and liberation.* South Hadley, MA: Bergin and Garvey.

Freire, P. (1995). *Pedagogy of hope: Reviving pedagogy of the oppressed.* New York: Continuum.

Freire, P. (1997). *Pedagogy of the heart.* New York: Continuum.

Geounuppakul, M., Butraporn, P., Kunstadter, P., Leemingsawat, S., & Pacheun, O. (2007). An empowerment program to enhance women's ability to prevent and control malaria in the community, Chiang Mai Province, Thailand. *Southeast Asian Journal of Tropical Medicine and Public Health, 38*(3), 546–559.

Gil, V. E. (1998). Empowerment rhetoric, sexual negotiation, and Latinas' AIDS risk: Research implications for prevention health education. *International Quarterly of Community Health Education, 18,* 9–27.

Gugushe, T. S. (1996). An overview of Paulo Freire's perspective on health education. *Journal of the Dental Association of South Africa, 51,* 734–736.

Hamilton, E., & Cunningham, P. M. (1989). Community-based adult education. In S. B. Merriam & P. M. Cunningham (Eds.), *Handbook of adult and continuing education.* San Francisco: Jossey-Bass.

Hartrick, G., Lindsey, E., & Hills, M. (1994). Family nursing assessment: Meeting the challenge of health promotion. *Journal of Advanced Nursing, 20,* 85–91.

Helitzer, D., & Wallerstein, N. (1999). A proposal for a graduate curriculum integrating theory and practice in public health. Health Education Research, *14,* 697–706.

Irwin, J. D., & Morrow, D. (2005). Health promotion theory in practice: An analysis of co-active coaching. *International Journal of Evidence Based Coaching and Mentoring, 3*(1), 29–38.

Kickbusch, I. S. (2001). Health literacy: Addressing the health and education divide. *Health Promotion International, 16,* 289–297.

Krawinkel, M. B., Mahr, J., Wuestefeld, M., & ten Haaf, J. (2005). Nutrition education for illiterate children in southern Madagascar: Addressing their needs, perceptions and capabilities. *Public Health Nutrition, 8,* 366–372.

Labonte, R. Feather, J., & Hills, M. (1999). A story/dialogue method for health promotion knowledge development and evaluation. *Health Education Research, 14,* 39–50.

Laver, S. M., van der Borne, B., & Kok, G. (2005–2006). Using theory to design an intervention for HIV/AIDS prevention in farm workers in rural Zimbabwe. 1994–95. *International Quarterly of Community Health Education, 25*(1–2), 135–148.

Laverack, G., & Labonte, R. (2000). A planning framework for community empowerment within health promotion. *Health Policy and Planning*, *15*, 255–262.

Levin, L. S. (1999). Patient education and self-care. *International Journal of Self Help and Self Care*, *1*, 21–31.

Liimatainen, L., Poskiparta, M., Karhila, P., & Sjögren, A. (2001). The development of reflective learning in the context of health counselling and health promotion during nurse education. *Journal of Advanced Nursing*, *34*, 648–658.

Mann, B. (1987). Working with battered women: Radical education or therapy? In E. Pence (Ed.), *In our best interest: A process for personal and social change* (pp. 104–116). Duluth: Minnesota Program Development.

McQuiston, T. H. (2000). Empowerment evaluation of worker safety and health education programs. *American Journal of Industrial Medicine*, *38*, 584–597.

Minkler, M., & Wallerstein, N. (1997). Improving health through community organizing and community building: A health education perspective. In M. Minkler (Ed.), *Community organizing and community building for health* (pp. 30–52). New Brunswick, NJ: Rutgers University Press.

Miranda, K. C., & Barroso, M. G. (2007). HIV/AIDS counseling: Analysis based on Paulo Freire. *Revista Latino Americana de Enfermagem*, *15*(1), 100–105.

Mishra, S. I., Chavez, L. R., Magana, J. R., Nava, P., Burciaga, V. R., & Hubbell, F. A. (1998). Improving breast cancer control among Latinas: Evaluation of a theory-based educational program. *Health Education and Behavior*, *25*, 653–670.

Monteiro, E. M., Neto, W. B., de Lima, L. S., de Aquino, J. M., Gontijo, D. T., & Pereira, B. O. (2015). Culture circles in adolescent empowerment for the prevention of violence. *International Journal of Adolescence and Youth*, *20*(2), 167–184.

Nutbeam, D. (2000). Health literacy as a public health goal: A challenge for contemporary health education and communication strategies into the 21st century. *Health Promotion International*, *15*, 259–267.

Plazas Mdel, P., & Cameron, B. L. (2015). Using Freire's participatory educational method to understand the experience of living with chronic illness in the current age of globalization. *Journal of Nursing Research*, *23*(2), 83–93. doi: 10.1097/JNR.0000000000000090.

Rindner, E. C. (2004). Using Freirean empowerment for health education with adolescents in primary, secondary, and tertiary psychiatric settings. *Journal of Child and Adolescent Psychiatric Nursing*, *17*, 78–84.

Roter, D. (2000). The medical visit context of treatment decision-making and the therapeutic relationship. *Health Expectations*, *3*, 17–25.

Rudd, R. E., & Comings, J. P. (1994). Learner developed materials: An empowering product. *Health Education Quarterly*, *21*, 313–327.

Rush, K. L. (1997). Health promotion ideology and nursing education. *Journal of Advanced Nursing*, *25*, 1292–1298.

Schillinger, D. (2001). Improving the quality of chronic disease management for populations with low functional health literacy: A call to action. *Disease Management*, *4*, 103–109.

Sharma, M. (2001). Freire's adult education model: An underutilized model in alcohol and drug education? [Editorial]. *Journal of Alcohol and Drug Education*, *47*(1), 1–3.

Sharma, M. (2002, July). *Using Freire's model for impact evaluation of coalitions in health and human services*. Paper presented at the summer residency of Walden University at Indiana University, Bloomington, IN.

Sharma, M., & Deepak, S. (2001). A participatory evaluation of community-based rehabilitation program in North Central Vietnam. *Disability and Rehabilitation*, *23*, 352–358.

Smith, M. K. (2005). *Paulo Freire*. Retrieved December 29, 2005, from http://www.infed.org/ thinkers/et-freir.htm

Travers, K. D. (1997). Reducing inequities through participatory research and community empowerment. *Health Education and Behavior*, *24*, 344–356.

United Nations Educational, Scientific, and Cultural Organization. (2003). *Peer approach in adolescent reproductive health education: Some lessons learned*. Bangkok, Thailand: Author.

Wallerstein, N., & Bernstein, E. (1988). Empowerment education: Freire's ideas adapted to health education. *Health Education Quarterly*, *15*, 379–394.

Wallerstein, N., & Sanchez-Merki, V. (1994). Freirian praxis in health education: Research results from an adolescent prevention program. *Health Education Research*, *9*, 105–118.

Wallerstein, N., Sanchez-Merki, V., & Dow, L. (1997). Freirian praxis in health education and community organizing. A case study of an adolescent prevention program. In M. Minkler (Ed.), *Community organizing and community building for health* (pp. 195–211). New Brunswick, NJ: Rutgers University Press.

Wang, C., & Burris, M. A. (1994). Empowerment through photo novella: Portraits of participation. *Health Education Quarterly*, *21*, 171–186.

Wang, R. (2000). Critical health literacy: A case study from China in schistosomiasis control. *Health Promotion International*, *15*, 269–274.

Waters, C. M. (2000). End-of-life care directives among African Americans: Lessons learned—a need for community-centered discussion and education. *Journal of Community Health Nursing*, *17*, 25–37.

Watt, R. G. (2002). Emerging theories into the social determinants of health: Implications for oral health promotion. *Community Dentistry and Oral Epidemiology*, *30*, 241–247.

Weinger, M., & Lyons, M. (1992). Problem-solving in the fields: An action-oriented approach to farmworker education about pesticides. *American Journal of Industrial Medicine*, *22*, 667–690.

Wells, K., Miranda, J., Bruce, M. L., Alegria, M., & Wallerstein, N. (2004). Bridging community intervention and mental health services research. *American Journal of Psychiatry*, *161*, 955–963.

Wittmann-Price, R. A. (2004). Emancipation in decision-making in women's health care. *Journal of Advanced Nursing*, *47*, 437–445.

NEWER THEORIES IN HEALTH EDUCATION AND HEALTH PROMOTION

Chapter 11

KEY CONCEPTS

- advantages
- attitudes
- autonomy
- behavioral confidence
- behavioral intention
- behavioral skills
- changes in physical environment
- changes in social environment
- coalition
- community coalition action theory (CCAT)
- competence
- disadvantages
- emotional intelligence theory
- emotional transformation
- empathy
- environment
- information
- information-motivation-behavioral skills (IMB) model
- initiation of behavior change
- integrative model of behavioral prediction (IM)
- managing relationships
- mood management
- motivation
- multi-theory model (MTM) for health behavior change
- norms
- participatory dialogue
- perceived behavioral control
- practice for change
- relatedness
- self-awareness
- self-determination theory (SDT)
- self-efficacy
- self-esteem
- self-motivation
- sexual division of labor
- sexual division of power
- skills and abilities
- structure of cathexis
- sustenance of behavior change
- theory of gender and power

AFTER READING THIS CHAPTER YOU SHOULD BE ABLE TO

- Describe the constructs and applications of the integrative model of behavioral prediction (IM)
- Explain the constructs and applications of emotional intelligence theory
- Explicate the constructs and applications of the information-motivation-behavioral skills (IMB) model
- Define the constructs and applications of self-determination theory (SDT)
- Explain the role of the construct of self-esteem in health education and health promotion
- Describe the community coalition action theory (CCAT)
- Explain the constructs and applications of the theory of gender and power
- Summarize the constructs of the multi-theory model (MTM) of health behavior change and apply them in designing a program of health education and promotion

The field of health education and health promotion has experienced tremendous growth in the past two decades. The emphasis on prevention in the health care sector, an aging population, a growing prevalence of lifestyle–related chronic and even communicable diseases, the success of health education and health promotion tools in controlling the HIV/AIDS epidemic, the success of health education and health promotion in reducing tobacco use in the United States, and improved training of health education specialists, dietitians, nurse educators, public health professionals, and health coaches have combined to advance the field to new heights. The theories described in this text have undoubtedly helped health education and health promotion reach its present stature. The theories have helped make the discipline an evidence–based practice field and led to translational research.

Most of the theories that we have discussed in this text emerged decades ago but have been extensively tested and applied since then. For example, the health belief model emerged in the 1950s (Rosenstock, 1974), was extensively tested in the 1970s and 1980s, and is still being applied today. The transtheoretical model emerged in the late 1970s (Prochaska, 1979); was tested in the 1980s, 1990s, and 2000s; and is still being applied. The theory of reasoned action emerged in 1975 (Fishbein & Ajzen, 1975) and was refined to the theory of planned behavior in 1991 (Ajzen, 1991). These theories have also been extensively applied in recent times. Theories of stress and coping emerged in the 1970s and 1980s and continue to be used (Lazarus, 1984; Selye, 1974). Social cognitive theory emerged in the mid-1980s (Bandura, 1986) from the earlier social learning theory and is popular even today. Social marketing started in the 1960s and is also still popular (Kotler & Levy, 1969). The diffusion of innovations theory, introduced in the 1930s, remains in use (Ryan & Gross, 1943). Finally, Freire's model of adult education, which originated in the 1970s, is still quite popular (Freire, 1970). So we see that most of the popular theories in health education and health promotion originated before 1991, with the theory of planned behavior being the most recent.

Since the 1990s several theories have been developed by basic sciences, and others have been refined from existing theories. These theories are still being tested. This chapter discusses some of the newer theories in health education and health promotion. It does not describe each theory in depth but rather provides an overview and some of their applications. These theories include the integrative model of behavioral prediction (IM), emotional intelligence theory, the information-motivation-behavioral skills (IMB) model, self-determination theory (SDT), the construct of self-esteem, community coalition action theory (CCAT), and the theory of gender and power. Finally, the chapter introduces a multi-theory model (MTM), which further elaborates constructs of health behavior change.

INTEGRATIVE MODEL OF BEHAVIORAL PREDICTION

Martin Fishbein, before his death in 2009, suggested a refined approach to his earlier theory of reasoned action (Fishbein, 1967) for explaining and predicting behavior. He called this modified approach an **integrative model of behavioral prediction (IM)** (Fishbein, 2008, 2009). The model summarizes constructs from the health belief model, social cognitive theory, the theory of reasoned action, and the theory of planned behavior. The IM has identified a definitive set of constructs that can account for a substantial proportion of the variance in any given behavior.

> The integrative model of behavioral prediction (IM) integrates constructs from the health belief model, social cognitive theory, the theory of reasoned action, and the theory of planned behavior.

CONSTRUCTS OF THE INTEGRATIVE MODEL

Like the theory of reasoned action and theory of planned behavior, the IM assumes that **behavioral intention** is the best predictor of behavior. Recall that behavioral intention is the thought to perform the behavior, which is an immediate determinant of the given behavior. The IM acknowledges the role of **environment** and **skills and abilities** in moderating the intention-behavior relationship. Recall that environment consists of the physical or social circumstances or conditions that surround a person. The skills and abilities relate to the person's aptitudes and capabilities. The IM also proposes that intentions are a function of **attitudes**, **norms** (perceived normative pressure), and **self-efficacy** or **perceived behavioral control**. Recall that attitudes are a person's overall feeling of like or dislike toward any given behavior; norms are one's belief that most of the significant others in one's life think one should or should not perform a particular behavior; self-efficacy is the behavior-specific confidence in one's ability to perform a given behavior; and perceived behavioral control is how much a person feels he or she is in command of enacting the given behavior. We have also seen that the attitudes are shaped by behavioral beliefs and outcome evaluations whereas norms are shaped by injunctive (i.e., subjective) and descriptive normative beliefs, and that self-efficacy (perceived behavioral control) is shaped by control beliefs and perceived power. The model also posits background influence of past behavior, demographics and cultural knowledge, attitudes toward targets, personality, moods, emotions, other individual differences, intervention exposure, and media exposure. These background influences shape the attitudes, norms, and self-efficacy, which then influence intention and behavior. A miniaturized depiction of this model is shown in **Figure 11-1**.

APPLICATIONS OF THE INTEGRATIVE MODEL

The IM has been used in the field of health education and health promotion. Some of its applications include evaluating the effects of anti-marijuana advertisements in adolescents (Zhao et al.,

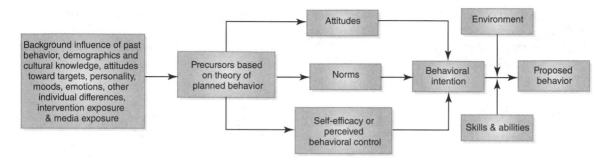

FIGURE 11-1 Miniaturized depiction of the integrative model of behavioral prediction (IM).

Adapted from Fishbein, M. (2009). An integrative model for behavioral prediction and its application to health promotion. In R. J. DiClemente, R. A. Crosby, & M. C. Kegler (Eds.), *Emerging theories in health promotion practice and research* (2nd ed., p. 221). San Francisco: Jossey-Bass.

2006), examining the role of religiosity in delaying the onset of coitus in virgin adolescents (Hull, Hennessy, Bleakley, Fishbein, & Jordan, 2011), explaining how adolescents seek sexual content in the media (Bleakley, Hennessy, & Fishbein, 2011), explaining how exposure to sexual media content influences adolescent sexual behavior (Bleakley, Hennessy, Fishbein, & Jordan, 2011), identifying psychosocial determinants of cancer-related information seeking among cancer patients (Smith-McLallen, Fishbein, & Hornik, 2011), improving sexual health communication (Hughes, Rostant, & Curran, 2014), predicting alcohol dependency in a sample of first-year undergraduate students (Atwell, Abraham, & Duka, 2011), predicting intentions to engage in cancer prevention and detection behaviors (Smith-McLallen & Fishbein, 2009), and predicting women's intention to be vaccinated against human papillomavirus (HPV) (Dillard, 2011). **Table 11–1** summarizes these applications.

Table 11-1	Applications of the Integrative Model of Behavioral Prediction (IM) in Health Education and Health Promotion
Evaluating the effects of anti-marijuana advertisements in adolescents	
Examining the role of religiosity in delaying the onset of coitus in virgin adolescents	
Explaining how adolescents seek sexual content in the media	
Explaining how exposure to sexual media content influences adolescent sexual behavior	
Identifying psychosocial determinants of cancer-related information seeking among cancer patients	
Improving sexual health communication	
Predicting alcohol dependency in a sample of first-year undergraduate students	
Predicting intentions to engage in cancer prevention and detection behaviors	
Predicting women's intention to be vaccinated against human papillomavirus (HPV)	

CRITIQUE OF THE INTEGRATIVE MODEL

Most of the studies with this model have been done to explain and predict behavior. Not much work has been done to develop health behavior interventions aimed at modifying health behaviors. More research in health education and health promotion is needed to operationalize this model in developing interventions and testing their efficacy and effectiveness. The model offers some advantages. First, it underscores the importance of intentions in predicting behavior. This line of thinking has been supported by the theory of reasoned action and the theory of planned behavior. Intentions are, indeed, important predictors of behavior. Second, it identifies salient constructs from four popular health behavior theories and integrates them into a single framework. This can boost the predictability of the model, although it has not yet been seen in intervention research. Finally, the IM acknowledges the role of environmental factors in predicting behavior. So, it is not just confined to personal-level factors but importantly acknowledges the role of environment in shaping the behavior.

One disadvantage of the IM is that it uses constructs from four different theories; thus there is a chance of overlap of constructs. The constructs should ideally be mutually exclusive. When constructs from different theories are combined we find that there is shared variance among constructs that interferes with statistical testing. Another disadvantage of this model is that there is limited evidence with regard to its predictability and not much with regard to interventions. Future research will tell how useful the model is in enhancing efficacy and effectiveness of health behavior interventions. Practitioners and researchers in health education and health promotion must utilize and test this model to build an empirical basis and evidence in favor of this model.

EMOTIONAL INTELLIGENCE THEORY

Peter Salovey and John D. Mayer (1990) first coined the term *emotional intelligence*, describing it as a type of social intelligence that involves the capability to observe and regulate one's own feelings and emotions, as well as those of others; to be able to differentiate among them; and to be able to utilize this information to channelize one's own thinking and behavior. The work of Salovey and Mayer was further advanced through a book by Daniel Goleman (1995) and several research studies. It was found that this aspect was more important than intelligence quotient (IQ) in predicting academic achievement and occupational status. Some researchers have broadened the theory of emotional intelligence to include it as part of a wider theory called "cultural intelligence" (Robertson, 2007, p. 14).

> **Emotional maturity is the essence of emotional intelligence theory and is considered as important as or even more important than intelligence.**

CONSTRUCTS OF EMOTIONAL INTELLIGENCE THEORY

Several researchers have defined the constructs of **emotional intelligence theory**. Lyusin (2006) identified four "branches" of emotional intelligence. These were identifying emotions, using emotions to make thinking more effective, understanding emotions, and guiding emotions. The more popular conceptualization of emotional intelligence theory is the personality model proposed by Goleman (1995). In this model, emotional intelligence is viewed as a set of emotional characteristics

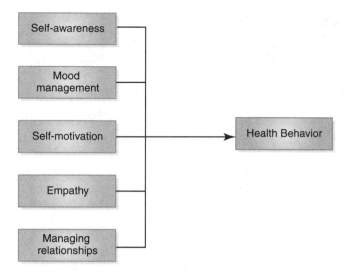

FIGURE 11-2 Constructs of emotional intelligence as applicable to health behavior research.

involving competencies. This has mostly been researched with regard to performance in the workplace. The constructs of emotional intelligence according to Goleman as applicable to health behavior research are depicted in **Figure 11-2**.

The first construct of emotional intelligence theory is **self-awareness**. This involves knowing one's emotions, recognizing feelings as they occur, and discriminating between them. The second construct is **mood management**. This entails handling feelings so that they become relevant to the current situation and one reacts appropriately. The third construct is **self-motivation** and includes "gathering up" one's feelings and directing oneself toward a goal, despite self-doubt, inertia, and impulsiveness. The fourth construct is **empathy**. This pertains to the ability to recognize one's feelings in others and tuning into their verbal and nonverbal cues. The final construct is **managing relationships**, which entails handling interpersonal interaction, conflict resolution, and negotiations. **Scale 11-1** illustrates how these constructs have been operationalized for measurement.

APPLICATIONS OF EMOTIONAL INTELLIGENCE THEORY

Emotional intelligence theory has been used in the field of health education and health promotion for a variety of applications. Some of these include bullying prevention (Casas, Ortega-Ruiz, & Del Rey, 2015), managing childbirth (Mohamadirizi, Fahami, Bahadoran, & Ehsanpour, 2015), predicting mental health (Branscum, Bhochhibhoya, & Sharma, 2013–2014), predicting postpartum depression (Rode, 2015), prevention of violence (Garaigordobil & Peña-Sarrionandia, 2015), relationship with substance abuse (Claros & Sharma, 2012), and understanding its role in motivation to help (Agnoli, Pittarello, Hysenbelli, & Rubaltelli, 2015). **Table 11-2** summarizes these applications.

Scale 11-1	Example of a Scale Measuring Emotional Intelligence					
		Never	Hardly Ever	Sometimes	Almost Always	Always
About your self-awareness						
1.	I know before I get angry.	☐	☐	☐	☐	☐
2.	I know before I get anxious.	☐	☐	☐	☐	☐
3.	I recognize feelings as they occur.	☐	☐	☐	☐	☐
4.	I can tell apart different feelings.	☐	☐	☐	☐	☐
About mood management						
5.	I manage my negative feelings.	☐	☐	☐	☐	☐
6.	I manage my positive feelings.	☐	☐	☐	☐	☐
7.	I react appropriately under anger.	☐	☐	☐	☐	☐
8.	I react appropriately under anxiety.	☐	☐	☐	☐	☐
About self-motivation						
9.	I direct my feelings toward a goal.	☐	☐	☐	☐	☐
10.	I overcome self-doubt in accomplishing any goal.	☐	☐	☐	☐	☐
11.	I overcome inaction in accomplishing any goal.	☐	☐	☐	☐	☐
12.	I overcome impulsiveness in accomplishing any goal.	☐	☐	☐	☐	☐
About empathy						
13.	I am adept at recognizing anger in others.	☐	☐	☐	☐	☐
14.	I am adept at recognizing anxiety in others.	☐	☐	☐	☐	☐
15.	I am adept at recognizing positive feelings in others.	☐	☐	☐	☐	☐
16.	I am adept at recognizing nonverbal cues associated with feelings in others.	☐	☐	☐	☐	☐
About managing relationships						
17.	I can easily handle interpersonal relationships.	☐	☐	☐	☐	☐
18.	I can easily resolve conflicts.	☐	☐	☐	☐	☐
19.	I can easily negotiate with others.	☐	☐	☐	☐	☐
20.	I can easily harness feelings to improve relationships.	☐	☐	☐	☐	☐

Table 11-2	Applications of Emotional Intelligence Theory in Health Education and Health Promotion
Bullying prevention	
Managing childbirth	
Predicting mental health	
Predicting postpartum depression	
Prevention of violence	
Relationship with substance abuse	
Understanding its role in motivation to help	

CRITIQUE OF EMOTIONAL INTELLIGENCE THEORY

Most of the work with regard to emotional intelligence theory has been in the areas of job performance and predicting and explaining behaviors, and there are few studies of its application in modifying health behaviors. Future practitioners and researchers must use this theory to modify health behaviors through interventions. The theory focuses primarily on emotions and thereby neglects the role of cognitive factors and environmental factors, which would limit its predictability. Perhaps this theory can be implemented in combination with other theories such as social cognitive theory, which emphasizes these factors. Waterhouse (2006) calls emotional intelligence a concept that has not yet been truly defined, beyond a "general mental ability" containing personality components, and advises that it would be hasty to incorporate emotional intelligence into educational curricula. In any event more research into this theory is needed.

INFORMATION-MOTIVATION-BEHAVIORAL SKILLS MODEL

In the field of HIV prevention a popular model is the **information-motivation-behavioral skills (IMB) model**. Fisher and Fisher (1992) first introduced this model in changing risk behavior for HIV/AIDS. Since then this model has been consistently used in the literature. It has served a useful purpose in the field of HIV/AIDS. It has also been applied to other fields such as breast self-examination and motorcycle safety (Fisher, Fisher, & Shuper, 2009).

CONSTRUCTS OF THE IMB MODEL

There are three constructs of this model. The first construct is **information**. Information refers to the collection of facts related to an action, idea, object, person, or situation. In the context of this model it pertains to the basic knowledge about a health condition that might include how the health condition or the disease develops, its outcomes, and strategies for its prevention and management. In the case of health behaviors this would be all the information regarding the positive or negative outcomes of the behavior, such as smoking, which is a negative behavior, or physical activity, which is a positive behavior; strategies for performing or not performing that behavior; conditions that foster or hinder that behavior; and so on. The prevention information that a person has is directly related to the preventive behavior. According to this model, the more information a person has, the greater would be the likelihood of his or her indulging in that preventive behavior.

> **According to the IMB model, the more information the person has, the greater would be the likelihood of his or her indulging in that behavior.**

The second construct of the IMB model is **motivation**. Motivation entails personal attitudes toward the behavior, perceptions of social support for that behavior, and the persons' perception as to how others behave. Motivation comprises two types of motivation: (1) *personal motivation* to practice preventive behaviors, such as attitudes toward practicing specific preventive actions; and (2) *social motivation* to engage in preventive behavior, such as perceptions of social support and perceptions as to how others behave. For example, in alcohol and drug education personal motivation would comprise one's attitudes about the benefits of not using alcohol and drugs and the value associated with those benefits, and social motivation would comprise one's perceptions about others' responses, such as a significant other's disapproval of alcohol and drug use. This construct has been influenced by constructs from social cognitive theory and the theory of reasoned action/theory of planned behavior.

The third construct of the IMB model is **behavioral skills**. This comprises an individual's objective ability and self-efficacy in performing the behavior. Self-efficacy is the confidence that a person has in his or her ability to perform a given behavior at the present moment. This construct has been influenced by social cognitive theory. For example, in the case of alcohol and drug education these behavioral skills would comprise techniques such as the ability to refuse drugs. This model is depicted in **Figure 11-3.**

APPLICATIONS OF THE IMB MODEL

In the field of health education and health promotion the IMB model has been used with several behaviors. Some examples of the application of this model include diabetes self-management (Song, Choi, Kim, Seo, & Lee, 2015), examining how students minimize harm to themselves and others when drinking (Howard, Griffin, Boekeloo, Lake, & Bellows, 2007), examining the severity of alcohol use and HIV sexual risk among juvenile offenders (Malow, Dévieux, Rosenberg, Samuels, & Jean-Gilles, 2006), examining substance use and sexual risk behaviors in men who

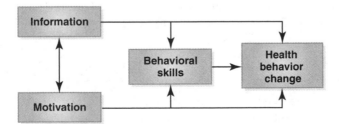

FIGURE 11-3 Depiction of the information-motivation-behavioral skills (IMB) model.

Table 11-3	Applications of the IMB Model in Health Education and Health Promotion
Diabetes self-management
Examining how students minimize harm to themselves and others when drinking
Examining the severity of alcohol use and HIV sexual risk among juvenile offenders
Examining substance use and sexual risk behaviors in men who have sex with men
HIV prevention
Preventing risky sexual behaviors
Reducing the rate with which men engage in sex under the influence of drugs or alcohol
Smoking cessation
Studying the effects of alcohol and expectancies on determinants of safer sex

have sex with men among those attending Mardi Gras celebrations in New Orleans (Benotsch et al., 2007), HIV prevention (Ybarra, Korchmaros, Prescott, & Birungi, 2015), preventing risky sexual behaviors (Bahrami & Zarani, 2015), reducing the rate with which men engage in sex under the influence of drugs or alcohol (Calsyn et al., 2010), smoking cessation (Cooperman, Richter, Bernstein, Steinberg, & Williams, 2015), and studying the effects of alcohol and expectancies on determinants of safer sex (Maisto, Carey, Carey, Gordon, & Schum, 2004). These applications are summarized in **Table 11-3**.

CRITIQUE OF THE IMB MODEL

One advantage of this model is that it is a parsimonious model. There are only three constructs and it is pretty straightforward to operationalize them. Another advantage is that the model has been thoroughly tested with HIV prevention behaviors and has shown adequate predictability.

Among the limitations of this model that have been mentioned in the literature is that the information construct of this model is a weak and inconsistent predictor of behavior (Fisher, Fisher, & Shuper, 2009). It can be said that information, while necessary, is not sufficient for behavior change. A second limitation is that information and motivation are often not mutually exclusive. Such interdependence poses problems in the testability of this model. Finally, the model lacks environmental and cultural factors, which are important in predicting and explaining behaviors and enhancing the predictability of any model. On the whole, however, the IMB model is a comprehensive conceptual framework that can be applied to a variety of health behaviors.

SELF-DETERMINATION THEORY

Self-determination theory (SDT) originated around the year 2000. It is an "organismic metatheory" (Ryan & Deci, 2000) grounded on the foundation that humans have an innate tendency toward growth, integration, and health. SDT proposes that humans have three basic psychological needs of autonomy, competence, and relatedness that must be satisfied within a social context in order for growth and well-being to be achieved (Fortier, Williams, Sweet, & Patrick, 2009). SDT is particularly focused on the processes through which a person acquires the motivation for initiating new health-related behaviors and maintaining them over time. This theory argues that developing a sense of autonomy and competence are critical to the processes of internalization and integration, through which a person comes to self-regulate and sustain behaviors conducive to health and well-being. Equally important is relatedness, as people are more likely to adopt behaviors promoted by those whom they trust (Ryan, Patrick, Deci, & Williams, 2008).

> **Self-determination theory (SDT) proposes that humans have three basic psychological needs of autonomy, competence, and relatedness that must be satisfied within a social context in order for growth and well-being to be achieved.**

CONSTRUCTS OF SELF-DETERMINATION THEORY

This theory presents itself through two mini-theories, *organismic integration theory (OIT)* and *cognitive evaluation theory (CET)*. OIT focuses on the motivational difference between autonomous (free) and controlled (regulated) behaviors, as situated on a continuum, and the degree to which behaviors are elective. This continuum includes behaviors that are intrinsically regulated, integrated regulated, identification regulated, introjection regulated, and externally regulated, respectively. Behaviors that are the least controlled and most autonomous are *intrinsically regulated*, meaning they are performed out of interest and enjoyment. *Integrated regulation* behaviors are executed due to congruence with other personal goals. In the middle of the continuum are less autonomous forms of regulation, *identification* and *introjection*, with identification referring to behaviors that are done out of importance and are personal, and introjection behaviors that are engaged in out of a sense of guilt or punishment. The most controlled and least autonomous are referred to as *externally regulated* behaviors, which are only performed to satisfy a demand or gain a reward. OIT suggests that positive outcomes are achieved by more autonomous forms of motivation versus those forms that are less autonomous. A final component of OIT is the process of internalization, by which an individual takes on greater autonomy for self-regulation over time (Fortier, Williams, Sweet, & Patrick, 2009).

CET is the part of SDT that suggests the essential needs of autonomy, competence, and relatedness for growth and well-being. **Autonomy** relates to the desire to be the regulator of one's actions and posits that behavior is volitional, **competence** describes the experience of feeling able to achieve a desired outcome, and **relatedness** refers to experiencing care and concern from and trust in important individuals and feeling connected and understood by others (Williams et al., 2011). In addition to the needs of autonomy, competence, and relatedness, CET considers the role of a **social context** in regard to internalization and self-regulation. Social context refers to the environment in which the behavior takes place. Individuals are more likely to regulate behaviors on their own and thus engage in lasting behavior change if there is social context support for autonomy, competence, and relatedness. Contexts can have a unique effect on whether behaviors are internalized; in particular, contexts delivered by health care professionals, who are in a position to prescribe positive health behaviors (Fortier, Williams, Sweet, & Patrick, 2009). A simplistic depiction of this theory is presented in **Figure 11-4**. It delineates the four main constructs of this theory—autonomy, relatedness, competence, and social context—in determining the health behavior.

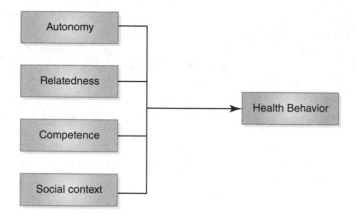

FIGURE 11-4 A simplistic depiction of the theory of self-determination.

APPLICATIONS OF SELF-DETERMINATION THEORY

SDT has been utilized with a variety of health behaviors, including tobacco abstinence, physical activity, weight loss, medication adherence, diabetes management, and cholesterol reduction (Fortier, Williams, Sweet, & Patrick, 2009). Williams, Niemiec, Patrick, Ryan, and Deci (2009) evaluated the effectiveness of a tobacco-dependence intervention based on SDT using a randomized cessation-induction trial. As a follow-up, Williams and colleagues (2011) completed a comparative effectiveness trial using three SDT-intensive tobacco-dependent interventions in which eligible participants were randomized to one of three treatment conditions intended for long-term maintenance of tobacco abstinence. Silva and colleagues (2010) implemented an SDT-based intervention for weight management, facilitating exercise adherence by enhancing the more autonomous forms of behavioral regulation. Patrick and Canevello (2011) used a computerized intervention based on SDT to better understand the psychological mechanisms in regard to physical activity frequency, intensity, and duration in sedentary young adults. Williams and colleagues (2009) applied SDT to predict medication adherence, quality of life, and psychological outcomes among diabetes patients using a mixed telephone-and-mail survey.

Some of the recent applications of SDT include facilitating weight loss (Wilson et al., 2015), improving cardiac rehabilitation (Rahman, Hudson, Thøgersen-Ntoumani, & Doust, 2015), motivating medical students to do research (Rosenkranz, Wang, & Hu, 2015), promoting dieting behavior (Katz, Madjar, & Harari, 2015), promoting physical activity and nutrition behaviors (Blackford et al., 2015; Moreau, Gagnon, & Boudreau, 2015), and promoting physical activity in the elderly (Morgan, Haase, Campbell, & Ben-Shlomo, 2015. These applications of SDT are summarized in **Table 11-4**.

CRITIQUE OF SELF-DETERMINATION THEORY

SDT is a well-supported theory that has been applied to many health education and health promotion contexts and diverse populations. It is an individual-level theory that focuses on individual factors that can be changed. Finally, SDT is a theory that can be used as a counseling approach

Table 11-4	Some Applications of Self-Determination Theory in Health Fields in 2015
Facilitating weight loss	
Improving cardiac rehabilitation	
Motivating medical students to do research	
Promoting dieting behavior	
Promoting physical activity and nutrition behaviors	
Promoting physical activity in the elderly	

with practitioners. SDT also has some limitations. As an individual-level theory, it cannot incorporate broader variables that affect health and health behaviors. However, as presented in this text, the construct of social context, if operationalized, can address this problem and provide this theory with greater predictive power. Secondly, it is possible that there is a "ceiling" effect with regard to the motivational variable that may warrant investigating this variable separately (Fortier, Williams, Sweet, & Patrick, 2009).

CONSTRUCT OF SELF-ESTEEM

In psychology **self-esteem** generally refers to a personal assessment by a person of his or her own worth (Hewitt, 2009). This construct has received attention since the 1950s, when Allport (1955) suggested that it was necessary for emotional well-being. A scale that measures self-esteem was developed by Rosenberg (1967, 1989) and is presented as **Scale 11-2**. Since the 1980s several programs have been introduced that build self-esteem for health and well-being.

Self-esteem has been linked to health behaviors. A cross-sectional study in Korea found that low self-esteem was significantly correlated with health risk behaviors (Kim, 2011). In a study of college students it was found that high self-esteem was indirectly linked to fewer alcohol-related problems (Backer-Fulghum, Patock-Peckham, King, Roufa, & Hagen, 2012). Another study in South African adolescents found that low self-esteem was linked to both adolescent smoking and alcohol use (Brook, Rubenstone, Zhang, Morojele, & Brook, 2011). Another study involving adolescents from Turkey showed that self-esteem was negatively associated with alcohol and illicit drug use (Kavas, 2009). A study of Hispanic adolescents in the United States found that self-esteem was the most important protective factor against substance use (Zamboanga, Schwartz, Jarvis, & Van Tyne, 2009).

> **Self-esteem refers to a personal assessment by a person of his or her own worth.**

CONSTRUCTS RELATED TO SELF-ESTEEM

In recent years a new theory, termed self-esteem enhancement theory (SET), has been proposed (Dubois, Flay, & Fagen, 2009). SET consists of five sets of constructs: (1) *contextual opportunities,* which include an individual's surrounding environment that supports development and sustenance

| Scale 11-2 | Rosenberg Self-Esteem Scale |

Instructions: Below is a list of statements dealing with your general feelings about yourself. If you strongly agree, circle **SA**. If you agree with the statement, circle **A**. If you disagree, circle **D**. If you strongly disagree, circle **SD**.

1.	On the whole, I am satisfied with myself.	SA	A	D	SD
2.*	At times, I think I am no good at all.	SA	A	D	SD
3.	I feel that I have a number of good qualities.	SA	A	D	SD
4.	I am able to do things as well as most other people.	SA	A	D	SD
5.*	I feel I do not have much to be proud of.	SA	A	D	SD
6.*	I certainly feel useless at times.	SA	A	D	SD
7.	I feel that I'm a person of worth, at least on an equal plane with others.	SA	A	D	SD
8.*	I wish I could have more respect for myself.	SA	A	D	SD
9.*	All in all, I am inclined to feel that I am a failure.	SA	A	D	SD
10.	I take a positive attitude toward myself.	SA	A	D	SD

Scoring: SA = 3, A = 2, D = 1, SD = 0. Items with an asterisk are reverse scored, that is, SA = 0, A = 1, D = 2, SD = 3. Sum the scores for the 10 items. The higher the score, the higher the self-esteem.

Rosenberg, M. (1989). *Society and the adolescent self-image* (Rev. ed.). Middletown, CT: Wesleyan University Press. The scale is under public domain but thanks are due to The Morris Rosenberg Foundation, c/o Department of Sociology, University of Maryland, 2112 Art-Sociology Building, College Park, MD 20742-1315. The scale is available at http://www.bsos.umd.edu/socy/research/rosenberg.htm.

of feelings of self-worth; (2) *esteem formation and maintenance processes,* which include cognitive, affective, and behavioral attributes that enhance self-worth; (3) *self-esteem,* which is global as well as domain specific; (4) *health and well-being,* which include influences from the cognitive, emotional, behavioral, physical, and social spheres; and (5) *modifying influences* from developmental, individual, and sociocultural differences.

APPLICATIONS OF SELF-ESTEEM

Several interventions have been designed using the concept of self-esteem enhancement. One such intervention is by Dalgas-Pelish (2006), who designed a self-esteem enhancement intervention in schoolchildren in fifth and sixth grades. The intervention consisted of four lessons on the topics of an overview of self-esteem, media influences, hiding emotions, and changes in self-esteem. It utilized a pretest/post-test design and used Coopersmith's (1967) Self-Esteem Inventory (SEI) to measure self-esteem. The girls who participated in the program had greater significant changes than boys in self-esteem scores. The results supported the effectiveness of this self-esteem enhancement program in girls as well as in children who had friends and children who were of lower socioeconomic status.

Another intervention that used self-esteem enhancement was conducted by Shiina and colleagues (2005) in a group of patients with bulimia. The intervention lasted 10 weeks and used Rosenberg's Self-Esteem Scale (1989) to measure self-esteem. The results demonstrated significant reduction in binge-eating behavior and improvement of social functioning.

Another prevention program aimed at promoting positive body image among university students also utilized self-esteem enhancement as part of its strategy (McVey et al., 2010). Besides self-esteem the program also included sessions on media literacy, stress management skills, and ways to recognize healthy versus unhealthy relationships. The results of the study revealed statistically significant improvements in body satisfaction between pretest and post-test measures.

Another study examined a 20-week weight-loss program for young participants implemented by a server-integrated smartphone app with health professional support and based on an addiction treatment approach that included self-esteem (Pretlow, Stock, Allison, & Roeger, 2015). The study measured body mass index (BMI), self-esteem, control over food, and the degree to which participants turned to food when stressed at four time points. Results showed a significant decrease in BMI, ratings of self-esteem, control over food, and a reduction in turning to food when stressed.

CRITIQUE OF SELF-ESTEEM

In my opinion, a certain amount of self-esteem is necessary for behavior change. However, it is not a sufficient construct in itself to cause the behavior to change. Unchecked or inappropriate self-esteem can be detrimental to behavior change. A bloated self-esteem can lead to a bloated ego such that the person may not want to change his or her behavior and may feel that his behavior is appropriate. This happens more often in the case of adolescents and well-established adults. Practitioners and researchers need to modify this construct in future interventions and test its efficacy with a wide variety of health behaviors in conjunction with other theories. The studies that have been done have used weaker designs such as pretest/post-test designs, and there is need to use the more robust randomized controlled trials (RCTs) in testing the efficacy and effectiveness of self-esteem. There is also a need to test this theory with different participants from different cultures and across different age groups. Most of the interventions that enhance self-esteem are designed for use with children and adolescents. There is need to explore their applicability in adults.

COMMUNITY COALITION ACTION THEORY

Our discussion of health education and health promotion theories would be incomplete if we did not include a community-level theory. The **community coalition action theory (CCAT)** is one such theory. A **coalition** is a group of several organizations working collectively toward a common goal while maintaining their individual identities. Coalitions have been developing rapidly over the past couple of decades in various sectors, including health, with the intention of creating opportunities that will benefit all members of the coalition. More specifically, community coalitions have been developed with the intention of achieving a common goal among the members of the community and have become common practice within the realm of health promotion. Although coalitions have become a popular means for soliciting health initiatives, it is difficult to measure their effectiveness owing to their inherent complexity. The CCAT identifies internal factors within the coalition that lead to the implementation of community change, and thereby provide an approach for assessing the efforts of coalitions (Kegler, Rigler & Honeycutt, 2010).

CONSTRUCTS OF CCAT

CCAT comprises 15 constructs and 21 practice-proven propositions that have been developed based on the constructs. The 15 constructs identified by Butterfoss & Kegler (2009) are *stages of development, community context, lead agency or convening group, coalition membership, processes, leadership and staffing, structures, pooled membership and external resources, member engagement, collaborative synergy, assessment and planning, implementation of strategies, community change outcomes, health/social outcomes,* and *community capacity*. The related propositions fall within the constructs and propose such things as the notion that "coalitions are heavily influenced by contextual factors in the community throughout all stages of development" (Proposition 3) and "participation in successful coalitions allows community members and organizations to develop capacity and build social capital" (Proposition 21) (Butterfoss & Kegler, 2009). These propositions summarize what is already commonly and empirically known about how community coalitions can improve health outcomes (Kegler, Rigler, & Honeycutt, 2010). For more details on the constructs and propositions, please refer to Butterfoss and Kegler (2009).

STAGES OF COALITIONS

CCAT posits that coalitions develop in stages, with the identified stages being formation, maintenance, and institutionalization. During the *formation stage*, the leading group or agency recruits an initial group of community partners who identify an issue of concern and then develop operating procedures. The *maintenance stage* involves preserving member involvement, generating group synergy, acquiring resources, and implementation, eventually leading to changes in practice and policy. Within the *institutionalization stage*, outcomes are produced as a direct result of effective strategies. These strategies can then become adopted by organizations or become part of a long-term coalition. It is important to note that these stages are not linear, but cyclical, which permits revolving back to earlier stages when new issues arise within the coalition (Butterfoss & Kegler, 2009).

APPLICATIONS OF CCAT

Although the use of community coalitions has become more prevalent in health promotion settings—a search of the literature demonstrated a plethora of studies using community coalitions to address obesity, physical activity, cancer, and diabetes prevention—the specific utilization of the community coalition action theory is limited.

Kegler and Swan (2011) used data from the California Healthy Cities and Communities (CHCC) program, a coalition of 20 communities, to test selected relationships in both the formation and maintenance stages of coalition development. They found that member characteristics, namely the number of community sectors engaged in the coalition, influence coalition outcomes, possibly due to collaborative synergy. Additionally, they found that coalition size in the formation stage was correlated with participation and dollars leveraged in the maintenance stage. Their findings supported the CCAT proposition that collaborative synergy leads to community change, thereby strengthening community capacity. Kegler, Rigler, and Honeycutt (2010), however, chose to purposely focus on the construct of community context and its related propositions, and how they influenced the formation of coalition for the same healthy community initiative previously discussed, CHCC. They found common themes among the related propositions that ultimately confirmed the impact that community context can have on community coalition formation.

In a very different application of the CCAT, Kluhsman, Bencivenga, Ward, Lehman, and Lengerich (2006) describe a coalition data collection system designed to monitor the impact of rural cancer coalitions in Pennsylvania and New York, where the 11 coalitions involved were conceptualized by the CCAT. These authors observed that over the 3-year study period, there were increasing trends in interventions, completed screenings, and documented community changes, which speaks to the effectiveness of coalitions, ultimately supporting the use of the CCAT. Kluhsman and colleagues (2006) reported that the 11 coalitions achieved more through their collective partnerships than any of the coalitions could have done alone, which supports the CCAT construct of pooling resources in an effort to improve the implementation strategies and, eventually, health outcomes.

Reed, Miller, and Francisco (2015) applied CCAT to examining how coalitions achieve HIV-preventive structural change. They examined data using content analysis from 12 coalitions to examine how contextual factors such as economic factors, collaborative factors, history-related factors, norm-related factors, and political factors augment or retard coalitions' success in achieving outcomes. They found history-related and political factors impacting structural changes in coalitions.

CRITIQUE OF CCAT

CCAT is the only comprehensive theory on functioning of coalitions, which is a strength of this theory. The constructs and propositions presented in this theory are grounded in nearly two decades of practice and research (Butterfoss & Kegler, 2009), which is also a strength of the theory. However, CCAT is a relatively new theory, and it does have some limitations. As previously stated, the breadth of the literature on the use of CCAT and health promotion initiatives is quite limited. The theory has not been operationalized in its totality. Future studies examining CCAT in health education and health promotion coalitions should consider addressing the theory in its entirety, as opposed to just single constructs. However, CCAT is not a parsimonious theory, making it challenging to operationalize in its entirety. Practitioners and researchers should consider examining more than the coalition functioning and look at the desired health behaviors and outcomes, including long-term sustainability. Community coalitions are complex, and attributing changes in health outcomes to community efforts is a difficult task, which is further complicated by numerous constructs that are complex on their own. Additionally, evidence to support the constructs and propositions is rare, and further research should aim to clarify the constructs and how they are linked.

THEORY OF GENDER AND POWER

One of the reviewers of this book suggested that the book would be incomplete without a feminist social structural theory such as the **theory of gender and power**, so this theory has also been included. The theory evolved from the work of Robert Connell, whose book *Gender and Power*

(1987) was a collection of writings on the theories of sexual inequality and gender and power imbalances. On the basis of these writings, Connell identified three major structures that he believed characterize the gendered relationships between men and women. These structures—the sexual division of labor, the sexual division of power, and the structure of cathexis—form the primary constructs of the theory of gender and power and exist at societal and institutional levels. The theory of gender and power has been used for HIV prevention interventions for women (Wingood, Camp, Dunkle, Cooper, & DiClemente, 2009).

CONSTRUCTS OF THE THEORY OF GENDER AND POWER

The first construct of the theory of gender and power is the **sexual division of labor**, which refers to the economic imbalances in the structure of our society that favor men (Connell, 1987; Wingood, Camp, Dunkle, Cooper, & DiClemente, 2009). At the *societal level* this pertains to the different allocations of occupations to men and women. At the *institutional level,* such as worksite, school, or family, one can also see the differences between the genders. In operationalizing this construct for health interventions one must pay attention to *economic exposures* of the participants, such as income, education, employment status, health insurance status, welfare status, and dependents, as well as *socioeconomic risk factors* such as race, age, economic hardships, and partner's economic status.

The second construct of the theory is the **sexual division of power**, which refers to the imbalances in authority and control pertaining to relations and roles in institutions in favor of men (Connell, 1987; Wingood, Camp, Dunkle, Cooper, & DiClemente, 2009). At the *societal level* this translates into greater power with men and at the *institutional level,* such as relations and the health care system, it also implies greater dependence on men. In operationalizing this construct for health interventions one must pay attention to *physical exposures,* such as relationship status, history of sexual abuse, history of physical abuse, gender discrimination, and racial discrimination, and *behavioral risk factors,* such as drug use, smoking/tobacco use, alcohol use, and coping with discrimination.

The final construct is **structure of cathexis**, which refers to social norms and affective connections between men and women (Connell, 1987; Wingood, Camp, Dunkle, Cooper, & DiClemente, 2009). At the *societal level* this means the normative expectations for men and women in the society and the emotional and sexual relations between men and women. At the *institutional level,* which includes family, relations, and faith-based institutions, there also are normative expectations that differ for men and women. In operationalizing this construct for health interventions one must pay attention to *social exposures,* such as in the case of HIV prevention sexual stigma, desire to conceive, and so on, and *personal risk factors,* such as distress, perceived gender norms, perceived influence of spirituality, and so forth. The theory of gender and power is depicted in **Figure 11-5**.

APPLICATIONS OF THE THEORY OF GENDER AND POWER

A qualitative study by Morison and Cook (2005) examined the midlife safer sex challenges for heterosexual women in New Zealand who were re-partnering or were in casual relationships. The study used interpretive phenomenological analysis in the context of the theory of gender and power to inspect the gender-normative assumptions and behaviors in women's narrations of unprotected sex and found that women were ill-informed and vulnerable with regard to sex. This study shows how this theory can be used qualitatively.

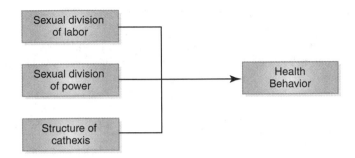

FIGURE 11-5 Diagrammatic depiction of the theory of gender and power for health behaviors.

Another qualitative study examined the gender context of sexual violence and HIV sexual risk behaviors among married women in Iringa Region, Tanzania, using the theory of gender and power (Nyamhanga & Frumence, 2014). The study classified the themes of focus group findings along the three constructs of the theory and found that HIV risk was increased because masculine sexual norms encouraged men to engage in unprotected sex. This account provides a good case study of how the theory of gender and power can be used to perform a thematic analysis of focus group data.

The theory of gender and power was used in an experimental study in African American men and women to examine the effects of alcohol, relationship power, and partner type on perception of difficulty in implementing condom use (Woolf-King, & Maisto, 2015). The study utilized a series of vignettes to record participant responses. This account provides a good case study showing how the theory of gender and power can be used to conduct an experimental study around different health behaviors.

Beckham, Shembilu, Winch, Beyrer, and Kerrigan (2015) utilized the theory of gender and power to enhance understanding of motherhood, sex work, and HIV in southern Tanzania. They used the qualitative research methods of focus groups and interviews, providing another example of how the theory can be used qualitatively.

Salud, Marshak, Natto, and Montgomery (2014) conducted a quantitative study using the theory of gender and power in Asian/Pacific Islander women for HIV-testing intentions. This study, interestingly, combined the theory with acculturation and the AIDS risk-reduction model (ARRM). This account shows how this theory can be combined with other models or theories in a quantitative paradigm.

CRITIQUE OF THE THEORY OF GENDER AND POWER

A major strength of this theory is that it brings to the surface the differences in the roles between genders and how they may affect the acquisition of health behaviors. Other theories have not focused on these differences. In this regard, the theory of gender and power is unique, and this uniqueness is a definitive strength of the theory. Presently, the theory is invaluable for understanding and changing sexual health behaviors, where it has been studied most. However, it needs to be further explored with respect to behaviors such as physical activity, substance abuse, and others.

One of the present limitations of this theory is that it does not consider macro factors, including the socioeconomic and political environments. However, Wingood, Camp, Dunkle, Cooper, and DiClemente (2009) note that this refinement to the theory is underway. Another limitation of the theory is that direct guidance of behavior change has not been provided by this theory. More research in this direction can help improve and refine this theory further.

MULTI-THEORY MODEL (MTM) FOR HEALTH BEHAVIOR CHANGE

In health education and health promotion we are interested in a theory that is exclusive to health behaviors, predicts health behavior *change*, is based on empirical evidence with health behavior changes, provides enough predictive power, is parsimonious, has constructs that are malleable, caters to both one-time and long-term health behavior change, and is applicable across cultures. Of all the theories presented in this text, the only one that is exclusive to health behaviors is the health belief model (Rosenstock, 1974). Unfortunately it does not have good consistent predictive power and is not about health behavior *change*. Only one theory is about behavior change, and that is the transtheoretical model. Unfortunately, it is not parsimonious, some of its constructs are not malleable, and its terminology and context are those of psychotherapy and not health education and health promotion (Prochaska, 1979). In this way we can discuss the merits and demerits of all the theories, but that is not our purpose in this section. Instead, we will explore a model for empirical testing that is exclusive for health education, has empirically tested constructs for health behavior *change*, is parsimonious, has constructs that are malleable, caters to both one-time and long-term behavior change, and is probably applicable across cultures: the **multi-theory model (MTM) for health behavior change** (Sharma, 2015). Although the constructs of this model have been tested individually, the model as a whole has not been tested.

> The multi-theory model for health behavior change is a proposition that predicts initiation of health behavior change using participatory dialogue, behavioral confidence, and changes in the physical environment; and sustenance of health behavior change using emotional transformation, practice for change, and changes in the social environment.

I have worked in the field of health education since 1981 and have experience with most of the theories presented in this text through projects in 13 countries around the world. I have authored more than 400 publications of which more than 150 have appeared in peer-reviewed journals. The multi-theory model for health behavior change is derived from my research and experience over this time. Based on my work with behavioral theories, I wish to dissect health behavior *change* into two components: **initiation of health behavior change** and **sustenance** (or continuation) of **health behavior change**. Initiation of the health behavior is the same as adoption of a one-time behavior such as receiving a vaccination. Sustenance, or continuation, of the health behavior, is the same as long-term performance of a health behavior (e.g., physical activity behavior) over the course of a lifetime. This differentiation is needed because the constructs that influence initiation are different from those that sustain the behavior. No such differentiation has been made by the theories that explain behavior, resulting in low predictive power when they are operationalized.

Let us look at the initiation of health behavior or performance of a one-time health behavior. Three main constructs influence this initiation of behavior. The first is the **participatory**

dialogue derived from Freire's (1970) model of adult education. For behavior *change* this participatory dialogue can be initiated by the health education specialist, nurse educator, dietitian, health coach, certified public health professional, or even by the health care provider. The important point is that the content of this dialogue must focus on **advantages** and **disadvantages** of the health behavior *change*. This is similar to the pros and cons of the transtheoretical model (Prochaska, 1979) or perceived benefits in the health belief model (Rosenstock, 1974). But it is somewhat different in the *process* because this dialogue is participatory, which means it must be a two-way communication or mutual exploration—a point that is emphasized by Freire but ignored by both the transtheoretical model and the health belief model. The construct of participatory dialogue is a very robust one that has been tested across cultures in all continents.

The second construct is **behavioral confidence**, derived from Bandura's (1986) self-efficacy and Ajzen's (1991) perceived behavioral control. There are three reasons for using the term *behavioral confidence* rather than the other two terms. The first reason is simplicity. I have conducted workshops in several parts of the world and no one, including attendees who were physicians, understood the meaning of the other terms on hearing them for the first time. Many of my students confuse self-efficacy with program efficacy. The second reason is that this construct has perhaps greater predictive power in the United States, but when utilized in my work in China (Murnan, Sharma, & Lin, 2006–2007), India (Sharma, Mehan, & Surabhi, 2008–2009), and Iran (Bagherniya, Sharma, Mostafavi, & Keshavarz, 2014–2015), it has shown either very modest predictive power or no predictive power—for obvious cultural reasons. The final reason is that this construct is slightly different from Bandura's self-efficacy and Ajzen's perceived behavioral control, which focus on learning a behavior. My conceptualization pertains to *changing* a health behavior; thus it is not about the "here and now" but instead about the "future." This construct is a projection of your certainty to perform a health behavior change in the *future*, not in the present.

The third and final construct for initiation of a behavior is the **changes in the physical environment**, which is derived from Bandura's (1986) construct of the environment, Prochaska's (1979) construct of environmental reevaluation, and environmental factors in Fishbein's (2009) integrative model, among others. This conceptualization pertains only to the physical and not the social environment and entails making changes to obtainability, availability, accessibility, convenience, and readiness of resources. This model is depicted in **Figure 11-6**.

Let us look at the sustenance or continuation of the health behavior or modification for long-term health behavior change. Three main constructs influence the sustenance of health behavior change. The first construct is derived from the self-motivation construct of emotional intelligence theory (Goleman, 1995), which involves "gathering up" one's feelings and directing oneself toward a goal, despite self-doubt, inertia, and impulsiveness. I call this construct **emotional transformation** because it involves converting or transforming emotions toward the health behavior change.

The second construct is derived from Freire's (1970) adult education model's praxis and is called **practice for change**. Praxis refers to active reflection and reflective action. Practice for change entails constantly thinking about the health behavior change and making mid-course corrections to one's strategy, overcoming barriers, and remaining focused on health behavior change.

The third and final construct is derived from constructs of the environment (Bandura, 1986), helping relationships (Prochaska, 1979), social support (House, 1981), and so on. It is called **changes in social environment** and entails creating social support from the environment. This change in social environment can be natural or artificial. The health education specialist, nurse educator, dietitian, health coach, certified public health professional, health care provider, or even a

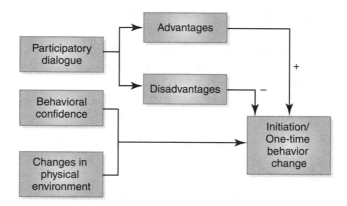

FIGURE 11-6 Constructs in initiation of health behavior change in the multi-theory model of health behavior change.

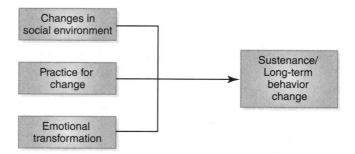

FIGURE 11-7 Constructs in sustenance of health behavior change in the multi-theory model of health behavior change.

lay health volunteer can provide help with change in the social environment. This model is depicted in **Figure 11-7**. The constructs, their definitions, and ways to modify each construct both in initiation and sustenance of health behavior change are summarized in **Table 11-5**.

I have presented this model based on my research and experience in the field with the various behavioral theories. The model has not been empirically tested, and I would urge the readers of this text, researchers in the field, and practitioners in the field to test and improve it further. I am not providing a critique of this model and leave it to the readers to do so.

APPLICATION EXERCISE

In this chapter we have introduced several theories and their applications. Choose a theory and an area of application that interest you. Locate and read the full-text article of that application and see how the theory was used in that context. One example is the application of the theory of emotional intelligence by Branscum, Bhochhibhoya, and Sharma (2013–2014) in mental health. This study

Table 11-5	Key Constructs of the Multi-Theory Model of Health Behavior Change	
Construct	**Definition**	**How to Modify?**
Participatory dialogue	Two-way discussion of the advantages and disadvantages of the health behavior change, with an emphasis on the process that helps in initiation of the change	• Small group discussion • Large group discussion • One-on-one interview • Culture circle • Photo voice • Brainstorming • Nominal group
Behavioral confidence	Projection of one's certainty to perform a health behavior change in the *future*, not in the present, that helps in initiation of the change	• Demonstration in small steps • Role play about the behavior change • Simulation of the behavior change • Psychodrama about the behavior change • Video about the behavior change with a credible role model
Changes in physical environment	Making modifications to obtainability, availability, accessibility, convenience, and readiness of resources that help in initiation of the change	• Networking • Fundraising • Lobbying • Coalition building • Collective effort
Emotional transformation	Converting or transforming emotions toward the health behavior change that help in sustenance of the change	• Role play • Psychodrama • Simulation • Small group discussion • Large group discussion
Practice for change	Constantly thinking about the health behavior change and making mid-course corrections to one's strategy, overcoming barriers, and remaining focused on health behavior change that help in sustenance of health behavior change	• Maintaining a diary • Keeping a journal • Recording on a technological tool
Changes in social environment	Creating social support from the environment that helps in sustenance of health behavior change	• Social support: natural (family, friends) or artificial (health education specialist, health coach, nursing educator, dietitian, certified public health professional, etc.) • Buddy • Peer-to-peer • Social media (e.g., Facebook) • Weekly or monthly meetings

tested the predictive nature of emotional intelligence with standardized measures of mental health to create a model that can be used to create more effective health promotion interventions. Stepwise multiple regression was used to predict mental health, which was measured using the Kessler K-6 scale. Also included in the model is type D personality, measured by Denollett's Scale of Negative Affectivity and Social Inhibition. Emotional intelligence with five constructs was measured by the scale presented in this text. The results revealed that while not all of the dimensions of emotional intelligence regressed significantly in each model, mood management was highly predictive of all mental health measures under investigation.

Read the full-text article on this study and prepare a 250-word critique. In writing the critique, pay attention to the psychometric properties (validity and reliability) of the scales used in this study (any measurement bias), the sample and sample size (any sampling bias), how the theory of emotional intelligence has been reified, data analysis used, and data interpretation, particularly generalizability of the study findings (any generalizability bias).

SKILL-BUILDING ACTIVITY

In this section we cannot show how each theory presented in this chapter can be applied, but we will be selective and choose to show how the multi-theory model of health behavior change can be used to modify physical activity behavior change in a group of Hispanic middle-aged adults. **Figure 11-8** depicts each of the constructs from the model and links these with educational processes and behavioral objectives to move sedentary participants to make the behavior change of becoming physically active.

Since both initiation and sustenance of this behavior are important we need to operationalize all six constructs of the model. The health education intervention would start by modifying the construct of participatory dialogue using the educational process of small group discussion or large group discussion to identify the advantages and disadvantages of making the health behavior change. Input would be two-way, with participants contributing as much, if not more, to the discussion. In order to build behavioral confidence the physical activity behaviors, such as riding a stationary bicycle, using a treadmill, and using other equipment in the gym, would be demonstrated in small, "doable," incremental steps. It would be emphasized how these steps can be used by the participants in the future. The third construct pertains to changes in the physical environment. A convenient, easily accessible gym that is reasonably priced or free would be made available to the participants. The health education specialist, certified health education professional, nursing educator, dietitian, or health coach can explore possibilities of organizational sponsorship or subsidization of the fee by the gym in this regard. These are the three constructs for initiation of physical activity behavior change and can be measured by three subscales that measure these constructs.

For sustenance of the physical activity behavior, which can be done in a second session, the first construct to be modified is emotional transformation. This could be modified through an affective educational method such as a role play, simulation, or psychodrama that shows the problems faced by a sedentary person and how dramatic change occurs when he or she switches to being physically active. The second construct for modification is practice for change, which is a reflection-based

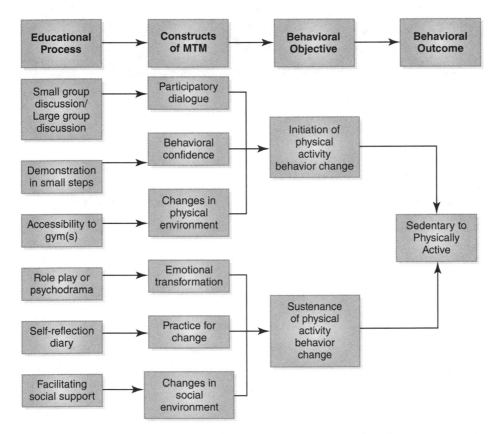

FIGURE 11-8 Diagrammatic depiction of the use of the multi-theory model (MTM) for health behavior change to modify physical activity behavior change in Hispanic middle-aged adults.

construct. The participants could be provided a diary, iPad, pedometer, or another technological tool to record their physical activity and keep a daily active reflection on this activity. The final construct is changes in the social environment. This could be built by facilitating social support, either natural or artificial. In artificial support the health education specialist, certified health education professional, nursing educator, dietitian, or health coach could regularly contact the participants to persuade them to meet their goals, help them overcome any barriers, and provide them with a listening ear.

Using this approach to the multi–theory model of health behavior change, plan a health education program for a behavior of your choice. **Table 11–6** provides a set of questions to assist you in choosing educational methods that correspond to different constructs of the model. **Scale 11–3** has been provided to measure changes in these constructs.

Table 11-6	Choosing Educational Methods that Correspond to Constructs of the Multi-Theory Model of Health Behavior Change

1. What is the best educational method to facilitate participatory dialogue?
   - Small group discussion
   - Large group discussion
   - One-on-one interview
   - Culture circle
   - Photo voice
   - Brainstorming
   - Nominal group
   - Other

2. What is the best educational method to facilitate behavioral confidence?
   - Demonstration
   - Role play
   - Simulation
   - Psychodrama
   - Video with a credible role model
   - Other

3. What is the best educational method to facilitate changes in the physical environment?
   - Networking
   - Fundraising
   - Lobbying
   - Coalition building
   - Collective effort
   - Other

4. What is the best educational method to facilitate emotional transformation?
   - Role play
   - Psychodrama
   - Simulation
   - Small group discussion
   - Large group discussion
   - Other

5. What is the best educational method to facilitate practice for change?
   - Diary
   - Journal
   - Recording on a technological tool
   - Other

6. What is the best method to facilitate change in the social environment?
   - Social support: natural (family, friends) or artificial (health education specialist, health coach, nursing educator, dietitian, certified public health professional, etc.)
   - Buddy
   - Peer-to-peer
   - Social media (e.g., Facebook)
   - Weekly or monthly meetings
   - Other

Scale 11-3	Instrument Based on the Multi-Theory Model (MTM) for Health Behavior Change to Measure Physical Activity Behavior Change

Directions: This survey is voluntary, which means you may choose not to complete it or not to answer individual questions. There is no direct benefit of this survey to you. All data from this survey will be anonymous and kept secret. Your responses will help in developing effective physical activity promotion programs. Please put an "X" mark by the response or fill the response that correctly describes your position. Thank you for your help!

1. During the past seven days, other than your regular job, how many minutes did you participate in any aerobic physical activities or exercises such as running, calisthenics, golf, gardening, or walking for exercise?

Monday	Tuesday	Wednesday	Thursday	Friday	Saturday	Sunday
____min.	____min.	____min.	____min.	____min.	____min.	____min.

Please add the total minutes up: _____ minutes/week

If your total is more than 150 minutes, you can stop taking this questionnaire. Thank you for your time.

....

2. Do you suffer from any medical condition, including any physical disability, that prevents you from being physically active?

☐ No
☐ Yes

If you answered yes, you may stop taking this questionnaire. Thank you for your time.

....

3. What is your gender? ☐ Male
☐ Female
☐ Other _____

....

4. How old are you today? _____ years

....

5. What is your race/ethnicity? ☐ White or Caucasian American
☐ Black or African American
☐ Asian American
☐ American Indian
☐ Hispanic American
☐ Other _____

....

6. What is your class? ☐ Freshman
☐ Sophomore
☐ Junior
☐ Senior
☐ Graduate

....

(continues)

Scale 11-3	Instrument Based on the Multi-Theory Model (MTM) for Health Behavior Change to Measure Physical Activity Behavior Change (*continued*)

7. What is your current overall GPA?
- ☐ Less than 1.99
- ☐ 2.00–2.49
- ☐ 2.50–2.99
- ☐ 3.00–3.49
- ☐ 3.50–4.00

8. Where do you live?
- ☐ On campus
- ☐ Off campus

9. Do you work?
- ☐ No
- ☐ Yes _____ hours/week (put a single number, not a range)

	Never	Hardly Ever	Sometimes	Almost Always	Always
Participatory dialogue: Advantages					
If you engage in more than 150 minutes of moderate- to vigorous-intensity aerobic physical activity every week you will ..					
10. . . . be healthy.	☐	☐	☐	☐	☐
11. . . . be relaxed.	☐	☐	☐	☐	☐
12. . . . get sick less often.	☐	☐	☐	☐	☐
13. . . . have more energy.	☐	☐	☐	☐	☐
14. . . . enjoy life more.	☐	☐	☐	☐	☐

	Never	Hardly Ever	Sometimes	Almost Always	Always
Participatory dialogue: Disadvantages					
If you participate in more than 150 minutes of moderate- to vigorous-intensity aerobic physical activity every week you will ..					
15. . . . be tired.	☐	☐	☐	☐	☐

Scale 11-3	Instrument Based on the Multi-Theory Model (MTM) for Health Behavior Change to Measure Physical Activity Behavior Change (*continued*)

	Never	Hardly Ever	Sometimes	Almost Always	Always
16. ... not have enough time for academics.	□	□	□	□	□

	Never	Hardly Ever	Sometimes	Almost Always	Always
If you participate in more than 150 minutes of moderate- to vigorous-intensity aerobic physical activity every week you will ..					
17. ... not have enough time for leisure.	□	□	□	□	□
18. ... have to pay for facilities.	□	□	□	□	□
19. ... get injuries.	□	□	□	□	□

	Not At All Sure	Slightly Sure	Moderately Sure	Very Sure	Completely Sure
Behavioral confidence					
How sure are you that you will be aerobically physically active with moderate- to vigorous-intensity for 150 minutes ...					
20. ... this week?	□	□	□	□	□
21. ... this week to complete all academic/work-related tasks?	□	□	□	□	□
22. ... this week while finding time for leisure?	□	□	□	□	□
23. ... this week without getting tired?	□	□	□	□	□
24. ... this week without getting injured?	□	□	□	□	□

(continues)

Scale 11-3	Instrument Based on the Multi-Theory Model (MTM) for Health Behavior Change to Measure Physical Activity Behavior Change (*continued*)				

	Not At All Sure	Slightly Sure	Moderately Sure	Very Sure	Completely Sure
Changes in physical environment					
How sure are you that you will...					
25. ...have a place to be aerobically physically active for 150 minutes per week?	☐	☐	☐	☐	☐
26. ...be able to afford a place to be aerobically physically active for 150 minutes per week?	☐	☐	☐	☐	☐
27. ...be able to use equipment to be aerobically physically active for 150 minutes per week?	☐	☐	☐	☐	☐

	Not At All Sure	Slightly Sure	Moderately Sure	Very Sure	Completely Sure
Emotional transformation					
How sure are you that you can...					
28. ...direct your emotions/feelings to the goal of being aerobically physically active for 150 minutes every week?	☐	☐	☐	☐	☐
29. ...motivate yourself to be aerobically physically active for 150 minutes every week?	☐	☐	☐	☐	☐
30. ...overcome self-doubt in accomplishing the goal of being aerobically physically active for 150 minutes every week?	☐	☐	☐	☐	☐

Scale 11-3	Instrument Based on the Multi-Theory Model (MTM) for Health Behavior Change to Measure Physical Activity Behavior Change (*continued*)

	Not At All Sure	Slightly Sure	Moderately Sure	Very Sure	Completely Sure
Practice for change					
How sure are you that you can...					
31. ...keep a diary to monitor total time of your aerobic physical activity every week?	☐	☐	☐	☐	☐
32. ...be aerobically physically active for 150 minutes every week if you encounter barriers?	☐	☐	☐	☐	☐
33. ...change your plan for being aerobically physically active for 150 minutes every week if you face difficulties?	☐	☐	☐	☐	☐

	Not At All Sure	Slightly Sure	Moderately Sure	Very Sure	Completely Sure
Changes in social environment					
How sure are you that you can get the help of a...					
34. ...family member to be aerobically physically active for 150 minutes every week?	☐	☐	☐	☐	☐
35. ...friend to be aerobically physically active for 150 minutes every week?	☐	☐	☐	☐	☐
36. ...health professional to be aerobically physically active for 150 minutes every week?	☐	☐	☐	☐	☐

(continues)

Scale 11-3	Instrument Based on the Multi-Theory Model (MTM) for Health Behavior Change to Measure Physical Activity Behavior Change (*continued*)				

	Not At All Likely	Somewhat Likely	Moderately Likely	Very Likely	Completely Likely
Behavior change: Initiation					
How likely is it that you will...					
37. ...increase your aerobic physical activity to 150 minutes in the upcoming weeks?	☐	☐	☐	☐	☐
Behavior change: Sustenance					
How likely is it that you will...					
38. ...Increase your aerobic physical activity to 150 minutes every week from now on?	☐	☐	☐	☐	☐

Thank you for your time!

SCORING

Construct of advantages: Scale: Never (0), hardly ever (1), sometimes (2), almost always (3), always (4). Summative score of items 10–14. Possible range: 0–20. High score associated with likelihood of initiation of behavior change.

Construct of disadvantages: Scale: Never (0), hardly ever (1), sometimes (2), almost always (3), always (4). Summative score of items 15–19. Possible range: 0–20. Low score associated with likelihood of initiation of behavior change.

Construct of behavioral confidence: Scale: Not at all sure (0), slightly sure (1), moderately sure (2), very sure (3), completely sure (4). Summative score of items 20–24. Possible range: 0–20. High score associated with likelihood of initiation of behavior change.

Construct of changes in physical environment: Scale: Not at all sure (0), slightly sure (1), moderately sure (2), very sure (3), completely sure (4). Summative score of items 25–27. Possible range: 0–12. High score associated with likelihood of initiation of behavior change.

Construct of emotional transformation: Scale: Not at all sure (0), slightly sure (1), moderately sure (2), very sure (3), completely sure (4). Summative score of items 28–30. Possible range: 0–12. High score associated with likelihood of sustenance of behavior change.

Construct of practice for change: Scale: Not at all sure (0), slightly sure (1), moderately sure (2), very sure (3), completely sure (4). Summative score of items 31–33. Possible range: 0–12. High score associated with likelihood of sustenance of behavior change.

Construct of changes in social environment: Scale: Not at all sure (0), slightly sure (1), moderately sure (2), very sure (3), completely sure (4). Summative score of items 34–36. Possible range: 0–12. High score associated with likelihood of sustenance of behavior change.

For **modeling** initiation, dependent variable can be item 37, and multiple regression can be used. For modeling sustenance, dependent variable can be item 38, and multiple regression can be used.

SUMMARY

Several new theories applicable to health education and health promotion have emerged in recent years. One such theory is the integrative model of behavior prediction (IM), presented by Fishbein. The model summarizes constructs from the health belief model, social cognitive theory, the theory of reasoned action, and the theory of planned behavior. Another theory is the emotional intelligence theory comprising five constructs; namely, self-awareness, mood management, self-motivation, empathy, and managing relationships. A third new theory is the information-motivation-behavioral skills (IMB) model. As described in this model, information pertains to the basic knowledge about a health condition that might include how the health condition or the disease develops, its outcomes, and strategies for its prevention and management. Motivation entails personal attitudes toward the behavior, perceptions of social support for that behavior, and the person's perception as to how others behave. Behavioral skills comprise an individual's objective ability and self-efficacy in performing the behavior.

A fourth new theory is that of self-determination (SDT). This is a behavior theory that proposes that humans have three basic psychological needs of autonomy, competence, and relatedness that must be satisfied within a social context in order for growth and well-being to be achieved. The construct of self-esteem or a personal assessment by a person of his or her own worth has also been used for predicting health behaviors in recent years.

A community-level theory is the community coalition action theory (CCAT), which identifies internal factors within the coalition that lead to the implementation of community change and thereby provides an approach for assessing the efforts of coalitions. Another new theory that has been used in health education and health promotion is the theory of gender and power. This is a social structural theory focused on three major social structures that characterize the gendered relationships between men and women: the sexual division of labor, the sexual division of power, and the structure of cathexis.

Finally, the text presents a new multi-theory model of health behavior change. According to this model there are two parts in health behavior change: initiation and sustenance. The constructs of participatory dialogue, changes in the physical environment, and behavioral confidence predict initiation, while the constructs of emotional transformation, practice for change, and changes in the social environment predict sustenance of health behavior change. Although the constructs have been well tested individually, this model needs to be empirically tested in its entirety.

IMPORTANT TERMS

advantages
attitudes
autonomy
behavioral confidence

behavioral intention
behavioral skills
changes in physical environment
changes in social environment

coalition
community coalition action theory (CCAT)
competence
disadvantages
emotional intelligence theory
emotional transformation
empathy
environment
information
information-motivation-behavioral skills
  (IMB) model
initiation of health behavior change
integrative model of behavioral prediction (IM)
managing relationships
mood management
motivation
multi-theory model (MTM) for health
  behavior change

norms
participatory dialogue
perceived behavioral control
practice for change
relatedness
self-awareness
self-determination theory (SDT)
self-efficacy
self-esteem
self-motivation
sexual division of labor
sexual division of power
skills and abilities
social context
structure of cathexis
sustenance of health behavior change
theory of gender and power

REVIEW QUESTIONS

1. Describe the integrative model of behavioral prediction (IM).
2. Define the five constructs of emotional intelligence theory.
3. Explain the information-motivation-behavioral skills (IMB) model.
4. Describe the self-determination theory (SDT).
5. Define self-esteem and explain how it has been used in health education and health promotion.
6. Describe the community coalition action theory (CCAT).
7. Explain the three constructs of the theory of gender and power.
8. Apply the multi-theory model of health behavior change to promoting intake of fruits and vegetables by schoolchildren.

WEBSITES TO EXPLORE

Application of the Information-Motivation-Behavioral Skills (IMB) Model

www.ncbi.nlm.nih.gov/pmc/articles/PMC3011990/

This website provides a link to the full-text article of a qualitative application of the IMB model to medication adherence by youth living with HIV. *Read this article. Do you agree with the findings? Do you find the account trustworthy (i.e., how much did the researchers adhere to procedures and exercise rigor)? Did they use triangulation (more than one method)? Are the results transferable to other settings? Summarize the answer to these and other reflections in a 250-word critique.*

Application of the Integrative Model of Behavioral Prediction

www.ncbi.nlm.nih.gov/pubmed/25431537

This website provides a link to the full text of an article entitled, "The Nature and Predictive Value of Mothers' Beliefs Regarding Infants' and Toddlers' TV/Video Viewing: Applying the Integrative Model of Behavioral Prediction." *Download the article and read it carefully. One of the research questions was which specific behavioral beliefs will most discriminate between mothers whose children view more TV/videos and those whose children view less? Find out the answer to this question and formulate it in your own words.*

Application of the Theory of Gender and Power

www.ncbi.nlm.nih.gov/pubmed/21553975

This website provides a link to a full-text article from *Health Psychology* that uses constructs from the theory of gender and power to establish associations with sexual behavior. *Download the full-text article and read it. How can this theory be used to guide an intervention in this area?*

Community Coalition Action Theory (CCAT)—Constructs, Propositions, and Diagrams

http://www.acha.org/documents/Programs_Services/webhandouts_2010/FR127-Lederer%20-%20CCAT%20Handout.pdf

For copyright reasons we have not provided you with the constructs, propositions, or diagram of the CCAT. But this website of the American College Health Association provides information on all three aspects. *Review this website. Choose any five constructs and related propositions of the CCAT. How can you modify these in order to improve the effectiveness of a coalition of your choice?*

Daniel Goleman—Emotional Intelligence

www.danielgoleman.info/topics/emotional-intelligence/

This is the website of Daniel Goleman, who popularized the concept of emotional intelligence. The website provides information about Goleman's background, the concept of emotional intelligence, and assessment tools for examining it, among other things. *Review this website and write down five things you learned about emotional intelligence or Daniel Goleman.*

How to Raise Your Self-Esteem

http://psychcentral.com/lib/how-to-raise-your-self-esteem/

This is an article by Dr. Stanley Gross that provides practical tips about how one can raise one's self-esteem. *Read this article and prepare a reaction paper as to how you will raise the self-esteem of your participants in a health education program.*

Self-Determination Theory

www.selfdeterminationtheory.org/

This is the website of self-determination theory. Links have been provided to details of the theory, including questionnaires, publications, and conferences based on the theory; faculty members who have developed it; and a listserv and news related to the theory. *Explore this website and summarize five things you learned about this theory.*

REFERENCES

Agnoli, S., Pittarello, A., Hysenbelli, D., & Rubaltelli, E. (2015). "Give, but Give until It Hurts": The modulatory role of trait emotional intelligence on the motivation to help. *PLoS One, 10*(6), e0130704. doi: 10.1371/journal.pone.0130704.

Ajzen, I. (1991). The theory of planned behavior. *Organizational Behavior and Human Decision Process, 50,* 179–211.

Allport, G. W. (1955). *Becoming: Basic considerations for a psychology of personality.* New Haven, CT: Yale University Press.

Atwell, K., Abraham, C., & Duka, T. (2011). A parsimonious, integrative model of key psychological correlates of UK university students' alcohol consumption. *Alcohol and Alcoholism, 46*(3), 253–260.

Backer-Fulghum, L. M., Patock-Peckham, J. A., King, K. M., Roufa, L., & Hagen L. (2012). The stress-response dampening hypothesis: How self-esteem and stress act as mechanisms between negative parental bonds and alcohol-related problems in emerging adulthood. *Addictive Behaviors, 37*(4), 477–484.

Bagherniya, M., Sharma, M., Mostafavi, F., & Keshavarz, S. A. (2014–2015). Application of social cognitive theory in predicting childhood obesity prevention behaviors in overweight and obese Iranian adolescents. *International Quarterly of Community Health Education, 35*(2), 133–147. doi: http://dx.doi.org/10.2190/IQ.35.2.d.

Bahrami, Z., & Zarani, F. (2015). Application of the information-motivation and behavioral skills (IMB) model in risky sexual behaviors amongst male students. *Journal of Infection and Public Health, 8*(2), 207–213. doi: 10.1016/j.jiph.2014.09.005.

Bandura, A. (1986). *Social foundations of thought and action.* Englewood Cliffs, NJ: Prentice-Hall.

Beckham, S. W., Shembilu, C. R., Winch, P. J., Beyrer, C., & Kerrigan, D. L. (2015). 'If you have children, you have responsibilities': Motherhood, sex work and HIV in southern Tanzania. *Culture, Health and Sexuality, 17*(2), 165–179. doi: 10.1080/13691058.2014.961034.

Benotsch, E. G., Nettles, C. D., Wong, F., Redmann, J., Boschini, J., Pinkerton, S. D., et al. (2007). Sexual risk behavior in men attending Mardi Gras celebrations in New Orleans, Louisiana. *Journal of Community Health, 32*(5), 343–356.

Blackford, K., Jancey, J., Lee, A. H., James, A. P., Howat, P., Hills, A. P., & Anderson, A. (2015). A randomised controlled trial of a physical activity and nutrition program targeting middle-aged adults at risk of metabolic syndrome in a disadvantaged rural community. *BMC Public Health, 15,* 284. doi: 10.1186/s12889-015-1613-9.

Bleakley, A., Hennessy, M., & Fishbein, M. (2011). A model of adolescents' seeking of sexual content in their media choices. *Journal of Sex Research, 48*(4), 309–315.

Bleakley, A., Hennessy, M., Fishbein, M., & Jordan, A. (2011). Using the Integrative Model to explain how exposure to sexual media content influences adolescent sexual behavior. *Health Education and Behavior, 38*(5), 530–540.

Branscum, P., Bhochhibhoya, A., & Sharma, M. (2013–2014). The role of Emotional Intelligence in mental health and Type D personality among young adults. *International Quarterly of Community Health Education, 34*(4), 351–365.

Brook, D. W., Rubenstone, E., Zhang, C., Morojele, N. K., & Brook, J. S. (2011). Environmental stressors, low well-being, smoking, and alcohol use among South African adolescents. *Social Science and Medicine, 72*(9), 1447–1453.

Butterfoss, F. D., & Kegler, M. C. (2009). The community coalition action theory. In R. J. DiClemente, R. A. Crosby, & M. C. Kegler (Eds.), *Emerging theories in health promotion practice and research* (2nd ed., pp. 237–276). San Francisco: Jossey-Bass.

Calsyn, D. A., Crits-Christoph, P., Hatch-Maillette, M. A., Doyle, S. R., Song, Y. S., Coyer, S., & Pelta, S. (2010). Reducing sex under the influence of drugs or alcohol for patients in substance abuse treatment. *Addiction*, *105*(1), 100–108.

Casas, J. A., Ortega-Ruiz, R., & Del Rey, R. (2015). Bullying: The impact of teacher management and trait emotional intelligence. *British Journal of Educational Psychology*, *85*(3), 407–423. doi: 10.1111/bjep.12082.

Claros, E., & Sharma, M. (2012). The relationship between emotional intelligence and abuse of alcohol, marijuana, and tobacco among college students. *Journal of Alcohol and Drug Education*, *56*(1), 8–37.

Connell, R. W. (1987). *Gender and power*. Stanford, CA: Stanford University Press.

Cooperman, N. A., Richter, K. P., Bernstein, S. L., Steinberg, M. L., & Williams, J. M. (2015). Determining smoking cessation related information, motivation, and behavioral skills among opiate dependent smokers in methadone treatment. *Substance Use and Misuse*, *50*(5), 566–581. doi: 10.3109/10826084.2014.991405.

Coopersmith, S. (1967). *The antecedents of self-esteem*. San Francisco: W. H. Freeman & Co.

Dalgas-Pelish, P. (2006). Effects of a self-esteem intervention program on school-age children. *Pediatric Nursing*, *32*(4), 341–348.

Dillard, J. P. (2011). An application of the integrative model to women's intention to be vaccinated against HPV: Implications for message design. *Health Communication*, *26*(5), 479–486.

Dubois, D. L., Flay, B. R., & Fagen, M. C. (2009). Self-esteem enhancement theory: Promoting health across the life span. In R. J. DiClemente, R. A. Crosby, & M. C. Kegler (Eds.), *Emerging theories in health promotion practice and research* (2nd ed., pp. 97–130). San Francisco: Jossey-Bass.

Fishbein, M. (1967). Attitude and prediction of behavior. In M. Fishbein (ed.), *Readings in attitude theory and measurement* (pp. 477–492). New York: Wiley.

Fishbein, M. (2008). A reasoned action approach to health promotion. *Medical Decision Making*, *28*(6), 834–844.

Fishbein, M. (2009). An integrative model for behavioral prediction and its application to health promotion. In R. J. DiClemente, R. A. Crosby, & M. C. Kegler (Eds.), *Emerging theories in health promotion practice and research* (2nd ed., pp. 215–234). San Francisco: Jossey-Bass.

Fishbein, M., & Ajzen, I. (1975). *Belief, attitude, intention and behavior: An introduction to theory and research*. Reading, MA: Addison-Wesley.

Fisher, J. D., & Fisher, W. A. (1992). Changing AIDS risk behavior. *Psychological Bulletin*, *111*, 455–474.

Fisher, J. D., Fisher, W. A., & Shuper, P. A. (2009). The information-motivation-behavioral skills model of HIV preventive behavior. In R. J. DiClemente, R. A. Crosby, & M. C. Kegler (Eds.), *Emerging theories in health promotion practice and research* (2nd ed., pp. 21–64). San Francisco: Jossey-Bass.

Fortier, M. S., Williams, G. C., Sweet, S. N., & Patrick, H. (2009). Self-determination theory: Process models for health behavior change. In R. J. DiClemente, R. A. Crosby, & M. C. Kegler (Eds.), *Emerging theories in health promotion practice and research* (2nd ed., pp. 157–184). San Francisco: Jossey-Bass.

Freire, P. (1970). *Pedagogy of the oppressed*. New York: Continuum.

Garaigordobil, M., & Peña-Sarrionandia, A. (2015). Effects of an emotional intelligence program in variables related to the prevention of violence. *Frontiers in Psychology*, *6*, 743. doi: 10.3389/fpsyg.2015.00743.

Goleman, D. (1995). *Emotional intelligence*. New York: Bantam.

Hewitt, J. (2009). The social construction of self-esteem. In C. R. Snyder & S. J. Lopez (Eds.), *Oxford handbook of positive psychology* (2nd ed., pp. 217–224). Oxford: Oxford University Press.

House, J. S. (1981). *Work, stress, and social support*. Reading, MA: Addison-Wesley.

Howard, D. E., Griffin, M., Boekeloo, B., Lake, K., & Bellows, D. (2007). Staying safe while consuming alcohol: A qualitative study of the protective strategies and informational needs of college freshmen. *Journal of American College Health*, *56*(3), 247–254.

Hughes, A. K., Rostant, O. S., & Curran, P. G. (2014). Improving sexual health communication between older women and their providers: How the integrative model of behavioral prediction can help. *Research on Aging*, *36*(4), 450–466. doi: 10.1177/0164027513500055.

Hull, S. J., Hennessy, M., Bleakley, A., Fishbein, M., & Jordan, A. (2011). Identifying the causal pathways from religiosity to delayed adolescent sexual behavior. *Journal of Sex Research*, *48*(6), 543–553.

Katz, I., Madjar, N., & Harari, A. (2015). Parental support and adolescent motivation for dieting: The self-determination theory perspective. *Journal of Psychology*, *149*(5), 461–479. doi: 10.1080/00223980.2014.903890.

Kavas, A. B. (2009). Self-esteem and health-risk behaviors among Turkish late adolescents. *Adolescence*, *44*(173), 187–198.

Kegler, M. C., Rigler, J. & Honeycutt, S. (2010). How does community context influence coalitions in the formation stage? A multiple case study based on the community coalition action theory. *BMC Public Health*, *10*(90), 1–11.

Kegler, M. C., & Swan, D. W. (2011). An initial attempt at operationalizing and testing the community coalition action theory. *Health Education and Behavior*, *38*(3), 261–270. Doi: 10.11777/1090198110372875.

Kim, Y. (2011). Adolescents' health behaviours and its associations with psychological variables. *Central European Journal of Public Health*, *19*(4), 205–209.

Kluhsman, B. C., Bencivenga, M., Ward, A. J., Lehman, E., & Lengerich, E. J. (2006). Initiative of 11 rural Appalachian cancer coalitions in Pennsylvania and New York. *Preventing Chronic Disease*, *3*(4), 1–10.

Kotler, P., & Levy, S. J. (1969). Broadening the concept of marketing. *Journal of Marketing*, *33*, 10–15.

Lazarus, R. S. (1984). Puzzles in the study of daily hassles. *Journal of Behavioral Medicine*, *7*, 375–389.

Lyusin, D. (2006). Emotional intelligence as a mixed construct: Its relationship to personality and gender. *Journal of Russian and East European Psychology*, *44*, 54–68.

Malow, R. M., Dévieux, J. G., Rosenberg, R., Samuels, D. M., & Jean-Gilles, M. M. (2006). Alcohol use severity and HIV sexual risk among juvenile offenders. *Substance Use and Misuse*, *41*(13), 1769–1788.

Maisto, S. A., Carey, M. P., Carey, K. B., Gordon, C. M., & Schum, J. L. (2004). Effects of alcohol and expectancies on HIV-related risk perception and behavioral skills in heterosexual women. *Experimental and Clinical Psychopharmacology*, *12*(4), 288–297.

McVey, G. L., Kirsh, G., Maker, D., Walker, K. S., Mullane, J., Laliberte, M., et al. (2010). Promoting positive body image among university students: A collaborative pilot study. *Body Image*, *7*(3), 200–204.

Mohamadirizi, S., Fahami, F., Bahadoran, P., & Ehsanpour, S. (2015). The effect of four-phase teaching method on midwifery students' emotional intelligence in managing the childbirth. *Journal of Education and Health Promotion*, *4*, 47. doi: 10.4103/2277-9531.157241.

Moreau, M., Gagnon, M. P., & Boudreau, F. (2015). Development of a fully automated, web-based, tailored intervention promoting regular physical activity among insufficiently active adults with type 2 diabetes: Integrating the I-change model, self-determination theory, and motivational interviewing components. *JMIR Research Protocols*, *4*(1), e25. doi: 10.2196/resprot.4099.

Morgan, G. S., Haase, A. M., Campbell, R., & Ben-Shlomo, Y. (2015). Physical ACtivity facilitation for Elders (PACE): Study protocol for a randomised controlled trial. *Trials*, *16*, 91. doi: 10.1186/s13063-015-0610-8.

Morison, T., & Cook, C. M. (2014). Midlife safer sex challenges for heterosexual New Zealand women re-partnering or in casual relationships. *Journal of Primary Health Care*, *7*(2), 137–144.

Murnan, J., Sharma, M., & Lin, D. (2006–2007). Predicting childhood obesity behaviors using social cognitive theory: Children in China. *International Quarterly of Community Health Education*, *26*(1), 73–84.

Nyamhanga, T. M., & Frumence, G. (2014). Gender context of sexual violence and HIV sexual risk behaviors among married women in Iringa Region, Tanzania. *Global Health Action*, *7*, 25346. doi: 10.3402/gha.v7.25346.

Patrick, H., & Canevello, A. (2011). Methodological overview of a self-determination theory based computerized intervention to promote leisure-time physical activity. *Psychology of Sport and Exercise*, *12*(1), 13–19.

Pretlow, R. A., Stock, C. M., Allison, S., & Roeger, L. (2015). Treatment of child/adolescent obesity using the addiction model: A smartphone app pilot study. *Childhood Obesity*, *11*(3), 248–259. doi: 10.1089/chi.2014.0124.

Prochaska, J. O. (1979). *Systems of psychotherapy: A transtheoretical analysis*. Homewood, IL: Dorsey Press.

Rahman, R. J., Hudson, J., Thøgersen-Ntoumani, C., & Doust, J. H. (2015). Motivational processes and well-being in cardiac rehabilitation: A self-determination theory perspective. *Psychology, Health and Medicine*, *20*(5), 518–529. doi: 10.1080/13548506.2015.1017509.

Reed, S. J., Miller, R. L., Francisco, V. T., & Adolescent Medical Trials Network for HIV/AIDS Interventions. (2015). The influence of community context on how coalitions achieve HIV-preventive structural change. *Health Education and Behavior, 41*(1), 100–107. doi: 10.1177/1090198113492766.

Robertson, S. (2007). Got EQ? Increasing cultural and clinical competence through emotional intelligence. *Communication Disorders Quarterly, 29*, 14-19.

Rode, J. L. (2015). The role of emotional intelligence in predicting postpartum depression. *Western Journal of Nursing Research*, pii: 0193945915590690.

Rosenberg, M. (1965). *Society and the adolescent self-image*. Princeton, NJ: Princeton University Press.

Rosenberg, M. (1989). *Society and the adolescent self-image* (Rev. ed.). Middletown, CT: Wesleyan University Press.

Rosenkranz, S. K., Wang, S., & Hu, W. (2015). Motivating medical students to do research: A mixed methods study using self-determination theory. *BMC Medical Education, 15*(1), 95. doi: 10.1186/s12909-015-0379-1.

Rosenstock, I. M. (1974). Historical origins of the health belief model. In M. H. Becker (Ed.), *The health belief model and personal health behavior* (pp. 1–8). Thorofare, NJ: Charles B. Slack.

Ryan, B., & Gross, N. C. (1943). The diffusion of hybrid seed corn in two Iowa communities. *Rural Sociology, 8*, 15–24.

Ryan, R. M., & Deci, E. L. (2000). Self-determination theory and the facilitation of intrinsic motivation, social development and well-being. *American Psychologist, 55*(1), 68–78. doi:10.1037//0003-066X.55.1.68.

Ryan, R. M., Patrick, H., Deci, E. L., & Williams, G. C. (2008). Facilitating health behavior change and its maintenance: Interventions based on Self-Determination Theory. *European Health Psychologist, 10*(1), 1–5.

Salovey, P., & Mayer, J. (1990). Emotional intelligence. *Imagination, Cognition, and Personality, 9*, 185–211.

Salud, M. C., Marshak, H. H., Natto, Z. S., & Montgomery, S. (2014). Exploring HIV-testing intentions in young Asian/Pacific Islander (API) women as it relates to acculturation, theory of gender and power (TGP), and the AIDS risk reduction model (ARRM). *AIDS Care, 26*(5), 642–647. doi: 10.1080/09540121.2013.841836.

Selye, H. (1974). *Stress without distress*. Philadelphia: Lippincott.

Sharma, M. (2015). Multi-theory model (MTM) for health behavior change. *WebmedCentral Behaviour, 6*(9), WMC004982. Available from http://www.webmedcentral.com/article_view/4982

Sharma, M., Mehan, M., & Surabhi, S. (2008–2009). Using social cognitive theory to predict obesity prevention behaviors among preadolescents in India. *International Quarterly of Community Health Education, 29*(4), 351–361.

Shiina, A., Nakazato, M., Mitsumori, M., Koizumi, H., Shimizu, E., Fujisaki, M., & Iyo, M. (2005). An open trial of outpatient group therapy for bulimic disorders: Combination program of cognitive behavioral therapy with assertive training and self-esteem enhancement. *Psychiatry and Clinical Neurosciences, 59*(6), 690–696.

Silva, M. N., Vieira, P. N., Coutinho, S. R., Minderico, C. S., Matos, M.G., Sardinha, L. B., & Teixeira, P. J. (2010). Using self-determination theory to promote physical activity and weight control: A randomized control trial in women. *Journal of Behavioral Medicine, 33*(2), 110–122.

Smith-McLallen, A., & Fishbein, M. (2009). Predicting intentions to engage in cancer prevention and detection behaviors: examining differences between Black and White adults. *Psychology Health and Medicine, 14*(2), 180–189.

Smith-McLallen, A., Fishbein, M., & Hornik, R. C. (2011). Psychosocial determinants of cancer-related information seeking among cancer patients. *Journal of Health Communication, 16*(2), 212–225.

Song, M., Choi, S., Kim, S. A., Seo, K., & Lee, S. J. (2015). Intervention mapping protocol for developing a theory-based diabetes self-management education program. *Research and Theory for Nursing Practice, 29*(2), 94–112.

Waterhouse, L. (2006). Multiple intelligences, the Mozart effect, and emotional intelligence: A critical review. *Educational Psychologist, 41*, 207–225.

Williams, G. C., Niemiec, C. P., Patrick, H., Ryan, R. M., & Deci, E. L. (2009). The importance of supporting autonomy and perceived competence in facilitating long term tobacco abstinence. *Annals of Behavioral Medicine, 37*(3), 315–324.

Williams, G. C., Patrick, H., Niemiec, C. P., Ryan, R. M., Deci, E. L., & McGregor Lavigne, H., (2011). The smoker's health project: A self-determination theory intervention to facilitate maintenance of tobacco abstinence. *Contemporary Clinical Trials*. doi: 10.1016/j.cct.2011.03.002.

Williams, G. C., Patrick, H., Niemiec, C. P., Williams, L. K., Divine, G., Lafata, J. E., Heisler, M., Tunceli, K., & Pladevall, M. (2009). Reducing the health risks of diabetes: How self determination theory may help improve medication adherence and quality of life. *Diabetes Educator, 35*(3), 484–491.

Wilson, D. K., Kitzman-Ulrich, H., Resnicow, K., Van Horn, M. L., George, S. M., Siceloff, E. R., et al. (2015). An overview of the Families Improving Together (FIT) for weight loss randomized controlled trial in African American families. *Contemporary Clinical Trials, 42,* 145–157. doi: 10.1016/j.cct.2015.03.009.

Wingood, G. M., Camp, C., Dunkle, K., Cooper, H., & DiClemente, R. J. (2009). The theory of gender and power: Constructs, variables, and implications for developing HIV interventions for women. In R. J. DiClemente, R. A Crosby, & M. C. Kegler (Eds.) *Emerging theories in health promotion practice and research* (2nd ed., pp. 393–414). San Francisco: Jossey-Bass.

Woolf-King, S. E., & Maisto, S. A. (2015). The effects of alcohol, relationship power, and partner type on perceived difficulty implementing condom use among African American adults: An experimental study. *Archives of Sexual Behavior, 44*(3), 571–581. doi: 10.1007/s10508-014-0362-7.

Ybarra, M. L., Korchmaros, J. D., Prescott, T. L., & Birungi, R. (2015). A randomized controlled trial to increase HIV preventive information, motivation, and behavioral skills in Ugandan adolescents. *Annals of Behavioral Medicine, 49*(3), 473–485. doi: 10.1007/s12160-014-9673-0.

Zamboanga, B. L., Schwartz, S. J., Jarvis, L. H., & Van Tyne, K. (2009). Acculturation and substance use among Hispanic early adolescents: Investigating the mediating roles of acculturative stress and self-esteem. *Journal of Primary Prevention, 30*(3–4), 315–333.

Zhao, X., Sayeed, S., Cappella, J., Hornik, R., Fishbein, M., & Ahern, R. K. (2006). Targeting norm-related beliefs about marijuana use in an adolescent population. *Health Communication, 19*(3), 187–196.

GLOSSARY

action stage: Stage of change in which a person has made meaningful change in the past 6 months with regard to adopting a healthy behavior or quitting an unhealthy behavior.

advantages: Construct of the multi-theory model of health behavior change that alludes to all positive things that can happen as a result of health behavior change.

advocacy: Health advocacy involves creating a shift in public opinion and mobilizing essential resources to support any issue or policy that affects the health of a community or constituency.

analytical epidemiology: Study of the determinants of health, such as behaviors and environments.

assessment protocol for excellence in public health (APEXPH) model: A public health planning model suitable for the local level that consists of three parts: organizational capacity assessment, community process, and completing the cycle.

attitude toward the behavior: A person's overall feeling of like or dislike toward any given behavior.

attitudes: Relatively constant feelings, predispositions, or set of beliefs directed toward an idea, object, person, or situation.

audience segmentation: Identifying distinct groups of people who are similar to each other in particular characteristics and thus likely to respond to messages in a similar way.

autonomy: A construct of the self-determination theory that relates to the desire to be the regulator of one's actions and posits that behavior is volitional.

awareness: Becoming conscious of an action, idea, object, person, or situation.

behavior: Any overt action, conscious or unconscious, performed by an individual that has a measurable frequency, intensity, and duration; a category of actions with a specification of target, action, context, and time (TACT).

behavioral beliefs: Belief that performing a given behavior will lead to certain outcomes.

behavioral confidence: A construct of the multi-theory model of health behavior change that is a projection of one's sureness to perform a health behavior change in the future, not in the present, which then helps in initiation of the health behavior change.

behavioral intention: The thought to perform the behavior, which is an immediate determinant of the given behavior.

behavioral skills: A construct of the information-motivation-behavioral skills model that comprises an individual's objective ability and self-efficacy in performing the behavior.

beliefs: Statements of perceived facts or impressions about the world.

CDCynergy: A multimedia health communication planning model developed by the Centers for Disease Control and Prevention, based on a CD-ROM with tailored versions, that comprises six phases: problem definition and description, problem analysis, communication program planning, program and evaluation development, program implementation and management, and feedback.

certified health education specialist (CHES): An individual who meets the required health education training qualifications, has successfully passed the certification exam of the National Commission for

Health Education Credentialing (NCHEC), and meets continuing education requirements.

certified in public health (CPH): A graduate from a Council on Education for Public Health (CEPH)–accredited school or program of public health who has successfully completed a knowledge and skill test in public health conducted by the National Board of Public Health Examiners (NBPHE).

challenge: A component of hardiness that refers to a willingness to undertake change, confront new activities, and obtain opportunities for growth.

change agent: An individual who influences a potential adopter's decision about an innovation in a favorable way.

changes in physical environment: A construct of the multi-theory model of health behavior change that pertains to making modifications to obtainability, availability, accessibility, convenience, and readiness of resources that help in initiation of the health behavior change.

changes in social environment: A construct of the multi-theory model of health behavior change that pertains to creating social support from the environment that helps in sustenance of health behavior change.

chronic strains: Chronic stressors that result from the responses of one social group to another, such as overt or covert, intentional or unintentional discriminatory behavior due to race, ethnicity, or so forth.

chronic stressors: Type of stressors that are ongoing and last for a sustained period of time. These include persistent life difficulties, role strains, chronic strains, community-wide strains, and daily hassles.

clarity of results: The degree to which outcomes of an innovation are clearly visible.

coalition: Grouping of separate organizations in a community united to pursue a common goal related to health or other matters affecting a large number of people.

code: A physical representation of an identified community issue in a form such as a case study, role play, story, slide show, photograph, song, or so on.

code of ethics for health educators: Written document for professional conduct of health educators that delineates responsibilities to the public, profession, and employers and responsibilities regarding the delivery of health

education, research and evaluation, and professional preparation.

codification: The process of creating codes to structure a discussion that highlights problems.

commitment: A component of hardiness that refers to the tendency to involve oneself in whatever one encounters, or a feeling of deep involvement in the activities of life.

communication channels: The links between those who have know-how regarding an innovation and those who have not yet adopted that innovation; the means by which messages are transferred between individuals.

community: A collection of people identified by a set of shared values.

community coalition action theory (CCAT): A community-level theory that identifies internal factors within the coalition that lead to the implementation of community change and thereby provide an approach for assessing the efforts of coalitions.

community development: A stage in which local initiative and leadership in a community has been organized and stimulated to a level at which change in health or other matters is occurring.

community empowerment: Process whereby individuals gain mastery over their lives in the context of changing their social and political environments.

community mobilization: Persuading community members to attend or participate in any activity planned by the health educator. Its purpose is to enhance awareness of a given issue at the community level.

community organization: Process in which community members identify needs, set objectives, prioritize issues, develop plans, and implement projects for community improvement in health and related matters.

community participation: When community members actively participate in planning or implementing projects.

community-wide strains: Chronic stressors that operate at an ecological level, such as residing in a high-crime neighborhood.

compatibility: The perception of an innovation's consistency with the values, past experiences, and needs of potential adopters.

competence: A construct of self-determination theory that describes the experience of feeling able to achieve a desired outcome.

complexity: The perception of the degree of difficulty in understanding and using a new idea, practice, or product.

comprehensibility: A component of the theory of sense of coherence that refers to the extent to which perceived stressors make cognitive sense, implying that there is some set structure, consistency, order, clarity, and predictability.

comprehensive health education model (CHEM): An older model of health education that consists of six steps: involving people, setting goals, defining problems, designing plans, conducting activities, and evaluating results.

conscientization: A term coined by Paulo Freire and a distinct construct of his ideology that refers to the process of identification of the root causes of any problem.

consciousness raising: An experiential process of change in the transtheoretical model that entails raising awareness of the causes, consequences, and cures for a particular problem.

contemplation stage: Stage of change in which a person is considering change in the foreseeable future, but not immediately; usually defined as between 1 and 6 months.

contingency management: See *reinforcement management*.

control: A component of hardiness that refers to the belief that one causes the events of one's life and can influence the environment.

control beliefs: Beliefs about internal and external factors that may inhibit or facilitate the performance of a behavior.

coping: Purposive, psychological mechanisms for dealing with stressors.

costs: In diffusion of innovations theory, the tangible and intangible expenses incurred in the adoption of a new idea, practice, or product.

counterconditioning: A behavioral process of change in the transtheoretical model that requires learning a new, healthier behavior in place of the old, unhealthy behavior.

critical consciousness: A construct of the Freirean model that refers to the development of the political organization of those adversely affected by the problem.

cues to action: Precipitating forces that make a person feel the need to take action.

daily hassles: Chronic stressors that include everyday problems, such as getting stuck in traffic.

decisional balance: The construct of the transtheoretical model that addresses the relative importance placed by an individual on the advantages (pros) of behavior change as opposed to the disadvantages (cons).

defense mechanisms: The devices that the mind uses to alter an individual's perception of situations that disturb the internal milieu or mental balance.

demonstrability: The degree to which an innovation may be experimented with on a limited basis.

descriptive epidemiology: Study of the time, place, and population attributes of a health problem through the collection of data such as mortality (death), morbidity (illness), and disability rates.

development of social norms: Creating social acceptance for a practice, behavior, condition, policy, law, or environment that may affect health in a community.

dialogue: A construct of the Freirean model that refers to two-way communication between learners and educators.

dietitian: An individual who is an expert in human nutrition or dietetics and the regulation of diet. A dietitian counsels people on what to eat in order to lead a healthy life or to pursue a specific health-related objective.

diffusion: The process by which a new idea, object, or practice filters through various channels in a community over time.

disadvantages: Construct of the multi-theory model of health behavior change that alludes to all negative things that can happen as a result of health behavior change.

dramatic relief: An experiential process of change in the transtheoretical model that enhances emotional arousal about one's behavior and emphasizes the relief that can come from changing it.

emotional coping: Techniques employed by a person to control the emotional and physiological states associated with acquisition of a new behavior.

emotional intelligence theory: A behavior theory that underscores the role of self-awareness, mood management, self-motivation, empathy, and managing relationships in predicting and explaining behavior.

emotional transformation: A construct of the multi-theory model of health behavior change that pertains to converting or transforming emotions toward the health behavior change that help in sustenance of health behavior change.

emotion-focused coping: Method of dealing with a stressor in which the focus is inward and involves altering the way one thinks or feels about a situation or an event.

empathy: A construct of emotional intelligence theory that pertains to the ability to recognize one's feelings in others and tuning into their verbal and nonverbal cues.

enabling factors: Antecedents to behavioral or environmental change that allow a motivation or environmental policy to be realized (e.g., availability of resources, accessibility, laws, or skills).

environment: Physical or social circumstances or conditions that surround a person.

environmental reevaluation: An experiential process of change in the transtheoretical model that involves both affective and cognitive components regarding how the behavior affects one's environment and how changing the behavior would influence the environment.

event-based models: Models of stress that underscore the role of life events in the causation of stress.

exchange theory: Marketing theory of voluntary transfer or transaction of something valuable between two individuals or groups.

forethought capability: The proposition that most behavior is purposive and regulated by prior thoughts.

formative research: In social marketing, collecting quantitative and qualitative data about a problem, its context, the attitudes and behaviors of the target audience, ways to reach the target audience, and existing messages and materials.

general adaptation syndrome: The three-stage physiological response (alarm reaction, resistance, and exhaustion) of any organism that encounters nonspecific stimuli.

goal setting: A determinant of behavior composed of setting goals and developing plans to accomplish chosen behaviors.

hardiness: A personality trait that is found to predict better coping with stressors; it consists of three components: commitment, control, and challenge.

health: A means to achieve desirable goals in life while maintaining a multidimensional (physical, mental, social, political, economic, and spiritual) equilibrium that is operationalized for individuals as well as for communities.

health behavior: Actions with a potentially measurable frequency, intensity, and duration performed at the individual, interpersonal, organizational, community, or public policy level for primary, secondary, or tertiary prevention. See also *preventive behaviors*.

health belief model (HBM): Theory designed to exclusively predict health behaviors based on the constructs of perceived susceptibility, perceived severity, perceived benefits, perceived costs, cues to action, and self-efficacy.

health coach: An individual who is trained in the field of health sciences and works one-on-one with a client to help him or her achieve a healthy lifestyle or a specific health behavior change objective.

health education: Systematic application of a set of techniques to voluntarily and positively influence health through changing the antecedents of behavior (awareness, information, knowledge, skills, beliefs, attitudes, and values) in individuals, groups, or communities.

health literacy: The capacity of an individual to obtain, interpret, and understand basic health information and services and the competence to use such information and services in ways that are health enhancing.

health promotion: Process of empowering people to improve their health by providing educational, political, legislative, organizational, social, and community supports.

helping relationships: A behavioral process of change in the transtheoretical model that entails developing caring, open, trusting, and accepting relationships that help in adherence to the healthy behavior.

homophily: The degree of similarity among group members.

illness behaviors: Actions taken by a person who feels sick and indulges in the behavior for the purpose of defining the state of his or her health and for discovering suitable remedies.

informal education: Type of education that uses experiential learning (i.e., learning from one's experiences) and simple conversation and can take place in any setting.

information: The collection of facts related to an action, idea, object, person, or situation.

information-motivation-behavioral skills (IMB) model: A health behavior model that emphasizes the role of information, motivation, and behavioral skills for effecting behavior change.

initiation of behavior change: According to the multi-theory model of health behavior change this refers to the starting of the health behavior change.

innovation: A new idea, object, or practice that is to be adopted.

integrative model of behavioral prediction (IM): A behavior theory that explains and predicts behavior based on myriad constructs derived from the health belief model, social cognitive theory, the theory of reasoned action, and the theory of planned behavior.

intervention mapping: A health promotion and education planning model that comprises six steps: needs assessment or problem analysis; creating matrices of change objectives; selecting theory-based intervention methods and practical strategies; developing an organized program; planning for adoption, implementation, and sustainability of the program; and generating an evaluation plan.

knowledge: Learning facts and gaining insights related to an action, idea, object, person, or situation.

legislation: A law passed by elected officials at the local, state, or federal level.

levels of change: Five distinct but interrelated levels of psychological problems that can be addressed in psychotherapy: symptom/situational problems, maladaptive cognitions, current interpersonal conflicts, family/system conflicts, and intrapersonal conflicts.

life change events: See *life events*.

life events: A distinct category of stressors that are discrete, major happenings affecting or having the potential to influence one's body, mind, family, or community (e.g., death of a family member); also known as life change events.

lobbying: Working with and influencing policy makers to develop an issue or policy that affects the health of a given community.

maintenance stage: Stage of change in which the person has maintained the changed behavior for a period of time, usually considered as 6 or more months.

manageability: A component of the sense of coherence that refers to the extent to which one feels that the resources under one's control are adequate to meet the demands posed by the stressors.

managing relationships: A construct of emotional intelligence theory that entails handling interpersonal interaction, conflict resolution, and negotiations.

marketing mix: The combination of product, price, place, and promotion.

master certified health education specialist (MCHES): An advanced-level health education/promotion practitioner who meets the required academic qualifications and has worked in the field for a minimum of five years, has successfully passed the competency-based certification exam of the National Commission for Health Education Credentialing (NCHEC), and meets continuing education requirements.

meaningfulness: A component of the sense of coherence that refers to the extent to which one feels that life makes sense emotionally and that at least some of the stressors in life are worth investing energy in and are worthy of commitment and engagement.

model: An eclectic, creative, simplified, and miniaturized application of concepts for addressing problems.

model for health education planning (MHEP): One of the older models of health education planning; it comprises six phases: program initiation, needs assessment, goal setting, planning/programming, implementation, and evaluation.

model for health education planning and resource development (MHEPRD): A five-phase model of health education planning developed in the 1980s that consists of the following phases: health education plans, demonstration programs, operational programs, research programs, and information and statistics.

mood management: A construct of emotional intelligence theory that entails handling feelings so that they become relevant to the current situation and one reacts appropriately.

motivation: A construct from the IMB model that entails personal attitudes toward the behavior, perceptions of social support for that behavior, and the persons' perception as to how others behave.

motivation to comply: Degree to which a person wants to act in accordance with the perceived wishes of those significant in his or her life.

multilevel approach to community health (MATCH) model: A health education planning model that consists of five phases: goals selection, intervention planning, program development, implementation preparations, and evaluation.

multi-theory model (MTM) for health behavior change: A proposition that predicts initiation of health behavior change using participatory dialogue, behavioral confidence, and changes in physical environment; and sustenance of health behavior change using emotional transformation, practice for change, and changes in the social environment.

networking: Creating interdependent relationships with individuals, groups, and organizations to accomplish mutually set objectives in health or other matters.

nonevents: Absence of events that have the potential for causing stress; these include desired or anticipated events that do not occur, desired events that do not occur even though their occurrence is normative for people of a certain group, and situations in which a person has nothing to do.

normative beliefs: A person's beliefs about how other people who are significant in his or her life would like him or her to behave.

norms: Beliefs that most of the significant others in one's life think one should or should not perform a particular behavior. See also *subjective norm*.

nursing educator: An individual who is a nurse or nurse practitioner by training and is involved in educating patients or community members about disease management or a healthy lifestyle.

opinion leaders: Influential individuals in a community who sway the beliefs and actions of their colleagues in either a positive or negative direction.

optimism: A personality disposition that refers to the tendency to expect the best possible outcome or think about the most hopeful aspects of any situation.

outcome evaluations: Value a person places on each outcome resulting from performance of a given behavior.

outcome expectancies: Value a person places on the probable outcomes that would result from performing a behavior.

outcome expectations: Anticipation of the probable outcomes that would ensue as a result of engaging in the behavior under discussion.

participatory dialogue: A construct of the multi-theory model of health behavior change that is a two-way discussion of the advantages and disadvantages of the health behavior change, with an emphasis on the process that helps in initiation of the health behavior change.

partnership: Establishment of collaboration with multiple partners who will work on the same issue.

PEN-3 model: A culturally appropriate planning model that is composed of three interrelated and interdependent dimensions, each with an acronym of PEN: (1) health education (person, extended family, and neighborhood); (2) educational diagnosis of health behavior (perceptions, enablers, and nurturers); and (3) cultural appropriateness of the health behavior (positive, exotic, and negative).

perceived barriers: Beliefs concerning the actual and imagined costs of following a new behavior.

perceived behavioral control: How much a person feels he or she is in command of enacting the given behavior.

perceived benefits: Beliefs in the advantages of the methods suggested for reducing the risk or seriousness of the disease or harmful state resulting from a particular behavior.

perceived power: A person's perception about how easy or difficult it is to perform the behavior in each condition identified in his or her control beliefs.

perceived relative advantage: The perception regarding how much better a new product, idea, or practice is than the one it will replace.

perceived severity: Subjective belief in the extent of harm that can result from an acquired disease or harmful state as a result of a particular behavior.

perceived susceptibility: Subjective belief regarding a person's likelihood of acquiring a disease or reaching a harmful state as a result of indulging in a particular behavior.

perceived threat: The combination of perceived susceptibility and perceived severity.

persistent life difficulties: Chronic stressors that include life events lasting longer than six months, such as long-term disability.

pervasiveness: The degree to which an innovation requires changes or adjustments by other elements in the social system.

place: The distribution channels, or where and how customers are going to get the product.

planned approach to community health (PATCH) model: A health planning model developed by the Centers for Disease Control and Prevention that comprises five phases: mobilizing the community, collecting and organizing data, choosing health priorities, developing a comprehensive intervention plan, and evaluating results.

policy: Creating the environmental supports needed to sustain a behavior change.

policy development: The process of developing a policy with ramifications for affecting the health of communities.

popular education: Type of education that is based on community needs, fosters equal relationship between learners and teachers, builds on a community's experience, and aims at social change.

practice for change: A construct of the multi-theory model of health behavior change that pertains to constantly thinking about the health behavior change and making mid-course corrections to one's strategy, overcoming barriers, and remaining focused on health behavior change that help in sustenance of health behavior change.

praxis: A construct of the Freirean model that refers to the method of tying together theory and practice; also known as active reflection or reflective action.

PRECEDE-PROCEED model: A health promotion and health education model with eight phases: social assessment and situational analysis, epidemiological assessment, educational and ecological assessment, administrative and policy assessment and intervention alignment, implementation, process evaluation, impact evaluation, and outcome evaluation. The acronym PRECEDE stands for predisposing, reinforcing, and enabling constructs in educational/ environmental diagnosis and evaluation. The acronym PROCEED stands for policy, regulatory, and organizational constructs in educational and environmental development.

precontemplation stage: Stage of change in which a person is not considering change in the foreseeable future, usually defined as the next 6 months.

predisposing factors: Factors that are antecedents to behavioral change and that provide motivation for the behavior (e.g., knowledge, beliefs, attitudes, values, perceptions).

preparation stage: Stage of change in which a person is planning for change in the immediate future, usually defined as in the next month.

preventive behaviors: Actions taken by a healthy person for the purpose of preventing disease or detecting disease in an asymptomatic phase. See also *health behavior*.

price: The tangible and intangible things that the target audience has to give up in order to adopt the new idea (product).

primary appraisal: A process in which a person determines the severity of the stressor and makes an assessment regarding whether he or she is in trouble; one of the constructs of theories of stress and coping.

primary prevention: Preventive actions that are taken prior to the onset of disease or an injury with a view to removing the possibility of their ever occurring.

problem posing: See *problematization*.

problematization: The essence of the Freirean methodology; it includes emphasis on raising questions without providing any predetermined answers. The participants have to reflect and arrive at answers themselves; also known as problem posing.

problem-focused coping: Method of dealing with a given stressor by one's ability to think and to alter the environmental event or situation.

product: In social marketing, the behavior or offering that is intended for the target audience to adopt.

promotion: The mechanism by which one gets a message across to a target audience.

publics: The primary and secondary audiences involved in a social marketing program.

purse strings: The amount of money available for a social marketing campaign.

reappraisal: The feedback loop by which a person determines whether the effects of the stressor have been effectively negated; one of the constructs of theories of stress and coping.

recent life events: Discrete major life happenings that have occurred within the past year.

reciprocal determinism: The triadic reciprocity of causation among personal factors, the environment, and behavior.

reinforcement management: A behavioral process of change in the transtheoretical model that utilizes reinforcements and punishments for taking steps in a particular direction.

reinforcing factors: Factors that follow a behavior and provide continuing rewards for sustenance of the behavior (e.g., family, peers, teachers, employers, health providers, community leaders, decision makers).

reinvention: The degree to which potential adopters of an innovation can adapt, refine, or modify the innovation to suit their needs.

relatedness: A construct of self-determination theory that refers to experiencing care and concern from and trust in important individuals and feeling connected to and understood by others.

remote life events: Discrete major life happenings that have occurred in the distant past, beyond one year.

response-based model: Model of stress that underscore the role of responses arising out of stress.

reversibility: In the diffusion of innovations theory, the ability and degree to which the status quo can be reinstated by ceasing to use the innovation.

role strains: Chronic stressors that include either strain from performing specific roles (such as parenting, working, being in a relationship) or performing a multiplicity of roles at the same time.

secondary appraisal: A process in theories of stress and coping in which a person determines how much control he or she has over the stressor. If control is high, then no stress develops; if control is low, then stress develops.

secondary prevention: Actions that block the progression of an injury or disease at its incipient stage.

self-awareness: A construct of emotional intelligence theory that involves knowing one's emotions, recognizing feelings as they occur, and discriminating between them.

self-control: See *goal setting*.

self-determination theory (SDT): A behavior theory that proposes that humans have three basic psychological needs of autonomy, competence, and relatedness that must be satisfied within a social context in order for growth and well-being to be achieved.

self-efficacy: The confidence that a person has in his or her ability to pursue a behavior.

self-efficacy in overcoming impediments: Confidence that a person has in overcoming barriers while performing a given behavior.

self-esteem: This refers to a personal assessment by a person of his or her own worth.

self-liberation: A behavioral process of change in the transtheoretical model that entails the belief that one can change and a commitment and recommitment to act on that change.

self-motivation: A construct of emotional intelligence theory that includes "gathering up" one's feelings and directing oneself toward a goal, despite self-doubt, inertia, and impulsiveness.

self-reevaluation: An experiential process of change in the transtheoretical theory that involves both affective and cognitive components and includes a person's assessment of his or her self-image with the new behavior.

self-reflective capability: Human attribute that entails analysis of experiences and thinking about one's own thought processes.

self-regulatory capability: Human attribute that entails setting internal standards and self-evaluative reactions for one's behavior.

sense of coherence: A theory that purports that comprehensibility, manageability, and meaningfulness in life improve coping with stress.

sexual division of labor: A construct of the theory of gender and power that refers to the economic imbalances in the structure of our society that favor men.

sexual division of power: A construct of the theory of gender and power that refers to the imbalances in authority and control pertaining to relations and roles in institutions in favor of men.

SHOWED model: A mnemonic acronym of the phases of the Freirean methodology for facilitating a discussion. The steps are as follows: What do we *see* here? What is really *happening*? How does the story relate to *our* lives? *Why* did the person acquire the problem? How is it possible for this person to become *empowered*? What can we *do* about it?

sick role behaviors: Actions taken for the purpose of getting well by people who are sick.

situational perception: How one perceives and interprets the environment around oneself.

skill: Act involving physical movement, coordination, and use of the motor function.

skills and abilities: A construct of the integrative model of behavioral prediction that refers to the aptitudes and capabilities that a person has.

social cognitive theory (SCT): Theory that posits a triadic reciprocity among behavior, the environment, and cognitive personal factors.

social context: A construct of self-determination theory that refers to the environment in which the behavior takes place.

social-ecological models: Planning models that consider intrapersonal, interpersonal, social, cultural, organizational, and policy/environmental levels in planning multilevel interventions.

social learning theory: Theory that posits that learning takes place from imitation, reinforcements, and self-control.

social liberation: An experiential process of change in the transtheoretical theory that refers to an increase in social opportunities or alternatives.

social marketing: The use of commercial marketing techniques to help in the acquisition of a behavior that is beneficial for the health of a target population.

social networks: Person-centered webs of social relationships or all the relationships that an individual has in his or her life.

social reality: Awareness of the context of facts. This context must be from the perspective of the participants or clients.

social support: The help obtained through social relationships and interpersonal exchanges.

social system: People in a society connected by a common goal.

stages of change: Discrete phases in the transtheoretical model through which a person transits when undergoing change of a behavior. The stages consist of precontemplation, contemplation, action, and maintenance.

stimulus control: A behavioral process of change in the transtheoretical model that involves modifying the environment to increase cues for healthy behavior and decrease cues for unhealthy behavior.

stress: The response of the body and mind, including behaviors, as a result of encountering stressors, interpreting them, and making judgments about controlling or influencing the outcomes of these events.

stressors: Various external events that pose actual or perceived threats to the body or mind.

structure of cathexis: A construct of the theory of gender and power that refers to social norms and affective connections between men and women.

subjective norm: One's belief that most of the significant others in one's life think one should or should not perform a particular behavior. See also *norms*.

sustenance of behavior change: According to the multi-theory model of health behavior change this refers to the continuation of the health behavior change.

symbolizing capability: Human attribute that entails the use of symbols in attributing meaning to experiences.

temptation: The urge to engage in unhealthy behavior when confronted with a difficult situation.

termination: The point in the transtheoretical model at which the person has completely quit the habit, has no temptation to relapse, and is fully self-efficacious to continue with the change.

tertiary prevention: Those actions taken after the onset of disease or an injury with a view to assisting diseased or disabled people.

theory of gender and power: A social structural theory according to which there are three major social structures that characterize the gendered relationships between men and women: the *sexual division of labor*, the *sexual division of power*, and the *structure of cathexis*.

theory of planned behavior (TPB): A theory of behavior that posits that intention precedes behavior and is determined by the attitude toward the behavior, subjective norms, and perceived behavioral control.

theory of reasoned action (TRA): A theory of behavior that posits that intention precedes behavior and is determined by the attitude toward the behavior and subjective norms.

time: In the diffusion of innovations theory, the interval between becoming aware of an idea and adopting it.

transactional model: Model of stress and coping that is characterized by the interaction of a person with the environment in four stages: primary appraisal, secondary appraisal, coping, and reappraisal.

transformation: A construct of the Freirean methodology that implies comprehension of the political and social causes of any given problem.

transtheoretical model (TTM): A model of behavior change that posits that people move through five stages of change, from precontemplation (not thinking about change) to maintenance (acquisition of the healthy behavior), in which they are aided through 10 processes of change and the constructs of decisional balance, self-efficacy, and overcoming temptation.

type A personality: Personality type that is characterized by a hurrying nature, exercising control over people and things, a sense of urgency, and a challenging nature.

type B personality: Personality type that is characterized by a more laid-back lifestyle and a more relaxed disposition than a type A personality.

value expectancy theories: Theories that postulate that a behavior depends on the importance placed by an individual on an outcome (value) and the individual's estimate of the likelihood that a given action will result in that outcome (expectancy).

values: Enduring beliefs or systems of beliefs that a specific mode of conduct or end state of behavior is personally or socially preferable.

vicarious capability: Human attribute that entails the ability to learn from observing other people's behavior and the consequences that they face.

INDEX

Page numbers followed by *b*, *f*, or *t* indicate material in boxes, figures, or tables, respectively.